Becoming a Nation

Becoming a Nation

Processes and Prospects

Papers Presented at the 41st Annual Research Seminar of ACPI Held at St. Albert's College, Ranchi, 20-23 October 2016

Edited by

Dolreich Pereira

Association of Christian Philosophers of India

&

Christian World Imprints™

ACPI Annual Philosophy Series No. 18

Series Editors: Keith D'Souza, John Peter Vallabadoss & Kurian Alumkal

First Published in 2017 by

Association of Christian Philosophers of India
through The Secretary, ACPI
Vijnananilayam, Janampet, Vijayarai PO
Eluru-534475, West Godavari Dt., A.P.
petercapu@gmail.com
www.acpiindia.com
Phone: +91 9698224321

&

Christian World Imprints™
Christian Publishing & Books from India
H-12 Bali Nagar, **New Delhi-110015**
info@christianworldimprints.com
www.ChristianWorldImprints.com
Phone: +91 11 25465925

ISBN: 978-93-5148-229-1 (HB) ISBN: 978-93-5148-230-7 (PB)

Cataloging in Publication Data--DK
Courtesy: D.K. Agencies (P) Ltd. <docinfo@dkagencies.com>

Association of Christian Philosophers of India. Annual Research Seminar (41st : 2016 : Rānchī, India)
Becoming a nation : processes and prospects : papers presented at the 41st Annual Research Seminar of ACPI held at St. Albert's College, Ranchi, 20-23 October 2016 / edited by Dolreich Pereira.
pages cm. -- (ACPI annual philosophy series ; no. 18)
Includes bibliographical references.
ISBN 9789351482291
ISBN 9789351482307

1. Nationalism--India--Congresses. 2. India--Politics and government--Congresses. 3. India--Social conditions--Congresses. I. Pereira, Dolreich, editor. II. Association of Christian Philosophers of India, organizer, publisher. III. St. Albert's College, Ranchi, host institution. IV. Title. V. Series: Association of Christian Philosophers of India. Annual series ; no. 18.

DS480.853.A87 2016 DDC 320.540954 23

Printed in India.

Contents

Editorial

"No nation has been on earth since the beginning of time and the very concept of nationhood is pretty recent. Despite that, most nations look upon their own existence as a self-evident destiny conferred by God, or by Nature, since time immemorial. Nations tend to think of their cultures and political systems, even their frontiers, as the work of Man, but they see their national existence as a transcendent fact, beyond all question"— Milan Kundera[1]

The word "nation" comes from the Latin word *natio* meaning birth. The Oxford Dictionary defines "nation" as "a large body of people united by common descent, history, culture, or language, inhabiting a particular state or territory;" whereas for the Dictionary of the French language, it is a "group of people living on a common territory, conscious of its unity (historical, cultural, etc.) and constituting a political entity". Right away we see that defining "nation" is a difficult task and the resulting confusion is widespread. The term "nation" has often been used as a synonym for "country", "state", or ethnic group" and it is frequently the case that this uncritical usage has consequently resulted in fierce disagreements on what constitutes national identity. As Andrew Heywood notes: "To claim the status of a nation is to make powerful political demands, notably about the right to self-government and, ultimately, sovereign independence".

The term nation has evolved over the centuries. In medieval times, it corresponded to a group of men having a common origin. Today, it includes a set of things; this combination leads to the creation of a sense of belonging together. The nation, and hence this feeling of belongingness can be transmitted often from generation to generation. It is therefore the will to live together of the people forming a nation that makes it possible to make it endure. We understand then that there is necessarily a long journey in order to arrive from the idea of nation to the historical reality of becoming a nation.

According to Ernest Renan (at the 1882 conference at the Sorbonne, entitled "What is a nation?"), the nation thus appears as a historical result,

1 Soren Frank, *Migration and Literature*, (New York: Palgrave Macmillan, 2008), 103.

"a soul, a spiritual principle".[2] Johann Gottfried Herder proposes a definition of the nation based on the soil and the common language. Finally, Johann Gottlieb Fichte also evokes language by demonstrating its significance, but also gives the people its importance in the constitution of a nation.

If these conceptions are variable, certain objective data can nevertheless make it possible to define a nation. We then compile certain notions such as ethnicity, language, religion, culture, territory and the state. The reality is not so simple since some states, like India, have several languages in their midst.

The concept is therefore difficult to grasp and it is understandable that it is ultimately more a political construct to ensure social cohesion than a true legal concept. Some proponents of the class struggle believe that the nation hides conflicts of interest between social classes, and hence there is no real national sentiment that animates a whole people. Nevertheless, the construction or "becoming of a nation" is historically well established; it is indeed a historical result. The creation of a nation has sometimes been necessary to lead to unity; this was the case during the French Revolution, when the revolutionaries shouted "Long live the nation", while the monarchy had just been overthrown. In our own situation, the idea of India as a nation was also proclaimed through the famous slogan of the freedom-fighters: "Jai Hind!" This example shows the necessity of a historical (r)evolution which eventually brought people together.

The historical result leading to the founding of a nation can take place in several ways: it may be the succession of monarchical dynasties (France), or a desire to unite territories like it happened in post-independent India. It is notably with centralization that the nationalist sentiment asserts itself. The idea of this concept has important consequences. The principle of nationality made it possible to establish a political balance in Europe. But, the idea of creating a nation is not only European; the colonized countries saw the nationalism of their inhabitants reinforced. Nationalism thus led to a mass decolonization and the emergence of new states.

If nationalism has led to decolonization, the term sometimes has a disturbing connotation. Nationalist feeling is often henceforth attached to a refusal of openness towards other people, to a feeling of hatred towards them, and to a confinement of the people upon themselves. But, nationalism differs

---

2 "A nation is a soul, a spiritual principle. Two things, which in truth are but one, constitute this soul or spiritual principle. One lies in the past, one in the present. One is the possession in common of a rich legacy of memories; the other is present-day consent, the desire to live together, the will to perpetuate the value of the heritage that one has received in an undivided form. Man, Gentlemen, does not improvise. The nation, like the individual, is the culmination of a long past of endeavours, sacrifice, and devotion." Ernest Renan, "Qu'est-ce qu'une nation" in *Nationalism*, eds. John Hutchinson and Anthony D. Smith (Oxford: Oxford University Press, 1994), 17.

from similar notions such as patriotism, which might lead some of us to think that nationalism engenders some violence. Yes, there is a difference between the nationalism of Hitler and the nationalism of Churchill; or the nationalism of those who fought for Indian Independence and that of our present-day rulers.

Nationalism, therefore, is not a word with imprecise contours that would designate any sort of political reference to the nation: it includes at least the following traits: the fear of decline due to a cause which is internal and/or external to the nation; the reaction against the present, which takes place by rewriting history to the advantage of nationalism and projects a nationalist future; the organic structure in which the individual is less important than the community and must be sacrificed to it when necessary, in the name of a higher power; the use of propaganda to maintain, and channel national sentiment and obtain political power. Thus understood, nationalism is not only a lie that covers an unavowed modernization; it is on the contrary very explicit and puts on its agenda the subject(s) of the persecutions that it plots against. Even though nebulous, ideological entities such as the nation are indispensable as soon as one wishes to introduce nuances. We may not know exactly what a nation is, but we know what nationalism means. And it is crucial to distinguish the right type from the wrong one. By conceiving nationalism from the nation, one understands how the nation can serve as an instrument for ideologies that are not at all nationalist in the good sense of the term. Religions, political and economic doctrines, racist and fascist ideologies may manipulate the nation for their own purposes which are not nationalist.

It is in this context that the Association of Christian Philosophers of India gathered at their 41st Annual Research Conference to discuss and debate "Becoming a Nation: Processes and Prospects". This meeting was hosted by St. Albert's Seminary, Ranchi, Jharkhand and took place during 20-23 October 2016. Through their varied views and dialogical discourses on this topic published in this book, the Christian philosophers of India offer a panoramic perspective on the diverse processes and prospects involved in becoming a nation.

This book has a tripartite division: the first part explores some of the ideological considerations underlying the terms "nation" and "nationalism". Using this as a springboard, the second part examines various aspects of nationalism using a multidisciplinary approach involving History, Science, Technology, Political Science, Media Studies, etc. Finally, the third part invites us to listen to new and old voices of Indian Nationalism – voices that are important but sometimes run the risk of being silenced in the raucous cacophony of extreme views on nationalism.

The first part contains eight essays. The first, entitled "Imagining a Nation: Postcolonial Perspectives" by **Nishant Alphonse Irudayadason**, highlights three important and inevitable aspects to imagining a nation: secular, pluralistic and cosmopolitan. The author focuses on the need for decimating and deconstructing colonial imagination and constructions in order to develop a creative and dynamic narrative of a nation while at the same time, critiquing a lopsided version of nation and nationalism programmatically constructed by Hindutva ideologues anchored in a colonial narrative of homogeneity and fixity. In his paper, "From Sovereignty to Solidarity: Redefining Identity Politics", **Keith D'Souza** contends that "sovereignty" needs to be understood in the context of a diversity of competing powers and virtual spaces, rather than merely and narrowly being associated with national and political geo spaces. He proposes different forms and forums of solidarity, within and across various social and national boundaries, as preferred modes of social connection to establish social harmony and optimal productivity and prosperity. **Jose D. Maliekal** analyses the multi-stranded and entwined phenomena of democracy, nation and the state in his paper: "Whose Nation? Whose State?": Subaltern Readings *into* Constitutional Trajectories". Raising many questions about the interpretation of the Constitution, the construction of the nation and the state, heundertakes a subaltern reading of the Constitution, constituting the Dalit Life-worlds, inscribed by the purity-pollution binary and the dominance of the touchables, who design social space. He suggests that the task of philosophizing, in these struggles and multiple and contested readings of the text that is Nation/State/Constitution is to be in touch with the political society of the dispossessed. **Peter Ladis F.** gives us a politico-legal perspective in "The Dialectics between Fundamental Rights and Directive Principles" wherein he looks at the core differences between fundamental rights and directive principles of the Indian legal system. He addresses the burning issue of whether any elected government in India can amend the Fundamental Rights to suit its party ideology and concludes in the light of various landmark judgments of the Supreme Court of India, that no elected government can impose its ideology on the Constitution of India. With the help of Georg Hegel's philosophy of the state, **Gregory Mathew Malayil** helps us to reflect on various nuances of the evolution of nation-states in "The Nation as an Evolution of Self-Consciousness: An Analysis Based on Hegelian Philosophy". Considered as an organic, internally differentiated and interrelated totality, a nation and the sovereignty of the nation-state are not external forces imposed on the people but the very extensions of the self-consciousness of man. **Gayatri Mendanha** explores Hannah Arendt's solutions to the evils of ethnic cleansing and ideological thinking in her essay, "Hannah Arendt: The Political Function of Thinking". In urging citizens to dialogue with the 'other', Arendt believed that when we "think what we are doing", we are shielded from committing inhuman, unthinking crimes. The objective of the paper, "The Role of Intellectuals and the Right to Dissent" by **Noel D'Costa** is to bring about an awareness and understanding that the line of attack used to stifle dissent is an important step to detect and assert the role of intellectuals in approaching and responding to challenges. Using Jacques Ranciere's epistemic consequence of dissent, the author contends that consensus can be an ideal in theory but dissent as proposed by Ranciere, is patriotic and a democratic nation should learn to agree to disagree for its social and political growth. In "Becoming an Indian Christian", **Victor Ferrao** elaborates the dynamism necessary for Indian Christians to overcome positivist, isolative, essentialist and static thinking in predetermined set moulds. In trying to understand the non-linear process of the inter-being of Indian Christians and other Indians, he attempts to discern the co-becoming, co-presencing, co-journeying and co-emergence of Indian Christians and Indians in general. Co-becoming occurs in an intertwined mode side by side where both Christians and Indians co-make each other while caring for each other.

In the second part of this book, seven papers examine various aspects of nationalism using a multidisciplinary approach. In his essay, "Deconstructing the Orientalist Imaging of 'Spiritual' India", **John Peter Vallabadoss** attempts to critique a one-dimensional picture of Indian reality and to illustrate the multi-dimensional aspects of India. Overemphasizing one aspect of Indian reality as only 'spiritual' damages its true nature and encourages mono-cultural, monolithic construction of Indian polity and socio-religious reality. By deconstructing the orientalists' imaging of India, he hopes to safeguard the true nature of Indianness that challenges a particular viewing of the Indian nation. In "Science: not to silence "Silence": Reflections on the role of Science in building a Holistic Nation", **S. Stephen Jayard** looks at India's huge contributions in science. The builders of our nation were really convinced that only science could take India ahead in economy, defence, self-sufficiency in food-production, removal of poverty, etc. The author pleads for strengthening the spiritual foundation of India so that this nation does not lose its "depth" in the world of science. The ultramodern India must be cautious about *not allowing science to silence the "silence" of our great nation,* as science and 'silence' are two great tools in nation building. In "Terrorism, Fundamentalism and Nationalism", **Jose Pennamparambil** argues that only nationalism has got a positive meaning. In a country that has many religions, religion and the state have to be separated. The challenge today is to appreciate the diversity of religions, ascertain the reasons behind confrontations and conflicts, and react to specific events and situations with informed, reasoned responses rather than predetermined presumptions and reactions. The full sense of how a nation is built comes through the recognition that is accorded to it by the international community writes **Francis Arackal Thummy** in his paper, "The Role of Soft Power and Hard Power in Nation Building". India as a nation is recognized as an emerging power in and through its soft power – democracy, diplomacy, culture, cultural products, economy, language, media, educational, software, and managerial skills – and hard power, exemplified through its military might. The author makes the case that in today's international relations, soft power is more helpful than hard power in building and showcasing India. In the context of nation building, what does it mean for citizens with different cultural identities, often based on ethnicity, race, language, gender or religion, to recognize themselves as equals in the way they are treated in a political and civil society? Are the reflections of Western thinkers open to the various achievements of different cultural eras or are their discourses poor and fixed in a monochrome perspective? These are some of the issues examined by **Dolreich Pereira** in his essay, "Multiculturalism and Recognition in the context of nation building: Western Questions and the Indian Experience", as he explores multiculturalism, its challenges and the politics of recognition which plague democratic societies today. In his paper, "Politics Governing the Reservation Policy", **S. Sekar Sebastian** attempts to highlight the politics behind the policy of reservation. He describes the evolution of the policy of reservation with the principle of representation, the policy of reservation in the private sector, the debate with advocates and antagonists of reservation, the legal prospects of reservation and other salient features. **Vianney Maria Joseph** in "Symbols of Indian Nationalism: past glory and present crisis" offers his reflections on symbols. They enrich our insights and their emotional associations with the 'motherland' helps to bind categories of peoples into a nation. However, they can become instruments that are manipulated by sectarian groups to stir the emotions of individuals, thus leading to communal unrest and divisions. This paper attempts to look at some of them in the light of the present day crises that we are witnessing.

Seven essays are presented in the final part of the book. **Ashley Miranda** turns our attention to the public debate on India's development between Amartya Sen and Jagdish Bhagwati in his paper, "Ushering in a New Dawn: Making Poverty History in India". The author contends that the difference between Sen and Bhagwati is more a difference of emphasis than of substance. Rather than saying one of them is right and the other is wrong, India needs people like Sen and Bhagwati to disagree, to dialogue and to point out directions that others lack the experience to see. While marking out his preference for Sen, the author concludes strongly that when it comes to the poor, it would not be an exaggeration to say that we must work for their interests first before attending to anything else. In "Winners and Losers in the Development Game", **Anthony Dias** asserts that "Development" is a complex game involving local, national and international players and it produces winners and losers. While there are indeed winners, there are many more losers whose losses are both tangible and intangible and which render them impoverished. They are the Project Affected Persons displaced and dispossessed by the draconian law of land acquisition. This article attempts to show that only the genuine praxis of sustainable development would guarantee protection of the rights of present and future generations and contribute to nation-building. In "Clash of Nationalisms: Calling for a Gandhian Alternative", **A. Pushparajan** invites us to re-examine the trans-religious approach of Gandhi and an interreligious dialogue and cooperation advocated by him. By being 'trans-religious' Gandhi meant that each one will be rooted in one's own religion and yet will go beyond it so as to co-operate with other religious believers. This pluriformic, yet trans-religious model will help establish a just and new society, by pooling the resources of all so that all human beings will be able to live in dignity, equality and in harmony. **Devasia M. Antony** presents "The Nation as an Antinomy: A Note on the Conceptual Logic of Tagore's Dissenting Voice on Nationalism" where he analyses the narrative of nationalism and the inbuilt problematic of exclusive predication and hermeneutic violence in the antinomy of the nation. After a brief description of the various nuances and significance of the twin concept "nation-nationalism", he explores the use of this concept in some of Tagore's works. The problem of relationality or relativity between the "Self" and its "Other" becomes very important in the context of 'domesticated' nationalism. The *advaya-advaita* model employed here calls for universal humanity and not a parochial humanity as nationalism is often taken to mean. In "Revisiting Narayana Guru, Periyar and Ambedkar for Secular Modernity in India", **James Ponniah** offers an overview of the initiatives and struggles of three leaders - Narayana Guru, Periyar and Dr. B. R. Ambedkar – who, basing themselves on the principles of equality, individual freedom and rationality, sought to make India a secular modern state, either through direct political activism (as in the case of Periyar and Ambedkar) or through spiritual activism (as in the case of Narayana Guru). Is there a "space" available for every individual in Indian society? **James D. Chellappa** responds to this question in his article "Subaltern "Space" within the Fabric of Contemporary Indian Society". The present Indian scenario has become difficult for subaltern communities to coexist with the hegemonic forces which are in power. Using a case study on the subaltern Ayyavalli cult of southern Tamil Nadu, he shows that the recent onslaught of Hindutva has made Ayyavalli into yet another form or strand of Hinduism. Originally strong reformers, they are now happy to assert their Hindu roots and traditions. The final essay "Sri Aurobindo: From Politics to Poetics in Post-Modern India" authored by **Kamladevi Kunkolienker,** attempts to deal with the foundation and his ideas of nationalism, his contribution in awakening the people of India towards the freedom movement, and his retirement as a yogi in Pondicherry.

Exploring the different facets involved in "Becoming a Nation" makes us realize the enormity of the project undertaken. These papers reflect attempts to study the subject from a multicultural, multi-religious perspective while adopting a multi-disciplinary approach. No single volume can do justice to this vast topic. While much has been discussed in the pages of this book, much more has been left unsaid. Hence, we refrain from attempting to form a synthesis of the various views presented and in keeping with the spirit of the Indian nation we celebrate our unity of positive purpose in the diversity of our views.

I thank all the contributors for their papers; they took time and trouble to write and re-write them in spite of their busy schedules. I also express my gratitude to Dr. Keith D'Souza, President of ACPI, and the Executive Committee of ACPI for entrusting me with the task of editing this book and for their constant support and guidance. Finally, I thank the publishers, Christian World Imprints, for their patience and professionalism in bringing out this book. This volume is only a beginning; may this work continue with the valuable support and encouragement of our readers.

Keynote Address

Dr. Alexius Ekka, SJ
Director, Xavier Institute of Social Service (XISS), Ranchi

Introduction

At the outset, I would like to thank the organizers for making me the Keynote speaker at this august gathering. I am not a philosopher like all of you, although I did philosophy at Jnana-Deepa Vidyapeeth, Pune, as part of my priestly training. I accepted to speak at the inaugural function of this seminar because its theme intrigued me the most – Becoming a Nation: Processes and Prospects.

So when I thought about this topic, a myriad questions and images flashed in my mind like a computer screen - staring at me and questioning me on the very issue of what it means to be a nation. Some of these images were the lynching of Akhlakh in Dadri at Muzzaffarnagar on 28 September 2015 by Hindu fanatics for allegedly eating cow meat, the manual scavenging by untouchables even in the twenty-first century in states like Bihar and Uttar Pradesh, the brutal gang rape and murder of Nirbhaya in Delhi in December 2012, the land grabbing spree of Adivasi territory by corporate houses and certain states to industrialise the country, the demolition of the Babri Majid on 6 December 1992, the Gujarat carnage of 2002, the communal violence against Christians in Kandhamal following the mysterious murder of Swami Laxamananda Saraswati on 23 August 2008 and the state sponsored violation of human rights under legislations like AFSPA[1] (Armed Forces Special Powers Act), the government's ploy to contain naxalism under the Salwa Judum in Chhattisgarh and the Operation Green Hunt in Jharkhand and finally the recent move by the Jharkand state government to create a "land bank" by annexing people's land without their consent in violation of the Fifth Schedule, the PESA Act[2] and the Forests Right Act[3] (FRA).

In such an exasperating scenario in India, how does one propose to become a nation? What does it mean to be a nation in the first place? My reflections to answer these questions make it necessary to first of all understand the meaning of becoming a nation. But to do so we first need to understand the very terms like nation, nationality, nationalism, state and citizenship. We can then discuss the processes and prospects of becoming a nation.

Nation, Nationality and Nationalism

A nation is a territorial entity to which its nationals have an emotional attachment and in which they invest a moral meaning; it is a homeland – whether ancestral or adopted. Nationality is the collective identity that the people of the nation acquire by identifying with the nation. For a nation to be sustainable its people should be in a position to communicate with one another, that is, they should have a common language. This need not be their ancestral language, it can be an alien tongue (e.g. Bahasa in Indonesia). On the other hand, it is not the case that all those who communicate in the same language necessarily make a nation. English, French, Spanish and Chinese, for example, are spoken by people inhabiting, different territories in different parts of the world. It is the combination, the fusion of territory and language, that makes the nation; a nation is a community in communication in its homeland.[4]

The Indian nation thus consists of over 125 crore population which is spread out in 29 federal states and seven Union Territories. They comprise Indo-Aryan, Dravidian, Mongoloid and other ethnic groups which adhere to many religions like Hinduism, Islam, Christianity, Sikhism, Jainism and Buddhism to mention only a few besides the belief systems of the indigenous peoples or tribals. They speak 19 different languages like Hindi, English, Bengali, Oriya, Punjabi, Gujarati, Tamil, Malayalam, Telugu, Kannada, Rajasthani, and Santhali among others, not to mention more than 400 odd tribal dialects and tongues. The Indian nationality thus consists of many regional ethno-linguistic groups, which reflecting the rich and complex history of India.[5]

State and Citizenship

A state is a legally constituted institution, which provides its residents with protection from internal insecurity and external aggression. Territory is common to the nation and the state. But there is a crucial difference between national and state territory; while the former is moral, the latter is a legal entity. A welfare or socialist state also provides for the social well-being of its residents. A democratic state is a community of people who participate directly or indirectly in the governance of the state. If the state and the nation are coterminous, we have a nation-state. But most states today are multi-national (meaning many nations), poly-ethnic, or a combination of the two.

It is not possible to extend measures of social well-being and the right of political participation to all residents of a state, because they are of two types – citizens and non-citizens. All citizens, by definition, are entitled to welfare and participation. Therefore, a polity ought to be a community of full-fledged citizens, although often this is not the case. Residents who are nationals are invariably citizens. The non-national residents, the ethnics, could also be citizens, although they encounter several problems in acquiring citizenship. Thus, one may speak of full-fledged citizens, nominal citizens and non-citizens.[6]

The Indian Constitution

Our constitution is a charter embodying the fundamental principles on the basis of which the state is to be governed.[7] It is indeed a majestic edifice of enduring human values. It is a record of the compromise of competing interests and values, which are cultural, linguistic, and religious and was arrived at by the erstwhile Constituent Assembly consisting of 318 members who debated and discussed all aspects of human values and societal activities, power sharing by the three major components of the State, the rights of the linguistic and religious minorities and various other aspects influencing the lives of Indian citizens in individual and collective endeavours.

On 25 November 1949, the eve of the formal adoption of the Constitution by the Constituent Assembly, Dr. B. R. Ambedkar observed: "Will Indians place the country above their creed or will they place creed above country? I do not know. But this much is certain that if the parties place the creed above the country, our independence will be put in jeopardy a second time and probably be lost forever. This eventuality we must all resolutely guard against. We must be determined to defend our independence with the last drop of our blood. If we wish to maintain democracy not merely in form but also in fact, what must we do? The first thing in my judgement we must do is, to hold fast to constitutional methods of achieving our social and economic objectives."[8]

Cultural rights are absolute and are not susceptible even to reasonable restrictions like other fundamental rights in Part III of the Constitution. The Supreme Court has held that the cultural rights are not only fundamental but also absolute and not amenable to restrictions. They are not largesse conceded by the majorities to the minorities. They are fundamental rights won by the minorities for the preservation and promotion of their cultural ideologies. It is not a patronage accorded by anyone in any sense of the term.[9]

Becoming a Nation

In the context of the present discussion, becoming a nation means how so many of us Indians live together in peaceful harmony, respecting one another, upholding the ideals and values enshrined in the Preamble of the Constitution, honouring the fundamental rights of citizens including the special provisions conferred upon the weaker sections and abiding by the norms and provisions for the governance of the country. It also means upholding the democratic principles in running the state, having a rule of law with impartial judiciary and implementing secularism without fear or favour. As regards happiness, prosperity and well-being of all the citizens of the country, we need to adopt and develop a holistic and sustainable paradigm, which caters to the care of the earth and its resources as well as the animal kingdom.

Processes and Prospects

Speaking of the processes and prospects of becoming a nation, we need to spell out the mechanisms through which we can attain the avowed objectives of liberty, justice, equality and fraternity as articulated in the Constitution of the country. Of the many areas that catch our attention, we will briefly discuss and reflect on four sectors which constitute the processes and prospects for becoming a nation – (1) secularism and peaceful coexistence, (2) sustainable development, (3) gender justice equity and (4) supporting people's movements.

1. Secularism and Peaceful Co-existence

In order to live dignified human lives, our Constitution has bestowed upon us the freedoms of conscience, religion and worship. This fundamental right gives an assurance to millions of Indians to practice their religions without fear. But the contrary is true. The cultural chauvinism advocated by the *Sangh Parivar* and the *Hindutva* lobby is a great disservice to the nation. There is so much communal violence being perpetrated and hatred being propagated every day in different ways by the Hindu fundamentalists especially against the Christian and Muslim minorities in different parts of the country that one begins to suspect the hand of the ruling party at the centre behind all the carnage and intimidation.

Cultural supremacy is an offshoot of religious fundamentalism and religious fundamentalism is a dangerous obsession. Instead of building bridges of understanding, fanatics are sowing the seeds of disharmony and anarchy, which is the surest way for secession and disintegration. Saffronization is bound to produce diseased minds and a sick and divided society. It will militate against national cohesiveness and undermine the unity and integrity of the nation besides hindering peaceful co-existence.

The minorities are equal partners in building the nation-state. Indian civil society built on the foundations of the rule of law and parliamentary democracy does not admit discrimination against cultural minorities. A single culture is not only opposed to the letter and spirit of the Constitution but also antithetical to the philosophy and text of the Constitution.

An Effort to Bring Communal Harmony in Society: Jharkhand Sadbhavna Manch

The Jharkhand Sadbhavna Manch (JSM) is an informal civil society organization comprising members of various religions, cultures and traditions in Ranchi. Its objectives are to foster peace and harmony in society as well as to strengthen the bonds of mutual respect, tolerance, understanding, fellow feeling among the peoples of different religions and cultures. Some of JSM's programmes and activities have been (1) to organize conferences, workshops and meetings to promote communal harmony, (2) to organize protest rallies against communal violence demanding justice along with the restoration of communal harmony, (3) to celebrate the annual World Peace Day and the festivals of different religions together, (4) to instil among students and the general public mutual tolerance and appreciation of each other's religion and culture and (5) to work for the protection of the rights of the minorities.[10]

Such efforts must be made at various localities in each district and state to ensure the religious freedom of the people and to understand the principles of secularism and experience the values of unity in diversity in the country.

2. Sustainable Development

Sustainable development is most commonly defined as: "... development that meets the needs of the present without compromising the ability of future generations to meet their own needs."[11] This concept however should be holistic and must include natural resources as a source of livelihood for tribal people who have a symbiotic relationship with them.

Ironically, the word development today has a bad connotation. It has come to mean the depletion of natural resources for ever increasing profits and insatiable greed of a few rich people at the cost of development which displaces the poor, particularly tribals and Dalits. It also causes irreparable ecological destruction leading to the extinction of many organisms and plant species and environmental pollution causing serious health hazards.

Pope's Critique on Development and Response

Pope Francis[12] himself in his Encyclical *Laudato Si'* has questioned the present paradigm of development, which is causing untold destruction to Mother Earth, our common home, through pollution and climate change, a shortage of fresh drinking water, loss of biodiversity, leading to the decline in the quality of human life and the breakdown of society and increasing inequality.

The Holy Father further offers a new vision of the world through the Gospel of Creation, where he discusses the human roots of the ecological crisis and proposes an integral ecology. Similarly, he speaks of the lines of approach and action through dialogue on the environment in the international community and dialogue for new national and local policies, to mention a few. At the end he sends out an invitation for ecological education and spirituality by adopting a new lifestyle, educating for the covenant between humanity and the environment, ecological conversion, etc.

Praxis of Sustainable Development: Organic Farming

The Jharkhand Alternative Development Forum (JADFO) is a civil organization and an informal association of people engaged in the alternative development process in the State. It is represented by people at the grassroots, social activists, NGOs, academicians, engineers, researchers, media persons and practitioners in the Small Scale Industries in Ranchi.

As a concrete measure of sustainable and holistic development, JADFO has started organic farming activities in the villages of Burmu Block of Ranchi district. The farmers (mostly tribals) attended short training programmes on organic farming at the agricultural laboratory of Dr. Vandana Shiva in Dehradun. The training consists of identifying various seeds, preparing compost manure, vermin compost and pesticides. They also learn to prepare the soil and to grow organic seeds, besides using horticultural techniques. After completing the programme they practice organic farming. This has brought about an awareness of the demerits of the use of the high yielding varieties of seeds, chemical fertilizers and pesticides. Their uncontaminated and non-genetically modified crops - rice, pulses and vegetables - are abundant and taste better. Plans are afoot to make organic farming a movement in the area and link it with proper marketing of their agricultural products.

Many other areas of sustainable development practices are also well known in the country. These are tree plantation and cleanliness drives, making of check dams and adopting watershed management techniques for agriculture including water harvesting for domestic use. Becoming a nation today would imply adopting sustainable life styles and caring for the Mother Earth, including its rich and abundant resources.

3. Gender Justice and Equity

Women are the twin victims of subordination and inequality. On the one hand, there are daily reports of horrendous injustices and indignities perpetrated on women. These include molestation, rape, domestic violence, dowry deaths and witch hunting as well as being treated unfairly at work, including the lack of equal remuneration, etc., to women who live in urban as well as rural areas. On the other hand, strong measures adopted by various organizations and institutions as well as by individuals for gender justice and equity. Thus, both men and women, boys and girls should be free to develop their abilities and make choices – without limitations set by rigid gender roles and prejudices – based on personal interests and capacities. In this regard, mention must be made about a Bangalore-based organization called VISTAR, which conducts an annual international programme on Gender Justice and Social Transformation. Apart from the social analysis including forms of patriarchy and women's role in economic aspects and power structure in society, the participants are made to share their experiences on gender discrimination. Through the month-long training participants acquire knowledge and insights on these issues and come out with better understanding of men and women as equal and partners.

4. Supporting people's movements

In a democracy like India, there are various ways to assert people's rights. People's movements for justice and equality are well known in the country. As an exercise of becoming a nation, we must also join various people's struggles – whether for women's rights, Dalits' rights or tribal people's rights. The following example of the Koel Karo People's Movement in Jharkhand highlights how struggling with the displaced people won them justice and human dignity.

This movement ended in 2010 with the Jharkhand Government shelving the mega hydro power project after nearly 40 years of people's struggles. Mooted in 1970s, the Koel Karo Hydro power was to generate 750 megawatts of power at the cost of displacing a tribal population of 50,000 and causing ecological destruction in the area. The project affected people resisted the mega project and many organizations joined their struggle including XISS. It helped them to file a PIL in the Supreme Court in 1984 against the upcoming project, which did not even have any resettlement and rehabilitation (R&R) policy. In its judgement the Supreme Court gave a stay order to the Government of Jharkhand until a proper R&R policy was in place. In order to continue the project the government did bring about an R&R policy, which was copied and modified from some other project. This only resulted in the people intensifying their agitation against the project. The police fired on these demonstrators in 2001 and killed eight people. This only made the project-affected people to offer more resistance. Many NGOs, and Community-based organizations, including academic institutions, continued to support the people's movement against the Koel Karo Hydro Power Project. In the end the Jharkand Government decided to cancel it during President's rule in 2010.

The case of Koel Karo is an example of engaging in democratic means to obtain justice. We may also join hands with many such protest movements going on in the country and show that it is also a just way to demand justice and prove that it is a proper sign of becoming a nation.

Conclusion

Becoming a nation to realize the aims and objectives of democracy by its citizens is a lifelong project. Our country depends on knowledgeable and thoughtful students and educators to build peace with freedom and justice among nations and peoples. We must continually discuss various issues and adopt ways and means to deal with them with the idea of promoting human dignity, ecological sustainability and peace and social harmony in society.

The twenty two papers to be presented do touch upon vital areas of life and these will certainly address them adequately and provide us with concrete measures of becoming a nation having processes and prospects.

Notes

1 Armed Forces (Special Powers) Acts (AFSPA), are Acts of the Parliament of India that grant special powers to the Indian Armed Forces in what each act terms "disturbed areas". According to the Disturbed Areas (Special Courts) Act, 1976, once declared 'disturbed', the area has to maintain status quo for a minimum of 3 months.

2 Panchayats (Extension to Scheduled Areas) Act, 1996 or PESA is a law enacted by the Government of India for ensuring self-governance through traditional Gram Sabhas for people living in the Scheduled Areas of India. Scheduled Areas are areas identified by the Fifth Schedule of the Constitution of India. Scheduled Areas are found in ten states of India which have predominant populations of tribal communities. The Scheduled Areas were not covered by the 73rd Constitutional Amendment or Panchayati Raj Act of the Indian Constitution as provided in Part IX of the Constitution. PESA was enacted on 24 December 1996 to extend the provisions of Part IX of the Constitution to Scheduled Areas, with certain exceptions and modifications. PESA sought to enable the Panchayats at appropriate levels and Gram Sabhas to implement a system of self-governance with respect to a number of issues such as customary resources, minor forest produce, minor minerals, minor water bodies, selection of beneficiaries, sanction of projects, and control over local institutions (See Ministry of Panchayati Raj-PESA, Government of India).

3 The Scheduled Tribes and Other Traditional Forest Dwellers (Recognition of Forest Rights) Act, 2006, is a key piece of forest legislation passed in India on 18 December 2006. It is also known as the Forest Rights Act, the Tribal Rights Act, the Tribal Bill, and the Tribal Land Act. The law concerns the rights of forest-dwelling communities to land and other resources, denied to them over decades as a result of the continuance of colonial forest laws in India (See the Scheduled Tribes and Other Traditional Forest Dwellers (Recognition of Forest Rights) Act, 2006 of Government of India).

4 See T. K. Oommen, "Citizenship, Nationality and Ethnicity". Cambridge: Blackwell Publishers, 2001, p. 19.

5 See K. S. Singh, "People of India: An Introduction (People of India National Series)". New Delhi: Oxford University Press, 2002.

6 See T. K. Oommen, "Citizenship, Nationality and Ethnicity". Cambridge: Blackwell Publishers, 2001.

7 See D.D. Basu, "Introduction to the Constitution of India". Gurgaon, India: Lexis Nexis, 2014.

8 See H. G. Balakrishna, "Cultural ideologies and the implementation of constitutional provisions", *Religion and Society,* 47, no. 3 (2000): 8.

9 Ibid, p. 9.

10 See Alex Ekka, "Jharkhand Sadbhavna Manch: Promoting peace and reconciliation", *Ranchi Jesuits Year Book 2015.* Ranchi: Ranchi Jesuit Society, 2015.
11 See WCED, "Our Common Future: Report of the World Commission on Environment and Development", 1987, p. 41. Retrieved from http://www.un-documents.net/ocf-02.htm
12 See Pope Francis, "Encyclical Letter *Laudato Si', praise be to you: On care for our common home*". Trivandrum: Carmel International Publishing House, 2015.

Part 1

Nation and Nationalism: Ideological Considerations

1

Imagining a Nation
Postcolonial Perspectives

Nishant A. Irudayadason
Jnana-Deepa Vidyapeeth, Pune

Abstract: This paper seeks to highlight three important and inevitable aspects to imagining a nation: secular, pluralistic and cosmopolitan. This imagination is worked through postcolonial and subaltern studies taking inspiration from many postcolonial thinkers like Edward Said, Frantz Fanon, Homi Bhabha Ranajit Guha, Dipesh Chakrabarty and Gayatri Spivak. From the reading of the works of these renowned scholars, this paper focuses on the need for decimating and deconstructing colonial imagination and constructions in order to develop a creative and dynamic narrative of a nation in what Bhabha calls the "third space." This paper also critiques a lopsided version of nation and nationalism programmatically constructed by Hindutva ideologues, by showing that this version is anchored in a colonial narrative of homogeneity and fixity. An attempt is also made to fire our imagination by introducing the concept of "positive mutual indebtedness" accompanied by a commitment to human rights and social justice.

Introduction

Imagination calls for creative thinking and imagining a nation demands a responsible creativity; responsible because the task is laborious. There is no one singular paradigm to imagine a nation. Today's political climate demands that we adopt a post-colonial approach in imagining a nation. The reflections that emerge from postcolonial perspectives are likely to provide us with some theoretical tool to counter essentialist theories and/or colonial political narratives on nation. Again there is no one perspective emerging from the post-colonial studies. This make our task of imagination a pleasant one as all postcolonial scholars do not speak in unison and rightly so as we shall see that the "post" in post-colonialism, just as in postmodernity, celebrates difference. Postcolonial thinking, like postmodernity, is not a school of thought but a critical thinking and questioning rather than a constitutive doctrine.[1] However, the post-colonial approach is consciously and deliberately undertaken both to resist the essentialist approach to the idea of nation provided by Anthony D. Smith[2] and to creatively appropriate the idea of Anderson's understanding of nation as "imagined communities."[3]

This paper is divided into three parts. The first one aims at imagining a secular nation by offering a substantial corrective to the homogenous colonial narrative of history. To achieve this purpose, we study the main precursors of postcolonial studies who engaged in the reversal of the colonial prism. The second part intends to imagine a pluralistic nation through the optic of hybridity, a term borrowed from Homi Bhabha, whose ideas are extensively discussed in order to deconstruct the colonial constructions of fixed cultures. The final part is an attempt to imagine a "cosmopolitan" or "transnational" nation through a dynamic narrative of a non-territorial "third space."

1. Decimating the Fallout of Colonial Imagination

The merit of those whom we can call precursors of postcolonial studies such Aimé Césaire and Frantz Fanon is to have revisited the colonial imagination and discourses with new perspectives and to have relativized what was presented to the colonized as absolute. The colonial perspective was partial and truncated because, first, it established a boundary between "we" the dynamic colonizers and "they" the static colonized, thus attributing dynamism and movement exclusively to the former; secondly, it presented the colonized as "benefactors" of a "civilizing mission," making them indebted to the colonizers for their generosity. The precursors of postcolonial studies tried to undo the image of the colonized as having a passive static existence and as eternally being indebted to the benevolent generous colonizers. The reversal of this colonial claim has two dimensions: first, it transforms the idea of a "passive recipient" as offensive, thus making the colonisers claim of a "civilizing mission" dubious and heinous; secondly it presents the colonized as having their own narratives that are significant.

The first dimension of this reversal is clearly present in the writings of Fanon, including in his work *The Wretched of the Earth*: "The colonized must be made able to see that colonialism never gives away anything for nothing."[4] Thus, he interprets the revolution in Algeria as the moment when "the people understand that wealth is not the fruit of labour but spoils from an organized protection racket. The rich no longer seem respectable men but flesh-eating beasts, jackals and ravens who wallow in the blood of the people."[5] Also, if there is a relationship of debt between Africa and Europe, it is clearly the latter indebted to the former. Fanon asserts that the opulence of European nations "was built on the backs of slaves, fed on the blood of slaves and it owes its very existence to the soil and subsoil of the underdeveloped world."[6]

However, the second dimension of the reversal, namely the colonized have their own narratives that have been ignored or distorted by the colonizers has not been much emphasized - at least in explicit terms in the writings of Fanon. This second dimension is more crucial than the first one for our purpose of imagining a nation. The colonial narrative of a nation is what has gained prominence and popular acceptance in many countries particularly in India. Thus, the colonizers sought to give a coherent history of colonized India dividing the historical periods of the politics in the Indian subcontinent as Hindu nation, followed by a Muslim nation before it became a British colony. This homogenization of Indian history done by colonial historians, particularly James Bill, has done violence to the Indian narratives not merely by silencing its heterogeneous, multi-linguistic, multi-cultural and multi-religious aspects, but more by creating a religious polarization in its attempt to present a monolithic periodization of Indian history on the basis of religion. The different narratives of nationalism that is echoed today – either due to non-knowledge imposed by colonial historians or deliberately orchestrated by the present day political class who are also partisans of religions – is of this type contrary to the secular imagination of nation. A renowned Indian historian laments that "although discarded by historians, those that still hold to the theory continue to support the required hostility between Hindus and Muslims."[7]

In imagining a nation from a postcolonial perspective, heterogeneity becomes a favourable difference; it has always been in the psyche of the subcontinent before and in spite of colonialism. It allows every individual to bring difference to public life; it is an inevitable part of a "secular imagination" that leads to a philosophy not merely of "live and let live," but also "live and help live." Thus, secularism is not the ideology of post-religious world: a total separation of church and state as acclaimed by the French laicity, but a positive acceptance of all religions. This does not imply that we blindly accept anything in the name of faith without the need to challenge faith when it vitiates its very foundation by threatening to undermine the "humanistic discourse on the inclusiveness through difference."[8] Rustom Bharucha notes pertinently: "One needs to strengthen secularism as a philosophy and life practice by unearthing and activating its insufficiently mobilized resources and potentialities in the public sphere. Only then would it be possible to shift the secular struggle from its defensive position to a more positive agenda, transcending the innate condescension of 'tolerance,' to arrive at new modes of respecting and living with difference."[9] Only when we make an effort to live with differences in a secular space, can we become creative in our understanding of others and change ourselves before we ask others to change.

2. Deconstructing the Colonial Constructions

One of the important goals of postcolonial thinkers was to deconstruct the hegemonic Western epistemology that disempowered other cultures and discourses. "Taking a contrasting stance to traditional anti-colonialism, which was more concerned with carrying out a political, economic and social criticism, they [postcolonial thinkers] went into a more epistemic criticism, a criticism that was based on the textuality of colonialism."[10] In the eyes of postcolonial thinkers, the national identity claimed by nationalists is colonial and therefore, reductionist in many respects. First, mirroring the colonial perspective, the idea of "we the nationalists" is essentialist and maintains the same opposition constructed by the colonizers between them and the colonized without even any critical regard that this was precisely a colonial invention and falsehood. Edward Said, inaugurating the postcolonial studies with his book *Orientalism* has consistently adopted a critical approach to all essentialisms. Thus, in Culture and Imperialism, he asserts that "to leave the historical world for the metaphysics of essences like negritude, Irishness, Islam or Catholicism is to abandon history for essentializations that have the power to turn human beings against each other."[11] Another important author of postcolonial studies, Homi Bhabha, also rejects any attempt to nationalize identities and all extreme forms to which such attempts can lead us: "the very idea of a pure, 'ethnically cleansed' national identity can only be achieved through the death, literal and figurative, of the complex inter-weavings of history, and the culturally contingent borderlines of modern nationhood."[12]

Another important criticism against a kind of colonial and reductionist nationalism comes from the subaltern perspective, namely this colonial nationalism has deprived its due place to the subaltern identities such as farmers, women, untouchables, etc. This is an important contribution of Ranajit Guha through his work *Elementary Aspects of Peasant Insurgency in Colonial India* on peasant revolts in colonial India and their contributions to the struggle for independence.[13] Another founder of subaltern studies, Dipesh Chakrabarty, observes that "the declared aim of Subaltern Studies was to produce historical analyses in which the subaltern groups were viewed as the subjects of history."[14] If this ambition seemed vain for some important writers of postcolonial studies, including for Gayatri C. Spivak, it has nonetheless two merits: first, the reintroduction of "concrete" history in the primarily textual and symbolic undertaking of postcolonial studies, and, secondly, to counter the colonial concept of a homogenous identity with a plural and complex identity. From the point of view of this second merit, Homi Bhabha shows that two readings of Fanon are possible: one giving pride to multiple and ambivalent identities. "For Fanon, the liberatory 'people' who initiate the productive instability of revolutionary cultural change are themselves the bearers of a hybrid identity."[15] Pouchepadass corroborates this view of Homi Bhabha by stating that the postcolonial studies are at least partly inspired by the chapter titled "The Trials and Tribulations of National consciousness" in Fanon's work, *The Wretched of the Earth*.

According to Achille Mbembe, the key element that characterizes postcolonial studies is "entanglement and concatenation, unveiled chiefly through its critique of identity and subjectivity."[16] This is especially true of Bhabha, who opposes the colonial idea of identity within sealed borders and its refusal of the dynamic nature of cultural facts. "An important feature of colonial discourse is its dependence on the concept of 'fixity' in the ideological construction of otherness."[17] Bhabha aims to deconstruct all binary oppositions in the heart of the colonial imagination, to show that what is presented as being separate is actually already entangled. He opposes the rigid colonial conceptions with identities and cultures taken in constant movement of interpenetration and the overlapping of each other.

Thus, Homi Bhabha is less interested in redefining the colonized in isolation, however radically different from the optic of the colonisers this redefinition may be.

> What is theoretically innovative, and politically crucial, is the need to think beyond narratives of originary and initial subjectivities and to focus on those moments or processes that are produced in the articulation of cultural differences. These 'in-between' spaces provide the terrain for elaborating strategies of selfhood – singular or communal – that initiate new signs of identity, and innovative sites of collaboration, and contestation, in the act of defining the idea of society itself.[18]

For him all identities – whether colonial or nationalist – are hybrid in nature, but their coming into contact with one another doubles derivations and entanglements. Thus, he shows that imitation or identification with the other is not the simple production of a resemblance, but an ambivalent process: "the very place of identification, caught in the tension of demand and desire, is a space of splitting."[19] Imitation is the production of what is almost the same, but not quite. In other words, the mimesis of colonial narratives is itself ambivalent. Colonization, in spite of itself, has produced hybrid identities: "the effect of colonial power is seen as the production of hybridization rather than the noisy command of colonialist authority or the silent repression of native traditions."[20]

Deconstructing the colonial construction of the idea of nation in present day India is an urgent task, more compelling than ever before as there is a retrieval of the colonial reminiscence of cultural nationalism that we are witnessing in our time. The unfolding series of events in the past two years – creating vociferous debates on 'national" and "anti-national," with an intent of popularising the idea of being a national, as accepting a standardized singular Indian culture, invoking the law of sedition on any person who challenges the hegemony of the state in its attempt to give a uniform cultural identity to the nation, targeting broad-minded intellectuals who want to uphold the secular fabric of the nation erected on the principle of respect for multiculturalism – all these point to the return of a colonial narrative of "fixity" to haunt our memory of the colonial era.

Sadanand Menon extensively dwells on this subject in one of his recent essays titled "From National Culture to Cultural Nationalism." He rightly observes that cultural nationalism is "the trope that legitimizes its unrepentant aggression on every instrument of democracy."[21] The idea of cultural nationalism in India evolved together with the idea of nationhood. Many leaders in pre-Independent India worked out a paradigm of cultural nationalism by attempting to construct a glorious history of India, pure and uncontaminated by external influence and articulating this version of nationalism conjointly with Hindu symbolism, and this is systematically and programmatically being done under the patronage of the present ruling class. The recent imagery of Prime Minster Narendra Modi as Ram destroying Ravana, soon after the much advertised claim of the surgical attacks of the Indian army on Pakistan exemplifies this.

Within this narrative of cultural nationalism, the Vedas have become the single normative reference. Surprisingly, in the court case of allowing women to go to the Ayappan shrine, the judge asked for a proof if Vedas denied entry of women into temple. Unfortunately, it seems the question of women's entry into the Ayappan temple can be resolved through the study of the Vedas, and it is even more unfortunate that cultural nationalism is invisibly and subtly at work in reducing all forms of Hindu worship to a set pattern of Vedic rituals. Along with this Vedic homogenization, comes the militarization of deities, the "ready-for-battle Krishna who will lead his chosen ones to victory."[22]

This cultural nationalism does enormous violence to women and Dalits – whose concerns must be echoed in our philosophizing – in many different ways. The victims of the aggressive turn of cultural nationalism are the Dalits along with members of minority religions. The ideological imposition of banning the eating of beef targets the Dalits and reinstitutes the principle of purity and pollution. Violence is done to the Dalits by ensuring their double exclusion from cultural purity: first, they are forced to deal with corpses of cows and bulls for their very survival, including skinning the dead cows to make leather goods by which they are excluded from nationalistic cultural purity;

secondly, by ensuring that they do such jobs, they are physically attacked, humiliated, publicly shamed and labelled "anti-national." The same ideology of cow sacralisation also targets the Muslim community - to weaken them economically and shame them as being "anti-national." Part of the assertion of cultural nationalism is lamenting being Hindu victims during the invasion of Moghuls. Romila Thapar rightly challenges this assertion: "They speak of the Hindus being enslaved for a thousand years by Muslim rule, but do not pause for a while to [the fact] that caste Hindus victimized the lower castes, Dalits and Adivasis for two thousand or more years, and most caste Hindus, with a few exceptions, regarded it as quite legitimate. Some continue to do so."[23] We may have to interrogate if the increase of deaths – often brushed aside as suicides – of the Dalit students on the campus of higher education point to this sad fact.

Purohit made a distinction between Hindu nationalism and Indian nationalism, namely "the former was exclusive, narrowly based, mixed with religion and partial […] The latter believed in a composite culture of India, […] One exalted a community over other communities while the other emphasized unity in the diversity of various communities. While one had great belief in centralised leadership and in militancy; the other was wedded to liberal and democratic traditions."[24] Based on this distinction of Purohit, Menon holds that the very notion of "Bharat Mata" is part of such exclusive Hindu Nationalism and when hard core cultural nationalists of the ruling dispensation proclaim those who do not shout in public "Bharat Mata ki jai" are anti-national to make a theatrical display of patriotism, they do not refer to "loyalty to Indian nationalism but to Hindu nationalism or Hindutva."[25] The dangerous fallout of this cultural nationalism, Hindutva is the excessive violence done to women in Indian society. The slogan "Bharat Mata ki jai," Menon holds is not an expression of patriotism but of patriarchy: "Excessive mother-love is a camouflage for extreme misogyny."[26] He substantiates his claim by enumerating a series of unimaginable horrors done to women from brutalities done to pregnant women in Gujarat in 2002 to the Nirbhaya case in Delhi in 2014.

From this informed point of view, it is imperative that we deconstruct such aggressive cultural nationalism which is "an imaginary homeland constructed out of imaginary enemies, who always belong to religions or regions which you believe is not your own. It is a strange, anxious individual who will not pay the slightest heed to one's proven hybridity. In history nothing stays 'pure.' Or as Salman Rushdie would have it, it's all subject to 'mongrelization'."[27]

3. Evolving Dynamic Narratives on Nation in the "Third Space"

In order to imagine a dynamic narrative of a nation based on the notion of "third space," we need to revisit Anderson's idea of a nation as "imagined communities." The three reasons he gives why nations are imagined communities has contributed to Homi Bhabha's "third space" of hybridity. Firstly, the nation is imagined as limited, as situated infinite borders and not co-extensive with humanity. Secondly, the nation is imagined as sovereign through the ideal of freedom and plurality of religions. Thirdly, the nation is imagined as a community conceived in the image of a horizontal relationship in spite of inequalities.[28] The intersection between the "third space" of Bhabha and the "imagined communities" of Anderson happens where the imaginary paradigm meets the demand of different universe of meaning binaries of classical metaphysics such as East/West, colonized/colonisers, imaginary/real, etc. Known for his "third space," the interstitial and liminal space exceeding dualities leading to hybrid and fluid cultures, Bhabha anchors his theory on the foundations laid by Anderson. He affirms that Anderson has opened the way to discover not only the profoundly discursive character of nations made from "textual strategies" and "metaphoric displacements" of "figurative ploys" but also the ambivalence of modern political forms subject to the inevitable contingency of language; "the act of composition" of narratives are necessarily seen as dynamic, creative, and therefore uncertain.[29]

This hybrid model was defined by Paul Gilroy based on the Black Atlantic, the true archetype of hybridity "as a non-traditional tradition, an irreducibly modern, ex-centic, unstable and asymmetrical cultural ensemble that cannot be apprehended through the Manichean logic of binary coding."[30] This hybridity model was influenced by Giles Deleuze – for whom "the imaginary isn't the unreal; it is the indiscernibility of real and unreal,"[31] – in the image of the rhizome as opposed to that of the root, that is to say, a world of dissemination and miscegenation as opposed to a world of filiation and inheritance. There is no hard core identity or continuity or tradition as in the community model but varying formations in rupture, obeying only the logic of miscegenation. This hybrid diaspora is organized around racial and cultural poles in which several definitions of identity are articulated. Cantered on the concept of negritude, the originality of this diaspora first lies in the fact that it has no direct affiliation with any society or territories of origin. It is distinguished by continental breadth and diversity of its territories of origin.

The recent migrants from many countries due to civil wars or political oppression form the new diaspora. They include Tibetans, Tamils of Sri Lanka, Syrians, etc. There are also others from many developing countries, including, India migrating to Europe and North America for a better life. They too form part of the new diaspora. The term "transnational community" is used to denote this new diaspora. Riva Kastoryano affirms that "transnational networks linking the country of origin to the country of residence and promoting participation in both locations challenge the single allegiance required by membership in a nation's political community. Transnationalism has led to the institutional expression of the multiple belonging in which a country of origin becomes a source of identity; a country of residence, a source of right; and the transnational space, a site of political action."[32] Defined through a "desire to transcend both the structures of the nation state and the constraints of ethnicity and national particularity,"[33] the diaspora, and with it all communities associated with cosmopolitanism, is located in a "non-nationalistic" space which is best expressed by James Clifford: "whatever their ideologies of purity, diasporic cultural forms can never, in practice, be exclusively nationalist."[34]

The writings of Pnina Werbner, a South African anthropologist, are equally nourished by the notion of hybridity, cosmopolitanism, transnationalism. According to her, "There are no fixed cultures in modern nation-states; only political imaginaries of pure or impure cultural horizon."[35] From the views of different postcolonial thinkers from Bhabha to Werbner, we realize that the "third space" transgresses the logic nation based on fixed boundaries and claimed territories. Thus, we can say that the imagination of Anderson spills over the idea of nation circumscribed in its European genealogy, first, because this new epistemological legitimacy is granted to non-European cultures and, secondly, because of the semantic force contained in the term "imagined communities" whose theoretical imprecision has made it easy to apply it a desired elusive domain. So it is not the idea of nation, now atrophied, but the multiple cultural formations localized inside or outside of the geographical territory of a nation.

The cosmopolitan idea of transnationalism of Immanuel Kant merits attention as it was a radical idea of his time. One of the important aspects of this cosmopolitanism for Kant rests on universal peace for which standing armies must be abolished. A nation that takes excessive pride in its military force makes a return to archaic chaos and is doomed to failure. No doubt there is a close link between territorial nationalism and extravagant military display of power. The Hindutva imagery of "Akand Bharat" is a militant version of nationalism investing itself in the ability of creating an enemy. In India, this is achieved by a consistent attempt to label Pakistan as an enemy state. Any Indian in good books with any civilian Pakistani is labelled anti-national. This is nothing short of a fascist nationalism. Romila Thapar observes: "Nationalism requires a far greater commitment to attend to the needs of the Nation than sloganeering, and that too with slogans *focusing on territory or ones that have limited acceptability* ... it is indeed ironic that an Indian who refuses to shout this slogan is immediately declared anti-national, but an Indian who has deliberately not paid his taxes or stashed away black money is not declared as such."[36]

Transnational identity and cosmopolitan imagination makes the issue of border and border security irrelevant. Human rights violations are on the increase in the Kashmir valley in the name of homeland security, a fact often hidden by the mainstream media. Any questions raised on excessive military presence in civilian regions – whether in Pakistan or in North-eastern states – is viewed as unpatriotic or even worse as anti-national. Questioning atrocities of military persons is equated with being ungrateful to the sacrifices made by some of them on the borders and no one is willing to ask if these sacrifices are necessary; if so for whose interest? Dissent is brutally silenced with state machinery including the police and in some cases the army. All these are fallouts of a territorial identity of nation that does not want to accept the present day reality of migration, mobility and fluidity of borders. Recalling the ever inspiring and challenging words of Rabindranath Tagore, who declared that "nation is the greatest evil," he explains it in the following words: "It is my conviction that my countrymen will gain truly their India by fighting against that education which teaches them that a country is greater than the ideals of humanity."[37]

Conclusion

Imagining a secular, pluralistic and cosmopolitan nation, from the perspective of postcolonial studies, opens up a new kind of relationship with the other and a new way to deal with otherness. We cannot help but recall what Edward Said wrote about relationship among people and peoples: "the history of all cultures is the history of cultural borrowings. Cultures are not impermeable. [...] Culture is never just a matter of ownership, of borrowing and lending with absolute debtors and creditors, but rather of appropriations, common experiences, and interdependencies of all kinds among different cultures."[38]

We need to imagine a nation where we no longer know who gives but everyone receives from the rich diversity of the world. This exemplifies a social relation of positive mutual indebtedness[39] in the words of Jacques Godbout, in which each person (or each people) estimates having received more than given. But this positive mutual indebtedness, the privileged relational moment, cannot rest on a simple recognition of the cultural contributions of everyone to the history of humanity. It should be maintained by a constant actualization of shared values such as equal rights and justice. In this sense, the imagining of a nation of positive mutual indebtedness is not separated from issues of economic equality and social justice. A national goes beyond simply shouting slogans, affirms Romila Thapar:

> There has to be something more substantial to give hope to those that live at the edge of nowhere, that there is a reality that makes up a nation, and this reality will take them away from the edge and bring them to the centre and make life worthwhile. [...] These are issues that are foremost in the minds of students, perhaps more so among Dalit students. We heard them raise these issues

> at Jawaharlal Nehru University (JNU) and other universities. They were not just shouting slogans. They were demanding a different society, a society that ensured human rights and justice for all – precisely the kind of society that converts a country into a nation.[40]

Imagining a nation is indeed a creative but laborious task insofar as it is responsible; responsible insofar as it makes incantation for justice-to-come, justice which is indeconstructible, but in the name of which everything else has to be deconstructed.

Notes

1 See Jacques Pouchepadass, *L'Orientalisme: L'Orient créé par l'Occident* (Paris: Seuil, 1980), 186.
2 Anthony D. Smith, *The Ethnic Origins of Nations* (Oxford: Blackwell, 1986); Anthony D. Smith, "The Origins of Nations," *Ethnic and Racial Studies*, 12, no. 3 (1989): 340-367.
3 See Benedict Anderson, *Imagined Communities* (London: Verso, 2006).
4 Frantz Fanon, *The Wretched of the Earth*, trans. Richard Philcox (New York: Grove Press, 2005), 92.
5 Ibid., 133.
6 Ibid., 53.
7 Romila Thapar, "Reflections on Nationalism and History," in *On Nationalism* (New Delhi: Aleph, 2016), 26.
8 Rajan Ghosh (ed), *Making Sense of the Secular, Critical Perspectives from Europe to Asia* (New York: Routledge), 18.
9 Rustom Bharucha, *In the Name of the Secular* (Delhi: Oxford University Press, 1998), 24.
10 Jacques Pouchepadass, and Jules Naudet, *The Anti-Establishment Impact of Postcolonial Studies: An Interview with Jacques Pouchepadass*, trans. Kate McNaughtan (December 9, 2013); http://www.booksandideas.net/The-Anti-Establishment-Impact-of.html (accessed on October 12, 2016).
11 Edward Said, *Culture and Imperialism* (New York: Vintage, 1994), 228.
12 Homi Bhabha, *The Location of Culture* (New York: Routledge, 2004), 7.
13 Ranajit Guha, *Elementary Aspects of Peasant Insurgency in Colonial India* (Delhi: Oxford University Press, 1983).
14 Dipesh Chakrabarty, *Habitations of Modernity: Essays in the Wake of Subaltern Studies* (Delhi: Permanent Black, 2004), 7.
15 Bhabha, *The Location of Culture*, 55.
16 Achille Mbembe, Olivier Mongin and Others, *What is Postcolonial Thinking?: An Interview with Achille Mbembe*, trans. John Fletcher; http://www.eurozine.com/articles/2008-01-09-mbembe-en.html (accessed on October 13, 2016).
17 Bhabha, *The Location of Culture*, 94.
18 Ibid., 2.
19 Ibid., 63.
20 Ibid., 160.
21 Sadanand Menon, "From National Culture to Cultural Nationalism," in *On Nationalism* (New Delhi: Aleph, 2016), 148.
22 Ibid., 119.
23 Thapar, "Reflections on Nationalism and History," 12.

24 B. R. Purohit, *Hindu Revivalism and Indian Nationalism* (Lucknow: Sathi Prakashan, 1965), 86.
25 A. G. Noorani, "Nationalism and its Contemporary Discontents in India," in *On Nationalism* (New Delhi: Aleph, 2016), 102.
26 Menon, "From National Culture to Cultural Nationalism," 120.
27 *Ibid.*, 112.
28 See Anderson, *Imagined Communities*, 7.
29 See Homi Bhabha (ed.), *Nation and Narration* (London: Routledge, 1990), 1-4.
30 See Paul Gilroy, *The Black Atlantic: Modernity and Double Consciousness* (London: Verso, 1993), 198.
31 G. Deleuze, "Doubts about the Imaginary," in *Negotiations, 1972-1990*, trans. Martin Joughin (New York: Columbia University Press, 1995), 67.
32 Riva Kastoryano, "Negotiations beyond Borders: States and Immigrants in Postcolonial Europe," *Journal of Interdisciplinary History*, 41 (2010): 95.
33 Gilroy, *The Black Atlantic*, 19.
34 James Clifford, "Diasporas," *Cultural Anthropology*, 9, no. 3 (1994): 307.
35 Pnina Werbner, "The Dialectics of Cultural Hybridity," in Pnina Werbner et Tariq Modood (eds.), *Debating Cultural Hybridity* (London: Zed Books, 1997), 23.
36 Thapar, "Reflections on Nationalism and History," 5-6 (emphasis mine).
37 Rabindranath Tagore, *Nationalism* (Madras: Macmillan Company, 1976), 17-18.
38 Edward Said, *Culture and Imperialism* (London: Vintage, 1993), 261-262.
39 Jacques Godbout, *L'esprit du don* (Paris: La découverte, 2007), 168.
40 Thapar, "Reflections on Nationalism and History," 53-54.

2

From Sovereignty to Solidarity
Redefining Identity Politics

Keith D'Souza
St. Pius X College, Mumbai

Abstract: The term "sovereignty" is usually understood in terms of national territoriality. While political sovereignty is only one of the many competing forms of social sovereignty, the term sovereignty, instead, needs to be understood in the context of a diversity of competing powers and virtual spaces, rather than merely and narrowly being associated with national and political geospaces. All of these virtual spaces find themselves shapeshifting in a globalized world in which the social landscape is undergoing constant and rapid change. Globalization has unfortunately led to the emergence of chauvinistic nationalism in many parts of the world. Patriotism would seem to be a comparatively healthier manner of affirming identity and sovereign interests. However, even a patriotic mindset would necessarily need to factor in the plural and interdependent socio-cultural global context in which we live. Rather than patriotism, then, I propose that different forms and forums of solidarity, within and across various social and national boundaries, emerge as preferred modes of social connection. Without national and international solidarity with the "other" it would not be easy to establish social harmony and work towards optimal productivity and prosperity

Introduction

The 2016 Summer Olympics was a profound testimony to identity politics in terms of national sovereignty. People cheered wildly for their own teams and expected the best from them. However, for the first time there was a team composed of refugee participants who had qualified for the Olympics. During the inaugural function, they got a standing ovation when they entered the stadium. This spontaneous gesture on the part of the spectators broke through the otherwise narrow and intense feelings of national affiliation. Instead, what was affirmed was the recognition of belonging to a wider human family, and the implicit acknowledgement of the need for fellow-feeling across borders.

Political sovereignty is one of many competing forms of sovereignty in the many overlapping social spaces in our globalized world. This essay attempts to depict the many ways in which a naïve and restrictive understanding of political sovereignty does not hold water in a situation of shared and shifting sovereign social spaces. Nevertheless, political sovereignty continues to be a resilient and even a necessary ingredient of contemporary international relations. In a multivalent world, enhanced and exacerbated by globalization, chauvinistic and violent forms of nationalism have manifested themselves by way of sovereign assertiveness. A softer form of this collective assertiveness may be expressed via healthy patriotism. However, in the light of the manifest plurality and interdependence within and between multiple communities, what seems urgent today is the cultivation of a spirit of solidarity which cuts across intra-national and international boundaries. This spirit of solidarity is applicable not only to the political realm, but also within other sovereign social spaces.

1. The notion of sovereignty

The word 'sovereign' could most easily be translated as "rule from above," as it comes from the conjunction of 'super' (Lt. above) and 'regnum' (Lt. rule). The English word "sovereign" has been in usage since around 1280, conveying the sense of "a superior, a ruler, governor, lord, or master."[1] It is derived from the root word "reign," which itself comes from the "Latin regnum [which means] dominion, rule, realm" related to Lt. *regere* (to rule, to guide).[2] It is related to the Sanskrit word *virajya*, and to the English word "right."[3] The suffix "ty" has to do with the formation of "abstract nouns from adjectives, meaning the fact, quality, or condition of being [sovereign]."[4]

But the identification of its origin is often conventionally associated with the "Peace of Westphalia" treaties of 1648, which attempted to put an end to the long and bloody religious wars in Europe. These treaties were aimed at restricting the interference of external forces and influences on the internal authority and administration of assumed, nominated, or elected political leaders, as well as on the territories they governed.

The notion of sovereignty has several features. Stephen Krasner points out to four primary aspects of sovereignty.[5] The first is "interdependence sovereignty," which has to do with the regulation of "goods, capital, people, and ideas" across international borders. The second is "domestic sovereignty," which refers to the "structure of authority within a state and to the state's effectiveness or control." The third is "international legal sovereignty," or the recognition of autonomy and authority by other states, "the basic rule being that only juridically independent territorial entities are accorded recognition." Finally, we have the historically-rooted notion of "Westphalian sovereignty," which refers to the Treaties of Westphalia in 1648 – the ostensible but contentious starting point of the historical notion of sovereignty – due to which a state may enjoy "autonomy of domestic authority structure – that is, the absence of authoritative external influences."

2. The limits of sovereignty

Sovereignty has to do with the nature and scope of the exercise of wielding political power, and specifically featuring concepts such as autonomy, independence, authority, supremacy and territoriality. While the notion of sovereignty is taken for granted in contemporary international relations, Krasner points out that, "A political entity can be formally independent but de facto deeply penetrated. A state might claim to be the only legitimate enforcer of rules within its own territory, but the rules it enforces might not be of its own making."[6] In the following subsections we will highlight the many ways in which sovereignty, which while recognized *de jure*, may be seriously compromised or at least severely limited in terms of the *de facto* functioning of a typical contemporary nation-state.

One of the sharpest critics of the notion of sovereignty is Adam Rosen, who points out to the conceptual contradiction latent in the very term itself: "Sovereignty harbors its own conceptual contradiction: the sovereign must be both absolutely untethered to the community over which she or he is sovereign and yet capable of enforcing her/his decrees within a community that recognizes the law of the sovereign as binding upon it."[7] However, this conceptual problematic related to sovereignty appears to be the least vexing, in the context of our contemporary situation of globalization, in which the classical notion of sovereignty seems very fragile and difficult to maintain. In the words of Rosen:

> In a world traversed by ever increasing flows of transnational capital, debt, and (im)migration, with nations disaggregated by overlapping authorities and divided loyalties, further disarrayed by diasporas, displaced persons, refugees, guest workers, semi-settlers, dual citizens (official or tolerated), and other varieties of more-or-less officially authorized inhabitants, borders seem to multiply beyond any calculability.[8]

There are numerous borders which exist in our world: political, economic, cultural and religious; and each of these borders defines a different social space within. Rosen thus cryptically points out that "The nation-state seems a nostalgic point of orientation set against the indefinite multiplicity of borders that cry out for our attention, each in their own way and in countless combinations."[9] Shyam Saran, a former foreign secretary of India, seems to concur: "The nation-state endures and will continue to do so in the foreseeable future. However, the concept of national sovereignty, which is the defining characteristic, is increasingly conditioned, and indeed constrained by the reality that the line between domestic and external is now hopelessly blurred."[10]

The very notion of a nation may be best understood in terms of the "imagined community" metaphor coined by Benedict Anderson.[11] While we may never know – or even agree with – other members of our national community, we nevertheless can conjure up a sense and spirit of community along national contours. This notion of "imagined communities" could well be applied to various other domains of social life, especially the cultural and the religious. Political sovereignty in fact applies to only one of several different functioning sovereign spaces, and thus needs to share influence and power with these other social spaces. Furthermore, there will likely be overlapping borders between these different spaces, and even these borders – pertaining to different realms of human experience and interest – may not be as fixed as they appear. This is precisely because of the interplay between these different social spaces, in the minds and hearts of individuals, in the structure of social relations within and between communities, in the way policies are arrived at and implemented in various fora and in the way numerous social institutions are designed and function. Thus, on account of both internal and external social dynamics, these different sovereign spaces and their borders undergo a lot of shapeshifting over time.

2.1 Sovereignty and politics

It may appear that the political boundaries of nation-states are written in stone. Yet, "between 1948 and 1976, over 90 new nation-states emerged from the rubble of European imperialism."[12] The vast majority of nation-states have been formed only in the last century. In our own century, we have seen the emergence of new nation-states such as South Sudan and East Timor.

John Grey points out that "The emergence of modern nations has done much to emancipate individuals from the tyranny of local communities, but this freedom has come at a heavy price. Nearly everywhere, large-scale violence has been an integral feature of the construction of nation-states."[13] Thus, even older nation-states have had a chequered history before they became established and recognized as sovereign states, with definitive borders. Rosen points out to the example of the United States, which "is founded on the all-but-forgotten bodies and worlds of indigenous peoples and is continually secured by a narrative constellation that reduces the decimation of people(s) to a clearing of space on which a sovereign nation could be constructed or within which it could evolve."[14]

New states emerge as a result of factors such as the desire for freedom from imperial or colonial occupation, or because of internal conflicts of an ethnic or cultural nature or other serious fissures. Internal conflicts arise for different reasons: a perceived sense of injustice with regard to the sharing of material resources, a sense of domination on the one hand or negligence on the other by the centre, cultural identity issues, etc. Not only regions like the Punjab, the Northeast and Kashmir have had serious issues along these lines, but also several states which find it difficult to share common resources with neighbouring states – examples of how people sometimes place regional affiliations and concerns above national integration. Our neighbouring nation-states too have similar problems (the complex issue of the status of Tamils in Sri Lanka being one of the most glaring).

Nation-states are also not as insular as one may think. From the early history of our own country, we have had the experience of paradoxically aligning ourselves with the Non-Aligned Movement. Today, there are numerous such geopolitical alignments, mostly for economic and security purposes. The presence and action of extra-governmental organizations, like the UN and its allied bodies, and the transnational activities of a plethora of non-governmental organizations bear ample testimony to the fact that sovereign nations – and those who govern and represent them – are not all that autonomous and powerful as they may appear. Nations are subject to various bodies and systems of intra-national and extra-national accountability.

Finally, identity politics may also be cross-border, in the sense that one's primary political identification may lean more towards a country of origin or of cultural affinity, rather than the country of one's citizenship. For example, PIOs (persons of Indian origin) and NRIs (non-resident Indians) may feel a greater affinity towards India – albeit at a safe, comfortable and more privileged distance – than towards their home or host countries, which they may migrate to largely on account of economic and lifestyle benefits. In some cases, while immigrants enjoy the multifarious welfares of Western democratic and liberal political spaces, they seem to prefer that the parallel socio-political space in India instead features a more traditional, conservative ethos, harking back to a nostalgic past which may be difficult, if not impossible – and doubtfully desirable, at least to the minorities and other marginalized communities – to restore. This phenomenon of a misplaced and misunderstood loyalty may arise from a sense of guilt of deserting the homeland for greener pastures, or from some other psycho-social compensatory mechanism, or for some economic or political benefit.

2.2 Sovereignty and economics

International trade between governments and non-governmental agents (or non-state agents) has been going on for millennia. This trade has taken on gargantuan proportions under the impetus of contemporary globalization, by which governmental regulations have often been bypassed at worst, or co-opted at best. The economies of most countries today are intricately and unavoidably intertwined into the economic processes of nations far removed from their limited geographical spaces. It seems unthinkable for a modern nation to conceive of its economic progress without factoring in exchanges of goods, services and information from outside its borders. This makes even economic heavyweights like the US and China heavily reliant upon and indebted to foreign interaction and exchange. Transnational monetary regulatory and lending institutions like the IMF and the World Bank have further enhanced the relativity of economic sovereignty, by imposing stringent fiscal measures in order to regulate investments profitably and to ensure a free or liberal flow of financial and material assets across borders.

Sovereignty is limited even within the boundaries of a nation-state. The state is not as free or able to create ideal economic conditions as the general populace may wish. Hence, many political promises related to economics – such as increased employment opportunities, reasonable taxation levies and special subsidies – leave the people disappointed. The thorny issue of black money is yet another indication of the lack of power associated with sovereignty – and the lack of allegiance to a sovereign state. Depositing black money in foreign banks to save taxation clearly points to a lack of concern for the development of one's nation, in favour of a concern for the development of one's restricted circle of self, family and personal affiliates. Finally, it is not uncommon that many people possess unaccounted foreign currency, which is sometimes not easily obtainable via official channels. Even more rampant is the desire to have access to foreign goods, which may be of a better quality, or even cheaper than local goods and services. These dysfunctional practices of citizens – including a good number of those engaged in active party politics – are indicators of the lack of appropriate loyalty to the nation, even though lip service pertaining to nationalism and patriotism is often offered for public consumption by some of these same erring citizens.

2.3 Sovereignty and culture

The political boundaries of most contemporary nation-states do not exactly coincide with the borders which define spaces of cultural community, collaboration and concern. Nation-states are often comprised of diverse cultural communities, some of which may form smaller sub-cultures within the state. It is not uncommon that cultural communities within any given state possess a sense of community which extends far beyond the political boundaries of the state within which they exist.

In today's geopolitical world of a resurgence of right-wing thinking and feeling, there seems no doubt that cultural affiliations and concerns seem to have gained much more significance, even in democratic societies, in which civic and community-neutral processes should have been much more prevalent. Ethnic loyalties seem to have created a situation of conflicting social spaces. Some of these conflicts play themselves out in the larger and assumedly more neutral and objective political space which is supposed to provide a common and just ground for the interplay of diverse sub-cultural forces.

Viewing this issue from the perspective of indigenous communities worldwide, Rosen states: "There are 5,000 indigenous peoples and 199 states; hence great and continuous efforts of national consolidation may be ever-pressing upon state concerns."[15] Arguing against "Kenneth Waltz's standard distinction between national politics as the realm of authority, of administration, and of law and international politics as the anarchic realm of power, of struggle, and of accommodation in the interest of pre-set state goals,"[16] Rosen instead refuses to adopt "the standpoint of sovereignty by presuming a legitimate order within the state and a violent disorder without."[17]

But it is not only indigenous and marginalized communities which have strong cultural affiliations, and problems with an assumed and neatly defined state-based sovereignty. Many Indians from different regions of the country have close ties with people from their own communities all over the globe, many of whom are not even Indian citizens. Even the news media often report outstanding successes of persons of Indian origin who have achieved these successes outside the motherland. In fact, some of these people featured are not even Indian citizens, even from their birth. Yet, many citizens of our country seem to take great vicarious pride in these extra-territorial achievements – a sign of a fundamental solidarity which transcends geographical and political borders.

2.4 Sovereignty and religion

Far more than cultural affiliation, religious kinship in many cases often extends far beyond the country's borders, to embrace a sense of affinity with co-religionists across the globe. For example, the Indian diaspora – which is perhaps one of the most widespread – has over the recent years built up a good number of places of religious worship to suit the needs of first and even later generations of those of Indian origin.

This sense of religious affinity may cause problems of one sort or another, and is especially problematic when a particular nation may want to retain a dominant cultural flavour which comes into conflict with what is perceived as a foreign religious sensitivity. This is why, in order to retain state-centric loyalties, it is argued that, "the principles of Westphalia, including the drive to delegitimize subsocietal identities and loyalties, seem more relevant for … states than ever before."[18] These "subsocietal identities and loyalties" may be cultural or religious.

However, even when there is cultural and religious homogeneity within a nation, there is no guarantee that internal conflict will not arise between different groups of co-religionists, for different reasons. Even in a theocracy like Pakistan, there may be various groups within Islam itself which may come into conflict with other groups which believe somewhat differently or which operate according to different power interests. Thus, mere religious – or even cultural – homogeneity does not automatically necessitate a peaceful political and social situation.

3. From sovereignty to solidarity

Political sovereignty, as we have seen, is seriously limited on various counts. We live in a world in which "the autonomy of sovereign states, the integrity of national bodies, and the reliability of the nation-state map as the primary object domain of global politics seem to be very much in question."[19] Besides the extra-territorial limitations and restrictions related to sovereignty, there are numerous domestic concerns related to the nature, scope and function of sovereignty. After highlighting a few of these concerns, we will indicate the main reasons why sovereignty nevertheless continues to be a resilient and attractive phenomenon, and may indeed be considered necessary within the present context of international relations. However, if sovereignty is to be affirmed and to function in a healthy rather than dysfunctional manner, there is need to cultivate a wholesome and inclusive spirit of solidarity with peoples across different sovereign boundaries, as compared to a more chauvinistic and vicious nationalism, and even a relatively healthier spirit of patriotism.

3.1 Domestic concerns regarding sovereignty

One of the most basic "internal" or domestic questions which challenges the notion of sovereignty is: "How are citizens' basic rights secured if, for whatever reason, their political representatives severely abuse their powers or fail to adequately fulfill their responsibilities?"[20] Carmen Pavel, who asks this question, arrives at the unsavory conclusion that "the state is an incomplete institutional setup, because its institutions cannot offer reasonable assurance over the long run that they can secure minimal protections of their citizens' rights."[21]

Another issue is the diminishment of the power and authority of the state or government when it relies heavily upon, or outsources some of its powers and functions to private or corporate organizations. Paul Verkuil laments that, "The government exercises sovereign powers. When those powers are delegated to outsiders [non-governmental agents], the capacity to govern is undermined."[22] Verkuil refers to the distinction Isaiah Berlin makes in *The Hedgehog and the Fox*[23] between the government – represented by the fox – and outsourcing agencies – represented by the hedgehog. Verkuil argues that the function of the fox – a metaphor associated with being wise and possessing a comprehensive understanding of the socio-political situation – should be assumed by the government. The government is the one that needs to steer the ship – using a mixed metaphor, while the hedgehog – representing the plodding manner of policy execution – should be the equivalent of the ancillary or subsidiary organizations which are given the function only to row. Verkuil contends that "the new bureaucrat [Government] must be a fox, not a hedgehog."[24]

Besides the abuse of power by elected representatives and the injudicious delegation of powers to vested interests – ostensibly for a price – there are numerous other domestic concerns which call for a qualified understanding of sovereignty, such as the status and loyalty of guest workers, semi-settlers, forced migrants or refugees, etc. However, in spite of all of these limitations and concerns, the status of national sovereignty continues to be a recognized and valuable constant within the panorama of international relations.

3.2 The resilient nature of sovereignty

Some form of sovereignty – in terms of recognized leadership and socio-political boundaries – seems to have always existed in human society. Why, in spite of so many limitations and concerns, is sovereignty still such an attractive proposition? There are many reasons for this. First of all, sovereignty provides the ability and the assurance of governmental negotiation with legitimate leaders of other governments. Hence, the wariness of an increasing tribe of "non-state actors." Whatever the nature of governance within a country, there is a growing acceptance of democratic processes of representation, negotiation and arbitration at the level of international relations. It is difficult to negotiate with non-state actors precisely because they do not share these commonly held democratic dispositions and practices. Secondly, while governments may change, sovereignty ensures the establishment of a stable and developed bureaucratic machinery to provide constitutional stability and continuity, and processes of negotiation and arbitration between states.

Within nations, sovereignty is one of the main bulwarks against external aggression. It fulfills the basic need for physical security between nations and within a nation. It also provides a platform or forum to regulate stability at various levels of social life: equality of status and opportunity at the social level, productivity and prosperity at the economic level, creativity and harmony at the socio-cultural level, justice at the legislative and juridical levels, and infrastructural and institutional optimization at the administrative level. It is the government's primary responsibility to coordinate human resources, ensure peace and social stability and enhance the material infrastructure within the state, so as to improve the quality of life for all citizens. In ideal situations, this platform is constituted by elected representatives who then provide legitimate leadership which upholds sovereignty.

Sovereignty is also important for the building up of a sense of national solidarity, fellow-feeling and collective wellbeing. For sovereignty to be sustained and better appreciated, it is important that, "states do and/or ought to take a more active role in inculcating a sense of shared nationality among its citizens."[25] The next section will explore different avenues of cultivating this "sense of shared nationality." I will argue that this sentiment of sharing needs to be manifested within and across several sovereign spaces, for national and international wellbeing to prevail.

3.3 Redefining identity politics

Given the resilience of sovereignty in terms of a felt need, how may one sustain this sense of sovereignty in a socially salubrious manner? The cultivation of a "shared nationality" usually takes two dominant forms: patriotism or nationalism. These terms may often be confused with one another, but need to be more sharply distinguished.[26] Brian Barry distinguishes between a civic and an ethnic form of nationalism. "Civic nationalism is supposedly organized around political ideals rather than around a culture," in which citizens find unity "in their common allegiance to shared political ideals and practices."[27] The assumed advantage with civic nationalism over ethnic nationalism – especially for a country like India – is that "civic nationalism is allegedly neutral about culture, and hence is, in principle, inclusive and universalistic rather than exclusive and parochial."[28] However, Will Kymlicka disagrees with this distinction, as he prefers to promote a basic cultural unity or integrity that is common to all citizens of any given nation. He argues in favour of a "thin" national culture or a "societal culture" which is "characterized by a shared language and a set of public institutions covering different areas of social life, including the law, education, and the economy, rather than a "thick" ethno-culture that is characterized by (say) shared religious beliefs, family customs, and personal lifestyles."[29]

The "civic nationalism" proposed by Barry seems ideologically attractive, but may be too liberal and abstract and thus may not resonate with many people at the emotive or affective level. On the other hand, the "thin nationalism" advocated by Kymlicka may degenerate into a form of majoritarianism, to the detriment of minority groups within a nation. A good midway position is that of the "liberal cosmopolitanism" advocated by Kok-Chor Tan, who is realistic enough to acknowledge that:

> Most cosmopolitan positions, when more carefully examined, do allow space for the exercise of patriotic commitments, even if on first impression these positions seem to rule out any space for such special concern. If there is any dispute between the patriots and the cosmopolitans, it is over the limits of patriotic concern and how this special concern is to be morally understood.[30]

Keeping these "limits of patriotic concern" in mind, Tan contends that "As nationalism needs liberalism to tame it and to set moral constraints on it, so liberalism needs nationalism in order to achieve its end."[31] What would understandably result is a healthy form of patriotism, as compared to a more raw or uncivilized spirit of nationalism. In the words of Gurcharan Das, "Patriotism enables one to proudly identify with one's nation as a default social disposition, as well as to rise above this strong identification for a greater good. Nationalism sees no greater good, and any rising above national identification as traitorous or seditious."[32]

However, even though patriotism seems to be the most salubrious manner of manifesting or giving expression to identity politics, in the light of the preceding arguments which demonstrate that a narrow sense of sovereignty is practically unwarranted, we need an alternative social disposition and way of life which will better represent both practical and ideal interpersonal and inter-community relations. Accordingly, what I wish to propose is that even beyond patriotism – which may also be divisive, though not as toxic as nationalism – what is more reasonable, practical and also morally superior is the cultivation of *solidarity* as the social glue that binds peoples together, both within and across several interweaving domains of social life.

4. The need for collaborative solidarity

The postmodern human condition, coupled with globalization – and exacerbated with the present phenomenon of mass migration and the refugee crisis – seems to have put the modern creation and assumption of the nation-state under severe pressure. Key aspects of nationhood such as political autonomy, economic regulatory activity, legislative power, and even territoriality will consequently need to be modified. As a result of these contemporary conditions of socio-political life, the absolute nature and significance of sovereignty – as we have seen – has given way to a relative understanding. In the words of Rosen: "If there are any limits to sovereignty, there is no sovereignty, or perhaps only an indefinite relay of quasi-sovereign functions that do not level any clear-cut claims to being thought as sovereign in any classical sense of the term."[33]

Political sovereignty is only one of the many forms of social constructs which are governed by power agents, forces or interests. We have seen how economic, cultural and religious interests and influences call into question the hegemony of political sovereignty. All of these spaces of human life also have their own sovereign territories, within which specific people live and form communities, both real and virtual. At the personal level, people occupy different sovereign spaces simultaneously. Paul Ricoeur would term this as a "prefiguration" or spontaneous enactment of roles and responsibilities within diverse narratives which are specifically related to each of these spaces, constituting "a preunderstanding of the world of action, its meaningful structures, its symbolic resources, and its temporal character."[34] One can accordingly be an Indian and a Christian at the same time, without denying one's regional, cultural and professional identities as well. Perhaps it is tempting to think in terms of a hierarchy of personal identities, but a strong rival to this way of thinking is that proposed by Amartya Sen, who foregrounds the notion of multiple, context-based identities.[35]

While writing this essay, perhaps the identity and responsibility associated with being a member of the ACPI – and beyond that, of belonging to the professional guild of philosophers – would be more evident or obvious, with professional standards to meet, keeping in mind rules and norms regulated by these professional associations. However, there are numerous other roles and responsibilities I need to assume and fulfill, besides being an Indian, a Christian and a philosopher. Not all of these are evident or manifest at all times, with equal intensity, frequency or duration. There is thus a need to recognize the existence and texture of differing sovereign spaces and forces, not only making claims within oneself, but also on the social level, stemming from different power groups and community interests. For both personal balance and social harmony to prevail, there is a need for appropriate reciprocity and justice between these differing and even competing sovereign ideological and geopolitical powers/spaces.

Furthermore, on account of the constant interplay between sovereign spaces of the same genre – and also between different genres – social processes and individual roles and responsibilities will keep on getting modified. This will concomitantly result in a need for "shapeshifting" or "remapping" of different sovereign domains. Thus, what it means to be an Indian or a Christian or a philosopher – or an Indian Christian philosopher – is not something which can be defined easily or essentially, but rather something which needs to be dynamically and interrelatedly understood, and something which is likely to change over time and in different locations.

In such a world, in which sovereign spaces need to be shared – and as a result keep shifting their contours – it is anachronistic and dysfunctional to speak in terms of a chauvinistic nationalism, or for that matter, of even a more refined patriotism. What needs to be enhanced is the recognition of a growing pluralism in terms of social identities – be they political, economic, cultural or religious. Within each of these social "locations" there may be quite different ways of existentially understanding and living out one's identity. Furthermore, what needs to be cultivated is the need for solidarity within and across these social spaces. This solidarity will be based upon the need for a sharing of resources which could in turn enhance the quality of life and relationships within all these aforementioned domains of social existence. This is why Shyam Saran contends against the duplicitous tendency in contemporary local politics: "a polity which seeks political gain through polarizing society domestically cannot at the same time pursue a foreign policy which embraces the logic of internationalism."[36]

The contours of solidarity within and across political, economic, cultural and religious domains could take various forms. As a foundational disposition governing social life, solidarity has well reputed intellectual and moral moorings. The intellectual foundations of solidarity are perhaps best formulated within the framework of Jurgen Habermas' "communicative rationality"[37] – and what follows from this, his "discourse ethics,"[38] especially as worked out in the political sphere.[39] Connecting this trajectory of Habermasian thought with the specific theme of solidarity, Max Pensky comments:

> If we are bound to one another by the formal structures of speaking and hearing, then underlying all we say and do – not despite but especially in our differences – we reaffirm, with each utterance, acts of ongoing inclusion. These acts of ongoing inclusion, transmitted from basic linguistic competence through the affects and attitudes of persons, through political institutions and ultimately into the ethos of a democratic form of social life, can be summarized as *solidarity*.[40]

This implicit intentionality of inclusion as part of who we are as linguistic creatures is more fully fleshed out in the moral tradition of Catholic social teaching: "Solidarity descriptively connotes the cohesion of the civil society for the benefit of individuals (i.e., for the common good). Prescriptively, it contains moral obligations to one another and may be seen as a call for social action/social change for the ends of social justice."[41] These catch words of "discourse ethics," "acts of ongoing inclusion," "the common good," and "social justice" are intrinsically connected to the nature and dynamics of solidarity. Given the flexible and interdependent nature of personal and social identities, it seems obvious that erstwhile notions supporting isolationist sovereignty need to give way to a more realistic and morally superior sentiment of solidarity which binds peoples together within different spheres of social life.

Summing up the need for an urgent new world order which recognizes both pluralism and the need for collaboration, Saran hopefully states:

> One does not pretend to know how one could bridge the disconnect between the reality of the One World we inhabit today and the wave of intolerance, sectarian and racial hatred and the grossness of political discourse which is sweeping across country after country in the world. Could India lead the way to shaping a new world order which is aligned with the challenges we confront as humanity? Through the ages, India has developed a civilisation whose attributes are what that new order requires: the innate syncretism of its accommodative and self-confident culture, its easy embrace of vast diversity and plurality with an underlying spiritual and cultural unity, and a deep conviction that to achieve greatness a nation must stand for something more than itself.[42]

While recent political developments in the country do not indicate a coherence with these traditional civilizational values, it is hoped that better sense prevails and that collective political will – both nationally and internationally – will help create more spaces for collaboration and solidarity, rather than succumb to bigotry, isolationism and conflict.

Conclusion

Political sovereignty is only one of many competing forms of social sovereignty. Other aspects of human life – such as economics, culture and religion – also feature their own sovereign spaces. These multiple sovereign spaces can be seen to overlap and mutually influence one another. They may also compete with each other over limited assets in terms of human and material resources. While political sovereignty continues to be a resilient and valid notion, allegiance towards one's nation may be better expressed in terms of a more benign and productive sense of patriotism, as compared to nationalism, which has had a chequered history and has sharp features such as rigidity, chauvinism and violence. However, a parochial form of patriotism may be found wanting, when one considers the many ways in which peoples have become interdependent globally. As national identity is only one of many social signifiers amidst a field of competing personal indices, what seems more socially responsible and practical – and morally superior – is the cultivation of a spirit of solidarity within and between different social communities. A refined form of solidarity will recognize and affirm the pluralism that is inherent within and between different social communities, as well as the necessity for interdependence and collaboration within and between these communities.

Notes

1 Robert Barnhart, ed., *Chambers Dictionary of Etymology* (New York: Chambers, 1988), 1038.
2 Ibid., 905.
3 Ibid., 929.
4 Ibid., 1179.
5 The quotations in this paragraph are from Stephen Krasner, "Problematic Sovereignty," in *Problematic Sovereignty: Contested Rules and Political Possibilities*, ed. Stephen Krasner (NY: Columbia University Press, 2001), 2.
6 Ibid.
7 Adam Rosen, "Scandals of Sovereignty," in *Ethical Perspectives: Journal of the European Ethics Network*, 14/3 (2007): 332.
8 Ibid., 312.
9 Ibid., 313.
10 Shyam Saran. "The Future is Still Global," *India Today*, January 16 (2017): 59.
11 See Benedict Anderson, *Imagined Communities: Reflections on the Origin and Spread of Nationalism*, rev. ed. (London: Verso, 2006).
12 Ibid., 320, referring to the data found in Herbert Schiller, *Communication and Cultural Domination* (White Plains, NY: International Arts and Sciences Press, 1976), 1.
13 John Gray, accessed on Oct 1, 2016, https://www.theguardian.com/books/2006/aug/05/highereducation.shopping1
14 Adam Rosen, "Off the Map, Beneath our Feet: Cartographic Amnesia and the National Body," in *Alternatives: Global, Local, Political*, 37/2 (2012): 133.
15 Adam Rosen, "Scandals of Sovereignty," 321.
16 Ibid., 322.
17 Ibid.
18 B.S. Heisler and M.O. Heisler, "Transnational Migration and the Modern Democratic State," *Annals of the American Academy of Political and Social Science* 485 (1999): 12-22.
19 Adam Rosen, "Scandals of Sovereignty," 314.
20 Carmen Pavel, *Divided Sovereignty: International Institutions and the Limits of State Authority* (Oxford University Press, 2014), 2.
21 Ibid., 1.
22 Paul Verkuil, *Outsourcing Sovereignty: Why Privatization of Government Functions Threatens Democracy and What We Can do About it* (Cambridge: Cambridge Univ. Press, 2007), 1.
23 Isaiah Berlin, *The Hedgehog and the Fox: An Essay on Tolstoy's View of History* (London: Weidenfeld and Nicolson, 1953).
24 Ibid., 159.
25 Kok-Chor Tan, *Justice Without Borders: Cosmopolitanism, Nationalism and Patriotism* (Cambridge: Cambridge University Press, 2004), 88.
26 Kok-Chor Tan, for example, allows for both nationalism and patriotism as healthy components in the process of nation building. He has two independent sections of *Justice Without Borders* on both of these ways of expressing national loyalty, in order to complement a more abstract and universal "cosmopolitanism."
27 Kok-Chor Tan, *Justice Without Borders*, 89, summarizing the position of Brian Barry, "Statism and Nationalism: A Cosmopolitan Critique," in Ian Shapiro and L. Brilmayer, eds., *Global Justice* (NY: New York University Press, 1999), 53-60.
28 Ibid.

29 Ibid., 90. See Will Kymlicka, *Liberalism, Community and Culture* (Oxford University Press, 1989).
30 Ibid., 139.
31 Ibid., 85.
32 Gurcharan Das, *TOI Sunday*, August 14, 2016.
33 Adam Rosen, "Scandals of Sovereignty," 331.
34 Paul Ricoeur, *Time and Narrative*, Vol. 1, trans. Kathleen McLaughlin and David Pellauer (Chicago: University of Chicago Press, 1984), 54.
35 Amartya Sen, *Identity and Violence: The Illusion of Destiny* (London: Allen Lane, 2006).
36 Shyam Saran, "The Future is Still Global," 59.
37 See Jurgen Habermas, *The Theory of Communicative Action*, Vols. 1 & 2, trans. Thomas McCarthy (Cambridge: Polity Press, 1984 & 1987).
38 See Jurgen Habermas, "Discourse Ethics: Notes on a Program of Philosophical Justification," in *Moral Consciousness and Communicative Action* (Cambridge, MT: MIT Press, 1992).
39 See Jurgen Habermas, *Between Facts and Norms: Contributions to a Discourse Theory of Law and Democracy*, trans. William Rehg (Cambridge, MT: MIT Press, 1996).
40 Max Pensky, *The Ends of Solidarity: Discourse Theory in Ethics and Politics* (NY: SUNY Press, 2008), ix, original italics.
41 Sally Scholz, *Political* Solidarity (University Park, PA: Pennsylvania State University Press, 2008), 7.
42 Shyam Saran, "The Future is Still Global," 61.

3

"Whose Nation? Whose State?"[1]

Subaltern Readings into Constitutional Trajectories

Jose D. Maliekal
St. John's Regional Seminary, Vizianagaram

Abstract: This paper attempts to analyse the multi-stranded and entwined phenomena of democracy, nation and the state. The events leading to Rohith Vemula's suicide and the student-unrest, especially of the Dalits that his death triggered in the country have raised many questions about the interpretation of the Constitution, the construction of the nation and the state. As Upendra Baxi indicates, in the context of modernity, constitutionalism has displayed, inbuilt within it, a propensity to violence. Even the Indian Constitution, being a product of modernity, is inscribed by power-violence and antagonism, and open, as a text, to many readings, *à la* Barthes. The truth that the Indian Constitution is not a seamless robe, is driven home, also by the recent events in Dadri or Una. After the introductory remarks of a methodological nature, the paper engages itself in a Subaltern Reading into the Constitutional Trajectory, with a subsection, under the thematic, "An Audit of the Expectations/ Experience: The Flawed Invention of Citizenship". This is followed by the final section, "Dalit Life-worlds Constituted and Constituting: An Exercise in Embodied Reading", which is again an audit of the Constitution, constituting the Dalit Life-worlds, inscribed by the purity-pollution binary and the dominance of the touchables, who are also the cartographers of the social space. The conclusion poses the question, "Where and what would be the task of philosophizing, in these struggles and multiple and contested readings of the text that is Nation/State/Constitution?, and responds that "It is to be tactile, in touch, with the political society of the dispossessed, supporting the emergence of a Homo

Dialecticus, within/against the Homo Hierarchicus, letting itself transform, as a Tactile Public Philosophy.

> 'To envisage politics as a rational process of negotiation among individuals is to obliterate the whole dimension of power and antagonism' – that is to say, it is to obliterate the 'political' itself. However, to negate the political does not make it disappear, it only leads to bewilderment in the face of its manifestations and to importance in dealing with them.'[2]
>
> "Much of the business of "modern" constitutionalism was transacted during the halcyon days of colonialism/imperialism. That historical timepiece marks a combined and uneven development of the world in the processes of early modernity... [C]onstitutionalism inherits the propensity for violent social exclusion from the "modern."[3]
>
> "... the text is not a line of words releasing a single 'theological' meaning (the message of an Author-God) but multi-dimensional space in which a variety of writings, none of them original, blend and clash. The text is a tissue of quotations drawn from innumerable centres of culture."[4] "... there is a place where this multiplicity is focused and that place is the reader, not, as was hitherto said, the author. The reader is the space on which all the quotations that make up a reading are inscribed ... a text's unity lies not in its origin but in its destination."[5]

Introduction

The above quotations, from Chantal Mouffe, Upendra Baxi and Roland Barthes, respectively, which form the frontispiece of this work, are programmatic in character. Though, I had earlier chosen to dwell on the theme of the Nation, under the title, "Inverting Democracies: Towards an Anatomy of the Homogenizing Ideologies", the events consequent to that[6] made me alter my decision and dwell on the same theme, with a different slant. Thus, the present title, "Whose Nation? Whose State? Subaltern Readings *into* Constitutional Trajectories", which would lend itself, to a more grounded analysis of the multi-stranded and entwined phenomena of democracy, nation and the state. The death of Rohith Vemula[7] and the arrest of Kanhaiya Kumar and other students, on charges of sedition and their subsequent release on bail and the response of the State, especially the Ministry of Human Resources Development raised many questions about the interpretation of the Constitution, the construction of the nation and the state and the boundaries between the nation and the state. [8] The politically coloured incidents in Dadri[9] and Una[10] too pose questions on the nature of democracy in India.

As Baxi would indicate, in the context of modernity, constitutionalism has inbuilt within it, a propensity to violence. Mouffe reminds us that politics, as the liberal democrats would have us believe, is not an entirely rational process, but one inscribed with dimensions of power and antagonism. Hence, even the Indian Constitution, though post-colonial, still a product of modernity, is inscribed by power-violence and antagonism, and open, as a text, to many readings, *a la* Barthes, as seen above. The truth that the Indian Constitution is not a seamless robe, is not without knots, pretensions to being otherwise, is driven home, by the events leading to Rohith Vemula's suicide and the student-unrest, especially of the Dalits, that his death triggered. As Bhattacharjee poignantly comments with hermeneutical perspicacity on the posture of the rising Hindu religious nationalism in the country and the hollowness of its universalism:

> Those who have most overwhelmingly suffered the barbarism of history – Dalits, people of colour, vulnerable women, workers – alone carry a genuine value of universality in them, and in their protests against injustice we see the true unfolding of that universal spirit that impresses upon our hearts. The claims to universality of those in power – white colonisers, caste Hindus – are essentially un-universal, bigoted and discriminatory. It is not in "universal gospels" that we find any real, universal capacity but in the spirit of those who suffer these gospels, the propaganda of spiritual and cultural supremacy, these lies. The lack of vindictiveness in Rohith's note is a historic lesson for nationalist and casteist hate-mongers.[11]

Against this background of the false universalisms in the garb of rising Hindu religious nationalism, which makes the citizens who are not votaries of Hindutva feel ill at ease, this article attempts at the possibility of a subaltern reading *into* the trajectory of the Indian constitution. This is aimed at bringing into relief the Subaltern utopias, especially the aspirations of the Dalits, which have been accommodated into the text and the texture of the constitution, and using the tool of hermeneutics of suspicion, engages itself in a socio-cultural and economic audit of the enfleshment/eclipse of those very utopias and aspirations.

I propose to unfold this task by attempting a subaltern reading of the constitutional trajectory and, in the ensuing section, applying the same to the ground realities of the Dalit life-worlds in India, with *touch* as a semantic axis, and concluding with a brief, methodological afterword.

Subaltern Reading *into* the Constitutional Trajectory

At the outset, a few hermeneutical considerations are in order. In any reading, the text is available to the readers only in the present moment and it is futile to uncover the intended meaning of the author. Moreover, reading is an act which is always differentially located in terms of power. Every act of interpretation demarcates and populates a landscape afresh, towards a specific end.[12]

In the wider horizon of political philosophy, critical social theorists are concerned with the problem of the 'constitution' of the constitutions, that is the social, symbolic, as well as the material labours of power/governance, and the peoples and processes by whose labours the constitutions are constituted. In the constitutive moment, the 'constitutive' and the 'constituted' stand in a dialectical relation. As already noted earlier, constitutions, in their founding and developmental movements, are inscribed by violence, and the construction of imperial spaces for nation-states leads to the destruction of many plural life-worlds and worldviews. An enquiry into the dialectics of the 'constitutive' and the 'constituted' is about the geographies of in/justice, legitimation of power and resistance, the distinction between the 'legal' and the 'popular' sovereign, the latter attributed the plentitude of constituent power.[13]

The view that the Indian Constitution is totally liberal in origin and in content has been debated in scholarly circles and come in for critical attention. In this context, a distinction can be made between civil society and political society. Civil society, according to Partha Chatterjee, is constituted by institutions of modern associational life, while political society is the domain of mediating institutions between civil society and the state. This hiatus between civil society and political society is the mark of non-Western democracy and democratic aspirations often violate the institutional norms of civil society.[14] The Indian state is bourgeois in its legal system, property structure, institutions of governance, as revealed in the Constitution, in its thrust towards reproduction of capital and development perspectives. The bourgeoisie exercise leadership functions in the coalition of classes which controls the state.[15]

While attempting a reading of the Indian Constitution, or any constitution, produced in the South, could they be read outside the optic of ideology (Marx), episteme (Foucault) and habitus (Bourdieu), read outside, this Eurocentric paradigm, through the grounded optic of a Mahatma or Mandela, or Ambedkar, the 'Aristotle' of the Dalits? The Indian Constitution produced in the middle of twentieth century, and the South African constitution, towards its end, stand testimony to the fact the knowledge production is possible outside the hegemonic state actors. This is not to deny that the constitutions furnish arenas of contested relationship between state and civil society, like the difference between civil society and political society we have seen above. Added to that, since the state formative processes are ongoing and indeterminate, it is necessary to distinguish between three layers of meanings of constitutions as texts, and constitutional law, and theory/ideology (constitutionalism). Notwithstanding these, it is to be noted that today the global capital defines 'democracy', 'good governance', 'rights' and 'development', giving rise to a new brand of economic constitutionalism.[16]

There is the politics of desire and the politics of representation at play in the making of the constitutions, almost all of which carry the democratic deficit, the constitution makers legitimating their narrative monopoly over the voice of the people. "Constitutions usually archive basic decisions made by elderly, homophobic, non-tribal, gender-biased, metropolitan, professional, political, and propertied males; their practices necessarily reflect special interests and specific constellations of power and ideology"[17] The practice of the reading of the Constitution must help us to archive the plurality and multiplicity of practices of representation generated by a whole variety of lawpersons and the non-law persons, whose views are generally obscured, and who are struggling to shed the weight of oppressive constitutional practices. The reading of/into the constitution as text, as law and ideology must make us cognizant of the juris generative constituent power of the people's insurgent practices – the passive constitutional revolution of the people.[18]

Against the background of the distinctions we have made between the Constitution as text, law and ideology, reading *into* the Constitutional trajectory is an exercise in archaeology, as well as a genealogy of the difference between the constitutional expectation of the people the constitutional experience of the people a socio-cultural politico-economic audit of the career and future of the constitutional practices in globalizing/glocalizing world.[19] For reasons of space, I will be only indicative in this process.

An Audit of the Expectations/Experience: The Flawed Invention of Citizenship

"A critique of the Indian state can be evolved if the post-independence constitutional discourse is seen simultaneously as an instance of contestations and as exemplifying the tension between neutrality and instrumentality."[20] Since the 1980s the state has been strengthening itself and its coercive powers, but it does not show any inclination to use these powers for 'the people'. Therefore, state practices can be critiqued both on grounds of tilting in favour of the privileged and on grounds of not doing enough for the underprivileged."[21] This critique of the state, tilting in favour of the rich, or not reaching up to the poor is reflected in their everydayness, as captured by Saddat Hassan Manto, in the epigrammic story of the rickshaw puller. He was elated by the news of a new Constitution for India, but was jolted into reality in the police station before being locked up, when summarily told by the police, "What rubbish are you talking? What new constitution? It is the same old constitution, you fool!"[22]

The making of a constitution heralds a revolution of expectations. But as in the case of Manto's rickshaw puller, there is enormous human violation and tragedy in the acts of *making* and *reading* the constitutions that mark the passage from normative constitutional *expectations* to lived constitutional *experience*. As already indicated, the constitution-makers had to embody subaltern expectations, negotiating avoidance of wholesale derangement of dominant expectations, through many compromises, which involved a blend of 'symbolic' and 'instrumental' strategies. Anterior expectations determined the construction of republican citizenship for all Indians, in ways that had few parallels in the history of modern constitutional ideology. This, together with the constitutional outlawry of untouchability, as a fundamental right (Articles 14, 15), abolition of agrestic serfdom (Article 23), and discrimination on the grounds of sex (Articles 14, 15), are results of a mass of anterior expectation, catalyzed by a radically heterogeneous freedom movement.[23]

The invention of citizenship, against the background of the traumatic event of the Partition of India, generating solicitude for Minority Rights, and Constitutional secularism,[24] that mandates the radical reform of 'majority' Hindu religious tradition is a proud and forward-looking achievement of the Indian Constitution. The recognition of indigenous, not merely cultural pluralism, but civilizational pluralism, is also another great achievement, taking the Indian Constitutional discourse, beyond the perfunctory and the conventional contemporary discourse of 'multiculturalism.'[25]

Coming to the constitutional experience, in contrast to the expectations enshrined in the text of the Constitution, as regards the rules and laws of implementation, there is structured innocence concerning the values of dignity and fraternity between the governors and the governed. The idea of republican virtues, especially respect for fellow-citizens, which is the matrix of democracy, is yet to be learnt by the citizens, though ideologically and as utopia, equality and fraternity are to be practiced and striven after. As stated, though the impact of *Homo Hierarchicus* inscribed by the binary of purity/pollution is outlawed, at the ground level, the idea of fraternity in association with dignity is in a deficit in the political fabric of India, as well as the practice of the idea of republican citizenship.[26]

The enforcement of 'constitutional patriotism', to borrow a phrase from Jurgen Habermas, set boundaries for the Indian post-swaraj discourse and praxis of human rights, right to free speech and expression, conscience and belief, movement and association, within the bounds of sedition/treason, and draconian security legislations rather routinely upheld and sustained by the Supreme Court of India. This leads to a culture of rightlessness, with militarized practices of governance continuously reproducing patterns of confiscation of Indian citizenship. Those whom the Indian state machinery can successfully stigmatize as constitutional outlaws stand wholly denied of their rights as citizens and human beings. It seems that the Indian constitutional theory and practice urges us to examine that human rights become intelligible only within the context of rightlessness. Sovereignty seems to manifest itself in excess. Subaltern perspectives of dissent interrogate the sovereign monopoly over constructions of security and integrity of the 'nation'-state, especially being constructed under majoritarian Hindu nationalism and Althusserian rendering of bourgeois constitutionalism.[27]

Beyond the constructs of 'security, integrity and unity', the theologies of development, in vogue in the Indian State reinforce the culture of rightlessness. Anti-developmental citizen activism gets constructed, even decreed as 'anti-national.'[28] Non-participatory developmental practices of politics also create conditions of rightlessness, celebrating the power of the few, as the destiny of the millions of human beings. Ideological practices of development by the dominant sections of society as a totalizing metanarrative, entails constitutional and political labour, producing 'symbolic capital' as well as material conditions of ongoing human deprivation. From a subaltern perspective and praxis, the fulfilment of conditions and capabilities that, in practice, are to affirm the worth of all citizens, are eternally deferred, showing the toothlessness of a much-gloried Constitution in the local configurations of power. The human rights of the citizens are inverted and the rights become the monopoly of the rich and the powerful.[29]

The developmental programmes, from large irrigation projects like Narmada and Tehri, to the Green Revolution, of which the Bhopal catastrophe is an archetype, have created infrastructure for development, as well as reproduction of rightless peoples. What dominant discourse constructs as the economy of scarcity, subaltern discourse constructs as the economy of excess. It is this political economy of developmentalist excess that confiscates the constitutionally enshrined human future of large masses of Indian citizens, now being contested through social action litigation and judicial activism, notwithstanding the fact that the Supreme Court of India remains insecure, parlous, and at times schizo-paranoid in its negotiation of its attempt at the reversal of the phenomenon of the reproduction of rightlessness caused through developmentalist inversion of the Constitutionally guaranteed human rights.[30] As Mahasveta Devi, satirically notes in her *Bashai Tudu*, "The Indian Constitution respected every citizen's fundamental right to become whatever he could become by the dint of his guts. The poor therefore had the right to become poorer still."[31]

Against this background of the differential between the Expectations and the Experience of the Constitution, in the next section we attempt at engaging ourselves in an audit of the Dalit life-world as constituted in the Constitution and now being constituted in the contemporary culture of rightlessness. We engage ourselves in this process, as an Embodied reading, through the optics of the experience of *untouchability*.

Dalit life-worlds constituted and constituting: An exercise in embodied reading

Though, the concern for secularism warrants the reaffirmation of the Indian Constitution, in the context of Hindutva designs, social justice must be invoked as an evaluative concept for the assessment of the Indian Constitution. It has to be noted that every successive amendment of the Constitution, ironically confirms the discursive capacity of civil society to escape the constitutional attempts that are otherwise aimed at coalescing the legal and moral realms of justice. To what extent, the provisions in the Constitution have succeeded in creating cultural conditions, within which, one could experience mutual recognition, the cultivation of republican virtues of respect of the other, as we had indicated earlier? To what extent have the state and its institutions succeeded in augmenting the moral stamina of society, so that it could accept the claims for recognition by the untouchables,[32] especially their pursuit for self-esteem and self-respect?[33]

The Constitution does seem to privilege legal rights over moral rights, in the sense that it is aimed at extracting a firm commitment to moral rights by enforcing legal rights through institutional mechanisms. It is as if the Constitution presupposes that the recognition of dignity may not easily come from the upper castes that it will have to be extracted from the twice-born civil society. The second assumption is that the positional good will automatically guarantee the cultural good. So, there are in the Constitution, provisions providing opportunities for achieving material parity with others. These provisions, which will help the lower castes to attain material benefits also involve a promise of the reorganization of society, along egalitarian lines. Thus the central government formulated the Anti-Untouchability Act in 1955 and in 1988, the more stringent and more comprehensive SC/ST Prevention of Atrocities Act. The Ministry of Welfare, Government of India, has already adopted the Act, prohibiting the employment of manual scavengers. There are provisions, both at the central and state levels, ensuring the dignity for those who are exposed to humiliation and indignity. Of course, these provisions were put in place not so much flowing from the ethical insight of the state as from the Dalit assertion for self-respect in certain parts of the country. Notwithstanding all these, the constitutional provisions achieve only limited success, as the upper castes have failed to take the moral lead in offering unconditional recognition to those groups deprived of this recognition. On the contrary, the upper castes seem to be using discursive methods to escape constitutional obligation.[34]

The experience of untouchability, which forms the basis of all the constitutional provisions and Acts (1955 Act, with amendments, and 1988 Act) insulates the source of untouchability and captures only the sites of untouchability. The upper caste person with a malignant capacity to inflict insults on the untouchables is the source of untouchability. In other words, it is necessary to treat untouchability as a phenomenon involving both the source of pollution and its object. Further, the second problem internal to the Constitution is that, while treating untouchability as a criterion of classification, it assumes that truth resides only in the body of the untouchable, and hence the untouchable becomes an object of classification. But in fact, it is the upper caste, the twice-born, who is the cartographer, who is empowered to demarcate the ritual spaces and confine some people as untouchables, within these spaces. It is the upper caste person who has the power of touch that he deploys to assign hierarchical meaning to the human body. In a kind of inversion, the touchable is found to be making himself/herself, supra-untouchable. The Indian Constitution is ill-equipped to produce that type of moral lexicon, evocative of the republican virtues of love, care and concern, by which the upper caste cartographer can redraw the boundaries of the touchable in social intimacy and overcome the anxiety projected on to the landscape of untouchability.[35]

Against the horizon of this anxiety related to the tactile, the lack of proximity between the touchable and un-touchable leads to the reification of the identities of both, inhabiting two spaces, but conceptually bound together. It is beyond the purview of the Constitution to classify people on the basis of the power that resides in the tension between the touchable and the untouchable. Untouchability as truth acquires power only when it resides in an active human being. Thus, the untouchable becomes a 'poison weapon' by which the upper caste is repelled in the social space.[36] Even if this be the case, the twice-born reserves the power to walk in and walk out of social relationships with Dalits who cannot force the upper castes to touch them. In other words, the upper castes control the moral/cultural resources that condition the use of the public sphere. The Indian Constitution, with its punitive provisions, offers limited promise in compelling the upper castes to share resources with the Dalits. The Constitution, with its egalitarian thrust, has not succeeded in penetrating the moral self of the upper caste. Untouchability is not something specific. It is all permeating and universal in character, as Ambedkar discovered 80 years ago. The details of his caste background reached the Baroda office, faster than his ontological being and his physical self, like many Dalit officers can testify even today, from their autobiographical sites.[37]

Constitutional provisions have paved the way for the achievement of positional good, by the Dalits, but not of cultural goods like recognition and dignity. Further, the Constitution does not automatically guarantee benefits of cultural justice. In fact, the Constitution creates tensions between positional and cultural notions of justice, as noted by Ambedkar. As he envisaged, even beyond cultural justice, justice as a principle has to be applied as a standard evaluator of the sphere of larger social relationships, where claims of equal worth are being framed and articulated. The Dalit life-worlds have been constituted in the text, legal provisions and the ideological trajectory of the Constitution. They are being reconstituted in the dialectical space/time of the quotidian subaltern struggles to contest the monopoly of touch appropriated by the twice-born.[38]

Conclusion

The struggle for cultural justice has to go on, on a quotidian note, as we have witnessed in the Dalit protests after the incidents at Una and elsewhere, as even before. Failing to launch such struggles leads to the reification of the issues of dignity enshrined as *expectations* in the constitutional documents. Everyday forms of protest,[39] creating little pockets of resistance,[40] leading to a democratic movement that is constantly and consistently interrogating the homogenizing forces that invert the text, context, texture and the thrust of the Constitution, are called for.[41] To facilitate this process of subaltern interrogation, we have to provide registers of interpretative practices by the citizenry, with their multiple readings of the Constitution, from their rhizoid locations, being aware of the ambiguities and tendencies towards co-option and counter-revolutionary tendencies. The emergence of these multiple readings gives hope that the fragments of the nation[42] are resilient against the culture of homogenization and the monolithic, economic Leviathan of Developmentalism.[43]

Where and what would be the task of philosophizing, in these struggles and multiple and contesting readings of the text that is Nation/State/Constitution? It is to be tactile, **in touch,** *with/in* the public sphere, supporting the emergence of a *Homo Dialecticus*, within/against the *Homo Hierarchicus*,[44] letting itself transform itself as a **Tactile, Public Philosophy**.[45]

Notes

1 This title, "Whose Nation? Whose State?" has been inspired by the title of an article by Felix Wilfred, "Whose Nation? Whose History?," Felix Wilfred and Jose D. Maliekal (eds), *The Struggle for the Past: Historiography Today* (Chennai: Department of Christian Studies, University of Madras, 2002), 71-96.

2 Chantal Mouffe, "Politics and the Limits of Liberalism," Chantal Mouffe, The Return of the Political (London: Verso, 1993), 140, as quoted in Nivedita Menon, "Citizenship and the Passive Revolution: Interpreting the First Amendment," Rajeev Bhargava (ed.), *Politics and Ethics of the Indian Constitution* (New Delhi: Oxford University Press, 2008), 198-99.

3 Upendra Baxi, "Constitutionalism as a site of State Formative Practices," *Cardozo Law Review*, 21, no. 4 (2000), 1184-5, as quoted in Menon, "Citizenship and the Passive Revolution," 198-99.

4 Roland Barthes, *Image, Music, Text* (New York: Hill and Wang, 1977), 146, as quoted in Menon, "Citizenship and Passive Revolution," 189.

5 Barthes, *Ibid*, p. 148, as quoted in Menon, "Citizenship and Passive Revolution," 189.

6 The events, under consideration are the death of Rohith Vemula, on 17 January 2016 and the widespread student protest and unrest in the Universities across the country, especially, Central University of Hyderabad, JNU, Delhi and Jadavpur University.

7 Manash Bhattacharjee, "The clarity of a suicide note," Lead Article, The Hindu, January 21, 2016, where the author comments on the suicide note of Rohith Vemula, and the socio-political circumstances, that drove him to his death.

8 See in this context, Zoya Hasan, "Redefining Indian Nationhood," Lead Article, *The Hindu*, February 24, 2016, where the author opines that the crackdown on JNU is in keeping with the right-wing project to ensure its world view becomes India's as well. Constructing the premier university as a space for anti-national thinking is crucial, for it gives this project a famous address and a justification to step in.

9 "A 50-year-old man, Mohammad Akhlaq, was beaten to death and his 22-year-old son severely injured on Monday night (28 September, 2015), in UP's Dadri, allegedly by residents of Bisara village, after rumours spread in the area about the family storing and consuming beef, police said. Six people were arrested in connection with the attack, around 45 km from Delhi, sparking protests that led to police firing, damage to vehicles and injuries to a 20-year-old welder who works for the National Thermal Power Corporation (NTPC) facility in the area. Police said they have sent samples of meat taken from Akhlaq's home "to the forensics department for examination. Akhlaq's daughter, Sajida, said the family had "mutton in the fridge" and not beef."As available on http://indianexpress.com/article/india/india-others/next-door-to-delhi-mob-kills-50-year-old-injures-son-over-rumours-they-ate-beef/, as accessed on 10 October, 2015.

10 "Four Dalit youths were severely beaten up and dragged on the road for nearly a kilometre in Gir Somnath district of Gujarat for allegedly possessing beef. The crime came to light after a video of the assault went viral on social media. Five persons were booked under Section 307 (attempt to murder), Section 395 (loot) of the Indian Penal Code and the Scheduled Castes and Scheduled Tribes Prevention of Atrocities) Act. Three of them were later arrested. The youths from Samadhiyala village, belonging to a community of leather traders, came to Una town in Saurashtra region to remove hide from a cow carcass. When they reached the town's bus stand on Monday, they were accosted by a group of men said to be Shiv Sena members. The youth were stripped half-naked, tied to a Sport Utility Vehicle in a crowded area and severely beaten up with iron pipes for over half an hour. No one from a large crowd of onlookers rescued the youth. The assailants, claiming to be working for cow protection, later dragged the youth to a police station a kilometre away and handed them over to police. After members of the Dalit community rallied at the police station, an FIR was registered against five men, including Pramodgiri Goswami, who claimed to be district president of Shiv Sena and an organisation working for cow protection. The injured youth were sent to a local hospital for treatment." (First Published On: Jul 12, 2016, 22:15 IST) – as available on http://www.firstpost.com/india/gujarat-four-dalit-youths-beaten-up-dragged-on-the-road-for-possessing-beef-3-arrested-2890118.html, as accessed on 15 August, 2016.

11 Manash Bhattacharjee, "The clarity of a suicide note."

12 Menon, "Citizenship and Passive Revolution," 190.

13 Upendra Baxi, "Outline of a 'Theory of Practice' of Indian Constitutionalism," Rajeev Bhargava (ed.), *Politics and Ethics of the Indian Constitution*, 92-3. In the context of the discussion of the constitutive power and popular sovereignty, see Michael Hardt and Antonio Negri, *Multitude: War and Democracy in the Age of Empire* (New York: The Penguin Press, 2004), wherein from a neo-Marxist viewpoint, the authors, in the context of globalized conflict, reimagine democracy from the idiom of Multitude, of Spinozan inspiration. Multitude, for these authors, is not the people, but rather the many peoples acting in network. Because of its plurality, innumerable and internal differences, the multitude contains the potential for true democracy. See also Michael Hardt and Antonio Negri, *Empire* (Cambridge, Massachusetts: Harvard University Press, 2001), of

which, *Multitude* is a sequel. *Empire* identifies a radical shift in concepts that form the philosophical basis of modern politics, concepts such as sovereignty, nation, and people. Hardt and Negri link this philosophical transformation to cultural and economic changes in postmodern society—to new forms of racism, new conceptions of identity and difference, new networks of communication and control, and new paths of migration. Looking beyond the regimes of exploitation and control that characterize today's world order, it seeks an alternative political paradigm—the basis for a truly democratic global society.

14 Menon, "Citizenship and Passive Revolution," 197.

15 *Ibid*, 200.

16 Baxi, "Outline of a 'Theory of Practice' of Indian Constitutionalism," 94-6.

17 *Ibid.*, 97.

18 *Ibid.*, 98.

19 *Ibid*, 99.

20 Suhas Palshikar, "The Indian State: Constitution and Beyond," Rajeev Bhargava (ed.), *Politics and Ethics of Indian Constitution*, 161.

21 *Ibid.*

22 Saddat Hassan Manto, *The Mottled Dawn*, Khalid Hassan (trans.) (Delhi: Penguin Books, 1997), 175, as quoted in Baxi, "'Outline of a 'Theory of Practice' of Indian Constitution," 100.

23 Baxi, "'Outline of a 'Theory of Practice' of Indian Constitution," 104.

24 For the considerations on the merits and the standing relevance of the Indian Constitution, and its innovative and revolutionary nature, from a liberal-democratic viewpoint, see Rajeev Bhargava, *Secularism and Its Critics* (New Delhi: Oxford University Press, 1999); Rajeev Bhargava, *The Promise of India's Secular Democracy* (New Delhi: Oxford University Press, 2010), where he joins issue with Sunil Khilnani's critique of Indian democracy, as expressed in his book, *Idea of India* (London: Hamish Hamilton, 1997). Also see Neera Chandhoke, *Beyond Secularism: The Rights of Religious Minorities* (New Delhi: Oxford University Press, 2000) and Sarah Joseph, *Interrogating Culture: Critical Perspectives on Contemporary Social Theory* (New Delhi: Sage Publications, 1998).

25 Baxi, "'Outline of a 'Theory of Practice' of Indian Constitution," 104.

26 *Ibid.*, 106.

27 *Ibid.*, 106-8. See Hannah Arendt, *The Origin of Totalitarianism* (New York: Harcourt Bruce, 1950). Romila Thapar, the eminent historian, in an interview given to Zia Us Salam, expressed the view that no majority community can claim monopoly over the nation or nationalism. See Zia Us Salam, "'Nationalism does not allow the Hindu in India to claim primacy,'" *The Hindu*, March 2, 2016.

28 See Akeel Bilgrami, "Gandhi (and Marx)" in Akeel Bilgrami (ed), *Secularism, Identity, and Enchantment* (New Delhi: Permanent Black, 2014), 143-45, where the author states that in the mood of the rejection of the anti-developmentalist mode of protest, former Union home minister P. Chidambaram calls for the rejection of counterculture against the use of natural wealth, the counterculture, which he wants to reject, being those who protest against the grabbing of land, by the mining and power projects. Even Amartya Sen, the most humane of the contemporary economists, who stands with the poor, in his "positional objectivity," was seen to be justifying the dispossession of agricultural land for "Development."

29 See Felix Wilfred, "Human Rights or The Rights of the Poor?: Redeeming the Human Rights from Contemporary Inversions," Asian Dreams and Christian Hope: At the Dawn of the Millennium (ISPCK: Delhi, 2000), 98-122, where the author critically analyzes the process, by which the human rights are being inverted by the dominant, in their favour, instead of being an instrument for the protection of the poor. Usually, inversion is a subaltern mode of appropriation of dominant structures of power or symbolic resources, causing a reversal of the existing order of things. Ranajit Guha, *Elementary Aspects of*

Peasant Insurgency in Colonial India (Delhi: Oxford University Press, 1977), 77-8. In the globalized world of today, instead of the subalterns using the tool of inversion, for reversal of structures, the dominant use it to appropriate for themselves, what is duly of the poor, in nexus with those in power and the interpreters of the law.

30 Baxi, "'Outline of a 'Theory of Practice' of Indian Constitution," 106-8. See Hardt and Negri, *Multitude*, 268-327, for a global cry for reforms in various areas of modern life, such as representation, rights and justice, economic grievances and bio-political grievances, all of which call for redressal, in a yearning for greater and grounded democracy, in the idiom of the Multitude, indicated earlier.

31 Mahasweta Devi, *Bashai Tudu* (Calcutta: Thelma Publication, 1990), 87.

32 Gopal Guru, "Constitutional Justice: Positional and Cultural," Rajeev Bhargava (ed.), *Politics and Ethics of the Indian Constitution*, 229-31.

33 Gopal Guru, "Liberal Democracy in India and the Dalit Critique," Social Research, 78, no. 1, Spring 2011, 99-122. See also Felix Wilfred, "Dalit Future: Future of the Nation," Asian Public Theology: Critical Concerns in Challenging Times (ISPCK: Delhi, 2010), 17-27.

34 Guru, "Liberal Democracy in India and Dalit Critique," 235-7.

35 *Ibid,* 241-2.

36 See Gopal Guru, "Rejection of Rejection: Foregrounding Self-respect," Gopal Guru (ed.), *Humiliation: Claims and Context* (New Delhi: Oxford University Press, 2013), 218.

37 Guru, "Liberal Democracy in India and Dalit Critique," 242 -3.

38 *Ibid*, 244. In this context, the grounded insight of Nirja Gopal Jayal, that, "The proclivity of official policy to cling to historical precedent even at the cost of ridiculous policy inconsistencies has meant that Muslim OBCs are entitled to quotas while Muslim and Christian Dalits are not." is very relevant to our discussion on radical justice for the Dalits. See Nirja Gopal Jayal, *Citizenship and its Discontents: An Indian History* (Ranikhet: Permanent Black, 2013), 256.

39 James Scott, *Weapons of the Weak: Everyday Forms of Peasant Resistance* (New Haven: Yale University Press, 1998).

40 David Harvey, *Spaces of Hope* (Edinburgh: Edinburgh University, 2000).

41 Guru, "Liberal Democracy in India and Dalit Critique," 245.

42 See Partha Chatterjee, "The Nation and its Outcastes" and "Communities and the Nation," Partha Chatterjee (ed.), *The Nation and Its Fragments: Colonial and Postcolonial Histories* (New Delhi: Oxford University Press, 2001), 173-99 and 220-239, respectively; also G. Aloysius, *Nationalism without a Nation in India* (Delhi: Oxford University Press, 1997), 214-28.

43 Baxi, "'Outline of a 'Theory of Practice' of Indian Constitution," 110-12.

44 Steven M. Parish, *Hierarchy and Its Discontents: Culture and the Politics of Consciousness in Caste Society* (Delhi: Oxford University Press, 1993), 100.

45 Emmanuel Wallerstein, the eminent social scientist speaks of a Public Sociology, like Public Theology. Public Sociology deals with the study of social processes and also processes of values. He says, "all sociologists – living or dead, or yet to be born - are public sociologists, cannot be other than public sociologists. The only distinction is between those who are willing to avow the mantle or those who are not," as quoted in Dan Clawson et al. (eds), *Public Sociology* (Berkeley: University of California Press, 2007), p.16, as quoted in Wilfred, "Introduction," *Asian Public Theology*, xi.

4

The Dialectics between Fundamental Rights and Directive Principles

Peter Ladis F.
Chanakya National Law University, Patna

Abstract: Dr. B. R. Ambedkar, Chairman of the Drafting Committee of the Constitution of India, said that there are certain things which are in conflict with Fundamental Rights in India. This definitely leads one to consider Rights as Fundamental Rights as against certain other Rights in conflict with fundamental rights. Thus, this research paper analyses the core differences between such rights defining the meaning of such rights and the dialectics between fundamental rights and directive principles emphasizing on the Indian legal system. The paper includes the classification of rights in the international scenario in comparison to the classification of rights under Part III and Part IV of the Constitution of India, i.e., Fundamental Rights and Directive Principles of State Policy. The paper addresses the burning issue of today as to whether any elected government in India can make such amendments in the Fundamental Rights as per its party ideology. In the light of various landmark judgments of the Supreme Court of India the study finds that the elected government cannot impose its ideology on the Constitution of India. In the present scenario, even if the Narendra Modi-led BJP government wants to impose the ideology of his party on the Constitution of India altering the rights, it cannot succeed, for the reason that the basic structure of the Indian Constitution cannot be amended as held in the case of *Kesavananda Bharati* v. *State of Kerala*, AIR 1973 SC 1461.

1. Introduction

> What are we having this liberty for? We are having this liberty in order to reform our social system, which is full of inequality, discrimination and other things, which conflict with our fundamental rights.[1] – Dr. B. R. Ambedkar.

Dr. B. R. Ambedkar, Chairman of the Constitution Drafting Committee, mentions certain things which are in conflict with Fundamental Rights in India. This definitely leads one to consider Rights as Fundamental Rights as against certain other Rights in conflict with fundamental rights. Thus, this research paper is an attempt to analyse the core differences between such rights defining the meaning of such rights and the dialectics between fundamental rights and directive principles emphasising on the Indian legal system. The burning issue today is whether any elected government in India can make such amendments in the Fundamental Rights as per its party ideology. This research addresses the issue in the light of various judicial pronouncements of the Supreme Court of India.

2. Role of State: A Historical Perspective

Human beings are rational beings. By virtue of their being human, they possess certain basic and inalienable rights, which are commonly known as human rights. Since these rights belong to them because of their very existence, they become operative with their birth. Human rights, being birth rights, are, therefore, inherent in all the individuals irrespective of their caste, creed, religion, sex and nationality. These rights are essential for all individuals as they are consonant with their freedom and dignity and are conducive to physical, moral, social and spiritual welfare. They are also necessary as they provide suitable conditions for the material and moral uplift of the people. Because of their immense significance to human beings, human rights are also sometimes referred to as fundamental rights, basic rights, inherent rights, natural rights and birth rights.[2]

With the emergence of the changing roles of the state from political state to *laissez faire*; from *laissez faire* to the welfare state, the state has taken upon itself every aspect of human life and ensures the welfare of every person and of society at large, viz., giving every person his or her due. Modern political philosophy regards the state as an organ to secure the welfare of the people, part of which is to secure social justice. India has envisaged this vision from the very inception of its Constitution giving the state a negative obligation under Part III, Fundamental Rights and a positive obligation under Part IV, Directive Principles of the State Policies. It is Part IV of the Constitution of India that mostly deals with the concept and contents of Social Justice. However, the responsibility of applying and broadening such a wider concept has been mainly shouldered by the judiciary. The Indian Judiciary has played the 'Father Figure' when it comes to establishing social justice among the various groups of people especially the underprivileged over the past decades. The leap that our judiciary has made to ensure social justice, needs a wider study and appreciation.

3. Rights: Broadly Classified Meaning

The Rights have been broadly classified into two categories on the basis of their importance in human lives. H. O. Agarwal in his book, 'International Law and Human Rights' explains the following classifications.[3]

3.1 Civil and Political Rights

Civil rights or liberties refer to those rights which are related to the protection of the right to life and personal liberty. They are essential for a person so that he may live a dignified life. Such rights include the right to life, liberty and security of a person, the right to privacy, home and correspondence, the right to own property, freedom from torture, inhuman and degrading treatment, freedom of thought, conscience and religion and freedom of movement.

Political rights may be referred to those rights which allow a person to participate in the government of a State. Thus, the right to vote, the right to be elected at genuine periodic elections, the right to take part in the conduct of public affairs, directly or through chosen representatives are some instances of political rights.

The nature of civil and political rights may be different but they are inter-related and interwoven, and, therefore, it does not appear logical to differentiate them. This reason alone led to the formulation of one covenant covering both civil and political rights, i.e., the International Covenant on Civil and Political Rights.

3.2 Economic, Social and Cultural Rights

Economic, social and cultural rights are related to the guarantee of minimum necessities of the life to human beings. In the absence of these rights their existence is likely to be endangered. The right to adequate food, clothing, housing and an adequate standard of living and freedom from hunger, the right to work, the right to social security, the right to physical and mental health and the right to education are included in this category of rights. These rights are included in the International Covenant on Economic, Social and Cultural Rights.

These rights are sometimes called positive rights because require active intervention, not abstentions, on the part of States. These rights are therefore counterpoint to the first generation or civil and political rights, with human rights conceived more in positive than in negative terms. The enjoyment of these rights requires a major commitment of resources and therefore their realization cannot be immediate as in the case of civil and political rights.

4. Classification of Rights: An International Perspective

Prior to 1948, the international community never had such classification of rights as the Universal Declaration of Human Rights. In that year they were incorporated into rights of the individual, which are both civil and political rights as well as the economic, social and cultural rights. In 1966 the United Nations came up with two international covenants.

4.1 The International Covenant on Civil and Political Rights

The United Nations International Covenant on Civil and Political Rights (ICCPR) attempts to ensure the protection of civil and political rights. It was adopted by the United Nations' General Assembly on 19 December 1966, and it came into force on 23 March 1976. The International Covenant on Economic Social and Cultural Rights, the Universal Declaration of Human Rights, and the ICCPR and its two Optional Protocols, are collectively known as the International Bill of Rights.

4.1.1 Purpose: The ICCPR recognizes the inherent dignity of each individual and undertakes to promote conditions within states to allow the enjoyment of civil and political rights. Countries that have ratified the Covenant are obliged to protect and preserve basic human rights and compelled to take administrative, judicial, and legislative measures in order to protect the rights enshrined in the treaty and to provide an effective remedy. There are currently 74 signatories and 168 parties to the ICCPR.

4.1.2 Content: The unifying themes and values of the ICCPR are found in Articles 2 and 3 and are based on the notion of non-discrimination. Article 2 ensures that rights recognized in the ICCPR will be respected and be available to everyone within the territory of those states who have ratified the Covenant (State Party). Article 3 ensures the equal right of both men and women to the enjoyment of all civil and political rights set out in the ICCPR.

4.1.3 The rights protected under the ICCPR

The following rights are included under the provisions of ICCPR:

Article 6 – Right to life.
Article 7 – Freedom from torture.
Article 8 – Right not to be enslaved.
Article 9 – Right to liberty and security of the person.
Article 10 – Rights of detainees.
Article 11 – Right not to be imprisoned merely on the ground of inability to fulfill a contractual obligation.

Article 12 – Freedom of movement and choice of residence for lawful residents.
Article 13 – Rights of aliens.
Article 14 – Equality before the courts and tribunals. Right to a fair trial.
Article 15 – No one can be guilty of an act of a criminal offence which did not constitute a criminal offence.
Article 16 – Right to recognition as a person before the law.
Article 17 – Freedom from arbitrary or unlawful interference.
Article 18 – Right to freedom of thought, conscience and religion.
Article 19 – Right to hold opinions without interference.
Article 20 – Propaganda for war shall be prohibited by law.
Article 21 – Right of peaceful assembly.
Article 22 – Right to freedom of association with others.
Article 23 – Right to marry.
Article 24 – Children's rights
Article 25 – Right to political participation.
Article 26 – Equality before the law.
Article 27 – Minority protection.

4.1.4 Limitations: Article 4 of ICCPR allows for certain circumstances for states parties to derogate from their responsibilities under the Covenant, such as during times of public emergencies. However, state parties may not derogate from Articles 6, 7, 8 (paragraphs I and 2), 11, 15, 16 and 18.

4.1.5 First Optional Protocol: This protocol allows victims claiming to be victims of human rights violations to be heard. The Human Rights Committee (Committee), which is established by the Covenant, has the jurisdiction to receive, consider and hear communications from victims. The first Optional Protocol came into force with the Covenant. There are currently 35 signatories and 115 parties to this protocol.

4.1.6 Second Optional Protocol: This protocol aims to abolish the death penalty. It was entered into force on 11 July 1991 and it currently has 37 signatories and 81 parties.[4]

4.2 The International Covenant on Economic, Social and Cultural Rights

The International Covenant on Economic, Social and Cultural Rights (ICESCR) was adopted on 16 December 1966 by the UN General Assembly and came into force 10 years later. The ICESCR, together with the Universal Declaration of Human Rights (UDHR) and the International Covenant on Civil and Political Rights (ICCPR), constitute the International Bill of Human Rights. The ICESCR defines a broad set of rights related to the economic, social, and cultural elements of life that states must provide to their citizens. Specific rights relate to:

- Housing
- Education
- Labour
- Environment
- Health
- Cultural rights (including language and religion)
- Self-determination

The ICESCR also requires state parties to submit reports on their implementation of the Covenant. Initially, the Economic and Social Council (ECOSOC) of the UN was responsible for the review of these reports. However, in 1985, the ECOSOC established the Committee on Economic, Social, and Cultural Rights ("the Committee") to assume all monitoring functions of the implementation of the ICESCR. The Committee is a group of 18 independent experts on economic, social, and cultural rights who meet twice a year in Geneva. The Committee provides guidance for and also monitors each state party's compliance with the ICESCR by drafting general comments on the scope of treaty obligations and conducting reviews of state parties' progress in implementing the treaty. In accordance with the Optional Protocol to the ICESCR, the Committee may also accept individual complaints and communications alleging a state party's violation of rights under the ICESCR.[5]

4.3 Generation of Rights

There are some scholars who have developed the theory of classification of rights into various generations – first, second generation and third generation of rights.

First generation human rights, often called "blue" rights, deal essentially with liberty and participation in political life. They are fundamentally civil and political in nature: They serve negatively to protect the individual from excesses of the state.

Second generation human rights are related to equality and began to be recognized by governments after World War II. They are fundamentally economic, social and cultural in nature. They guarantee different members of the citizenry equal conditions and treatment.

Third-generation, "collective-developmental" rights of peoples and groups held against their respective states aligns with the final tenet of "fraternity." They constitute a broad class of rights that have gained acknowledgment in international agreements and treaties but are more contested than the preceding types.

5. Classification of Rights under the Indian Constitution

Under the provisions of the Constitution of India, 1950, rights have been incorporated mostly under Part III and Part IV and these rights have been so classified that it resembles the classification of rights as discussed under Civil and Political Rights, and Economical, Social and Cultural Rights.

5.1 Concept of Fundamental Rights - Their Origin and Development

Part III of the Constitution of India, titled as "Fundamental Right" secures to the people of India, certain basic, natural and inalienable rights. These rights have been declared essential rights in order that human liberty may be preserved, human personality developed and an effective social and democratic life promoted.

Bhagwati J. in the case of *Maneka Gandhi* v. *Union of India*[6] held that these fundamental rights represent the basic values cherished by the people of this country since Vedic times and they are calculated to protect the dignity of the individual and create conditions in which every human being can develop his personality to the fullest extent. They weave a pattern of guarantees on the basic structure of human rights, and impose negative obligations on the state not to encroach on individual liberty in its various dimensions.

The aim behind having a declaration of fundamental rights is to make inviolable certain elementary rights appertaining to the individual and to keep them unaffected by the shifting majorities in the legislatures. It is to preserve certain basic human rights against interference by the state.

The inclusion of a chapter on fundamental rights in the constitution is in keeping with the trend of modern democratic thought. The guarantee of certain basic human rights is an indispensable requirement of a free society. The purpose is to preserve, for the benefit of the people, their fundamental rights against infringement by the institutions created by the constitution.

The framers of the Indian constitution followed the American model in adopting and incorporating the fundaments rights for the people of India. The constitution, not only secures the fundamental rights, but also, provides a speedy and effective remedy for their enforcement. A significant feature of the Indian Bill of Rights is that the remedy for the enforcement of the fundamental rights is itself declared a fundamental right and is included in the very chapter on fundamental rights. An act of the state whether legislative or executive, if inconsistent with a fundamental rights is declared to be null and void the nullity of such an act does not rest upon judicial pronouncement but upon the express provision contained in Article 13.

The very purpose of withdrawing certain subjects from the changing pattern of political controversy is to place them beyond the reach of a majority in a legislature and officials in the government and to establish them as legal principles to be applied by the courts. A dominant group of legislators could pass any discriminatory or unjust legislation and prejudice the interests of considerable sections of the people. This could amount to tyranny by the legislative majority. One's right to life, liberty and property, to free speech and free expression, freedom of worship and assembly and other fundamental rights are not subjects to be submitted to vote. They should not depend on the outcome of elections.

5.2 Directive Principles of State Policy

Part IV articles 36-51 of the Indian Constitution is about directive principles of state policy. The inspiration to include these principles of state policy is drawn from the constitution of Ireland. It sets forth the ideals and objectives to be achieved by the state for setting up a social welfare state, as distinguished from a mere police state, which aims at social welfare state, as distinguished from the common good and the secure to all its citizens, justice socio and economic.

6. A Journey from Directive Principles of State Policy to Fundamental Rights

The conflict between the rights under Part III and the rights under Part IV emerged from the very beginning of the Indian Constitution. Judges were left with very few options and they had to act according to the needs of the hour. They had to try to do social and economic justice without hurting their judicial conscience. The court in certain cases has followed the policy of reasonable restrictions in view of these directive principles. For instance, in the case of *State of Bihar* v. *Kameshwar Singh*[7] the court upheld the *jamindari* abolition in view of directive principles. It held that where two judicial interpretations are acceptable then the interpretation favouring the directive principles must be adopted. In the case of *Putthama v. State of Kerala*[8] it was held that the Kerala Agriculture Act is valid, it fulfils the purpose of Articles 38 and 39 of the constitution. In the case of *U.B. Uttar Var* v. *State of Maharashtra*[9] the court held that the interpretation that substitutes directive principles should be followed. Further in the case of *Kasturi Lal v. State of J.K*[10] the court held that every law or executive action must be reasonable and within public interest, and the yardstick of public interest and reasonableness is to be found in the directive principles.

The relationship between Part III and Part IV caused a lot of difficulties initially as the courts adopted a strict and literal interpretative approach to show that when there is a conflict between these two parts, the Fundamental Rights would prevail over the Directive Principles of State Policy.

> The Directive Principles of the State Policy, which by Art. 37 are expressly made unenforceable by a court cannot override

> the provisions found in Part III (Fundamental Rights) which, notwithstanding other provisions, are expressly made enforceable by appropriate writs, orders or directions under Art. 32. The Chapter on Fundamental Rights is sacrosanct and not liable to be abridged by any legislative or executive act or order, except to the extent provided in the appropriate article in Part III. The Directive Principles of State Policy have to conform to and run as subsidiary to the Chapter on Fundamental Rights.[11]

However, over a period of years, the Supreme Court brought changes in its own style of thinking and opened its arms to consider that the rights given under both the parts should be given effect as much as possible.[12] It was in 1970, in *Chandra Bhavan Boarding and Lodging, Bangalore v. State of Mysore*, that the Supreme Court accepted that there is no conflict between the Fundamental Rights and the Directive Principles. "They are complementary and supplementary to each other."[13] This journey from Part IV to Part III has paved way to consider all the rights towards forming a welfare state ensuring social justice to its citizens.

7. The Present Indian Scenario of Classification of Rights

Under Article 21, which is 'protection of life and personal liberty' many rights have been incorporated by the judiciary. The insertion of the word 'due' had made a lot of sense in the US Fifth Amendment and this was followed by the Indian Judiciary to give flesh and blood to the mere skeleton of words under Article 21.

Article 21 includes very many rights and following are the few examples:

Rights of the Arrested Man: The arrested man has a right that a relative or friend of his be informed about his arrest and the place of his detention. He has a right to consult a lawyer privately. Arrest should be made not merely on suspicion but only after a reasonable satisfaction reached after some investigation as to genuineness and bona fides of the complaint and a reasonable belief as to the person's complicity and even as to the need to effect arrest.[14]

Speedy Trial: Speedy trial has been held to be part and parcel of the right to life and liberty under Article 21 and the Supreme Court has observed:

> No procedure which does not ensure a reasonably quick trial can be regarded as 'reasonable, fair or just' and it would fall foul of Article 21. There can, therefore, be no doubt that speedy trial and by speedy trail we mean reasonably expeditious trial, is an integral and

essential part of the fundamental right to life and liberty enshrined in Art. 21.[15]

Subsequently, there have been many cases where from time to time the Supreme Court has laid down guidelines upholding the interests of vulnerable groups of people, like prisoners.

Right to Legal Aid: The Supreme Court has emphasized on the right to legal aid for poor prisoners who are not in a position to hire the services of learned counsel. Other than *Hussainara Khatoon's* case, in *Khatri* v. *State of Bihar*[16] the Court has explicitly mentioned that right to legal aid is a constitutional obligation cast on the State Government that cannot be denied.

Right against Police Torture: There are many cases where the policemen have misused their power and have caused great harm to the lives of vulnerable groups especially to prisoners and women. In *Francis Coralie Mullin* v. *Union Territory of Delhi*, the Supreme Court has condemned the act of torture as against Article 21. Special provisions are to be made for women prisoners by the State including separate lock-ups, toilet facilities, etc., and the interrogation of females should be carried out only in the presence of female constables.[17]

Compensation for Damages: *Rudal Shah* v. *State of Bihar*[18] cannot be forgotten for the gross negligence of the State Government where an individual was kept in jail for 14 years after his acquittal by the Criminal Court for which a compensation of Rs. 35,000/- was ordered to be paid to the victim.

The well-known Bhagalpur blinding case burnt the hearts of those who love humanity. It was alleged that the police had blinded certain prisoners. The Supreme Court of India rightly ordered adequate compensation and ordered the State to meet the expenses of housing these men in the blind home in Delhi.[19]

When a Bangladeshi woman was gang raped by some railway employees in the railway premises at Howrah Railway Station, it was with a Public Interest Litigation by an Advocate that the foreign national got justice by way of compensation too.[20] Such examples could be multiplied where the rights of the underprivileged has been upheld to ensure that their basic rights could not be violated.

Right to Health: The situations in some of the leading hospitals were very pathetic and first aid to the injured was denied as they did not fulfil certain formalities. Taking note of such inhuman practices the Supreme Court brought out certain guidelines to the hospitals where preservation of life is of paramount importance, the primary motive and the primary duty.[21]

8. Conclusion

The Indian legal system has set an example to the international community in classifying the rights into enforceable and non-enforceable rights. At present these rights are construed in such a way that the individual rights have been given utmost interest while upholding the common interest. What is the need for such classifications? The answer lies in the practical application of the rights whereby the basic rights are to be given utmost importance and the directive principles depend on the available resources of the State.

As per the research question whether the elected government can infringe on the rights so enshrined under Part III of the Constitution, the answer is found in the enforceable nature of Fundamental Rights in India. The apex court has made it crystal clear that the basic structure of the Constitution can never be amended. Therefore, in the light of the above discussion the study finds that the elected government cannot impose its ideology into the Constitution of India. In the present scenario, even if the Narendra Modi-led BJP government wants to impose the ideology of BJP in the Constitution of India altering the rights, it cannot succeed, for the reason that the basic structure of the Indian Constitution cannot be amended.

Notes

1 http://www.brainyquote.com/quotes/authors/b/b_r_ambedkar.html visited on 12.06.2016
2 H. O. Agarwal, *International Law and Human Rights,* (Allahabad: Central Law Publications, 2006), 705.
3 *Ibid.* pp.707-709.
4 https://ccla.org/summary-international-covenant-on-civil-and-political-rights-iccpr/ visited on 12.07.2016.
5 http://www.hrichina.org/en/international-covenant-economic-social-and-cultural-rights-icescr. Accessed on 12.07.2016.
6 AIR 1978 SC 597.
7 AIR 1952 SC 252.
8 AIR 1978 SC 771.
9 AIR 1977 Bombay 99.
10 AIR 1965 SC 1039.
11 *State of Madras* v. *Champakam Dorairajan* AIR 1952 SC 226.
12 See, *Kerala Education Bill,* AIR 1958 SC 956.
13 AIR 1970 SC 2042 at 2050. Similar view was taken by the Supreme Court in *Golak Nath v. State of Punjab*, AIR 1967 SC 1643 and in *Kesavananda Bharati* v. *State of Kerala*, AIR 1973 SC 1461.
14 *Joginder Kumar* v. *State of Uttar Pradesh*, AIR 1994 SC 1339.
15 *Hussainara Khatoon* v. *Home Secretary, State of Bihar (I),* AIR 1979 Sc 1360.
16 AIR 1981, SC 928.
17 See, *Sheela Barse* v. *State of Maharashtra* AIR 1983 SC 378.
18 AIR 1983 SC 1086.
19 *Khatri* v. *State of Bihar*, AIR 1981 SC 928.
20 *Chairman, Railway Board* v. *Chandrima Das*, AIR 2000 SC 988.
21 *Parmanand Katara* v. *Union of India,* AIR 1989 SC 2039.

5

The Nation as an Evolution of Self-Consciousness
An Analysis Based on Hegelian Philosophy

Gregory Mathew Malayil
Dharmaram Vidya Kshetram, Bengaluru

Abstract: A nation comes into existence as a consequence of an evolution which has social, historical as well as political dimensions. In the context of India, civilizations and regional kingdoms acted as the nuclei of the evolution. The quest for an indivisible nation, many a time worked as the under-current during this evolutionary process. George Hegel's philosophy of the state helps us to reflect on various nuances of the evolution of nation-states. The interpenetration of the universal with the particular will through a complex system of social and political mediations is what forms the self-consciousness of the nation-state. It is considered as an organic, internally differentiated and interrelated totality. A nation and the sovereignty of the nation-state are not external forces imposed on the people but the very extensions of the self-consciousness of man. The evolution of a nation in space and time is not a one-time process, but an ongoing one.

Introduction

The terms state and nation are often used as synonyms though there are differences between them. 'Nationalism' generally denotes the attitude that the citizens of a nation have when they care about their national identity which is often defined in terms of common origin, ethnicity, and cultural ties.[1] A nation consists of an ethnic or cultural community, whereas a state is a political entity with a high degree of sovereignty. Physical elements play an important role in the birth of a state. The division and the reunion of Germany is a good example. The 'United Nations' is an organization of nation-states. In this paper, nation and state are used with the same meaning: nation-state.

Nationalism came into the focus of extensive philosophical debate a few decades ago, mainly as a consequence of the internal clashes in several nations including the former Soviet republics.[2] National awakening and struggles for political independence are often both heroic and cruel. The formation of a nation-state, in general, responds to deep popular sentiment but sometimes results in inhuman consequences, from violent expulsion and 'cleansing' of non-nationals, leading to organized mass murder. The formation of a nation-state can be viewed from various perspectives such as historical, social, political, etc. Theories of methodological nationalism and universalism analyse the nation-state in relation to society.[3] Classical, modernist and contemporary social theories[4] threw light on the fabric of the nation-state, trying to explain the dynamics of its present status. All these perspectives in one way or the other imply that a nation is evolving from something that has already existed[5] and this evolution is a gradual and slow process as it takes place in the context of biological evolution.

Certain Evolutionary Features

The evolution and existence of any nation-state is associated with space, time and culture. During the past two centuries, the nation-state has been deified and demonized in equal measure.[6] Nation-states underwent several changes and variations; they have gone through experiences of unification, totalitarian terror, occupation, division, and then re-unification; and they have been legitimized around ethnic/racial, republican, monarchic, liberal, democratic, federal and even class principles. In spite of all these variations, the nation-state succeeded, to an important extent at least, in presenting itself as a solid, stable and ultimately the necessary form of social and political organisation in modernity.[7] We see that all nations are going through a process of evolution. We try to see this process in detail, with our own nation, India, as an example.

India: Evolution from Civilizations to the Republic

Civilizations are the outcome of primitive man's attempts to transgress the limits set by nature. A search for the origin of present India, will take us to the early civilizations of the North-West. With his tools and vision it is not only the limits set by nature which are transgressed but also the limits of human experience and cognition. From elementary adaptation to the natural environment to the establishment of great civilizations, the horizon of experience and the regional extension of human relations constantly expanded. The hunter, food gatherer, peasant and civilization are the different stages of this evolution. But a change of climate or a devastation by invaders was sufficient to cut off the roots of their existence and identity. Indian history provides excellent examples of this evolution.[8] Pre-historic sites with stone tools were almost exclusively found in the region between Udaipur and Jaipur, the valley of the Narmada River, the eastern slopes of the Western Ghats, the region between the rivers Krishna and Tungabhadra, and a few other places which were not centres of the great empires of the later stages of history.[9]

During the later advanced stages of civilizations, a similar process took place in the political environment too. The established regional kingdoms had to face a lot of threats from their neighbouring kingdoms as well as from various militant invaders. Gradually all this havoc contributed to the unification of regional kingdoms. The invasion by colonial powers again indirectly worked as a unifying factor. A spirit of "we-feeling" spread over the subcontinent which worked as fighting power against the colonial establishments. Consequently, we see India emerging as a nation as part of an evolutionary process, which is not deliberately designed or controlled systematically and progressively by anybody.

The state of India is based on a great tradition. The small kingdoms of the Gangetic plains, the great empires of antiquity, the regional kingdoms of medieval times, the Mughal Empire, the British Indian Empire and finally the Union of India, mark the different stages of political development and evolution.[10] The nucleus of this development was the Indus Valley and similar civilizations and the pre-civilization forms of settlements around 6000 BC, including Neolithic settlements in Baluchistan. But gradually it encompassed all parts of the vast country. The political development spread over the geographical space in course of time. In fact, the parliamentary system as well as secularism, evolved as part of this age old evolution.

Parliamentary Form of Government and Secularism

The present Indian parliamentary form of government actually emerged from the Mughal and British Systems.[11] In ancient India, kings enjoyed unparalleled authority. They were like umpires who could interfere in local conflicts and settle issues. The modern territorial state in India was introduced by the great Mughals whose strategies of administration were imitated by their enemies and successors. The British, who took over the Mughal structure, "civilized" it by replacing the military officer with the civil servant. Local autonomy as well as the royal umpire were superseded by judges. British legislation and jurisdiction made an impact on Indian life. The process of devolution of power by which the British continuously postponed the grant of full-fledged parliamentary democracy made the Indian nationalists strive for the goal of a national parliamentary government even more strongly.[12] As both the Mughal and the British Indian political tradition was highly centralist, this centralism was followed by the Indian nationalists.

The regional kingdoms and empires of ancient as well as medieval India had the noble attitude of religious tolerance. They might have been influenced by Vedic or Upanishadic ideologies. When the British conquered India they did not make it a Christian empire; similarly, when the Indian National Congress challenged British rule, they took great care to retain a secular character. The British policy of 'divide and rule', which finally led to the partition of India, confirmed the Indian National Congress even more in its adherence to secularism, which then also became the guiding principle of the Union of India. Jawaharlal Nehru saw in this secular republic the true school of the Indian nation in which it would grow up in terms of modern national solidarity.[13] This process is still on going and there are many obstacles which are to be overcome by concerted efforts.

Limits of Historical and Social Approaches

Historical as well as Social approaches would provide an account of the various events that took place in the processes of evolution of a nation-state. Although, the different theories related to them explain the dynamics and governing forces of the formation of a nation-state, certain issues remain unattended to a great extent. On reviewing and analysing the evolution and existence of India or any nation-state, a few questions may arise. What prompted ancient man to form civilizations? Why did the freedom fighters and nationalists sacrifice their lives? How does a nation-state get sovereignty? Is sovereignty bestowed on any arbitrarily selected individual? Now we see the increase in the state's control over its population through nationalisation policies such as literacy campaigns, schooling, taxation and military recruitment. If a sovereign state curtails the rights of an individual, who would compensate it? Is there any limit to the power that a nation-state can exercise over its citizens? Tracing back the paths traversed by any nation from its present would reveal the truth that each nation-state is in a process of constant becoming. To understand the nuances of this becoming, the basic 'entity' which undergoes the process of evolution needs to be unravelled. Reflections in the light of Hegel's philosophy would help us in this direction.

Hegel: State as an Ideal

According to Hegel the very existence of the state is part of a divine strategy, not a merely human arbitrary artefact. In the original German his words are as follows: "*Es ist der Gang Gottes in der Welt, dass der Staat ist.*"[14] This has been variously rendered into English as "The state is the march of God through the world." The existence of the state is the presence of God upon earth or "the march of God in the world that is what the state is."[15] What Hegel meant to say was not that the state is the 'March of God' on earth or anything of this nature but to highlight the divine element reflected in the sovereignty of the state. Furthermore, it has to be pointed out that Hegel's theory does not refer to any existing state. It is the idea of the state with which Hegel is dealing and any existing state cannot be anything but a mere approximation to the idea. In this context he explains the relevance of rational freedom and the role of man's self-consciousness.

Rational Freedom

Hegel's political philosophy begins with the common assertion that we all are striving for freedom. In Hegel's sense, we enjoy freedom when we successfully pursue ends larger than our own or anyone's private good. As rational and thinking beings, we relate ourselves universally to the whole of the social world. Our freedom is not fully actualized until we are with ourselves in ends which are universal. Through corporations, the individuals in society acquire ethical ends which go beyond their self interest. These ends pass over in turn to the absolutely universal end, the state.[16]

Hegel distinguishes 'the political state proper' from the state in a broader sense, the community as a whole with all its institutions.[17] He regards the state in the latter sense as the individual's final end. Hegel asserts that the individual's highest freedom consists in membership in the state.[18] Accordingly, the highest consciousness of freedom is the consciousness of this membership, in what he calls the 'political disposition' or 'patriotism'. He says patriotism is nothing more than a habit of leading one's normal life and doing one's ethical duty, while taking the state as one's 'substantial basis and end.'[19] Hegel locates the absolutely universal end in the state because it alone is a self-sufficient individuality, not part of any larger whole. To those who would relate their actions to some still larger entity ('humanity at large', a 'cosmopolitan world society' or 'all sentient creation') Hegel points out that such entities are not real, but only abstractions. We actualize our freedom by relating ourselves to something real which truly actualizes the power of reason in the world. The state, Hegel says, is 'the absolute power on earth.'[20]

The state, is not made by any contract, but rather grows out of history. Hegel says that our general understating of freedom as the unhindered capacity to do as we please without any restrictions is abstract and unsatisfactory. We must rise above petty personal interests and short term comforts in order to achieve long-term goals. A child may feel that if she were completely free she could stay home from school and play video games. However her parents force her to go to school. By restricting her immediate choices her parents are actually maximizing her freedom, because education will enable her to pursue a career and make meaningful choices in the future. As with the child, we can be self-actualized and concretely free individuals only rising above our personal impulses and serving universal and community ends embodied in the rational organization of the state.[21] Being a member of a family or a member of one's profession always involves some sacrifice of immediate pleasures and interests. But for most of the people, these are not burdens imposed on them, for they find personal satisfaction and have inner-joyfulness in carrying out the duties of parenthood or career. It is this quality, but transformed to a higher realm that motivated Mahatma Gandhi and other leaders to move ahead with the independence movement, sacrificing their own lives.

When Hegel talks about the state, he sees it as community fulfilling a positive ethical purpose. Of course, the government consists of bureaucracies and agencies that enforce laws, making the state appear as a coercive authority standing over us. He refers to this aspect of society as civil society or the external state which has the negative function of maintaining order. However, the political and economic structures of a society are but the skeleton that supports the real life of the state, which is the spiritual activity of the people manifested in their language, law morality, science, art, music, poetry, architecture, religion and philosophy. "For the state is not the abstract confronting the citizens, they are parts of it, like members of an organic body where no member is the end and none is its means. It is the realization of freedom, of the absolute, final purpose and exists for its own sake."[22]

Self-Consciousness

According to Hegel, as we have already seen, the rationality which permeates the world of man becomes apparent for the first time in the state. The rationality will be hidden behind feeling and sentiment in the family and it will be the means to achieving individual self-interest, in civil society. The family represents a moment of universality in the sense of undifferentiated unity. Civil society represents moments of particularity.[23] The state represents the unity of the universal and the particular. Instead of undifferentiated unity we find in the state differentiated universality or unity in difference. And instead of sheer particularity, we find the identification of the particular with the universal will. To put the matter in another way, in the state, self-consciousness has risen to the level of universal consciousness.[24] The individual is conscious of himself as being a member of the totality in such a way that his selfhood is not annulled but fulfilled. The state is not an abstract universal standing over and against its members; it exists in and through them. At the same time by participating in the life of the state the members are elevated above their sheer particularity. The state is an organic unity. It is a concrete universal existing in and through particulars which are distinct and one, at the same time.

The state is said to be the self-conscious ethical substance. 'The state is the actuality of the ethical idea. It is ethical mind qua the substantial will manifest and revealed to itself, knowing and thinking itself, accomplishing what it knows and in so far as it knows it ... self-consciousness ... finds in the state, as its essence and the end and product of its activity, its substantive freedom.'[25]

The state is the actuality of the rational will when this has been raised to the plane of universal self-consciousness. Rights are established and maintained as the expression of the universal self-consciousness and morality obtains its content. That is to say, a man's duties are determined by his position in the social organism. This does not mean that a man has duties only to state and none to his family. For the family is not annulled in the state: it is an essential, if subordinate, moment in the state's life. Hegel doesn't mean to imply that a man's duties are determined once and for all by an unchangeable social position. Though he insists that the welfare of the whole social organism is paramount, he also insists that the principle of individual freedom and personal decision is not annihilated in the state, but will be preserved.[26]

It is clear that Hegel speaks of the state in the most exalted terms. However, he has no intention of suggesting that historical states are immune from criticism and he makes this point quite clear. 'The state is no ideal work of art; it stands on earth and so in the sphere of caprice, chance and error and bad behaviour may disfigure it in many respects. But the ugliest of men, or a criminal or an invalid, or a cripple, is still always a living man. The affirmative, life, subsists despite his defects, and this affirmative factor, which is our theme here.'[27] Hegel highlights the positive element, life, which remains in spite of the privation and says that it is with the positive element that we have to see the state. Based on rational freedom, the state is organized in such a way as to enable each to realize his freedom in conjunction with others.

"The state is absolutely rational in as much as it is the actuality of the substantial will which it possesses in the particular self-consciousness once that consciousness has been raised to consciousness of its universality. This substantial unity is an absolute unmoved end in itself, in which freedom comes into its supreme right. On the other hand, this final end has a supreme right against the individual, whose supreme duty is to be a member of the state."[28] External conformity with the law, however, is by itself an empty ritual, since it lacks the moment of consciousness. When Hegel says in the preface to the Philosophy of Right that the state is 'reason as it actualized itself in the element of self-consciousness'[29] this implies that institutions are not conceived as externally imposed organs but become extensions of man's own self-consciousness.

The self-consciousness of any present Indian citizen has been formed after a long process of evolution. The ancient Indians who were part of the great civilizations, the medieval Indians who underwent the rule of different emperors and kings, and the modern Indians, who fought against the colonial powers, all together contributed to the self-consciousness of present day

Indians. In spite of the ancient, medieval or modern contexts, man always looks for rational freedom which is the driving force of the mainstream and that unites the people together. Now though there are no threats of invasions or colonial powers as unifying factors, people are brought together through travel and communication promoted by business, agriculture, opportunities for education, employment, tourism, pilgrimages, etc. These interactions result in forming a collective or universal consciousness which is the very substratum of present India. Ideally, the various developmental projects or reforms in consideration are extensions of this collective consciousness. At the same time, as Hegel himself said, the state is not an ideal work of art and hence there are chances of distortions and antinational tendencies.

Unity in Diversity and Self-Consciousness

India is a land known for its unity in diversity. Among Indian citizens we find numerous religions, castes and, linguistic and ethnic groups. Different regions observe variations in climate and culture. They celebrate different festivals and perform varied religious rites. In spite of these diversities, Indians feel a sense of unity and oneness among them. Since ancient times, powerful kings were inspired with the ideal of one, indivisible India. This prompted them to make conquests of lands - stretching from the Himalayas to the seas. The Indian consciousness always quested for unity. The Indian consciousness was ready to embrace various cultures and religions. It was this consciousness which enkindled patriotism and accelerated the integration of various regional kingdoms. We enjoy the rational freedom as Hegel interpreted, which is provided by the state, which always takes into account the freedom and existence of the other.

Conclusion

We have seen from the historical evolution of India that a nation is not a product of any deliberate design or plan. The nation comes into existence as an evolution. Though, almost all the nations externally remain static, all are in one way or another passing through a process of becoming. Internal conflicts, such as regionalism, religious fundamentalism, terrorism, etc., are some of the factors that destabilise the existence of any nation. At the same time, these threats arouse the feeling of patriotism which counteracts against the destabilising factors. The nation, the sovereignty of the nation-state, law, constitution, etc., are not external forces imposed on the people. As we see from Hegelian philosophy, all these things are actually evolved from the self-consciousness of the people which strives for rational freedom. Hegel's philosophy of the ethical dimensions of a nation-state may be questioned or criticised on certain grounds; however, a deep understanding of Hegel's concept of self-consciousness would contribute to a better insightful understanding of the factors that drive the evolution of a nation-state.

Notes

1 "Nationalism", Stanford Encyclopaedia of Philosophy, revised on 15 Dec. 2014, https://plato.stanford.edu/entries/nationalism/.
2 *Ibid.*
3 Wagner Peter, *A Sociology of Modernity Liberty and Discipline* (London: Routledge, 1994), 19-194.
4 Castelles Manuel, "Materials for an Exploratory Theory of the Network Society," *British Journal of Sociology* 51, no. 1 (2000): 5.
5 Castelles Manuel, "A Rejoinder to Abell and Reyniers' 'Failure of social theory,'" *British Journal of Sociology* 52, no. 3 (2001): 541.
6 Daniel Chernilo, *A Social Theory of the Nation-State* (Oxon: Routledge, 2008), 1.
7 *Ibid.*
8 Hermann Kulke and Dietmar Rothermund, *A History of India* (London: Routledge, 1998), 1.
9 *Ibid.*
10 *Ibid.*, 333.
11 *Ibid.*
12 *Ibid.*
13 *Ibid.*, 334.
14 Shlomo Avineri, *Hegel's Theory of the Modern State* (Cambridge: Cambridge University Press, 1994), 176.
15 *Ibid.*, 177.
16 Allen W. Wood, *Elements of Philosophy of Right*, trans. H. S. Nisbet (Cambridge: Cambridge University Press, 2000), 274.
17 Georg Wilhelm Friedrich Hegel, *Philosophy of Right*, trans. T. M. Knox (London: Oxford University Press, 1942), 267.
18 *Ibid.*, §258.
19 *Ibid.*, §268.
20 *Ibid.*, §331.
21 William F. Lawhead, *The Voyage of Discovery: A History of Western Philosophy* (Washington: Wordsworth Publishing Company, 1996), 389.
22 Georg Wilhelm Friedrich Hegel, *Reason in History: A General Introduction to the Philosophy of History*, trans. Robert S. Hartman (Indianapolis; Library of Liberal Arts, 1953), 52.
23 Frederick Copleston, SJ, *A History of Philosophy, Vol. VIII: Modern Philosophy* (New York: Image Books, 1994), 212.
24 *Ibid.*
25 Hegel, *Philosophy of Right*, trans. T. M. Knox, § 257
26 Frederick Copleston, SJ, *A History of Philosophy, Vol. VIII: Modern Philosophy*, 212.
27 Hegel, *Philosophy of Right*, trans. T. M. Knox, addition to §258.
28 *Ibid.*, §258.
29 *Ibid.*, 12.

6

Hannah Arendt
The Political Function of Thinking

Gayatri Mendanha
Symbiosis School for Liberal Arts, Pune

Abstract: India is a land of diverse beliefs, value systems, cultural and social traditions. Yet, when there is a call for ethnic cleansing, and 'other' ways of living are attacked, it breeds violence and fear among citizens. In this paper, I shall explore Hannah Arendt's solutions to this 'evil'. Arendt's work transcends her time to speak to us in an Indian context today. The dangers of ideological thinking, the problem of evil, the co-existence of a diverse people and the role of a citizen are issues that we find ourselves confronted with. Arendt urges citizens to allow for a public-political space where they can dialogue with the 'other'. She also believed that when we "think what we are doing", we are shielded from committing inhuman, unthinking crimes. I will discuss the political function of thinking, the questions her ideas raise to the Indian citizen, and its relevance to our situation today.

Introduction

On 9 February 2015, the Supreme Court of India stated that "we don't know for how long it [India] will remain a secular country."[1] In the face of the demolishing of the Babri Masjid on 6 December 1992, the Godhra riots in 2002, the lynching of 52-year-old Mohammad Ikhlaq on 28 September 2015 and the the call for a Hindu *rashtra*, we need to attempt to understand the reasons for these 'evils' and look for solutions. As we look back into our nation's past and head towards an uncertain future, we ponder awhile in the present to re-look at our processes and prospects.

India is a land of diverse beliefs, languages, literatures, cultural and social traditions and value systems. Yet, when there is a call for ethnic cleansing, and 'other' ways of living are attacked, it breeds violence and fear among citizens. Amartya Sen tells us that, "Experiencing pluralism can be effortless and automatic, but practicing it and defending it against organized attack cannot but be a serious intellectual exercise."[2] In this paper, I will explore Hannah Arendt's ideas and discuss the political function of thinking in an Indian context. Arendt, one of the most influential political philosophers of the twentieth century, wrote extensively on Nazi Germany, the effects of a totalitarian regime and the horror of the incomprehensible concentration camps. After the death camps, the world was forced to confront what ordinary human beings were capable of doing. Arendt, herself had come face to face with the problem of evil and the use of violence to settle political conflicts. One of her solutions to the problem of evil was to "think what we are doing."[3] Arendt does not construct a framework for us, but understands our engagement with the political as a "specific type of activity and a specific kind of experience."[4]

In trying to understand the violence that some Indian citizens subject each other to, at the altar of ethnic cleansing, this paper will begin by exploring Arendt's writings on the role of ideological thinking in producing blind allegiance and will look at her solutions to combating it. We will then attempt to understand the 'Eichmanns' of the world, who were not motivated by ideological thinking, yet commit inhuman crimes. In confronting Adolf Eichmann's thoughtlessness, Arendt began to wonder if thinking was the antidote to not-thinking and the banality of evil. We will explore her ideas on the political function of thinking and look at its relevance to our situation today.

I. Ideological thinking

Ideologies are theories that people blindly believe for fact and are willing to go to great lengths to defend. These ideologies offer "promises to explain all historical happenings, the total explanation of the past, the total knowledge of the present, and the reliable prediction of the future."[5] The illogical conclusions that these ideologies arrive at, with regard to other communities and cultures, can be extreme and inhuman. In a diverse country such as ours, there will be divisive forces and ideologies that will attempt to alienate citizens from each other. Some citizens will be defined as more 'Indian' than others. Its lopsided worldview has resulted in isolated groups becoming tools in the hands of politicians. We have seen how ideological thinking is used as a tool to manipulate reality and brainwash people into committing inhuman crimes.

One wonders who these unthinking people are, who are willing to sacrifice free thought at the altar of ideological thinking. Unthinking people seek ideologies, because ideologies gives people answers to questions of their own destiny and identity. In this alternative reality they are not alone but are a part of a larger vision. It is better to belong and act in accordance with an ideology, rather than being an invisible nobody. Brian McClinton highlights Koestler's argument: "that mass crimes of violence committed for selfish, personal motives are historically insignificant compared to those committed out of a self-sacrificing devotion to a flag, a leader, a religious faith or a political conviction."[6] In this deep, unquestioning commitment the fundamentalist is willing to step into the shoes of a terrorist. Even an act that is otherwise morally reprehensible is looked upon as morally right within the framework of those principles. Within certain ideological frameworks, even God would reward inhuman acts. Koestler maintains that "we have a peculiar capacity to become emotionally committed to beliefs which are impervious to reasoning, indifferent to self-interest and even to the claims of self-preservation."[7] This is the peculiar situation in which so many people are in and allow themselves to become tools that wreak havoc and destroy peace.

Arendt's Solutions:

1) Human Spontaneity

Arendt believed that, "The real obstacle, and enduring opponent, of the totalitarian system is human spontaneity."[8] In spontaneous thought and action, the individual breaks away from the clutches of ideological thinking and forms a unique identity for her/himself. This embracing of pluralism opens multiples ways of seeing and experiencing the world. Moving away from a singular worldview, makes it difficult for governments to make tools of people, to be used for their own political gains. Governments gain from an unthinking mob that is bound together and sees the world from one perspective. Arendt was a champion of the individual, who in the midst of plurality, lived as "distinct and unique being among equals."[9]

2) A Public-Political Space

Politics, for Arendt, is the creation of a space where diverse people can articulate their concerns publically, allowing for an exchange of ideas and different perspectives. She argues for a sophisticated political discourse and meaningful dialogue among citizens that is oriented towards inter-subjectivity. Unfortunately, most citizens reduce their political engagement to just their private, anonymous vote. Arendt concludes that totalitarian movements triumphed because the majority had been indifferent. They were, "neither the result of circumstances beyond human control, nor of history's inexorable march, but happened because of the concerted failure of ordinary people to act to stop them."[10] It proved that "a democracy could function according to rules which are actively recognized by only a minority."[11]

We are reminded that "although there were countless 'inward opponents' of Nazism in the Third Reich, for instance, their objections to the death camps were inconsequential since they were not voiced in public."[12] In India today there are many 'inward opponents' who are too afraid to voice their opinions or engage in a political debate. In the creation of a public-political space citizens can freely and collectively deliberate. It is here that "their differences as well as their commonalities can emerge and become the subject of democratic debate."[13] Maurizio Passerin D'Entrèves writes that, "As an alternative to a system of representation based on bureaucratic parties and state structures, Arendt proposed a federated system of councils through which citizens could effectively determine their own political affairs."[14] This would be a space for multiple standpoints and voices. She envisioned a more enlightening political discourse. As Arendt says, judgment "cannot function in strict isolation or solitude; it needs the presence of others 'in whose place' it must think, whose perspective it must take into consideration, and without whom it never has the opportunity to operate at all ... judgement, to be valid, depends on the presence of others."[15] In being able to put oneself in the shoes of the other to take in multiple perspectives, one's own reasoning and thought expands. In the landscape of power and politics, Arendt encourages dynamic critical thinking and questioning. It is a move away from ideological thinking, towards evolving worldviews and perspectives.

The German playwright, Bertolt Brecht harshly admonishes the apolitical citizen stating that, "The worst illiterate is the political illiterate, he doesn't hear, doesn't speak, nor participates in the political events ... The imbecile doesn't know that, from his political ignorance is born the prostitute, the abandoned child, and the worst thieves of all, the bad politician, corrupted and flunky of the national and multinational companies."[16] In a democracy citizens must be empowered with a sense of effective political agency and efficacy. Arendt recognised the importance of power sharing. She urged ordinary people to enter the political realm as active citizens and be capable of making decisions that would direct the course of their collective lives. The Indian Constitution is a masterpiece, but it is finally up to its citizens to turn it into a reality. As citizens of India, would we be willing to engage in a public-political dialogue? What is our role in the affairs of our state? How do we participate in the governance of the state? Is the majority indifferent? Do we just pursue our own individualistic needs and simply ignore governmental excesses?

3) Disinterested Reflection

Arendt philosophises on the role of citizens and their relationships with each other in the public realm. When citizens are intimately bound together by ties of communal feelings, and look at themselves as a collective, what is sacrificed are the "public values of impartiality, civic friendship, and solidarity."[17] Canovan writes, that Arendt envisioned a "formal, artificial public realm in which what mattered were peoples' actions rather than their sentiments; in which the natural ties of kinship and intimacy were set aside in favour of a deliberate, impartial solidarity with other citizens; in which there was enough space between people for them to stand back and judge one another coolly and objectively."[18] This was essential for the kind of public political discourse that she envisioned. It was not meant to be impassioned, deeply emotional hot-headedness but required an "enlarged mentality" and disinterested reflection.[19]

While Arendt sought ways to bind people together, she was against the notion of a nation. In a letter to Karl Jaspers she celebrated the demonstration of freedom in America. On January 29, 1946, she wrote in a letter to Karl Jaspers, "There really is such a thing as freedom here [in America] .... The republic is not a vapid illusion, and the fact that there is no national state and no truly national tradition creates an atmosphere of freedom ..."[20] She demonstrated her thinking in her own life when she looked at the love for the Jewish people. She writes in a letter to Scholem, "I have never in my life "loved" any people or collective - neither the German people, nor the French, nor the American, nor the working class or anything of that sort. ... the only kind of love I know of and believe in is the love of persons."[21] Rabindranath Tagore also recognised the beauty and value in transcending a blind devotion to India and embracing a love and respect for all humanity. He writes, "It is my conviction that my countrymen will gain truly their India by fighting against that education which teaches them that a country is greater than the ideals of humanity."[22] It is these thinkers and their "enlarged mentality" that show us the path ahead.

II. The Eichmann Trial

Although, ideological thinking is a potent tool, one must also consider the Eichmanns of the world who may not always be motivated by ideology, yet commit inhuman crimes. With Eichmann's trial, Arendt extends her political thought to include questions of morality and personal responsibility. *Eichmann in Jerusalem* was originally commissioned as a series of articles written for The New Yorker magazine. It consisted of Arendt's reflections when attending Eichmann's trial in Jerusalem. Otto Adolf Eichmann was a German Nazi and one of the major organizers of the Holocaust. He was charged by Reinhard Heydrich with facilitating and managing the logistics of mass deportation of Jews to ghettos and extermination camps in German-occupied Eastern Europe.[23]

During Eichmann's trial, Arendt observed that although the crimes Eichmann had committed were monstrous, he himself was 'banal', marked by a profound thoughtlessness and lack of conviction. It made Arendt re-look at moral responsibility and moral judgment. This man, so distanced from reality, had also admitted that "officialise" (Amtssprache) was his only language.[24] In a totalitarian bureaucracy, in which an inverted morality prevailed, Eichmann was surrounded by people who were *for* the implementation of the Final Solution. Having taken an oath, he accepted the premises of his state and to the best of his ability worked on carrying out orders. What disturbed Arendt was that the crimes committed were not the product of a mad, inherently evil sociopath, but an ordinary human being who was simply unable to think, unable to put himself in someone else's shoes, unable to allow for a new perspective or to consider alternatives. To Arendt, Eichmann was terrifying because he was "thoughtless." The real trouble, she believed, was there were so many like him, terrifying normal people who made evil banal.

An Indian Eichmann: Ashok Mochi

Who were these 'ordinary' citizens who marched blindly against their defenseless fellow citizens to wreak havoc and destruction? Ordinary street cobbler Ashok Mochi's photograph came to symbolise the terror of the 2002 carnage that took place during the Gujarat riots. He was seen wearing a saffron head band and holding an iron rod, marching very aggressively. He was accused of looting and burning Muslim homes and shops in the area, was charged under sections 435 and 436 of the Indian Penal Code (crimes of arson and causing destruction by fire), and arrested. Yet, like in the case of Eichmann, this was banal. Tied down by poverty and the boundaries of his caste, he had worked as a sweeper, a security guard, a house painter, and many other trades, but in none could he establish himself. On the morning of 28 February 2002, when news of the horrific Godhra incident hit the headlines, there was tension in the air with newspapers printing pictures of charred bodies. Yet, Mochi's worry was that the riots would swallow up his earnings for weeks, even months. Not many Hindu men sported beards. He was afraid that the mob would mistake him for a Muslim and attack him. Unable to find a barber to shave his beard, even after a desperate search, he tied a saffron scarf on his forehead to mark himself as a Hindu. He joined other young men at the Shahpur Chowk, where the Vishwa Hindu Parishad had installed months earlier a board announcing that Gujarat was a Hindu Rashtra. He found himself in the midst of the riots and marched on, shouting slogans. Similar, to Eichmann's confession, he was neither ideologically inclined nor fostered a strong hatred for Muslims, holding that he become one of the rioters just by coincidence.[25]

In both these cases, in which the individuals claimed not to be emotionally tied to an ideology, we can question as to how their conscience allowed them to commit these crimes. Arendt points out that "conscience is tied to the public world. Eichmann's problem was that he found no one, absolutely no one, 'who actually was against the final solution.'[26] In the absence of the dialogical other, there is a flawed sense of reality. We also see how, when one's safety is at stake, "customs or behaviour patterns … could be changed as easily as table manners."[27]

1. The Political Function of Thinking

While we are able to put ourselves in Eichmann's and Mochi's shoes and to understand their choices, we must also look at the other side of the coin, at people who are unwilling to fall prey to these 'evils'. While the 'banality of evil' is intriguing, what is also interesting is how certain individuals in a totalitarian regime are unwilling to participate or actively resist committing these crimes. Arendt draws attention to these individuals who were capable of moral judgement and independent choices, even in the midst of the collapse of all other social and political structures. They are the ones that stand out for her, because of their refusal to be swept away. She writes, "That under conditions of terror most people will comply but some people will not … Humanly speaking, no more is required, and no more can reasonably be asked, for this planet to remain a place fit for human habitation."[28] It was this ability to discriminate between right and wrong, even when the only criteria is their own judgment that is representative of Arendt's political thinking.

Lawrence Vogel, in emphasizing the responsibility of 'thinking' in dark times, writes, "The practical implication of Arendt's view is that the Eichmanns of the world are guilty of negligence for their failure to think, for thinking is not the special province of intellectuals, much less professional philosophers."[29] When we live in unpredictable, uncertain times and an inverted morality is the order of the day, we can still expect the individual to be capable of free and independent thought. The individual can still freely resist evil against all odds. Dagme Barnouw writes, "No political order, no matter how perverse, conditions its citizens totally and Eichmann must be presumed to have been free to reject the final solution."[30]

Arendt insisted that care for the world is superior to care for the self. She appealed to the morality of a shared citizenship to resist public evil. The fate of our fellow citizens must concern us. Barnouw writes that, "Though he failed ultimately as a human being, Eichmann failed also as a public citizen, as a member of the realm of plurality."[31]Arendt also harshly critiques the Christian ideal of goodness, which she considered to be an essentially unworldly quality, since "many of those who want to be good ultimately care little for the world."[32]

She writes that most of Machiavelli's arguments against religion were directed against those who love their own salvation, more than the world.

Arendt's moral "absolute" is: "that we ought to share the world with other people."[33] Hence, in the case of Eichmann she offers the following judgement:

> Just as you supported and carried out a policy of not wanting to share the earth with the Jewish people and the people of a number of other nations--as though you and your superiors had any right to determine who should and who should not inhabit the world--we find that no one, that is, no member of the human race, can be expected to share the world with you. This is the reason, and the only reason, you must hang.[34]

Thinking as the Antidote

In *Eichmann in Jerusalem*, Arendt explores the horrors that human beings become capable of when they lose their ability to think. Kathleen Jones reminds us, that without thinking, "we become quite literally homeless because we imagine both the strangers sitting next to us and even our kin to have become unbearably threatening. These "others," may become as much afraid of us as we are of them. And when that happens, it becomes possible for any one of us to do awful things."[35] We have witnessed both in India and around the world the effects of this paranoia.

Confronting Eichmann's thoughtlessness, Arendt began to wonder if *thinking* was the antidote to the *not-thinking* and the banality of evil. She writes:

> Might the problem of good and evil, our faculty for telling right from wrong, be connected with our faculty of thought?...Could the activity of thinking as such, the habit of examining whatever happens to come to pass or attract attention, regardless of results and specific contents, could this activity be among the conditions that make men abstain from evildoing or even actually 'condition' them against it?[36]

Arendt believed that if the answer to this question was a yes, then we should demand the exercise of thinking from every sane person. She believed that thinking was both universal and necessary to living responsibly. She believed that thinking and critical reflection were capable of protecting us from committing evil. For Arendt, thinking is a soundless, internal dialogue that a person has with him/herself. "It is a Socratic dialectical interchange, consisting of questioning and answering not of others, but of ourselves. This internal dialogue leads the person to act in accordance with sound moral judgments and to avoid committing evil."[37] This faculty of judgment, our ability to distinguish the right from the wrong, is not something we automatically inherit or possess. It is always in a state of becoming, it has to be deconstructed and recreated perpetually through public discourse. Else, even the best of us, will find ourselves sliding into dogmatism and ideology.

Thinking is a process by which one destroys unexamined ideals and morals, and by using one's imagination is able to construct one's own frameworks and worldviews. In this deconstructive reconstructing, "withdrawn from the world, like Penelope spinning her web, the process undoes each night what seemed conclusive the day before."[38] This activity of thinking can condition us against evil because of its effect on the thinker. It acts as a shield even against socially sanctioned evil. When one thinks, one is forced to reflect on one's actions and on what one is doing. In this dialogue with the self the conscience is evoked and one strives for harmony with the self. "It's better to suffer wrong than to do wrong, Arendt claims, because you can't befriend and live together with an evildoer, though you can remain friends with a victim."[39] Thinking also enables us to take into consideration a plurality of perspectives. We are able to put ourselves in the shoes of the other, which broadens our horizons and aids our judgement.

Yet, if we admit this and hold that thinking is possible for everyone, then people who are "thoughtless" should be responsible for their choices and actions. If we believe that the human mind is capable of revolting against and rejecting extreme evil, even without recourse to metaphysics, then we believe that blind atrocities will be resisted. "Even under the circumstance of "total moral collapse," where "every legal act is immoral and every moral act a crime," there remains something within our nature that we can rely on, namely the call of conscience, awakened by the activity of "thinking without banisters", empowering one, at the very least, to resist the tide of socially sanctioned murder."[40] This implies that the individual is responsible for acting in accordance with an inverted morality, rather than resisting it. The task of acting and resisting socially sanctioned murder, finally falls to each individual citizen who will always be confronted with choices.

Conclusion

In our world we still bear witness to mindless horror, because sometimes "thinking" isn't easy. Even if we have platforms like Facebook and Twitter in where we can dialogue with the 'other' we would rather engage only with a small circle of like-minded individuals who will not challenge us to think differently. Arendt's ideas have been presented to the reader to recognise the political function of thinking and dialogue. She recognised the importance of power sharing, and urged ordinary people to enter the political realm as active citizens capable of making decisions that would direct the course of their collective lives.

Notes

1 Anand, Utkarsh. 2015. http://indianexpress.com/. 5 February. Accessed October 1, 2016. http://indianexpress.com/article/india/india-others/not-sure-for-how-long-india-will-stay-secular-sc/.
2 Amartya Sen, "Indian Pluralism," India International Centre Quarterly, 1993, 37.
3 David Watson, "Hannah Arendt and the American Republic," Transactions of the Charles S. Peirce Society 28, no. 3 (summer, 1992): 429, http://www.jstor.org/stable/40320370.
4 "The Political Thinking of Hannah Arendt," The Political Thinking of Hannah Arendt, University of Bergen, accessed October 2, 2016, http://www.uib.no/en/fof/100013/political-thinking-hannah-arendt.
5 Hannah Arendt, *The Origins of Totalitarianism* (New York: Harcourt Brace Jovanovich, 1973), 470.
6 Brian McClinton, "Eichmann, Kant and the Banality of Evil," Humanism Ireland, no. 131 (Nov. & Dec. 2011): 13.
7 As cited in Brian McClinton, "Eichmann, Kant and the Banality of Evil," Humanism Ireland, no. 131 (Nov. & Dec. 2011): 13.
8 Eric Helleloid, "Hannah Arendt's Phenomenology of the Will: Contingency, Temporality, and the Nature of Moral Judgment," Ph.D diss., The University of Georgia, 2014, 10.
9 Kathleen Jones, *The Political Theory of Hannah Arendt: The Problem of Evil and the Origins of Totalitarianism*, Summer Seminars and Institutes for School Teachers, 7.
10 Ibid., 5.
11 Hannah Arendt, *The Origins of Totalitarianism* (New York, 1951), 5-6.
12 Hannah Arendt, *Eichmann in Jerusalem: A Report on the Banality of Evil* (New York: The Viking Press, 1965), 103.
13 Maurizio Passerin D'Entrèves, *The Political Philosophy of Hannah Arendt* (Taylor & Francis, 2001), 17.
14 Ibid., 21.
15 Hannah Arendt, The Crisis in Culture: Its Social and Its Political Significance, in Hannah Arendt, Between Past and Future: Eight Exercises in Political Thought (Harmondsworth: Penguin, 1977), 220-21.
16 A quote by Bertolt Brecht," Goodreads, accessed October 2, 2016, http://www.goodreads.com/quotes/541442-the-worst-illiterate-is-the-political-illiterate-he-doesn-t-hear.
17 Maurizio Passerin D'Entrèves, *The Political Philosophy of Hannah Arendt* (Taylor & Francis, 2001), 146.
18 Ibid., 146.
19 Hannah Arendt, 'Truth and Polities', Political Theory and Social Change, ed. David Spitz (New York: Atherton Press, 1967). 128.
20 "News," Hannah Arendt Center News, accessed October 2, 2016, http://hac.bard.edu/news/?p=9580.
21 Hannah Arendt, *The Jew as Pariah* (New York, 19780), 246.
22 Rabindranath Tagore, *Nationalism* (Madras: Macmillan Company, 1976), 17-18.
23 "List of major perpetrators of the Holocaust," Wikipedia, February 12, 2017, accessed February 14, 2017, https://en.wikipedia.org/wiki/List_of_major_perpetrators_of_the_Holocaust.
24 Dagme Barnouw, "The Secularity of Evil: Hannah Arendt and the Eichmann Controversy," Modern Judaism 3, no. 1 (February 1983): 85, http://www.jstor.org/stable/1396167.

25 Harsh Mander, "From Godhra to Una: The face of the Gujarat riots has attached his name to the Dalit cause," Scroll.in, August 28, 2016, accessed November 7, 2016, https://scroll.in/article/813919/from-godhra-to-una-the-face-of-the-gujarat-riots-has-attached-his-name-to-the-dalit-cause.

26 Dagme Barnouw, "The Secularity of Evil: Hannah Arendt and the Eichmann Controversy," Modern Judaism 3, no. 1 (February 1983): 46, http://www.jstor.org/stable/1396167.

27 Lawrence J. Biskowski, "Practical Foundations for Political Judgment: Arendt on Action and World," *The Journal of Politics* 55, no. 4 (November 1993): 882, http://www.jstor.org/stable/2131940.

28 Eric Helleloid, "Hannah Arendt's Phenomenology of the Will: Contingency, Temporality, and the Nature of Moral Judgment," Ph.D diss., The University of Georgia, 2014, 11.

29 Lawrence Vogel, "The Responsibility of Thinking in Dark Times: Hannah Arendt versus Hans Jonas," Graduate Faculty Philosophy Journal 29, no. 1 (2008): 4.

30 Dagme Barnouw, "The Secularity of Evil: Hannah Arendt and the Eichmann Controversy," Modern Judaism 3, no. 1 (February 1983): 178, http://www.jstor.org/stable/1396167.

31 *Ibid.,* 178.

32 Lawrence J. Biskowski, "Practical Foundations for Political Judgment: Arendt on Action and World," *The Journal of Politics* 55, no. 4 (November 1993): 884, http://www.jstor.org/stable/2131940.

33 Dagme Barnouw, "The Secularity of Evil: Hannah Arendt and the Eichmann Controversy," Modern Judaism 3, no. 1 (February 1983): 179, http://www.jstor.org/stable/1396167.

34 Hannah Arendt, *Eichmann in Jerusalem: A Report on the Banality of Evil* (New York: The Viking Press, 1965), 279.

35 Kathleen Jones, *The Political Theory of Hannah Arendt: The Problem of Evil and the Origins of Totalitarianism*, Summer Seminars and Institutes for School Teachers, 9.

36 Hannah Arendt, Thinking, of the Life of the Mind (New York: Harcourt Brace Jovanovich, vol. 1 (1977): 5.

37 Brian McClinton, "Eichmann, Kant and the Banality of Evil," Humanism Ireland, no. 131 (Nov. & Dec. 2011): 13.

38 Lawrence Vogel, "The Responsibility of Thinking in Dark Times: Hannah Arendt versus Hans Jonas," Graduate Faculty Philosophy Journal 29, no. 1 (2008): 3.

39 Ibid., 4.

40 Ibid., 5.

7

The Role of Intellectuals and the Right to Dissent

Noel D'Costa
Patriarchal Seminary of Rachol, Goa

Abstract: The idea of a multicultural India with diverse religious beliefs seems threatened by the process of absorption, domestication and homogenization, and pruned and reshaped by a certain ideology. When this process is threatened by the intellectuals holding positions in institutions and society through their writings, speeches and symbolic actions, the ruling governing authority uses media, deception and the politics of loyalty and betrayal to stifle the opposition. The objective of the paper is to identify the role of the intellectuals amidst the above mentioned tactics to throttle dissent and their right to dissent. I analyse that being aware and understanding the line of attack used to stifle dissent is an important step to detect and assert the role of intellectuals in approaching and responding to challenges. I further argue using Jacques Ranciere the epistemic consequence of dissent. I contend that consensus can be an ideal in theory but dissent as proposed by Ranciere, with its own method and ethics, is a practical solution for any vibrant democratic nation. I conclude that dissent is patriotic and a democratic nation should learn to agree to disagree for its social and political growth.

Introduction

The role of intellectuals and the right to dissent has come to the fore in discourse because there were deeply disturbing trends in India that threatened to tear asunder the *pluriversal, diversal* and multicultural fabric of the country.

Various intellectuals[1] had returned the Sahitya Akademi awards conferred upon them. An executive board member of Sahitya Akademi, K. Satchidanandan resigned from all bodies of the Akademi. They were protesting against the killing of M. Kalburgi, Narendra Dabholkar, Govind Pansare, and Mohamed Akhlaq. Kalburgi, Dabholkar and Pansare were writing and educating the people against a particular ideology. Their killing hallmarked the murder of India's culture of diversity and deliberation. There were also recent incidents of summoning Arundhati Roy for criticizing government policies. Some student leaders from universities, like JNU, were arrested. People were detained for dissenting with the government using social networking sites.

These glaring instances by government bodies were seen as the abridgment of the fundamental right of speech and expression. Instead of swift action from the government, there was a deafening silence and rhetoric against the intellectuals. The growing intolerance left no scope for dissent. There seemed to be a systematic strategy to mute opposition and control public opinion.

These incidents lead us to discuss the role of intellectuals and their right to dissent in a democratic nation. A democracy has essential elements like "limited government, strong civil society, the independence of autonomous institutions, the encouragement of dissident opinion and wide-ranging debate."[2] Should intellectuals continue to dissent or come to a consensus? What are the epistemic consequences of the dissent? Is there a reasonableness of dissent? These questions will be discussed through a dialectical method in the paper.

I argue that *dissensus* in consensus is an important element of a healthy, democratic nation. A leadership which does not subscribe to dissent will use media, politics of loyalty and betrayal and deception to control opinion. The role of the intellectual lies in braving and challenging the above mentioned means used.

1. Conceptualising Dissent

Dissent is an essential feature of human thought and activity. As has been acknowledged, informed dissent was fundamental to the progress of humankind. Dissent has been understood in varied ways. Naman Mody and Arnapurna Rath would say it is a "complex interplay of multiple subjectivities."[3] It is concurrent with critical thinking, where the subject along with the others have the competence to differ and disagree with the accepted viewpoint. It can result in simple disagreement or opposition to civil disobedience.

The original sense of the word dissent was apostatizing. It was some sort of an opposition, revolt or complete renunciation through criticism in a religious context. Noam Chomsky uses the word dissent to speak of an intellectual tradition involving the prophets. They were like dissenters who would condemn and criticize the then existing system. The word gradually went on to refer to a renunciation of a non-religious belief like a political party.

It was seen as a questioning or an open repudiation of the official ideological doctrine of the state party due to the breach of the original values.[4]

Mody and Rath view dissent as an act which "centres on 'withholding assent' or 'disagreeing' because of an espousal of a different view."[5] Hamid Ansari recognized that the need to accept a differing opinion was an essential ingredient of plurality in a democratic society. He says that "the right of dissent also becomes the duty of dissent since tactics to suppress dissent tend to diminish the democratic essence."[6] Though, this definition seems to be an expansive way of understanding dissent, Detlef Pollack and Jan Wielgohs comprehend dissent as all discourses and activities critical of the state to openly deny the state a full control of public life. The person against whom dissent is carried out is the state or the authority or the government. The endeavours of dissent "were not aimed primarily at the removal of the regime, but rather foremost at expanding the sphere of autonomous action under the conditions existing."[7] The location of dissent takes place in the public space which is open to all.

There are some intellectuals who stand out with dissenting voices. If Chomsky is identified as the dissenting voice in the Western political contexts, then we have Arundhathi Roy as indicative of the voices in the South Asian contexts. Roy's dissent is based on what she calls "The Greater Common Good". Her basic contention is that "the state is failing in its pursuit of the objectives it was set up for."[8] The state only provides privileges to the powerful but gives a deaf ear to the marginalized. The dissenting voice prevents an ideology or opinion to be pushed through various means for polarization of the people. As Ansari asserts that dissent is a "democratic right to object, oppose, protest and even resist."[9] Therefore, intellectual dissent can also be patriotic.

So, the notion of dissent can take shape in various forms. The understanding of intellectual dissent in this paper is an expressive or outspoken rebellion through the views, opinion, ideals and actions against established or proposed norms, ideals or entity by the state. A person or a group is unwilling to work together with a recognized social cultural or governmental authority. It arises from the strong personal belief that a particular view, proposal, doctrine, etc., is flawed and must be opposed. We shall see in the next section how the process of clobbering dissent takes place.

2. Clobbering Dissent

Dissent is never liked by the power players in authority. They will use all their know-how to stifle dissent. The way intellectual dissent has been clamped down in India is a cause of concern. The usual modus operandi is to connect dissent with disloyalty to the nation and guard the ideological interests with the veil of patriotism. They use the controlled media to bombard intellectuals by an act of subterfuge. What is the role of the intellectuals when the authority uses media, deception and the politics of loyalty and betrayal to throttle dissent?

We shall see in this section the ways and means used to curtail dissent and how dissenting intellectuals can play their role.

2.1 Role of Media

Mass Media, especially print and television have been a powerful tool in making and shaping public opinions. Print and television today are being disproportionately owned by the large corporations, which have created a system or a structure where journalistic ethics are kept in a safety locker. The power players in the corporate world and the ruling political leaders have become inseparable bedfellows. The way news is generated and dissenting voices are targeted speak volumes about this relationship. Simon Colte claims that "how the news media frame protests; how they display their spectacle and drama; how they give voice to the oppositional views, values and grievances that drive them and the contention that surround them – all are integral to the media politics of dissent."[10]

James Halloran and others introduced a notion of 'inferential framework.'[11] They narrate how the media construe and portray a peaceful dissent through the framework of violence. We can see the televised framing in India which "trivialized, polarized, marginalized and disparaged"[12] the dissenters and their aims, and highlighted the violence of the dissenters.

Some national television stations which trumpet themselves to be the voice of the nation have resorted to sensationalising and public trials of the dissenters. They accuse the dissenting intellectuals as being anti-nationals by cherry-picking the statements of their speeches and writings. They astutely twist their formulations without taking into consideration the whole story to charge them of being against the nation. Those who read print media or watch television are fed with a distorted picture of the dissenting intellectual or institution, they represent. There are also dissenting voices which are sidelined. The media ensures that the genuine voices of dissenters do not reach the audience.

Writers like Arundhati Roy, actors like Shah Rukh Khan and Aamir Khan, student leaders like Kanhaiya Kumar and others were frequently targeted in India for dissenting against the government by the media. They were labelled as anti-India and pro-Pakistan. The issues which they had raised were cleverly sidelined by amplifying the 'anti-national' sloganeering. The right-wing ideological sympathizers were used to repeatedly vent the hateful labels. These repulsive utterance were given a prominent place in the print media and sound bites on prime time television. Today's media has failed to foster the culture of discussion, deliberation, agreement, and dissent.

The understanding of the problem invites a response. The role of intellectuals in this situation is very challenging. Their dissenting voices with clarity of viewpoints to connect with the people need a medium. The powerful media in India are television and print. Social media when used effectively can make contact with a sizeable number of people. The intellectuals not only have to voice out but get their ideas to reach the people. They have to find out ways and means to communicate their viewpoint. The process of creating a network of people through social media to dissipate their point of view is an essential element to make known the dissenting voices to the larger audience.

Intellectuals also have to critique the corporate-influenced media and empower people to be critical of media which is powerful. Dissenters should critically assess the medium through which opinions are fabricated. They should focus on reforms to regulate the policy of media and to advocate its public interest obligation. Promoting and supporting media outlets with different kind of structures and creating networks to be vigilant and think critically are some of the ways that intellectuals can contribute and play their role in the process of dissent.

2.2 Result of Deception

Deception is an art to put on an act to make a person believe that which is untrue. One finds deception in every field of life. Political deception is no exception and is used as a means to achieve political goals. It is still a big problem worldwide and it can take many forms. The usual ploy used is discussed in the previous section of how the meaning of a comment which was never intended is taken out of context to portray the utterer in a bad light.

Deception is a tool which is often used to manipulate opinion. The state or the political parties, ruling or otherwise manipulate people's opinion by inducing them to accept the manipulated claim. The purpose is to win elections or throttle a certain ideology through deception. The faculty to carry out the process is what Hannah Arendt calls 'imagination'. She writes, "The deliberate denial of factual truth – the ability to lie - and the capacity to change facts - the ability to act - are interconnected; they owe their existence to the same source: imagination."[13]

The manipulator has an advantage. As Arendt says: "Lies are often much more plausible, more appealing to reason, than reality, since the liar has the great advantage of knowing beforehand what the audience wishes or expects to hear."[14] This is seen in the context of the 2014 general elections in India. The then opposition party[15] promised the people what they wanted to hear. The tag line of 'Achhe Din'[16] or transferring Rs. 15 lakhs into the bank account of each voter or marching to Lahore to defeat Pakistan were some of the deceptive promises made. After winning the election, these deceptive promises were considered as 'Jumlas.'[17] The manipulated promises are considered as legitimate way to achieve political results. Arendt considers that, "Lies have always been regarded as justifiable tools in political dealings."[18] The gulf between what was promised and what ought to have been is the raison d'être for the dissent.

Deception is also carried out by suppressing information through government employees who were prohibited from freely communicating through social media on matters of serious consequences to the public. The use and abuse of the system to silence the voices of the non-government organisations, if they take on the government is also seen. The common strategies employed were bullying, harassment, intimidation, public denigration and the threatened withdrawal of funding.

By knowing how deception takes place is essential to reversing its outcome. The role of the intellectual lies in targeting the hollowness of the promises by calling attention to the discrepancies. When information belonging to the public domain is withheld, people can become an easy target of deception. The naive public should be made aware of the government lies and cover-ups. Intellectuals can collaborate with RTI[19] activists to get the factual data from different government agencies. This collaboration becomes a powerful association for the intellectuals to bring about an atmosphere of trust among the people. Citizens will be able to view the claims of government agencies with skepticism.

2.3 Politics of Loyalty and Betrayal

Another form of striking dissent is contrasting loyalty and betrayal. The argument presented is that if you are not consenting to the ideology of the political party governing the state, then you are betraying the nation. Those intellectuals who protested against the murder of Kalburgi or at Dadri or the suicide of Rohith were trolled by political groups as being 'pseudo-intellectual, anti-national or pro-Pakistani'. Their loyalty to the nation was questioned by comparing it with the soldiers fighting on the borders against Pakistan. Their dissent was seen as disloyalty to the nation.

The politics of identity is at the core of this distinction. Politics of identity is a movement of affirmation of a group as a race, religion or a nation. In the process of recognition of one's identity, the identity of the other person is demonized. The intellectual dissenters' views are not only seen as wrong or misguided but their identity is cloned with the identity of those demonized. This becomes an easy ploy to sweep the view of the intellectuals beneath the carpet and their distorted demonized identity is magnified. The projected demonized identity given to the dissenting intellectuals is seen as an act of betrayal even though they have all the requirements to fit in one's own identity. It becomes an act of loyalty to the nation for those supporting the powers to defeat the dissenting intellectuals to affirm the self-esteem of their own identity. The dissenting intellectuals find themselves in a peculiar position to ascertain their loyalty to the nation and at the same time to continue to critique.[20]

The politics of identity is seen in many cases in India whether it was the opposition to the re-writing of History of India by Romila Thapar, or the verbal and physical attack on Kanhaiya Kumar, who was propounding an idea of India that has the intellectual freedom to discuss, deliberate and dissent. Both of them and many others with similar views were termed as anti-national. There were also cases of sedition filed against some dissenting individuals. Sedition is construed as betrayal towards the nation. Andreas Kalyvas writes that the pursuit for uniformity or homogeneity leads to the implication of those advocating plurality and difference. They consider proponents of plurality and difference as a threat that fragment and weaken the nation and justify the clampdown of dissent as an act of nationalism.[21]

Clive Hamilton and Sarah Maddison reflect upon the method employed by the government in Australia in targeting dissent. They claim that this method consists in allocating an 'attack dog' role to some functionaries of the government. These functionaries deploy the staff of government to uncover aspects of the past of the opposition that can be used to denigrate them.[22] This seems to be very evident in India as Anand Sharma alleges that the present government is "selectively leaking confidential documents to certain news channels to target the opposition."[23] There have been also some ruling party functionaries of India who use classified information whether it is from the Ministry of Defence (MoD), the Central Bureau of Investigation (CBI) or the Enforcement Directorate (ED) to target the life of the intellectual. The carefully selected leaks portray a malicious portrait of the intellectuals in the public sphere.

The ideology which associates the identity with loyalty has to be challenged. Intellectuals have the duty to shift the discourse from the sacrifices made not only by the soldiers but the everyday sacrifices made by the citizens and can be some sort of civic type of nationalism. The interrogation of the means employed in clobbering dissent becomes important to understand the stifling of dissent by maligning and vilifying the intellectuals. The assertion of the right to dissent has led intellectuals to be in a piquant situation. The ruling powers were able to silence some intellectuals and shield their interests beneath the rubric of nationalism by using the media, deception and the politics of loyalty and betrayal to overpower dissent. The intellectuals are challenged to respond to the tactics used by those governing the nation.

3. 'Dissensus' in Consensus for Healthy Democracy

The political process of decision-making is conceived as disputing, opposing and contesting, which finally leads to a triumph of one over the other. In a democratic nation, should the deliberations by intellectuals come to a consensus, or continue to dissent? The question of the right to dissent is very fundamental in this discussion. We shall explore in this section whether dissent is an essential tool for a democratic state or consensus to make it an ideal.

3.1 Consensus: A Theoretical Ideal?

A simplistic understanding of the process of decision-making in a democratic nation seems to be grounded on consensus. This notion of democracy having a communal society based on collective decisions is projected as an ideal. The absence of dissent suggests an agreement among all the stakeholders of the state with regards to rules, norms and values.

Though, Jurgen Habermas is cited as an exponent of consensus as a democratic principle, his position is what some would call 'epistemic proceduralism'. It is a "model of 'procedural rationality' by which we could judge the legitimacy of procedures for argumentation, agreements and compromises."[24] It would mean to come to a decision with some sort of conjecture of reasonableness. It is done as David Estlund would argue through the application of intellect in the course of deliberations and interpersonal reasoning. There may be negative consequences that arise due to disagreement. Richard Feldman and Ted Warfield write that "some sort of revision or abandonment of belief is epistemically required in light of revealed peer disagreement."[25]

The making of the Constitution of India is one such process of coming to such reasonableness. The deliberations that took place were not only about settling disputes over the competing proposals of what India should be but formulating laws within which an Indian citizen accommodates himself despite the disagreement. Though, the process of drafting the laws took place a long time ago, the amendments or change can occur only in the institutionalized deliberations of lawmakers. So consensus seems to be the hallmark of a democratic nation.

3.2 Dissent: A Practical Solution?

Jacques Ranciere helps us to understand the dynamics of dissent for a democratic nation. Democracy for Ranciere is a "'power of the people' simultaneously legitimizes and de-legitimizes it."[26] On one hand, there is a legitimization that takes place through self-government whereas on the other hand there is also a dissent that takes place. He calls it a 'democratic paradox'. It is "as a form of government is threatened by democracy as a form of social and political life and so the former must repress the latter."[27] The society through dissent represents the central idea of politics and individuals in the community affirm the power through destabilization of the public spaces. The establishment of democracy needs what Ranciere writes as "a new topography, the creation of a space made of disconnected places against the aristocratic space that connected the material privilege of the landowners with the symbolical power of the tradition."[28] Ranciere says that "Politics is always manifested through a distortion of this logic."[29]

3.2.1 Outline of 'Dissensus'

Ranciere in his paper 'The Thinking of Dissensus: Politics and Aesthetics[30] brings out the concept of 'dissensus' as "a difference between sense and sense: a difference within the same, a sameness of the opposite."[31] Dissent is not only about speaking but of people confronting their interest and values. Speaking implies sense in what is uttered. Ranciere writes that there is no agreement on what sense means. The conflict lies in, as he writes "who speaks and who does not speak, about what has to be heard as the voice of pain and what has to be heard as an argument on justice."[32] The conflict that happens in the Indian context between the intellectuals and the state is not only about differing ideological interest but the conflict about what an 'interest' is. It is the tussle between those elected to govern the state as and how they would prefer and those supposed to co-operate in the governance.

Dissent is not deliberation happening due to difference of opinion or misunderstandings but "everything to do with unequal power relations within consensus-democratic public spheres."[33] He writes that everyone is assigned a fixed place and function in society. When someone tries to blur the boundaries of these fixed places and functions, there is dissent taking place. Dissent is not unlimited but it is to "a specific relationship, a specific measure of incommensurables."[34]

3.2.2 Method of 'Dissensus'

Disagreement for Ranciere is not only an object of theorization but also its method, and challenges this idea of consensus or purity through his concept of 'politics'. Politics happens when there is a disruption, opposition and interruption to the police order.[35] Politics is a disruptive force for Ranciere unlike a space for Arendt. It means that there is politics when the natural order of power is broken "by the affirmation that the power belongs to those who have no qualification to rule – which amounts to saying that there is no ground whatever for the exercise of power."[36] His method involves interventions into particular situations, specific instances in which ideas are at work and also an interruption and redistribution of spaces of what Ranciere calls "distribution of the sensible – that allots to each his or her proper role and function."[37]

He calls his method 'thinking of "dissensus"'. He writes that "genuine political or artistic activities always involve forms of innovation that tear bodies from their assigned places and free speech and expression from all reduction to functionality."[38] The power in the political assigned space is held by the state. For Ranciere, power of the people is not the power of the state. Democracy implies a tension between the power of thinking and acting exercised by the people and the appropriation of the power by the state, which justifies its power as the power given to them by the people. The responsibility of people in a democratic nation lies in recovering the democratic values by affirming their capacities to think, judge, decide and dissent. This process has to be done through the public spaces of discussion, where information is circulated, motives are spelt out and the action directed. This is what Ranciere calls, "The power of the citizens is the power to act for themselves, to have autonomous force"[39] This action will not provide answers but reveal the dissent at the core of every consensus.[40]

3.2.3 Ethics of Dissensus

Should the action of dissent be regulated by ethics or based on certain principles of ethics? Does dissent have a moral force? The debate about dissent as being ethically right or wrong cannot be settled. Nevertheless, it can be processed as "the conceptualization of exception, wrong or excess apart from any kind of ontology."[41] Ranciere writes that "Ontology requires a modality of action whose real name is ethics: to will the unwilled ... A proclamation which, by affirming chance and choosing what has been, insists on an ethics of becoming in which the and ... and ... of multiple assemblages is contrasted against the either ... or ... of active wills pursuing their goals in opposition to other goals."[42]

Todd May argues that the politics of Ranciere has a principle of equality. The Politics of Ranciere involves action of people. These actions see themselves as equal.[43] The ethics of the action lies in the presupposition of equality. According to May, justifying the ethics of equality through political action lies "only to the extent to which it is accepted by those alongside whom and against whom one struggles."[44] Jean-Philippe Deranty points out that Ranciere's political action "is close in spirit to the program of the ethics of recognition. He writes that recognition can only be achieved through struggles for recognition."[45]

Conclusion

Dissent is at the very core of democracy and enhances the system of governance. The progress of any democratic nation, whether social or political, hinges on dissent. The intellectual dissenters through their ideas, perspectives and agendas challenges the given way of thinking and acting and provide a means for informed decision-making and opportunities to examine and enrich understandings, which results in progress.[46] Those who govern the nation-states employ media, make use of deception and bring into play the politics of loyalty and betrayal to stifle dissent. The role of the dissenting intellectual lies in understanding the means employed and in providing an appropriate response.

The dialectics of dissent sees this criticism as a form of dialogue. Dialogue provides the dissenting voices space to discuss, deliberate, oppose and ultimately appreciate the differences. Dialogue does not mean that it should result in consensus. Political space sees in consensus the right to dissent. The political obligation in a democratic nation is the right to political participation. This right includes the right to dissent. The Constitution of India has protected this fundamental right by Article 19(1) (a) of every citizen to express dissent. Even the Supreme Court of India has observed that "the restrictions on the freedom of speech must be couched in the narrowest possible terms," i.e., the restrictions have to be 'reasonable' and cannot be arbitrary, excessive or disproportionate.[47]

The right to dissent demands a shift of the notion of democracy of Habermas as a space of deliberation and dialogue, which results in consensus to Ranciere's proposition of the impossibility of rational deliberation that is free from power.[48] Dissenting intellectuals should be able to discern their roles in this power equation. The suppression of dissenting intellectuals is the suppression of the position they occupy in the power reckoning. The one who curbs dissent in a democratic nation is concerned about his position to yield power and can be termed as unpatriotic. The politics of dissent demands that we agree to disagree.

Notes

1 Like Uday Prakash, Nayantara Sahgal, Ashok Vajpeyi, Krishna Sobti, Sarah Joseph and many more.

2 Clive Hamilton and Sarah Maddison, eds., *Silencing Dissent: How the Australian Government is Controlling Public Opinion and Stifling Debate* (Australia: Allen & Unwin, 2007), ix.

3 Naman Mody and Arnapurna Rath, "Author-Activism: Philosophy of Dissent in the Writings of Arundhati Roy," *Asiatic* 7, no. 1 (June 2013): 56.

4 Detlef Pollack and Jan Wielgohs, eds., *Dissent and Opposition in Communist Eastern Europe* (Aldershot: Ashgate Publishing Limited, 2001), viii.

5 Mody and Rath, "Author-Activism: Philosophy of Dissent in the Writings of Arundhati Roy," 58.

6 Hamid Ansari, "First Ram Manohar Lohia Memorial National Lecture in Gwalior," Vice President Office http://vicepresidentofindia.nic.in/speechesinterviews/address-shri-m-hamid-ansari-honourable-vice-president-india-first-ram-manohar.

7 Pollack and Wielgohs, *Dissent and Opposition in Communist Eastern Europe*, ix.

8 Mody and Rath, "Author-Activism: Philosophy of Dissent in the Writings of Arundhati Roy," 69.

9 Ansari, "First Ram Manohar Lohia Memorial National Lecture in Gwalior."

10 Simon Cottle, "Reporting Demonstrations: The Changing Media Politics of Dissent," *Media, Culture and Society* 30, no. 6 (Oct 2008): 854.

11 James D. Halloran, Philip Elliott, and Graham Murdock, *Demonstrations and Communication: A Case Study* (Harmondsworth: Penguin Books, 1970).

12 Cottle, "Reporting Demonstrations: The Changing Media Politics of Dissent," 856.

13 Hannah Arendt, *Crises of the Republic: Lying in Politics, Civil Disobedience on Violence, Thoughts on Politics, and Revolution* (Florida: Harcourt Brace and Company, 1972), 5.
14 Ibid., 6.
15 Now, the ruling party.
16 It is a Hindi word translated in English as 'Good Days.'
17 'Jumla' is a Hindi word which means an "empty promise which is merely some words strung together which are only to be taken at face value and with no significance attached to them."
18 Arendt, *Crises of the Republic: Lying in Politics, Civil Disobedience on Violence, Thoughts on Politics, and Revolution,* 4.
19 RTI is a Right to Information Act, which was brought in force by the previous government in India.
20 Ira Chadha-Sridhar, "Reflections on Dissent - How is Hannah Arendt Relevant for Contemporary Israel and India?," Kafila, https://kafila.org/2016/07/28/reflections-on-dissent-how-is-hannah-arendt-relevant-for-contemporary-israel-and-india-ira-chadha-sridhar/.
21 Andreas Kalyvas, *Democracy and the Politics of the Extraordinary: Max Weber, Carl Schmitt, and Hannah Arendt* (Cambridge: Cambridge University Press, 2008), 222.
22 Hamilton and Maddison, *Silencing Dissent: How the Australian Government is Controlling Public Opinion and Stifling Debate,* 4.
23 IANS, "BJP's 'Dirty Tricks Department' Targeting Opposition: Congress," *The Times of India* May 13, 2016.
24 Luke Goode, *Jürgen Habermas: Democracy and the Public Sphere* (London: Pluto Press, 2005), 62.
25 Richard Feldman and Ted A. Warfield, eds., *Disagreement* (New York: Oxford University Press, 2010), 4.
26 Jacques Ranciere, *Dissensus on Politics and Aesthetics*, trans. Steven Corcoran (London: Continuum, 2010), 53.
27 Ibid., 47.
28 Jacques Rancière, "The Thinking of Dissensus: Politics and Aesthetics," in *Reading Ranciere*, ed. Paul Bowman and Richard Stamp (New York: Continuum, 2011), 6.
29 Jacques Ranciere, interview by Unknown, 2012.
30 Rancière shows the relationship with his research on politics and aesthetics as "an attempt to think a specificity of politics as disagreement and a specificity of the aesthetic heterogeneity that break away from the absoluticization of the dissensus as wrong or disaster." Rancière, "The Thinking of Dissensus: Politics and Aesthetics."
31 Ibid., 1.
32 Ibid., 2.
33 Nicole Doerr, "Between Habermas and Rancière: The Democracy of Political Translation," *Transversal* (2013), http://eipcp.net/transversal/0613/doerr/en.
34 Paul Bowman and Richard Stamp, eds., *Reading Rancière* (London: Continuum, 2011), 12.
35 Police order is "an order of bodies that defines the allocation of ways of doing, ways of being, and ways of saying, and sees that those bodies are assigned by name to a particular place and task; it is an order of the visible and the sayable" Jacques Ranciere, *Disagreement: Politics and Philosophy* (Minneapolis: University of Minnesota Press, 1999), 29.
36 Rancière, "The Thinking of Dissensus: Politics and Aesthetics," 3.
37 Bowman and Stamp, *Reading Rancière,* xii.
38 Ranciere, *Dissensus on Politics and Aesthetics*, 1.
39 "Jacques Rancière Interview: "Democracy is Not, to Begin with, a Form of State"."
40 Bowman and Stamp, *Reading Rancière,* xvii.

41 Ibid., 11-12.
42 Ranciere, *Dissensus on Politics and Aesthetics*, 87.
43 Todd May, "Jacques Rancière and the Ethics of Equality," *SubStance* 36, no. 2 (2007): 24.
44 Ibid., 27.
45 Jean-Philippe Deranty, "Jacques Ranciere's Contribution to the Ethics of Recognition," *Political Theory* 31, no. 1 (2003): 145.
46 Stephen P. Banks, ed. *Dissent and the Failure of Leadership,* New Horizons in Leadership Studies (Massachusetts: Edward Elgar, 2008), viii.
47 Ansari, "First Ram Manohar Lohia Memorial National Lecture in Gwalior."
48 Doerr, "Between Habermas and Rancière: The Democracy of Political Translation."

8

Becoming an Indian Christian

Victor Ferrao
Patriarchal Seminary of Rachol, Goa

Abstract: Becoming Indian is a complex dynamic inter-relational process. To enter this dynamism of Indian Christians we have to overcome positivist, isolative, essentialist and static thinking that black box both Indian-ness and Christian-ness in predetermined set moulds. Moving away from the indologocentric thinking, we try to understand the non-linear process of the inter-being of Indian Christians and other Indians. We then attempt to discern the co-becoming, co-presencing, co-journeying and co-emergence of our Indian Christians and Indians in general. Co-becoming occurs in an intertwined mode side by side where both Christians and Indians co-make each other while caring for each other. This leads us to the dynamic co-translative process of becoming Indian Christians and Indians in general.

Introduction

Christians in our country along with the other minorities are facing a profound crisis. It is complex and resists every shade of its reduction in logocentric terms. It is as though with the rise of the militant Hindu right, Christians with the other minorities seem to be challenged by an emergence of a void that "unhomes" them in their own country. But this discomforting experience provides several possibilities to an Indian Christian. The experience of "deterritorialisation" can be productive and bring a new impetus to them. To arrive at a new territorialisation, it is imperative that we understand that this "únhoming" is arising from a gap that is constituted by a retroactive construction of both our

Indian-ness and Christian-ness by the right wing forces. There is an exteriority and interiority of our Indian-ness and Christian-ness. These dimensions become existent/external through an immanent analysis.

The immanent analysis opens the space of a power differences in our society. We can trace several lines of hegemonic formations that cross religious, regional and caste boundaries. Hence, there are several competing semiologies that we can construct with each overlapping as well as marking its difference with the other. Just like the colonizers in the sixteenth century judged and ranked human civilizations based on the benchmark of alphabetic writing, particularly in Latin America, and constructed what is known as colonial difference[1] and legitimated their colonial imperialism so also a power differential is generated by the right-wing Hindu groups based on the possession of a Hindu religion/culture. The hegemonic formation that flows from this cleverly crafted gap seems to have successfully constructed an imagination that has Hinduism/Hindu culture as central to the exclusionary nationalism that is championed by them. Hence, it is important to understand how these discourses retroactively recreate the interests that they claim to represent in their followers. Besides, the immanent analysis that we strive to engage in this study opens us to the (dis)location of being an Indian Christian in the midst of this totalitarian nationalism.[2]

Therefore, the immanent analysis deals with the presence of Christianity in India, which is marked by an obscure sense of survival where Christians have to negotiate complex processes of identity and difference. To understand this complex presence we have to move away from what may be called indologocentric underpinnings of our thinking. Having abandoned static, essentialist and logocentric mode of thought, we attempt to enter into the complex and dynamic becoming of Indian Christians. Next, we analyse the becoming of an Indian Christian from a libidinal economy and the economy of co-emergence. Finally, we attempt to evolve a growing shareable space through the co-becoming of Indian Christians and the other Indians.

Moving away from a logocentric analysis of Christianity in India

The essentialized, positivist and fixated conceptualization of Christianity in India in foreclosed boundaries remains logocentric and exorcises the dynamic presencing/copresencing of Christianity. Hence, in this context, we try to resist the temptation of representing and describing Christianity and Indian-ness merely in static and objectifying modes of understanding and move into a journey that remains sensitive to the mode of becoming an Indian Christian. This takes us way from what can be called Indologocentrism. It is an attempt to stay in the mode of saying and not in discursive practices that suffer foreclosures. While engaging the copresencing and becoming of Christianity in India, we remain humble and admit that our effort to remain in the "saying" rather than in the "said" may often be haunted by the mode of the "said" which cannot be totally discarded.

Cartography of the embedded and embodied position

The processes of becoming Indian Christian are complex and non-linear and cannot be adequately grasped through linear, logocentric logic of the same. The alternate figuration of this complexity can open us to several dimensions that might otherwise remain opaque to the positivist and essentialized modes of thinking. Hence, we have the challenge to glide into thinking through flows and inter-connected emergence. The alternate figuration that we need to undertake is not figurative ways of thinking but materialistic mapping of the embedded and embodied positions. This new approach can dwelve into the complexity of spatio-temporal processes in terms of a dual dimension of power as restrictive (*potestas*) and affirmative (*potential*) and not in a static (inertia) mode.[3] Though, the complex processes in our society resist representation of these pulls and pushes, an analysis of these with critical attention can open the in-between states and stages of transition, hybridization and nomadization of Indian Christians. It is a challenge to map the living in a dynamic state of being both Indian and Christian at the same time. This means the cartographies that we strive to open up reveal how Christians in India are indexed, otherized and unhomed. Thus, it strives to manifest how power-relations and structures affect the becoming of Indian Christians at the national, regional and local levels. This depicts the Indian Christian as a subject-in-process and unveils the power locations they have to negotiate, interrogate and resist.

Non-linear approach

The dynamism of society cannot be captured in a linear conceptual apparatus. The complexity that we are faced within our understanding of the becoming of Indian Christians challenges us to move towards a non-linear mode of thinking. This approach leads us to cross the boundaries of our habituated linear thinking. This means that non-linear thinking opens us to the complex dynamism of multiple flows that irrupts or rather disrupts the leaps that transpose and mutate. This takes us away from a static, fixated and linearized mode of thinking to a radiating, rippling and even reverse modes of non-linear rhizomatic thinking.[4] Thus, the non-linear modes of thinking take us into the leaps of codes, fields or axis. This means non-linear thinking resists being imprisoned in fixed structures of instrumental rationality. Hence, this approach brings us to the pushes, pulls and expulsions that shape the becoming an Indian Christians. That is why a non-linear mode of thinking may be a good way of getting fully immersed in the becoming(s) of Indian Christians. The immersion into the becoming(s) of Indian Christians brings us to the consideration of our co-presence and co-emergence in inter-relatedness with the rest of our fellow

Indians. It takes us away from the phallic logic that constructs all difference through the hierarchical logic of sameness. This hierarchical logic pathologizes difference(s) and marks it out as a lack or absence of what is essentialized as a standard of sameness. Hence, we are enabled to contest the cartographies that map the Indian Christians through markers of absence and legitimate their exclusion and marginalization.

Non-phallic logic

The phallic (il)logic constructs its other through foreclosures. It creates substitutes for the phallus, driven by the desire of the lost object. We are schooled to think of subjectivity through the prism of castration that Freud named as the legendary Oedipus complex. Non-phallic logic contests the imperialism of Oedipus and dismantles the triangulation of the oedipal orbit which represses desire.[5] Oedipalization results into an endless repression of desire and the installation of the supremacy of the Phallus which introduces this lack into desire. This lack then controls desire and castrates its productivity, leading it to foreclosed resignations through triangulations of the 'holy family' of Freud: the Father, the Mother and the Son. We can trace this triangulation at work in the becoming of the Indian Christians. Often Indian Christians, under the fear of castration (orphaned), submit to the law of the father and undergo resignation or latency. This Oedipalization of the becoming of Indian Christians results in the loss of self. Hence, against this oedipalizing phallic logic, we have to consider what Deleuze and Gauttari proposed as "schizophereization" which opens the flow of production and views desire not through the prism of lack but of production. Deleuze and Gauttari even suggest that we need to come to a de-anthropomorphization that takes us to a becoming of animals.[6] Some scholars claim that phallic logic also is able to detach itself from the oedipal moorings and drift fearsomely and aggressively against the *jouissance de femme.*[7]

Understanding the becoming of Indian Christians

The becoming of Indian Christians is inter-webbed, hybrid and liminal. We have to distance our analysis from the power of the logic of the "same" and open our horizons to the immanent dimensions of being an Indian Christian. The logic of the "same" frames the dynamic and diverse becoming of Indian Christians in subject positions that are static, inferiorized and obtained by multiple subtractions. These discourses view the becoming of Indian Christians as deviant and pathological. Therefore, we need to overcome this indologocentric master code which operates as a map of semiotic inscriptions and culturally enforced codes that filter what passes of as Indian and as Christian in our society. Hence, becoming Indian Christians would become profoundly visible to our immanent analysis if we understand the zone of becoming Indian Christians as the point for the flow of energies or the surface of intensities.

Becoming an Indian Christian, a political project

We have to view the historizing or the becoming of Indian Christian as also spatializing or territorializing. This embodied being and becoming of the Indian and Christian is profoundly political and cannot be solely viewed as the other of the same (other Indians). If viewed as the other of the same, we shall become blind to inter-connected flows that bring about co-emergence in diverse ways of being both Indian and Indian Christians. By differently historizing and territorializing, the Indian Christians make a difference to the Indianizing of various other Indians which itself is plural and cannot be conceptualised in an Indologocentric master code. This means the becoming of both the Indians and Indian Christians is a creatively active and a symbiotic co-project. It is therefore, profoundly co-Indianizing. Hence, this co-Indianizing might be viewed as a space of plenitude and not of lack. Unfortunately, the indologocentric master code views the becoming of Indian Christian through the lens of lack and nails it as not national enough. It views the Christian Indian as the other of the Indian(s) by the introduction of lack. The injection of lack pathologizes the different historizing of Indian Christians. But this "otherising" of the Christian Indian fails to capture their dynamic and complex co-historizing and co-territorializing and hence, the Indian Christian remains the "othered" Other. Behind this veil of otherising, the Indian Christian lives and historizes/territorializes as the other that is "othered". Thus, the historizing become ex-centric leading to the transformation of an Indian Christian as one who is exiled (*Homo Sacer*)[8] in his/her own country.

Becoming an Indian Christian, a site of co-becoming

The zone of becoming of an Indian Christian is a dynamic field of interface where several material and symbolic forces intersect. It is a space that enacts the becoming of an Indian Christian, a space of praxis, of being an Indian Christian. It is a site where we can locate the desire of an Indian Christians which itself is plural and cannot be totalised. This means both the Indianizing and Christianising of the Indian Christian is plural. It is a space of being alongside with other Indians. The Indian Christians in their in-depth becoming remain present to and journey with other Indians. Hence, there is a symbiotic becoming of Indians and Indian Christians. This means there is mutual becoming where we might locate a joyful affirmation of one's enjoyment of being in India alongside other Indian(s). But unfortunately this dimension of co-journeying is not understood by indologocentric approaches.

The embodied nature of all human becoming occurs in a site of subject formation. It introduces the person into a dynamic process of subjectification where both the repressive (potestas) and the empowering (potentia) aspects are intersecting. The repressive power often pushes the becoming of an Indian Christian into an oedipal mode. This oedipal mode of becoming an Indian Christian operates on the institution of lack which is accepted as a marker of Indian-ness. Hence, the absence of this marked Indian-ness becomes a difference that legitimates both oedipal closure of Indian Christians and their pathologization by imperially motivated significant minority among the Indians. But we can also trace the empowering power that can lead to a free and joyful enjoyment of being an Indian Christian alongside of others. This mode of historizing of an Indian Christian might be called affirmative deconstruction.

Becoming an Indian Christian, an entangled dynamism

Becoming an Indian Christian is not merely given. It is an intertwined, entangled and a porous process. The becoming of Indian Christians, being an affirmative deconstruction cannot be insulated from the becoming of the rest of Indians. The Indian Christians are made, as much as they make other Indians and others in the world. It is through the immersion into the plural ecologies of Indian society that we have the emergence of Indian Christians. Here, we may step into the larva stage of becoming an Indian Christian. This opens the process of becoming, the incubation stage of the being of the Indian Christians which flows from the virtual to the actual. Actuality is always side by side with virtuality. There is never an actual Indian Christian without the cloud of the virtual. The virtual orients, conditions and engenders the becoming of Indian Christians. Within this virtual realm, we can trace a continuous and complex negotiation with caste, religious beliefs and practices of other Indians, economic and political practices and systems, technological and scientific values, terrorism, violence and fear etc., resulting in an emergence of the subjectivity of an Indian Christian. Hence, we do not have the luxury of thinking that the Indian Christian is in a unitary mode of Indologocentric framework. The being of an India Christian is not a closed container. Like every other Indian, an Indian Christian is a subject-in-becoming alongside of other subjects. The subjectification of an Indian Christian has to pass through the constant processes of transition, hybridization and normadization that characterize their ways of being-in-the-world.

Libidinal economy of Indian Christians

There is an enjoyment (*Jouissance*) factor in the becoming process of all the ways of being-human-in-the-world. That is why the understanding of becoming an Indian Christian unfolds an economy of enjoyment. The understanding of enjoyment was understood in the sense that it can be disruptive of social coherence. This position is based on the view that prohibition is the glue of our society and maintains social order. But developments in psychoanalysis today enable us to contest this belief and it has become clear that far from mere prohibition, society arises out of enjoyment.[9] Even prohibition becomes a way of enjoyment as subjects derive enjoyment from their sacrifice while others do so from its enforcement as well as their rebellion against it. But this happens through restrained enjoyment and neither through complete renunciation nor complete freedom over enjoyment.

The symbolic order(s) and enjoyment(s)

The several lines of prohibition of enjoyment that are inscribed in the symbolic order(s) that conditions the becoming of Indian Christians introduce the possibility of enjoyment. In fact, the multiple forms of prohibitions are grounded in phallic logic. They produce barriers relative to which enjoyment can constitute itself. This means without the law of the father that demands renunciation of enjoyment, no enjoyment is possible. It is in giving it up that we retrospectively create the enjoyment we never had. This is why Lacan rewrites Dostoyevsky's declaration which states that 'without God everything is permitted' as 'without God nothing is permitted.'[10] Hence, within its several constraints, from among Indian(s), Indian Christian(s) trace a joy in both their Indianizing and Christianizing becoming as Indian Christian(s). The Indian symbolic order(s) becomes the law of the father and can produce an oedipal or anti-oedipal response of becoming Indian Christian(s). For instance, the Brahminic symbolic order produces what has been christened as sanskritization or rebellious de-sanskritizations of several hues among the Indians. Besides, there are other symbolic order(s) that influences Indian Christian(s). This means the becoming of Indian Christians is not free from its share of entanglement in these symbolic order(s). The Indian Christians have to give up a part of themselves which did not exist until it is given up and becomes a lacking subject that produces several lines of becoming that strive to overcome the loss. The loss and recovery dynamism is produced by a desire which is, in its turn, produced by what Lacan calls object petit a. Thus, for instance, we might identify the object petit a of Indians as the lure of brahminhood, the original forbidden fruit of Indian(s). It is this lure of brahminhood(s) (mimetic desire of Brahmin(s)) that produces us Indian(s) as desiring subjects. We have introduced Brahminhood(s) because it is differently imagined as an object petit a by Indian(s). But, there is not just a singular object petit a. There are other object petit a(s) like the lure of Europe, Science and Technology(s), Nation(s), Hindu Rashtra(s), etc.

Desire in the becoming(s) of Indian Christians

The paradox of being a desiring subject is in the very giving up of enjoyment(s). Lacan teaches that object petit a is the cause of the subject.[11] Indeed, following

Deleuze, we may assign it as the cause of the larval subjects by taking a plunge into the non-unitary notion of subject. That is, we will have to admit that there are plural ways of becoming an Indian Christian both individually and collectively. Within this complex dynamism, we might trace an oedipal response that led the leadership of Indian Christian(s) to opt for the saffronizing of liturgy by adopting the codes of the Brahminical order. We may also trace the oedipalization in the choice of silence of the Christian leadership in India to several intolerant voices/vigilantes for fear of being disowned/ orphaned by the right wing forces/power elite in our society. Besides the familiar oedipal responses, we can trace an anti-oedipal response which challenges the reign of the law of the father in plural ways. The Dalit Christians contestation of the Brahminical symbolic order(s) can be taken as an illustration of the anti-oedipalizing mode of becoming among Indian Christians. Moreover, the modes of becoming(s) that seem to lead several Christian(s) serving caste rather than Christ can be discerned through the enjoyment of death drive. The death drive can illumine why like other Christians, Indian Christians may become unfaithful to Christ whom they claim to follow. Moreover, the "fort-da" analysis of Freud can open us to several ways in which the Indian Christians seek substitutes/ fetish in their becoming(s).

Enjoyment and symbolic recognition

All becoming being co-becoming is essentially marked by re-cognition, which is always conferred by the symbolic order(s). Recognition is a way of enjoying one's social status. Perhaps, the way money produces recognition might illumine this complex process. The value of money does not lie so much in the enjoyment of the things it can buy but in the recognition it can bring. This is why rich people part with money to gain access to the enjoyment of recognition. One can derive recognition in the acts of benevolence as well as in acts leading to de-recognition of the other. Thus, in the very discrimination and subjection to ill-treatment of Dalits, there is enjoyment of the supremacist Brahmins and other upper castes. It is as if in the acts of de-recognition that we recognize ourselves as different and mark our boundary and space. Through, the complex project of recognition/de-recognition of the other, the self becomes what it is (in a non-unitary sense). The becoming of Indian Christians is marked by making boundaries and creating cartographies. But in this very project of self-creation which also entails the enjoyment of symbolic recognition, one realises that recognition primarily depends on the other. Thus, as Hegel argues, it is the salve that authorises the mastery of the master.[12] It is in this paradox of mutuality that human relations emerge, flourish and disintegrate. We can trace this mutuality in the multiple emergence(s) of Indian Christians and Indians.

The economy of mutual emergence and Indian Christians

All becoming of human beings happens in a field of mutuality which might be termed as the field of resonance. It is here that the becoming(s) of Indian Christian(s) and other Indian(s) take place. It is a space where we can trace sources of the self of Indian Christian(s) as well as that of other Indian(s). It brings co-emergence in differentiation and grounds their aesthetico-ethical sensibilities which can be contested and re-directed.

Co-poietic differentiation in co-emergence

The self-creation/auto-poiesis is a co-poiesis where the processes of difference occur, leading to the manifestation of difference. It is a border-linking space where the co-becoming of the Indian Christians occurs and where it does not reach the fixity of an object but remains a transject. Hence, the co-poiesis leads to the emergence of us as subject(s) side by side. It is an event in which we inscribe the "other" in us and us in the other. These traces can never die with our death because they are inscribed in the others who outlive our death. Thus, we carry the traces of the other in us and vice versa. This brings us to a shareable space that we continuously build. Hence, there is no pure Indian Christian completely isolated and other to Indians. Though, the encounter is side by side it is a transgressive and invasive. It might be oedipalizing or anti-oedipalizing in the presence of a difference that co-merges. Besides, it can lead to the cognizing of the self and its other. It is in the co-presence of the other Indians, that the Indian Christians recognize both themselves and their Other(s). This leads us to a shareable space that is transmissible and translatable by our mind that receives the encounter. Thus, the unconscious is not logocentric space-seated in the core of the self but it is a border space between the self and its other. Hence, we can understand how Indian Christians come to a plural cross inscribing of psychic traces of themselves into the other Indian(s) as well as receive the imprints of the other(s). This inscribing of the traces of each in the other is part of the ongoing co-poiesis of differentiation that co-flourish into the co-emergence of all Indians.[13]

Contesting the asthetico-ethical sensibilities

The traces of the other in the self can lead to a sharing and exchanging of these traces forming a continuous co-poietic web. In the encounter with the self with its other, they come to a co-sharing and co-wit(h)nessing of each other.[14] This encounter can lead to the co-becoming of each other's co-contesting where the self is reduced to a partial self of a larger subjectivity. Thus, the co-presence of other Indians, the Indian Christian becomes a partial subject (larval subject in Deleuze), part of a larger subject and each is somehow fragilized. This link with the larger subject brings us to a space of shareability and severalty[15] which can trigger resistance or compassion. Sometimes this response becomes a point of discord or communion, which produces roles that are enacted and they produce memory traces that are accumulated over a period of time, in the horizon of which each partial subject is transformed and springs forth into co-becoming. This fragile shareability produces aesthetic-ethical sensibilities rooted in compassion which leads to reciprocal responsibility for each other among Indian Christian(s). The reciprocal responsibility is co-responsibility. The ethics of co-responsibility emerges as a trace of the present that challenges anyone placed in this horizon. But this may not always be always compassion. When the self and its other(s) focus on the severalty and accumulate the traces of difference, the other of the self, the partial subject begins to look like an enemy who has no space of shareability. Hence, co-poiesis that occurs can produce aggression. This can explain why Indian Christians are often fragilized, alienated and de-nationalized and are pushed into the domain of what Kristeva calls abjects.

Co-fragilization and partial subjects

The co-emergence of the partial subjects/larval subjects that produce the shareable space transmit/exchange the traces of each other which are rooted in the conductible capacity of our mind. When transmission is made impossible by the pathos of trauma, we are rendered open to the zone of translatability. Lacan teaches that trauma is an event that we cannot handle with the resources of our imagination and symbolism. Trauma is first addressed through the imaginary producing the phantasmatic images that remain far from the real. This triggers an attunement of the spiralic metamorphic translatability that converts the co-emergence into a ping pong game. But the response of the other(s) of the self that occurs at the other end of the spiral, but still within the sharable space, cannot be easily predicted. It can take merely edited forms of mimesis like the individualist character of worship acquires a communitarian dimension and is being re-enacted in the other Indian contexts of worship. This means whether the sharing/ exchange of the traces unite or divide, the self co-emerge(s) with its other as partial/larval subject(s). In the encounter of each other, the self and its other co-create each other and co-fragilize each other. Fragilization is a kind of creation of the partial selves mainly in the contest of its other. This means the Indian Christians and other Indians co-emerge and co-fragilize and become partial/larval selves that are always in the process of co-becoming.[16] Co-fragilization as partial subjects/larval selves can generate both compassion and re-resistance and aggression. When fragilization is viewed as inferiorization, resistance and aggression may result.

Co-emergence and translation

Often there is an imitation of the desire of the other. The self mimes its other(s) as it shares or exchanges its traces with its other(s). This brings us into the realm of transmission and translation. This copying and mimesis is complex and non-linear and becomes translative. The becoming of Indian Christians being fragilizing can produce resistance through translation. Hence, it can lead to what may be viewed as a trans-becoming.

Translative co-becoming

Lacan has opened our vistas to the trans-individual character of the unconscious by teaching us that the unconscious is the discourse of the other and is structured like a language. This means the unconscious comes into being through the introduction of the person into language. Lacanian psychoanalysis helps us to understand how a collective unconscious becomes a discourse of the other(s) that affect, afflict and shape the co-becoming(s) of the Indian Christians and rest of the Indians. Here, we shall try to apprehend the tensive processes of translative co-becoming(s). Language is a signification system and operates on two axes. The vertical axis is viewed as the paradigmatic axis and the horizontal is called the syntagmatic axis. Lacan says that the elements in the unconscious like wishes, desire (desire to copy the other) images, etc., form signifiers and these signifiers form the signifying chain where one signifier has meaning only because it is not the other signifier. There is nothing that the signifier ultimately refers to. He further says that positive relations of significations do not exist. There are only negative relations (value significations) among signifiers where one signifies what it is, only because it is not something else.[17] These negative relations can be discerned in the fragilization and the co-becoming of the partial selves of the Indian Christians and the other Indians. The way the Indian Christians or other Indians view their relations on the horizontal axis (syntagmatic) axis offers them many options to generate their co-emergence in difference. Hence, the tensive translative processes that we have discerned here are profoundly complex, non-linear and marked by emergence and resist all kinds of predictions and pre-determinations.

Trauma and tensive translations

Lacan teaches that self is an excentric self. It identifies with its image in the mirror (imaginary). That is why a self comes into being through a movement of ecstasies. The self can mutate into several larval subjects/partial subjects in the encounter with the other who becomes the mirror. This mutation into several partial selves is a result of translations which can be likened to a child within six to 18 months, translating its discomforting fragile and fragmented self as congruent with the image in the mirror. Hence, in the encounter that carries the accumulated traces of traumatic memory of its other(s) (which itself may be a phantasmatic image) can trigger further fragilization which in turns translates into a chain of larval selves/partial selves. There are several translations that have generated a chain of larval selves/partial selves among Indian Christians and other Indians. This means, their co-becoming becomes co-translations which may be called co-transbecomings. When we become aware of this tensive translative processes, that informs and shapes our becoming/(un)becoming, we might arrive into a therapeutic zone that will heal the transbecoming/trans(un)becoming of both Indian Christians and other Indians. This therapeutic zone can generate an ethics of compassion that will influence our aesthetico-ethical sensibilities and a sense of co-journeying may lead to an emergence of dialogical co-becoming of both Indian Christians and other Indians.

Therapeutic translative co-becoming

The awareness of the co-becoming has the seeds of reversing the processes that may have become(un)becoming in the face of co-fragilizing of both Indian Christians and other Indians. This (un)becoming is a co-(un)becoming. Hence, a heightened awareness about it can indeed be therapeutic and generate an ethics of compassion which can foster a co-wit(h)nessing among Indian Christians and other Indians. This has the power to open us to the complex and dynamic processes of mutual mutations of the self into its partial selves/larval selves in the horizon of it's other(s). Hence, a co-wit(h)nessing can bring both Indian Christians and other Indians to a new level of ethics of compassion that overcomes erasures of dynamic co-becoming where disclosures of self or that its other(s) are foreclosed into reductive configurations leading to conflictual becoming among the Indian Christians and other Indians. Hence, awareness can generate an ethics of care and can take us to a leap of consciousness that might enable the self to see its trace in its other(s) and vice versa. Hence, the Indian Christian(s) carries other Indian(s) in them and vice versa. Fragilizing can be positively viewed as the carrying of the other in the self. Therefore, fragilizing may not be merely viewed as a mutating process of partial selves, but one that carries the larval self of other(s) in oneself.

Conclusion

Our study has tried to unearth the complex, non-linear and dynamics of co-becoming(s) of both Indian Christians and other Indians. We tried to avoid the indologo-centric fixation of both Indian-ness and Christian-ness and approach the process of co-becoming in multiple modes of both Indianizing and Christianising of Indian Christians in dialogue with the other Indians. The co-becoming(s) of both the Indian Christians being co-transbecoming can move into plural paths of becoming and (un)becoming. Hence, through a mutual co-wit(h)essing we hope to rise to an ethics of care that is grounded in the realization of the co-presence of each in the other and, each with the other.

Notes

1 See Walter D. Mignolo, *Coloniality, Subaltern Knowledges and Border Thinking: Local Histories/Global Designs* (New Jersey: Princeton, 2000), pp 13-18.

2 See Victor Ferrao, "Totalitarian Nationalism is Taking Shape in India" in *UCANEWS http://www.ucanews.com/category/author/victor-ferrao*, accessed on29/9/2016.

3 Rosi Baraidotti, *Metamorphoses: Towards a Materialist Theory of Becoming* (Cambridge: Polity Press, 2002), p. 2.

4 Ibid., p. 8.

5 Gilles Deleuze and Felix and Gauttari, *Anti-Oedipus: Capitalism and Schizophrenia* (Minneapolis: University of Minnesota Press, 2000).

6 Ibid.

7 Juliet Flower MacCnnell, *Hysteric's Guide to the Future Female Subject* (Minneapolis: University of Minnesota Press, 2000), pp. 218-219.

8 George Agamben, *Homo Sacer: Sovereign Power and Bare Life* (Stanford: Stanford University Press, 1998).

9 See Todd McGowan, *The End of Dissatisfaction? Jacques Lacan and the Emerging Society of Enjoyment* (Albany: State University of New York Press, 2004).

10 Ibid., p. 16.

11 Ibid.

12 Ibid., p. 26.

13 The Notions of copoiesis, copresence wit(h)nessing and coemergence are derived from the work of Bracha Ettinger. See http://www.ephemerajournal.org/sites/default/files/5-Xettinger.pdf, accessed on29/9/2016.

14 http://jordancrandall.com/main/+UNDERFIRE/site/files/q-node-562.html accessed on 29/9/2016.

15 See http://professorvj.blogspot.in/2013/03/transgressive-shareability.html accessed on 29/9/2016.

16 http://www.oslit.nl/beheer/wp-content/uploads/2012/03/Program-Bracha-L.-Ettinger.pdf, accessed on 29/9/2016.

17 See Ian Parker, *Psychoanalytic Culture: Psychoanalytic Discourse in Western Society* (London: Sage Publications, 1997), p. 195.

Part 2

Voices of Indian Nationalism

9

Deconstructing the Orientalist Imaging of 'Spiritual' India

John Peter Vallabadoss
St. Joseph's Capuchin Philosophical College, Kotagiri

Abstract: Any study on Indian reality surprises, especially the non-Indian orientalists, colonial and post-colonial writers. While wondering at its diversity and changes, a tendency of reducing it to a one dimensional character has often been expressed in their approach giving rise to certain imaging of 'spiritual' India. Orientalists' imaging had its context, ideological constraints, and commercial and political projects. The denial of Indian diversity and plurality in all aspects becomes a threat perpetuated by spiritualizing Indian reality. The paper attempts to critique a one dimensional picture of Indian reality and to illustrate the multi-dimensional aspects of India. Overemphasizing one aspect of Indian reality as only 'spiritual' damages its true nature and encourages mono-cultural, monolithic construction of Indian polity and socio-religious reality. By deconstructing the orientalists' imaging of India, we hope to safeguard the true nature of Indianness that challenges particular viewing of the Indian nation. Becoming a nation needs a national building project on the true foundation of Indian diversity.

Introduction

Incredible India's diversity fascinates. Instead of appreciating its diversity and changes, a tendency of reducing it to one dimensional character has often been expressed. A certain imaging of a 'spiritual' India, constructed with orientalists' imagination using facts and fiction, data and interpretations has continued for the last few centuries to rule the mind of anyone who views, picturizes and studies Indian reality. The heritage of India constructed as 'spiritual' has always been upheld either in a form of reaction to Western materialism or of finding a justification for tradition-bound Indian society. Conveniently following the orientalist interpretation of Indian reality, many native scholars, both in colonial and post-colonial periods, have been rightly calling it as '*sanskrativistaar*,' cultural renaissance[1] along with spiritualizing everything Indian as a national project of self-preservation. Critiquing such an imaging of India, makes us think 'how' and 'what' of such construction and 'why' of its carrying forward. The paper attempts to highlight orientalist imaging as leading to mono-culturalism and tries to counteract it by illustrating the multi-dimensional aspects of India.

1. Engagement with India's Past

Authoritative projections, explorations and enquiries, have always been contested in postcolonial sensibilities, aiming to negotiate and rework on resources at the core of shifting configurations of social worlds. The clamour over the past for assertion of authority provides appropriations and enunciations of the past with certain visions with contending validities in the making of their world. Possibilities of critical ferment and creative expression in history writing, varieties of history, based on plural perspectives, intellectual disagreements, and ethical contentions, are necessary.[2] New perspectives on India's past are needed in times of contesting over the past through controversies over history books and monuments, and through contentions over the heritage of communities. We experience the inadequacy of historical narratives to represent all aspects of India. When we are burdened by issues of crafting of Indian history, with one's own particular bias, there is a need for scrutiny on historical scholarship that had specific visions of the state and nation, the West and modernity, and the colony and post-colony.[3] The past has returned to haunt the present, finding novel manifestations and escalating assertions. Demands on the past have been central to many assertions of culture, identity and tradition. Many crave a particular picture of the Indian past to suit their ideology. Critiquing the orientalist and colonial engagements in imaging India in certain categories and entities, we try to explore the concepts and process in the past and their impacts in the present. Unraveled productive possibilities which suited are continued, like spiritual India, but that which is not suited to vested interests, are denounced.

Post-colonial historiography entails cultivation of a critical questioning of colonial orientations, and acknowledges and articulates vital conceptualizations of the true nature of India and its people. Probing into orientalist dispositions in creating 'spiritual' imaging of India, we find the limitation of presenting only a certain aspect and neglecting the other equally important dimensions of Indian tradition. The expressions of tradition are understood by orientalists with given, prominent, surface level information they received both from their own viewing and from their informants. These elements have become sources of certain imaging 'spiritual' India. Sometimes, imaginative explorations of pasts with calculated conceptions ended up with certain manifestations. Critical and imaginative renderings of modern and colonial knowledge need serious requirements of evidence and fidelity to facts, even though the historical always sift historical evidence through critical filters and construe facts rather than deal with them as they are. As dialogue with the sources is at the heart of the historian's craft, a historian without linguistic skill and literary abilities and sensibilities would be no historian at all. For example, in K. A. Nilakanta Sastri's attempt at using the summaries of inscriptions available from reports of the Archaeological Department, rather than reading and interpreting by oneself from the inscriptional sources that are available in the field.[4] The cultural history of India has been always written in the colonial period by non-Indians and in foreign language. When such writings became text books and source books, difficulty arose in the ability of acquiring historical knowledge which is in foreign language and also due to the absence of advanced historical works in our vernaculars.[5] Orientalists' imaging is scrutinized from this angle of understanding the Indian reality from their own perspective and from their informants.

Further the intellectuals in colonial India had worked out a dichotomy: material/spiritual and outer/inner, man/woman and world/home, etc. Operating from the mindset of the enlightenment era of European modernity, the Oriental scholars on India had a partial vision. The west was seen to be superior in the material sphere,[6] and the orient as 'spiritual,' – a dichotomy serving the schemes of modernity. Many of the salient aspects of the tradition under their study have not been given opportunity for articulation as they were not in the everyday spaces and public places of their informants and of their own area of study. Today with increased awareness of plural contentions within history writing, critical questioning about orientalist knowledge and imaging of India, initiates procedures of demystification of 'spiritual' India. They take the side of the apparent epistemic breach, vigorously opposing oriental imaging. Demanding and overthrowing conventions of orientalist or colonial history in favour of replacement by subversions of the myth of a 'spiritual' India has been done by scholars to bring in fresh research and accounting for true Indianness. Without the critical enquiry into such imaging that neglected the historical differences, we run the risk of suffering from mind-numbing sameness.[7] Historical sensibilities offer lessons and insights into rethinking of past for the present of the country. The becoming of nation depends on such necessary reconfigurations.

2. India enchanting the Orientalists

The transformation happening in India is towards reliving the past, taking pride in the ancient past. The entire project of imaging spiritual India pictured ancient wisdom providing basic truths of life useful to anyone searching for lasting peace and liberation. The ancient *Rishi*-s (seers, in Sanskrit) and *Arijnar*-s (wise people, in Tamil) have always charmed and delighted foreigners with their clairvoyant visions and perceiving though the cosmos, the minutest, distant and hidden mysteries. Justifying the cultural, religious, ritual symbols that have deeper meaning, East has attracted the West constantly. The 'symbolic,' the 'mystical' and the 'spiritual' of India have evoked a sense of awe in the highly rationalized, materialized and secularized West.[8] The ordinary is extraordinary indeed, having a deeper sense of the inner world, hidden and unknown aspects of the apparent, the seen and the visible. The trans-empirical approach of the Indian mind found the sacred in the secular. Sacred symbols involved in rituals and ceremonies as essential ingredients are chosen from the 'profane' and the 'secular' to reveal the mysteries of nature in the universe. Through spiritualizing, symbols from the physical gain a deeper meaning in the metaphysical sense.[9] The orientalists and the Westerners have noted this aspect of Indian traditions and admired their veracity and depth of understanding of reality.

Western missionaries who encountered Indian culture needed knowledge of Indian languages, beliefs and conduct. The production of European scholarly knowledge of India by missionary-scholars helped the orientalist and colonial writers.[10] David Lorenzen opined that in some degree the knowledge of British-Indian orientalists was better, as it was built upon the pioneer works of missionaries before 1770.[11] In sum, the new orientalist knowledge of British India was of a higher quality and had greater effect. Orientalists had a different orientation from that of the missionaries, as a secular and enlightenment-tinged character of orientalist research made for greater openness to India and Indian religion. More than the missionaries, the orientalists had direct and prolonged access to Indian scholars. Indian people themselves became the engine propelling the orientalist project. The East India Company and later the Empire, financed the institutions that supported orientalist research. Not only orientalist scholars but also Indian scholars as assistants and sometimes those establishments were supported by the British Indian government.[12] Orientalists like Abbe Dubois, Max Muller, William Jones, etc., are best examples of imaging 'spiritual' India.

3. Critique of Project Orientalism

Orientalism is critiqued today not as a spontaneous approach of the west towards the east, but as a project that helped legitimization of imperial powers. Orientalism, as Edward Said categorically affirmed, is a discourse to divide Persians, Indians, Chinese and South Asians as the 'other,' as the non-European.[13] "The relationship between Occident and Orient is a relationship of power, of domination, of varying degrees of a complex hegemony...."[14] The projected inferiority of the east with myths, religions and primitive morality, justifies the superiority of the west with technology, enlightened reason and discovery of scientific revolutions. James S. Mill said that the great Indian heritage was decadent; only by imperialist intervention can it be restored. Orientalism was on a civilizing mission through commerce and industrialization at least in the early British period in India. The orientalist discovery of India as a changeless and stagnant society was resisted by Indians.[15] The search for a true Indian knowledge system and of its past was taken up by Indian *pandits,* the intellectuals. Institutions like the Asiatic Society encouraged the active role of local informants and *pandits* who 'remembered' their past and recalled Indian past glory and interpreted it to move forward.[16] Responding to the later shift from orientalism to westernization, Indian orientalists have come up with discoveries glorifying the Indian past. They even went to the extent of glorifying the Indian past by claiming all modern disciplines, fields and sciences were found in the Indian past, like astronomical science, mathematics, atomic science, democracy, etc. In a way it led to 'worship' of the Indian nation which is supposed to be different from 'love' for the nation.[17]

History becomes one of the sources for every community and nation, providing not only a specific outlook of their past, but also constructing a particular national identity.[18] The middle class aspiration to cope with the influx of western ideologies and to secure a comfortable space for their existence in British India, found in orientalism a source for identifying itself as 'spiritual' as opposed to the 'material' western society. A new sense of social awareness for creating an identity was well supported by the orientalists' construction. Although, such a construction has positively contributed to Indian identity, it still was a monolithic, one-dimensional narration of India as only "spiritual". Even modern gurus found it profitable for their personal gains and to develop their organizations in the spiritual market and thus, orientalist imaging was given a greater scope to manipulate the constructed past of India as spiritual and idealistic.

4. Critique of Orientalist-Colonial Historiography

Following the orientalists' imaging of India, the colonial interpretation of Indian history has been very influential in the construction of the Indian identity as 'spiritual.' The evolution of nationalist ideas was seen to be attached to colonialist construction.[19] The cultural beginning of India, as seen in contemporary research shows that diversity of world views, philosophies, and traditions beautified Indian reality. The history of religions in medieval India provides a picture of diversity of religious sects and not that of monolithic religion. In pre-colonial times, there were multiple identities of caste, language, religious sects, political ambitions that were in constant war. Religious identities were based not on monolithic religion but on religious sects. Neglect of such character is unwarranted not only in the interpretation of the Indian past, but also in assessing the anti-colonial and post-colonial emergence of Indian identity creation. The colonial reading of Indian history, denied this diversity; for instance, J. S. Mill's *History of British India*, published in 1818, divided Indian civilization in terms of monolithic religious identities as Hindu, Muslim and British civilizations. Colonial writers continued the categorization as history of two nations, Hindu and Muslim Nations. Emerging from the empiricist tradition, Mill exhibited contempt for religion, but while writing Indian history he centered on religious identity; specifically he essentialised one religious identity at every age, reducing the differences into simply one.[20] For him, the religion of the ruler becomes a category for history. For him, many other characters do not matter at all. Thus, his monolithic presentation of Indian history in the category of religion is a typical example of orientalism.

The British saw this hostility as convenient for their rule in helping both politics and colonial policy. Strengthened by the construction of majority and minority communities, as distinct, consolidated and monolithic religious identities, colonial writers continued the polarization.[21] Nationalist historians like Chaudhary, R. C. Majumdar, Nilakanta Sastri challenged some colonial theories, like orientalist despotism, yet accepted religious periodization. Labels got changed, but divisions and reasons for divisions remained as 'religious.' Aryan theory and history, as held by some Indologists like Max Muller, constructed the Vedic tradition as a foundation for Indian civilization. Olcott's theory of Aryan expansion also helped the idea that India had a single history. K. C. Sen and Max Muller were of the same view, and held the Aryans as a superior race - both European and Indian.[22] Such one sided colonial Indology drew its inspiration from Orientalism and completely neglected the other aspects of pre-Vedic, non-Vedic, non-religious and non-spiritual traditions of India, from Ancient through Medieval to Modern periods of Indian history.

5. From 'Spiritual' to 'Hindu' India

The appropriation of orientalist and colonial imaging of India by Hindutva forces to suit their political agenda is disturbing. The religious politics of Hindutva claims to cleanse the cultural pollution of Indian historians influenced by western ideologies, forget that its foundations are well rooted in colonial ideologies. The core of Hindu mono-culturalism lies in the identity of 'hindu,' constructed as emerging in the land of ancestry as *pitrubhumi,* and in the land of religion as *punyabhumi.* Non-Hindus are labelled as foreign in the claim of treating Hindus as primary citizens. The question of what kind of nation India should be engaged India's leadership immediately after Independence, and were centered on the options of being secular or Hindu, capitalist or socialist. Defined as a secular democracy committed to serving the well-being of all its people, regardless of religion, region, caste, gender or race, India gave a decisive answer in its new constitution in 1950. The use of the idea of India as a Hindu nation has become jargon to challenge the reality of India as a modern, secular, pluralistic nation.[23] Continuing the convenient construction of 'spiritual' India, to be Hindu India and that too Vedic India, deliberate attempts are made in postcolonial writings on the origins of Indian Civilization as the Harappan civilization and Aryans as settlers not invaders, imposing Sanskrit as the mother tongue, and Hinduism as *Sanatanadharma* to be the religion of the country. They lacked critical reading but served the religious politics of imaging a *Hindurastra.*

6. Deconstructing Singular Dimensional India

For most non-Indian scholars and writers, the Indian subcontinent is full of spiritual insights, of deepest truths about reality and the self. The voices of India speak of her rich philosophical and religious traditions, revealing many wonderful secrets of the human heart and mind, enriching personal existence and illuminating Western culture.[24] All postcolonial Western writings about India have such fascination and rendering. They seek Indian insights as the process of self-discovery and pilgrimage along the Indian way. Images of such notions persist and predominate although India had its past with wonderful accomplishments in sciences like astronomy, chemistry, medicine, mathematics and humanistic thoughts of Jain and Buddhist systems. India's political, linguistic, geographical and racial diversities are matched by the diversity of her thought. Some Indian philosophers are materialists, other idealists; some are monists, others dualists or pluralists; some emphasize empirical knowledge, others meditational insight. Religious thought is also equally diverse. Some were atheistic like Jainism and Buddhism, some are theistic like Vaishnavism and Saivism. For John Koller, there is probably no more diverse and pluralistic culture in the world than the Indian and certainly no one image or description could possibly capture the rich diversity.

Nevertheless, acknowledging Indian diversity, many orientalist and colonial scholars are obsessed with religions and seeing the continuity, not the changing cultural spheres. They crushed the diversity to fit into a monolithic and unchanging pattern. "Beneath the manifold diversity of physical features ethnic groups, languages and dialects, and religions in India there has always been an underlying uniformity of life."[25] Spiritual transformation has constituted the ultimate aim in life for most of the Indian people over the ages. This underlying vision of participation in the ultimate reality and the aim of spiritual transformation of human existence have guided much of

Indian philosophy and religious thought.[26] The central systematic philosophy in India is said to be asceticism, yoga, devotion, ritual, truthfulness, supra rationalism. In light of this continuous pattern of change and diversity, it would be exceedingly rash and unwise to claim that there is one unchanging way of thinking and acting that is exclusively and uniquely India. Such a claim would represent an implicit attempt to reduce the rich and changing diversity that is India to a single simple formula. Due to the tendency of seeing something as a unity in Indian plurality, many writers and thinkers have ended up with mono-cultural outlooks.

7. Daya Krishna's Critique of Indian 'Spiritual' Image

The concern of Daya Krishna is to rescue those traditions from the long spiritual quest of India with which they have become associated and entangled. Due to the diverse exigencies of history from the late eighteenth century to the first half of the twentieth century, such suffocation has been experienced by the non-spiritual aspects of India. He says, "The interests of western Indological studies combined with the search for a spiritual self-identity in the face of overwhelming western superiority in all fields of knowledge seemed to have led to the creation of a certain picture of India's philosophical past which has become fixed in the minds of successive generations of students and teachers, both in India and abroad, through innumerable text-books which render it almost impossible to question the picture or build a different one."[27] Trying to break the picture, its outlines and patterns and foci, he decries that even questioning the textual traditions of the Indian past and a critical examination of concepts, positions of traditions in India have not taken place. Even scholars are accustomed to see things in a certain way, and habituated to entertain a certain picture of India's philosophical past.[28] Much more reluctance is witnessed among scholars to question and critically view the 'texting' of orientalists and western scholars about the picturing of India as 'spiritual'. The orientalist production of texts has clearly given a picture of 'spiritual' India. Daring to question it and attempts to deconstruct its imaging become a task needed to secure a holistic vision of India as such.

The claim of India as 'spiritual' in nature, that distinguishes it from western philosophy, and making it something unique and apart, has never been put to the test as it is claimed to be self-evident with no requirement for any argument or evidence on its behalf. No one dreams of questioning it. Reality is dichotomized in such a way that only the 'spirit' is real and matter is only an appearance, illusory and unreal. Although, it is true that most of Indian philosophical schools recognize the ultimate reality of spirit in one form or another, they can hardly be characterized as being 'spiritual' in character as they equally recognize the ultimate reality of matter in some form or the other.[29] The Jainas, the Vaiśeṣikas and the Sāṁkhyans recognize the reality of matter besides Cārvākās.

8. Indian Thought: Not merely Idealistic and Spiritual

We need to necessarily doubt the reiterated claim that the philosophical tradition of India was one of unbroken idealism or spiritualism. S. Radhakrishnan claimed that the characteristic of Indian thought is that it has paid greater attention to the inner world of man than to the outer world.[30] The non-idealistic trends on Indian thought like materialism, naturalism and dualism are clearly evident. The problems are faced by Indian materialists for their space in the history of Indian thought by writers[31] deliberately dissociating themselves from materialism and explicitly writing from the idealistic point of view. The conventional standpoint of an idealistic view with a monolithic interpretation of Indian thought led to convenient dogmatism and over-simplifications of systems of India, with highly consistent interpretation of a diversified Indian heritage from the uncompromisingly idealistic standpoint. Of course, their effort enjoyed the widest popularity both in and out of academic circles. We need to frequently question the validity of such conclusions and propose a re-examination. The works of D. P. Chattopadyaya are commendable in this regard, in tracing the 'lost' resources of Lokayata, the Indian materialist tradition.[32]

We find in the atomism of the Vaisesikas, *Ajnanavada, Bhutavada, Ajivika* and the Buddhist *Sarvastivadi* important elements of Indian materialism. There are references to non-idealistic trends from Tantrism, Samkhya philosophy and ancient Indian characteristic ideology of 'Mother-right.' Even though, there is also a remarkable similarity between the Lokayata tradition and the more archaic stratum of the Vedic tradition, materialist tradition was presented in such a contemptuous way that agrees with the notions of the contemporary prejudices against materialistic philosophy in general, such as Madhavacarya who considered Lokayata as the lowest system of philosophy[33] and as the cult of crude people who little understand the higher values of human existence. Such a notion is also reflected in the attitude of the modern scholars on materialism as a mere perversion. The very fact that almost all thinkers and writers in India levelled severe criticism against it, stands as a witness that Lokayata cannot be taken to be as simple a philosophy as it might appear. Lokayata meant not only the philosophy of the people but also the philosophy of 'this-worldliness.'[34] The interpretation of all ancient systems in India requires a constructive effort in both deconstructing the conventional interpretation and reconstructing concrete factors of Indian non-idealistic thought patterns to lay siege to the ideological citadels built around the history of Indian thinking, enabling a deconstruction of 'spiritual' India.

Concluding Remarks

If orientalists' imaging helped create a fascination in the West towards its Eastern orientation, as a part of positioning the emerging 'Other' of the Euro-centric 'Self,' natives found it favorable for Indian 'self-identity' with certain peculiarities in the process. English educated Indian intellectuals saw a greater opportunity to exploit it for consolidating anti-colonial sentiments during the British period and for nation building in the post-Independence period. Such imaging deliberately denies the holistic and comprehensive viewing of Indian reality. The denial of Indian diversity and plurality in all aspects becomes a threat perpetuated by spiritualizing Indian reality. The diversity of India is unique. Anchoring ourselves on Indian diversity, and critiquing 'spiritualizing' and 'idealizing' Indian traditions, we attempted to highlight the other dimensions of Indian reality neglected by orientalists-colonialists and some contemporary Indian writers. Overemphasizing one aspect of Indian reality as only 'spiritual' damages its true nature and encourages a mono-cultural, monolithic construction of Indian polity and socio-religious reality. By deconstructing the orientalists' imaging of India we hope to safeguard the true nature of Indianness that challenges the particular viewing of the Indian nation. Critically analyzing the traditionally conceived self-evident claims about Indian culture we assert that national identity is to be based on reliable history, and not on anyone's passion for the past. Nationalism has to do with identity of citizens and it cannot be an identity claimed by any single unit. Deconstructing 'spiritual' India raises critical questions for India today in shaping its nationhood on the lines of a monolithic religious identity.

Notes

1 Jhaver P. Shreeniwas, Preface, *Spiritual Heritage and Cultural Symbols of India* (Delhi: Jaico Publishing House, 2009), x.

2 Saurabh Dube, Foreword, in A. R.Venkatachalapathy, *In those Days there was No Coffee: Writings in Cultural History* (New Delhi: Yoda Press, 2006), xvii.

3 Saurabh Dube, Foreword, in A. R. Venkatachalapathy, *In those Days there was No Coffee,* ix.

4 Sanjay Subrahmanyam, "Whispers and Shouts: Some Recent Writings on Medieval South India," *The Indian Economic and Social History Review,* 38 (4), 2001, 461.

5 Refer, Jadunath Sarkar, "Confessions of a History Teacher,' *Modern Review* (December 1915), 662-667.

6 Partha Chatterjee, "The Nationalist Resolution of the Women's Question," in Kumkum Sangari and Sudesh Vaid (eds), *Recasting Women: Essays in Colonial History* (New Delhi: Zubaan Books, 1989), 6.

7 Saurabh Dube, Foreword, in A. R. Venkatachalapathy, *In Those Days there was No Coffee,* xii.

8 Jhaver P. Shreeniwas, Preface, *Spiritual Heritage and Cultural Symbols of India,* xii.

9 Adherence to its outward form alone without comprehending their inner meaning degenerates into superstition. Such practices and belief systems have been the areas of

justifications for Western criticism of Hindu superstitious beliefs and practices. Seen as irrational beliefs and superstitious practices, these render a sorry picture of the Indian religious milieu even among the Orientalists and Western scholars.

10 Thomas R. Trautmann, *The Clash of Chronologies: Ancient India in the Modern World* (New Delhi: Pearson, 2006), 189.

11 Refer, David Lorenzen, *Ancient to Modern: Religion, Power and Community in India,* ed., Ishita Bannerjee-Dube and Saurabh Dube. (New Delhi: Oxford University Press, 2008).

12 Thomas R. Trautmann, *The Clash of Chronologies,* 191-193.

13 Edward Said, *Orientalism* (1977 reprint, London: Penguin, 2003), 108.

14 Edward W. Said, "Orientalism," in *The Post-Colonial Studies Reader,* ed. Bill Ashcroft, et.al. (London: Routledge, 1995), 89.

15 Bhaskar Chakraborty, "Colonial State and its Ideology Orientalism," Video Lecture https://www.youtube.com/watch?v=3gO8BnAznik accessed 12th July, 2016.

16 The earlier notion of forgetting the past that let down the Indians was held as a spontaneous reaction of many Indian English educated persons. Later Indian scholars took pride in the Indian past and defended Indian reality using the same category of the orientalist construction of 'spiritual' India. Spivak's and Said's question of nature and content of the 'speech of subalterns' reveals the fact that even if subalterns are allowed to speak or empower themselves of capability of speech, they would speak only in the language of the superiors; in the present case the colonizers.

17 The making of '*bharatamata*' Mother India was a religious personification of the land by the communal nationalists. In fact, Bankim Chandra Chatterjee's slogan of '*vande mataram'* – worship to the mother, became a catchphrase, rousing Indian consciousness for the independence movement.

18 Romila Thapar, "The Nation and History: Then and Now," Lecture in JNU on 5th March, 2016 https://www.youtube.com/watch?v=YvLdkKj36t0 accessed on 13th July, 2016.

19 Refer Romila Thapar, "India: The Colonial Roots of Hindutva 'Nationalism,'" in http://www.sacw.net/article12848.html accessed on 15th Feb, 2017.

20 Harbans Mukhia, "The Nation and History: Then and Now," Lecture in JNU on 5th March, 2016, https://www.youtube.com/watch?v=YvLdkKj36t0 accessed on 13th July, 2016.

21 Orientalists' polarization of India as 'spiritual' and the Occident as 'material,' was prior to colonial polarization of Indian history and society on religious identities.

22 Romila Thapar, "The Nation and History: Then and Now," Lecture in JNU on 5 March 2016.

23 John M. Koller, *The Indian Way: An Introduction to the Philosophies and Religions of India* (New Delhi: Pearson, 2006), 354-355.

24 John M. Koller, Preface, *The Indian Way,* iv, 1-4.

25 P. Raghunadha Rao, Preface, *Indian Heritage and Culture* (New Delhi: Sterling Publishers, 1988), v.

26 John M. Koller, *The Indian Way,* 10.

27 Daya Krishna, Preface, *Indian Philosophy: A Counter Perspective* (Delhi: Oxford University Press, 1991), vii.

28 *Ibid.*, ix.

29 *Ibid.,* 4.

30 Refer S. Radhakrishnan. *An Idealist View of Life* (London: George Allen & Unwin, 1932).

31 Like S. Radhakrishnan, S. Dasgupta, M. Hiriyanna.

32 Refer Debiprasad Chattopadhyaya, *Carvaka/Lokayata: An Anthology of Source Materials and Some Recent Studies.* New Delhi: ICPR, 1990; While at least the major texts of the other schools are preserved for us, all the original works of the Lokayatikas are lost beyond the prospect of any possible recovery. What we are actually left with are merely a few

fragmentary survivals of the Lokayata, but all these are preserved in the writings of those who wanted only to refute and ridicule it. Debiprasad Chattopadhyaya, *In Defence of Materialism in Ancient India* (New Delhi: People's Publishing House, 2008).

33 Debiprasad Chattopadhyaya, *Carvaka/Lokayata*, 423.

34 Debiprasad Chattopadhyaya, *In Defence of Materialism in Ancient India,* 27.

10

Science: Not to Silence "Silence" *Reflections on the Role of Science in Building a Holistic Nation*

S. Stephen Jayard
Jnana-Deepa Vidyapeeth, Pune

Abstract: Science is important for any modern society. Lasting changes are possible only with the backing of science as exemplified in the French Revolution of 1789 and in the post-colonial period of India around 1940s. In Part I, we take a cursive look at India's huge contributions in science - from the ancient times until today. The builders of our nation were really convinced that only science could take India ahead in economy, defence, self-sufficiency in food-production, removal of poverty, etc. Unfortunately, the benefits of science have not reached all citizens and only those at the top rung of society enjoy them. Ironically, in spite of great strides in science we still find astrology and superstitions strongly influence large sections of the population in India. Even the University Grants Commission (UGC), the body for higher education in India, has unfortunately made efforts to introduce astrology in the universities as a science. Part II, therefore, discusses some factors to show that astrology does not qualify to be a science. The concluding section focuses on the dire need of strengthening the spiritual foundation of our nation so that India does not lose its "depth" in the world of science. The ultramodern India must be cautious about *not allowing science to silence the "silence" of our great nation,* as science and 'silence' are two great tools in nation building.

1. Science Shaping India and India Shaping Science

Science does play a marvelous role in the make-up of any modern society. Real and lasting changes are very often possible only with the backing of science as exemplified in the 1789 French Revolution and in the post-colonial period in India around the 1940s. By the eighteenth century, science totally changed the face of the Western world with the supply of coal and steam energy, which replaced animal energy; railroads and automobiles made traveling much faster; the telegraph and telephone made communication quicker and more far-reaching. These days innovations in computer technology, communications through optical fibre and other modern day marvels have had a dramatic change on society. There are constant efforts to "effectively translate scientific and technical understanding into the techniques, tools, and insights that improve the quality of our lives"[1]

Science is no stranger to India. Centuries before the emergence of modern science in the West, India was known for inventions and discoveries:[2] for example, buttons on our dress is a great innovative idea by India, about 5,000 years ago. India's contributions in the fields of mathematics, trigonometry, algebra, calculus, the usage of π are amazing. In fact, the invention of the zero, greatly astounded great minds like Albert Einstein. Aryabhata, an Indian mathematician and astronomer, in 500 AD, made several significant contributions in mathematics. Chess is India's valuable creation to the world. Another example to showcase Indian genius: Jagdish Chandra Bose (1858-1937), a famous physicist, made studies on plant physiology, which later came to be known as bio-physics. His famous lecture at the prestigious Royal Institute in May 1901, challenged the traditional boundaries of natural science and the distinctions between living and non-living entities. About this Margaret Noble wrote to Tagore later, "We realized that at long last, India established the excellence of her wisdom before an assembly of western scientists and emerged as the preceptor and not as a disciple, not even as an equal."[3]

Science emerged as an 'event' in Europe bringing about lots of changes in their culture, ideologies, life-styles and belief-systems; God was sent into exile or even declared dead. But in India science easily gelled with the Indian psyche and society. Since, India has been exhibiting a very strong spirit of rational inquiry, along with its emphasis upon morals and spirituality, the emergence of modern science did not distract India from its spiritual traditions. India has never bifurcated science from intuition or morals. Murli Manohar Joshi, a professor of Physics and former Union Minister for Human Resources Development, makes it clear: "A significant aspect of Indian epistemology which distinguishes it from the dominant western discourse is the inseparable link between epistemology and ontology and of both with ethics ... no dichotomy is seen between the empirical, rational, and analytical modes of knowing and the mystical and intuitive modes."[4]

The West, being taken up by the glamour of modern science, saw science as a value in itself. That is why, "in the name of scientific progress it [the West] justifies development of weapons of mass destruction, rapacious consumption of energy and materials oblivious to the consequential devastation of the environment, appropriation of traditional community-owned knowledge to achieve intellectual property rights by individuals and firms."[5] But India has always seen science as a great means to augment the lives of individuals and society; science was seen as valuable in the midst of social concerns; whatever was not conducive to the holistic growth of humanity and nature, India was not keen on it, no matter how attractive that science might be. Shruti Kapila's analysis shows that India did not allow science to replace religion, nor to declare the death of God, as it happened with Europe; nor did science get 'spiritualized' through science, as happened with the Orientals.[6] The inherently spiritual nature of the Indian soil was not drowned by the waves of science. While in Europe, the Enlightenment led society to a definite disenchantment with God, in India such things did not happen; rather people in India were helped to revisit their religious ideologies and beliefs with the help of science so as to give their relationships with God a new footing. Spiritually enlightened persons, like Vivekananda, had the scientific temperament as their basis for their efforts for reform in religious practices; for them, "Science was to nourish and condition the transformation of religion, an agenda that was effected through vigorous propaganda in the latter half of the nineteenth century and beyond."[7]

The impact of modern science upon India is very significant. Post-independence, India tried to stand tall in the world. Visionaries and statesmen like Jawaharlal Nehru took charge of the ministry of science and technology, so that he could personally supervise this important area of development. He was convinced that real changes would not come about with the force of law, but "... you can create an atmosphere where his [man's] actions are governed by scientific approach."[8] As Meghnad Saha, the editor of Science and Culture, rightly observed in his editorial of the first issue, "... India is passing through a critical stage in her history ... It is necessary that at such a juncture the possible effects of increasing the application of discoveries in science to our national and social life should receive very careful attention; for if the present is the child of the past, it may with equal emphasis be said that the future will be the child of the present."[9] Those visionaries saw in science huge power and potential that would emancipate the individuals from their wrong beliefs and practices, and that would empower the state in modern times; they decided to use its capacity to bring in socio-economic changes in India, which had just come out of colonial clutches.[10]

We need to realize, therefore, that science is for society and it is an emergent from society. Science has to be seen in its totality. The knowledge-content of science cannot be bifurcated from the value-considerations. Science is a response to the needs of society of a given time; society and science are inter-related: "Sciences are research traditions with complex histories and distant and widespread roots. 'Science' is the institution which sustains organized research, the ideology which posits a unity of science, a social principle which determines what reliable and authoritative knowledge is."[11]

In the past two decades India has emerged as a strong power in both its economic and scientific research prowess. The Chandrayaan-1 mission to the Moon in 2008, the Mars Orbiter Mission in 2014, its huge investments in the domains of biotechnology researches, competing with the international standards with ease, the incredible growth in the medicines and the amazing achievements in astrophysics and astronomy – are some of the noteworthy strides made by India.

2. Astrology – Astonishingly Unscientific!

India has now emerged as a strong power in the domains of science but, unfortunately, the influence of astrology and superstitions[12] are still very strong. On the one hand, India has made great strides in space exploration but, on the other, before launching its rockets into space, religious ceremonies (*poojas*) at the auspicious time for the success of the project are a must! Lots of people still believe in the power of a lemon, tied to the bumper of their vehicle to avoid accidents!

In India, astrology has been recently seen as a 'Vedic Science' (Jyotirvigyan) and therefore, the University Grant Commission (UGC) has proposed to establish such a department in our Indian Universities. But research shows that Vedic literature does not have anything to do about astrology, though it has lots to do about astronomy. Jayant Narlikar[13] explains some of the reasons as to why astrology is neither Vedic, nor scientific. He further analyses the usual reasons given to argue that astrology is a science. For instance: a) astrology relies on information obtained by astronomy, which is taken to be a science, hence, why not treat astrology as science?; b) some astrologers' predictions do occasionally come true; c) Some scientific disciplines like meteorology, medicine do also go wrong, so why not accept astrology as a science, in granting that it goes wrong sometimes?; d) some astrologers may make mistakes, but the discipline can still be scientific; and e) scientists don't have the patience and humility to study the discipline of astrology, but reject it blindly. But Narlikar systematically shows that all these arguments don't hold water and he concludes that astrology is not a science.[14]

Lawrence Jerome criticizes astrology as having no scientific validity; though it has survived for about 6,000 years, it is only a magical system.[15]

The ancient Greek astronomy of geocentricism, the perfect circular paths of the planets, and introduction of epicycles to tackle some of the discrepancies in their orbits – all such claims were dropped or corrected with the arrival of the helio-centricism of Copernicus, Galileo, Kepler and Newton. However, the idea of planets having their own power to move as they like and even to affect humans on the earth, somehow persisted deep in the human psyche.

It is sad that while, on the one hand, the UGC encourages and propagates nuclear physics and agricultural biotechnology, on the other, it tries to introduce superstitious beliefs and practices. If this continues we may unfortunately go back to burning women as witches, and offer human sacrifices to get a male baby! Article 51(A) (viii) of the Constitution underlies the 'fundamental duty' enjoined by every citizen, "to develop a scientific temper". Astrology is not just about predicting one's future. It must be seen in its larger perspective as something that affects social activities and status. While reading the horoscopes for marriages, D. Parthasarathy and R. Robinson point out the idea of inter-generational continuity of privilege, status and rituals define purity; further, "women, widows and the 'dalit-bahujans' are prevented from being included and even benefiting from the world of divinely ordained destiny. Closure, discrimination and stasis mark the system" - this reason must also be taken seriously to stop astrology and it is not enough to argue that astrology is not scientific.[16]

Astrology may be useful only as a psychotherapeutic exercise to find consolation in the world of uncertainties and anxieties that we live in. As long as we have uncertainties in life there may be a need to find some solace in astrology, but let us be aware that it is not scientific.

Concluding Remarks: The Need for Science and "Silence" for Nation Building

Today religious intolerance is dangerously on the increase. There is a move towards uniformity in all domains of life, be it in language, religion, culture or education, which threatens the real holistic growth of India and her long-cherished diversities. Such moves even have the danger of taking India back several centuries, jeopardizing all the blood and sweat of the visionaries of the past and the present, who toiled to keep India on the top of the world, not only in science but also in spiritual wealth.

While India gives paramount importance to the growth of science it must also take steps to look into the aspects that grant inner peace and make lives worthwhile. With the desire for spiritual enrichment on the increase, this sense of spirituality cannot be equated to religions in the ordinary sense. A religion may lead to spirituality but "fundamental spirituality" in its genuine sense, means "the inherent noble qualities of an individual's spirit or character, including morals and ethics, regardless of external influences."[17] Such authentic spirituality is the need of the hour, especially where we have lots of self-proclaimed God-men and God-women, and there is a general tendency to see 'morality as the lack of opportunity'.

In a consumerist society companies decide the taste and the needs of the people who are made to treat their wants as their needs. As this tendency gets deep rooted, we tend to sacrifice human relationships and even our total well-being in order to boost our self-image with a false sense of pride in possessing these must have gadgets. Further, modern technology has brought in 'instant culture', which is another substantial challenge that has to be faced in modern times. As everything can be done or achieved instantly, the same tendency also permeates in matters of relationships and spirituality.

Einstein had already warned that if we allow technology to dominate our human relations, society will be full of idiots. Too much of dependence on gadgets is gravely detrimental to the holistic development of children and it affects their exposure to natural environment and their artistic creativity.[18] Being fully aware of these dangers, Steve Jobs (1955 – 2011), an American information technology entrepreneur and inventor and co-founder of Apple Inc. did not allow his three children to use an iPad at home.[19]

The *fundamental spirituality* is in realizing the 'universe of consciousness', about which even scientists speak about. Apollo 14 astronaut and engineer Edgar Mitchell, on his way back to the earth from the moon, had a great feeling and conviction that all of us, and also the whole universe are participating in a 'consciousness'. This motivated him to establish the Institute of Noetic Sciences in 1973.[20] He was not alone in having such sublime feelings. Several quantum physicists have the same awareness of consciousness as they reflect upon the massively vast universe up there or the miniature world of the sub-atomic particles, deep within matter (or energy!). Consciousness is fundamental for some of them, like Erwin Schrodinger, Max Planck, etc.;[21] And with this realization of the universal consciousness one can easily be rooted in fraternity, which would in turn lead to peace and harmony in the world. Thus fundamental spirituality can be seen as entailing, "personal responsibility regardless of anything; developing our own humility and sincerity; guarding our integrity; taking in stride what each day has to offer; correcting what we can and accepting graciously what we cannot; showing consideration and respect for others and serving selflessly; thinking constructively and seeking truth and spirituality; being a channel of good; and expressing love, beauty, and spirituality at every opportunity; many of these contain common components with moral and ethical values."[22] The sense of fundamental spirituality can certainly restore ecological consciousness as well.

A nation can take real pride, as India does, in its past cultural heritage and spiritual traditions. It is no doubt praiseworthy. But to make any nation relevant in the global arena and to make its citizens keep pace with the fast-changing global scenario of science and technology, a nation must focus on science. Unless it tries to increase its scientific competence and contributes towards discoveries and inventions, the identity of a nation in the modern world will be lost. To make genuine contributions to humanity, a nation has to take science seriously, but at the same time must not allow science to silence the spiritual and inner dimensions of that nation; it is because, "... national identity is rooted in a tradition of invention as well as in the invention of tradition."[23] India must cherish and deepen its tradition of spirituality, in spite of its scientific developments.

Notes

1 "Science and Technology in Modern Society," in *Science, Technology and the Federal Government: National Goals for a New Era* (Washington DC: The National Academies Press), 1993.

2 The term 'science' and 'scientist' were coined by William Whewell, a historian and philosopher of science at Cambridge University, in 1844. Until then 'Natural Philosophy' and 'Natural Philosopher' were used respectively. This is another factor to show how science and philosophy have umbilical cord relationships.

3 V. Mukherji, *Jagadis Chandra Bose, Builders of Modern India Series*, Ministry of Information and Broadcasting, New Delhi, 1983, 38-39.

4 Murli Manohar Joshi, "Inaugural Address on the Occasion of Inauguration of Debate on National Policy for Research in Social Science and Related Issues", mimeo, Chandigarh, February 11, 2000.

5 Murli Manohar Joshi, "Inaugural Address on the Occasion of Inauguration of Debate on National Policy for Research in Social Science and Related Issues", mimeo, Chandigarh, February 11, 2000.

6 Cf. Shruti Kapila, "The Enchantment of Science in India", *Isis*, (The History of Science Society, The University of Chicago Press), Vol. 101, No. 1, March 2010, 120-132.

7 Shruti Kapila, "The Enchantment of Science in India", *Isis*, (The History of Science Society, The University of Chicago Press), Vol. 101, No. 1, March 2010, 120-132, 129.

8 Jawaharlal Nehru, *Selected Works of Jawaharlal Nehru*, ed. S. Gopal, 2nd ed. (New Delhi, 1987), 6:347; as quoted by Carol E. Harrison and Ann Johnson, "Introduction: Science and Notational Identity", *OSIRIS*, 2009, 24:1-14, 1.

9 As quoted by Itty Abraham, The Contradictory Spaces of Postcolonial Techno-Science", in *Economic and Political Weekly*, Jan 21, 2006, 210-216, 211.

10 David Arnold, "Nehruvian Science and Postcolonial India", *Isis* (The History of Science Society, the University of Chicago Press), Vol. 104, No. 2, 360-370.

11 Avinash, "Science and Society – What Kind of Mediation?", *Economic Political Weekly*, 7 February, 2004, 538-540, 539.

12 Astrology is generally defined as a study of occult influence of planets and stars on human affairs, whereas Astronomy is understood as a systematic study of heavenly bodies. Astronomy is a science in the modern sense as it bases itself on experiments and observations. Superstition is understood as excessive willingness to believe in the supernatural and widely held irrational beliefs in supernatural influence.

13 See: Jayant V. Narlikar, "Vedic Astrology or Jyothirvigyan", *Economic and Political Weekly*, June 16, 2001, 2113-2115.

14 See: Jayant V. Narlikar, "Vedic Astrology or Jyothirvigyan", *Economic and Political Weekly*, June 16, 2001, 2113-2115.

15 See: L. E. Jerome, "Astrology and Modern Science: A Critical Analysis", *Leonardo* 6, 121 (1973).

16 D. Parthasarathy and R. Robinson, "Science, Astrology and Democratic Society", in Economic and Political Weekly, August 18, 2001, 3186-87, 3186.

17 Sukhmander Singh and John Finnemore, "Restoring Inner Peace in a Science Dominated Society", *The International Journal of Religion and Spirituality in Society*, Vol. 6, Issue 1, 2015, 41-46, 42.

18 Sue Palmer, *Toxic Childhood* (London: Orion Books, 2006); Richard Louv, *Last Child in the Woods: Saving Our Children from Nature-Deficit Disorder* (Chapel Hill, NC: Algonquin Books, 2008); and *The Nature Principle: Reconnecting with Live in a Virtual Age* (Chapel Hill, NC: Algonquin Books, 2013).

19 Sukhmander Singh and John Finnemore, "Restoring Inner Peace in a Science Dominated Society", *The International Journal of Religion and Spirituality in Society*, Vol. 6, Issue 1, 2015, 41-46, 43.

20 As reported by, Sukhmander Singh and John Finnemore, "Restoring Inner Peace in a Science Dominated Society", *The International Journal of Religion and Spirituality in Society*, Vol. 6, Issue 1, 2015, 41-46, 43.

21 For more details on this, please see my paper: "Mysticism and Quantum Physicists – Friends or Foes?," in *Omega – Indian Journal of Science and Religion,* Vol. 3, No. 2, 2004. 89-106.

22 Sukhmander Singh and John Finnemore, "Restoring Inner Peace in a Science Dominated Society", *The International Journal of Religion and Spirituality in Society*, Vol. 6, Issue 1, 2015, 41-46, 43.

23 Carol E. Harrison and Ann Johnson, "Introduction: Science and Notational Identity", *OSIRIS*, 2009, 24:1-14, 3.

11

Terrorism, Fundamentalism and Nationalism

Jose Pennaparambil
Diocese of Thamarassery, Thamarassery

Abstract: India, our mother country, is the cradle of many civilizations and religions and she bears within herself diverse cultures, traditions and customs. But, in modern India we can see that there are some negative factors, like fanaticism, fundamentalism, racism and terrorism, which have crept into our country and are trying to destroy the unity and uniqueness of our motherland. In the process of becoming a nation, the themes of terrorism and fundamentalism play an adverse role in its making. Among the three themes of our discussion, nationalism, fundamentalism and terrorism, only nationalism has got a positive meaning. The problem in India is that the nation continues to keep religion and the state intertwined. In a country that has many religions, the government and the people must realize that religion and the state have to be separated. Such balancing requires careful and measured degrees of impartiality, neutrality, syncretism, and tolerance. The challenge today is to appreciate the diversity of religions, ascertain the reasons behind confrontations and conflicts, and react to specific events and situations with informed, reasoned responses rather than predetermined presumptions and reactions. What is needed in the Indian context is the peaceful coexistence of different religions. The core of Hinduism is tolerance: tolerance for other faiths, tolerance for others' opinions, tolerance for different and opposing points of view, tolerance for other races and ethnicities, tolerance for other creeds.

Introduction

India, our mother country, is the cradle of many civilizations and religions and she bears within herself diverse cultures, traditions and customs. People of different origins, castes, religions, colour, and languages are living together as a coherent unity. In ancient Vedic India there was the caste system, which divided man into different categories on the basis of work, and some elements of this system exists even today. However, we can see in India an underlying unity in diversity and the country is known as the greatest secular and democratic nation in the world. But, amidst all these good qualities in modern India we can see that there are some negative factors, like fanaticism, fundamentalism, racism and terrorism, which have crept into our country and are trying to destroy the unity and uniqueness of our motherland.

India being a multi-religious country, what separates belief-based religions from one another breeds antagonism and hostility even though the sameness they share is remarkable. Equally, the sameness between the nation-state and these book religions lies in their similar functions: these religions and the modern nation-state believe they have the right to fulfil their destiny, and they promise to protect their people and avenge any wrong against them. In exchange it is expected that their subjects' rights of expression will be compromised for the good of the state or religion.[1]

It is our experience from history that, once a people share a common bond of religious feeling, a nation is born and becomes powerful as it plays out its destiny in history. The nation-state ignores religious feelings and replaces it with the bond of patriotism which is awakened when the state is threatened or attacked. In a secular state it is the nation's flag, instead of the symbol of the cross or the crescent that is honoured and excites the spirit as it is unfurled in the wind.[2]

India being the biggest democratic and secularist country in the world, the central point of our discussion is to see it becoming a new nation in the modern world by varied processes and perspectives, and in this process of becoming, the themes of terrorism and fundamentalism play an adverse role in its making. A person can be a terrorist because of a deep emotional need and high order of motivation on grounds of 'nationalism' 'on religious sentiment' 'for deprivation' and 'for a revolution'. The cause of nationalism is a very strong feeling to take up terrorism. Hence, in this brief paper, I would like to see them in an Indian perspective. These themes are very much interconnected; however I would like to treat them one after another.

1. Terrorism

Defining terrorism is not very simple. Various interpretations and definitions of terrorism have come up in recent times. States have generally focused on talking of terrorism in terms of acts of violence and the death of innocents at the hands of non-state actors. In popular parlance in some regions and some circles, such acts of terror are legitimized as acts of political campaign. Terrorism may be understood as 'an act of violence against unarmed civilians, as a means of bargaining politically over specific demands or making a general statement.'[3]

This term has its origin from the Latin term '*terrere*' (to make another tremble with fear). In its political context, the term 'terrorism' has been used since the last decade of the eighteenth century, beginning with the French revolution. According to Pravin N. Sheth, "any philosophy or action that resorts to violent and illegal action or treatment with the aim to shake up an established civil order, legal political arrangement and to make a person/people experience fear and harassment or tremors is known as terrorism."[4] In other words, terrorism is a systematic unpredictable mode of violence pitted against the innocent public in order to terrorize individuals or even a government to attain political objectives. Terrorism has been used by political organizations both, rightist and leftist; and also by nationalistic and ethnic groups, in the name of revolution.[5]

According to the Home Ministry, terrorism in India poses a significant threat to the people of India. The regions with long-term terrorist activities are Jammu and Kashmir, east-central and south-central India (Naxalism) and the Seven Sister States.[6] In August 2008, National Security Advisor M. K. Narayanan said that there are as many as 800 terrorist cells operating in the country.[7] As of 2013, 205 of the country's 608 districts were affected by terrorist activity. Terror attacks caused 231 civilian deaths in 2012 in India, compared to 11,098 terror-caused deaths worldwide, according to the State Department of the United States; or about 2% of global terror fatalities while it accounts for 17.5% of the global population.[8] Media reports have alleged that terrorism in India is sponsored by Pakistan, particularly through its Inter-Services Intelligence (ISI). In 2012, the US accused Pakistan of enabling and ignoring anti-India terrorist cells working on its soil; however, Pakistan has denied its involvement. In July 2016, Government of India released data on a string of terror strikes in India since 2005 that claimed 707 lives and left over 3,200 injured.[9]

1.1 Types of Terrorism

Terrorism found in India includes ethno-nationalist terrorism, religious terrorism, left wing terrorism and narco-terrorism, etc. However, according to Gerald Chaliand, there are many types of terrorisms.[10]

a) Terrorism as liberation movements: National Liberation Front of Tripura (NLFT), People's Liberation Army of Manipur (PLAM), United Liberation Front of Assam (ULFA), etc.

b) Anti-imperialist or revolutionist terrorism: People's Revolutionary Party of Kangleipak (PRPK), Communist Party of India (Maoist), all Naxalite groups in India, etc.
c) Terrorism of Political sects: Communist Party of India (Marxist–Leninist), People's War Group and all its formations and front organisations, etc.
d) State or Para-state terrorism: International Sikh Youth Federation (ISYF), Khalistan Commando Force (KCF), Khalistan Zindabad Force (KZF), Liberation Tigers of Tamil Eelam (LTTE), Tamil Nadu Liberation Army (TNLA), etc.

Besides the above listed groups I would like to add one more, viz.

e) Religious terrorism: Most of the Islamic and Hindu terrorists groups fall in this category: Hizb-ul-Mujahideen (HM), Indian Mujahideen (IM), Jaish-e-Mohammed (JeM), Lashkar-e-Taiba (LeT), Students Islamic Movement of India (SIMI), Bajrang Dal, RSS. The last two are not labelled as terrorist groups but are connected to Hindu terrorism.

From among all these types, state terrorism is to be mentioned specially because of its effects on society. Hence, I mention it separately.

State Terrorism

State terrorism refers to acts of terrorism conducted by a state against a foreign state or people, or against its own people. According to global terrorism expert Amy Zalman, "State terrorism" is as controversial a concept as that of terrorism itself. She says, terrorism is often, though not always, defined in terms of four characteristics: (1) the threat or use of violence; (2) a political objective; the desire to change the status quo; (3) the intention to spread fear by committing spectacular public acts; (4) the intentional targeting of civilians.[11] It is this last element of targeting innocent civilians that stands out in efforts to distinguish state terrorism from other forms of state violence. Declaring war and sending the military to fight other militaries is not terrorism, nor is the use of violence to punish criminals who have been convicted of violent crimes.[12]

In the opinion of Zalman, state terrorism is a "terrifically slippery concept in large part because states themselves have the power to operationally define it. Unlike non-state groups, states have legislative power to say what terrorism is and establish the consequences of the definition; they have force at their disposal; and they can lay claim to the legitimate use of violence in many ways that civilians cannot, on a scale that civilians cannot."[13] A number of conflicts between states and their opposition have a rhetorical dimension. Palestinian militants call Israel terrorist, Kurdish militants call Turkey terrorist, Tamil militants call Sri Lanka terrorist.

A terrorist is not a coward. They are committed individuals who carry out horrific acts at the cost of their own life. But terrorist acts beget counter-terrorists acts only. The solution remains a far cry. Terrorism shows the brutality of a human being and this is the basic element of terrorist psychology. Since terrorism is an uncured sore in modern human society, its reasons are also varied. Here, we try to understand some of the reasons which are also applicable to religious fundamentalism.

1.2 The Reasons or Causes of Terrorism

A terrorist can kill an innocent man, woman, or child. He can even commit suicide to fulfill his task. What is the force hidden in him, which incites him to do all these desperate acts? He can take immense trouble and risk as well. There are myriads of reasons which tempt or force or even provoke him to do so.

1.2.1 Religious Reasons

Fanatic religious sentiments, which are the creation of a fundamentalist attitude, can inspire an individual to be a terrorist. Terrorists and fundamentalist leaders play the cards of religious sentiments in order to woo credulous youth into terrorist activities and make them *Hezbollah* (Warriors of God). Similarly, the RSS (Rashtriya Swayamsevak Sank) or the Bajrang Dal are training Hindu fundamentalists to attain the goal of establishing Ramarajya, a land only for Hindus. These groups pose a perennial threat to the peace and tranquility of India.

1.2.2 Political Reasons

Terrorism is a tactic, a function, and a method whose driving force is an ideological and political goal. Without such a driving force, terrorism would dry up and fail.[14] Some political powers are promoting violence or terror for sustaining or maintaining their power or hegemony over their respective areas. Some become terrorists because of their pledges to a political cause.

In a terrorist group everyone does not plant bombs or shoot at targets. Most of them are involved in setting up a network. Some are fund collectors, some arrange safe havens, some collect and disseminate information, some are technicians to prepare bombs, and some are recruiting agents and the like. So everyone in a terrorist group cannot be of the same psychology, though they may be like-minded. Some ambitious and courageous youth get fascinated with political power and involve themselves in terrorism initiated by towering political leaders who were initially inclined towards terrorism, like Nelson Mandela, Yasser Arafat, etc.

1.2.3 Social Reasons

A human being by nature is curious. Some are head-strong and stubborn. Some are more curious for legal title of rights or take pride in attaining qualities of command. But equal quantum of wisdom is not gifted to everyone. Greater numbers of people are influenced by passion, greed, intolerance, and instincts of anger. Such a man is easy prey to misguidance, becomes obstinate and pig-headed, and thus he goes far beyond normalcy and his return to a normal life becomes inconceivable. Most of the terrorists fall into this category.

The second topic of our discussion is fundamentalism. According to Mohammad Mohaddessin, both terrorism and fundamentalism are two sides of the same coin.[15] Hence, most of the facts about terrorism are also applicable to fundamentalism.

2. Fundamentalism

Fundamentalism and terrorism are not two different entities and we cannot make a water tight compartment or demarcation between them. Terrorists and fundamentalists alike do not have any hesitation or fear to use the name of God to step on all values and to cross any lines in order to advance their evil intentions. So, to a certain extent they are one and the same.

The problem with fundamentalism is the notion that one side is right and the other is wrong. If the religionists involved adhered to the concept that the purpose of religion is to teach tolerance, love and compassion, such conflict would not exist. But they are justified by the fundamentalist, because he believes that God is on his side and will reward him for his acts that in any other context, he himself would condemn.[16] Members of fundamentalist movements see themselves as saviours of society. The problem of fundamentalism knows no borders, and it is a common enemy of humanity.

The term 'fundamentalism' was originally coined to describe a narrowly defined set of beliefs that developed into a movement within the Protestant community of United States in the early part of the twentieth century.[17] The *Concise Oxford English Dictionary* defined fundamentalism as "the strict maintenance of traditional protestant belief"[18] and strict maintenance of ancient or fundamental doctrines of any religion, especially of Islam. The term *fundamentalist* has since been generalized to mean strong adherence to any set of beliefs in the face of criticism or unpopularity, but has by and large retained religious connotations.[19] Almost in all religions we see this fundamentalist attitude.

Whether Christian, Islamic, or of any other denomination, religious fundamentalism is by its very nature in opposition to democracy and a free society. It is an important source of social retardation. Since, India is a secular democratic country it obstructs the growth of a rational, secular morality-based on human desires and needs. It has been a major source of violent conflict in society.

The Indian experience with fundamentalism has been bloody and traumatic. Mahatma Gandhi fell victim to a Hindu fundamentalist's bullets. Former Prime Minister Indira Gandhi was gunned down by her own Sikh bodyguard in the aftermath of the Sikh fundamentalist movement in Punjab. A female suicide bomber of the Tamil fundamentalist group from Sri Lanka blew up Indira's son Rajiv Gandhi. According to Asghar Ali Engineer, the assassinations of the Mahatma, Indira, and Rajiv serve as stark reminders of what happens when contractual bonds holding together the complex social elements composing the body politic are broken and when political affiliations are weakened.[20] In present day India we can see fundamentalist attitudes that are far and wide.

S. L. Verma observes:

> One is not fundamentalist or extremist if he believes in religious tenets, observes ritual or worships of God in form he likes, or spreads teachings at his individual conscience level and without hurting others. When they give shape in the form of action, organization, community identity and influence, they do not reflect religion, but material interest, power and politics.[21]

A fanatic follower of religion acts doggedly in the prescribed fashion and does not care for the result. Some people go on supporting such acts in the name of religion. A person is not a fundamentalist when he voluntarily helps the police, intelligence services and other public agencies so as to isolate the elements of fundamentalism, before and after the occurrence of riots or communal disturbance in any form.

3. Nationalism

Among the three themes of our discussion, nationalism, fundamentalism and terrorism, only nationalism has got a positive meaning. Nationalism is a great democratic ideal which continues to live as the strongest force and continues to inspire struggle for national liberation in different parts of the globe. It stands for the nation-state and love for the nation-state, and advocates that every nationality has a right to have its own state. It maintains that every distinct human group possesses some special qualities which must be preserved and developed for the common good of humanity. This can be achieved only if that group is free to develop its own laws and institutions.

For both the British masters who quit the Indian subcontinent in 1947, and Mahatma Gandhi 'the Father of our Nation' and his followers who forced the colonial power out, nothing was perhaps dearer to their hearts than the desire for the foundation of secular democracies in South Asia that were free from the tumult of caste and religious hostility. But from the very dawn of independence, sectarian rivalries have undermined that aspiration.[22] Since then, most nations of South Asia have constantly been plagued by increasingly violent political turmoil due to a growing intolerance toward their minorities. Regional experts now fear that religious fundamentalism and militancy are not only destroying South Asia's ethnic diversity, but also are putting the region's political secularism in danger of collapse. Hindu extremists in India, Tamil militants in Sri Lanka, and Islamic fundamentalists in Afghanistan, Pakistan, and Bangladesh pose a threat to the region's secular fabric.[23]

Although, Hindu nationalist organizations were active in some parts of India since independence, their growth and rising popularity has been closely linked to the rise and increased activities of Islamic fundamentalists and vice versa, for example, the destruction of Babri Masjid in Ayodhya. While occasional Hindu-Muslim riots did occur at a few places at irregular intervals, these were a result of localized frictions and often perpetrated by narrow-minded individuals out to gain some petty motives.[24]

Containing these twin evils of terrorism and fundamentalism is a herculean task. Here are some of proposals.

4. How can we contain the evils of terrorism and fundamentalism?

It is perhaps next to impossible to find a universal remedy or a tailor-made solution for all kinds of terrorism encountered presently in the world today. If all state authorities or leaders of every country or religious heads do not deprive or suppress any sections of the people, I am hopeful and confident that 95% of terrorist acts of torture and turmoil will be well under control. To achieve that goal, senior citizens, teachers, guardians, students and religious people will have to be determined to abolish terrorism forever from the face of the earth.

Israel could be a model for India in learning to deal with terrorists, because Israel has been facing terror attacks since its inception. The maxim of Bageura, a security company in Israel, which trains soldiers and civilians to counter terror, can be taken as a means to curb terrorism. "We do not negotiate with terrorists, we react accurately and decisively. This is not a game, they are not playing, and neither are we. You don't just accept it, you fight and eliminate it."[25] Hence, to deal with the terrorists decisive steps should be taken.

The fight against terrorism must be treated not only as a 'proxy war' but as a war which could be long, multifaceted, more fierce and complicated. It is not merely terrorism as such. It is intermixed with religious fundamentalism. In the view of S. L. Verma there are two ways to fight terrorism. Firstly, it has to be met by force, if possible, before its occurrence, otherwise after it. The second way provides a long term solution. It requires the separation of religion from religious fundamentalism and its variants. In place of religion one may also have absolute faith in some ideology. Separating religion from religious fundamentalism or fanaticism is much more difficult. This separation has to be defined, supervised, enacted and properly implemented.[26] A step further that is needed is the separation of religion from politics or state, as done in Europe.

According to Gerald Chaliand, the basis for any effective action (prevention, infiltration, neutralization, manipulation, liquidation) is intelligence. There are two different aspects of intelligence: collecting information, which is the vital basic task and inevitably involves a significant number of false leads; and interpreting information, which is above all a matter of sociological and political analysis. This demands knowledge of the adversary's ideology, organization, methods and potential.[27]

Conclusion

Clearly, to bring all nation-states into a single order that can adjudicate the conflicts between all states is essential. A system of law that protects against military expansion and economic exploitation is essential. It was only when the nation states of Europe realized that their fates hinged upon cooperation with each other that they formed the European Union. A similar need exists among religious systems and especially among belief-based religious systems. The is a clear need to curtail their efforts towards promoting religious wars, evangelizing populations, and dominating and restricting the development of culture, since these are the goals of all belief-based religions.

The problem in India is that the nation continues to keep religion and the state intertwined. In a country that has many religions, the government and the people must realize that religion and the state have to be separated. Mixing the two has never worked, and it never will. The stability of the state system depends critically on the state's role in balancing and mediating relationships between thousands of separate communities. Such balancing requires careful and measured degrees of impartiality, neutrality, syncretism, and tolerance.

The challenge today is to appreciate the diversity of religions, ascertain the reasons behind confrontations and conflicts, and react to specific events and situations with informed, reasoned responses rather than predetermined presumptions and reactions. As long as religion is used to batter people into political submission, the poor and uneducated masses will remain in their shackles.

What is needed in the Indian context is the peaceful coexistence of different religions. The core of Hinduism is tolerance: tolerance for other faiths, tolerance for others' opinions, tolerance for different and opposing points of view, tolerance for other races and ethnicities, tolerance for other creeds. There is nothing wrong with the religions; it is only those who exploit them for their territorial or temporal purposes who are guilty.[28]

Similarly, one cannot deal with Muslims as supporters of tyranny and opponents to democracy, both in terms of philosophical and political discourses and of real politics. In the opinion of Moussalli, a new reading of Islam must be the basis to start a modern process of reformulating Islamic history and reforming Islamic civilization.[29] Thus, Muslims must be realistic and try to reinterpret their laws for the benefit of the faithful as well as for the entire humanity, considering the modern pluralistic religious situation of the world.

In short, I dream of a world where all religions coexist in a tolerant manner and in an attitude of give and take, work together for the peace, tranquility and the wellbeing of mankind in a passion of love and brotherhood. Inspired by the words of Rabindranath Tagore, I pray and wish that, "Into the heaven of freedom, my Father, let my human race awake."

Notes

1 Pirrie Grimes, Philosophy, *Religion, the State, and the Problem of Terrorism,* 2001, http://www.openingmind.com/prst.htm.
2 Ibid.
3 Ram Puniyani, *Terrorism versus Reality*. Thiruvananthapuram: Mythri Books, 2010, 13.
4 Pravin N. Sheth, *Global Terrorism*. New Delhi: Rawat Publications, 2005, 365.
5 Ibid., 4.
6 National Investigation Agency, Ministry of Home Affairs, Govt of India (2013).
7 M. K. Narayanan, "800 Terror Cells Active in Country", Times of India, 12 August 2008.
8 "Country Reports on Terrorism 2012", Department of States, United States, (May 2013).
9 K. Alan Kronstadt, Pakistan-U.S Relations Congregational Research Service (USA), 24 May 2012, 22-24, 39-41.
10 Gerald Chaliand, *Terrorism from Popular Struggle to Media Spectacle*. London: Saqi Books, 1985, 80-84.
11 Amy, Zalman. *State Terrorism Uses Violence and Fear to Maintain Power*, 2016. *http://terrorism.about.com/od/whatisterroris1/a/StateTerrorism.htm.*
12 Ibid.
13 Ibid.
14 Mohammad Mohaddessin, *Islamic Fundamentalism: The New Global Threat,* New Delhi: Anmol Publications Pvt. Ltd., 2003, xix.
15 Ibid.
16 Ibid., 29.
17 Asghar Ali Engineer, *Islam: Challenges in 21st Century*. New Delhi: Gyan Publishing House, 2004, 79.
18 *Concise Oxford English Dictionary*, 8th edition, 1989 s.v. "Fundamentalism," by R. E. Allen.
19 *The Harper Collins Dictionary of Religion*, s.v. "Religious Fundamentalism," by S. Jonathan.
20 Krishna Kumar, *Religious Fundamentalism in India and Beyond,* 2002, http://www.carlisle.army.mil/usawc/parameters/Articles/02autumn/kumar.pdf.
21 S. L Verma, *Beyond Hindutva*. Jaipur: Rawat Publications, 2008, 219.

22 Krishna Kumar, *Religious Fundamentalism in India and Beyond,* 2002, http://www.carlisle.army.mil/usawc/parameters/Articles/02autumn/kumar.pdf.
23 Krishna Kumar, *Religious Fundamentalism in India and Beyond,* 2002, *http*://www.carlisle.army.mil/usawc/parameters/Articles/02autumn/kumar.pdf.
24 Ibid.
25 Varghese, "Learn from Israel," *The Week*, 10 August, 2008, 10.
26 S. L. Verma, Beyond *Hindutva*. Jaipur: Rawat Publications, 2008, 220.
27 Gerald Chaliand, *Terrorism from Popular Struggle to Media Spectacle*, London: Saqi Books, 1985, 98.
28 Chinmaya R. Gharekhan, "To be a Fundamentalist Hindu." *The Indian Express*, 28 July 2014.
29 Moussalli, Ahmad S. "Islamic Democracy and Pluralism" in *Progressive Muslims,* ed. Omid Safi. 286-305. Oxford: One Word Publications, 2006, 296.

12

The Role of Soft Power and Hard Power in Nation Building

Francis Arackal Thummy
Amity University, Gurgaon

Abstract: Until the 1990s, the international community seemed to have been aware only of hard power, even when they weren't familiar with the term 'hard-power'. Joseph Nye is credited with coining the term 'soft power'. The term arose from a deeper reflection of the effectiveness of the foreign policy of his country – the US – in those times. Since then the term has caught everyone's attention, especially that of the diplomatic community. The full sense of how a nation is built comes through the recognition that is accorded to it by the international community. For instance, the US is considered a super-power and China a rising power by the international community. India has been an inherently soft power country, with its soft power credentials going back millennia, though it might have never been recognized as such. India-born religions, its culture, and diaspora have influenced various parts of the world as perhaps no other country has done. At present India as a nation is recognized as an emerging power in and through its soft power – democracy, diplomacy, culture, cultural products, economy, language, media, educational, software, and managerial skills – and hard power, exemplified through its military might. The paper would like to argue that in today's international relations soft power is more helpful than hard power in building and showcasing India.

1. Introduction

Every nation on earth has its unique soft and hard power that is used to build itself up. While awareness about hard power was generally widespread, almost in every nation, it was not so about soft power. This came home to me while I was teaching Master's students in Journalism and Mass Communication. The students weren't even aware of what 'soft power' is. "India has soft power in abundance", exclaimed an editorial in *The Economist*.[1] The weekly while describing soft power also mentions hard power.

For, soft power cannot easily be separated from hard power. According to *The Economist*: "Although, poorer and less economically dynamic than China, India has soft power in abundance. It is committed to democratic institutions, the rule of law and human rights. As a victim of jihadist violence, it is in the front rank of the fight against terrorism. It has a huge and talented diaspora. It may not want to be co-opted by the West but it shares many Western values. It is confident and culturally rich. If it had a permanent Security Council seat (which it has earned by being one of the most consistent contributors to UN peacekeeping operations) it would not instinctively excuse and defend brutal regimes. Unlike China and Russia, it has few skeletons in its cupboard. With its enormous coastline and respected navy (rated by its American counterpart, with which it often holds exercises, as up to NATO standard) India is well-placed to provide security in a critical part of the global commons."[2] While the international community acknowledges the soft and hard power of India, the million dollar question is how India will use these powers to build the nation up in the days and years to come.

2. Clarifying Terms

2.1 Soft Power

Joseph S. Nye Jr. was the first to develop the concept of 'soft power' in *Bound to Lead* published in 1990. Nye was of the view that his country the United States was the strongest nation not only in military and economic power, but also in a third dimension which he called 'soft power.'[3] According to Nye, "It is the ability to get what you want through attraction rather than coercion or payments. It arises from the attractiveness of a country's culture, political ideals, and policies. When our policies are seen as legitimate in the eyes of others, our soft power is enhanced."[4] Soft power rests on the ability to shape the preferences of others. Soft power is about a world in which international institutions matter, in which war is not the only way to settle conflicts and in which the ones to succeed are the most powerful, in terms of natural, economic and financial resources and are not necessarily the best equipped. In this sense a state, an organization or a single person can exercise power with means other than violence and force. Persuasion, example, seduction, and myth: these are the resources of soft power.

"Soft power is a staple of daily democratic politics. The ability to establish preferences tends to be associated with intangible assets such as an attractive personality, culture, political values and institutions, and policies that are seen as legitimate or having moral authority."[5] Soft power has to be distinguished from influence since influence can also rest on the hard power of threats or payments. Soft power is also to be distinguished from persuasion though it is an important part of it. In fact, soft power has the ability to attract … "in behavioural terms soft power is attractive power."[6] Since the 1990s, when the concept entered into public discourse, it has been used by diplomats, political leaders, editors, as well as academics around the world.

2.2 Hard Power

Hard power is symbolized by military and economic might, which "often get others to change their position."[7] "Hard power can rest on inducements ("carrots") or threats ("sticks")."[8] Hard power is commonly associated in International Relations with realism, as if there is no other alternative in dealing with another country – enemy, rogue, and other undesirables. So the use of power politics, force, threat, and violence is seen as being the only option and therefore justified. Hard power is, to a certain extent, the oldest form of power and history is replete with examples of its use. It is connected to the idea of an anarchic, untamed international system (a "State of Nature" as it were), where countries do not recognize any superior authority. It is the situation of free-for-all; might is right. Order is the result of competition for power and wars.

2.3 Smart Power

Smart power is a new and to a certain extent popular concept, which was coined by Nye and is used to describe a new way of dealing with and managing power. Nye conceptualizes smart power as something lying somewhere between hard and soft power, a sort of "third way" in the complex jungle of power relations. Nye stresses that smart power is something "beyond" hard and soft, a sort of new approach that fits particularly well into the realm of international relations and foreign politics. In other words, the ability to seamlessly combine soft and hard power is smart power.[9]

3. Nation

A nation is "a large aggregate of people united by common descent, history, culture, or traditions, language, who recognize common interests and the need for a single sovereign, inhabiting a particular country or territory."[10] A nation is a cultural entity whereas a state is a legal entity. Max Weber provided the classic definition of the state: A state is a human community that (successfully) claims the monopoly of the legitimate use of physical force within a given territory. Note that "territory" is one of the characteristics of the state. Specifically, at the present time, the right to use physical force is ascribed to other institutions or to individuals only to the extent to which the state permits it.[11] A nation is very much hinged on to the concept of nation-state. A nation-state is a political entity (a state) associated with a particular cultural entity (a nation). Further it can be described as a political unit consisting of an autonomous state inhabited predominantly by a people who share a common culture, history, and language. India is a new type of nation-state, because its people were not all of the same ethnicity, culture, and language, as had been thought to be the case when the concept of nation-state was earlier defined.

3.1 Nation-Building

Nation-building is a normative concept that means different things to different people. It is important to look at the evolution of theories of nation-building and at the other concepts which it has both supplanted and included. Many people believe that nation-building is evolutionary rather than revolutionary, that it takes a long time and is a social process that cannot be jump-started from outside. In its preliminary meaning nation-building is equated with the formation of a nation. For instance, the evolution of the Italian city-states into a nation, the German city-states into the Zollverein customs union and later a nation, the multiple languages and cultural groups in France into the nation of France, the development of China from the warring kingdoms, the stitching together of India from nearly 500 kingdoms.

Such formation took a very long time, and was the result, not only of political leadership, but of changes in technology and economic processes (the agricultural and then industrial revolutions), as well as communication, culture and civil society, and many other factors.[12] There has been a tendency to impose nation-building from outside: "The use of armed force in the aftermath of a conflict to underpin an enduring transition to democracy."[13] This was the case with Germany, Japan, Somalia, Haiti, Bosnia, Kosovo, Afghanistan, and Iraq in which American military power was used in the aftermath of a conflict to underpin the importance of democratization. Another very significant understanding of nation-building is that it is the work of the people within a nation. This is the sense that has been used in this paper. Although, India is a new type of nation-state, as mentioned earlier, there is a shared common national identity and part of nation-building is the building of that common identity.

Nation-building is essential because a strong state is necessary in order to provide security, and the building of an integrated national community is important in the building of a state. Nation-building implies democratization, not from without but from within. It stems from the democratic peace hypothesis. The seventeenth century philosopher Immanuel Kant is said to have put forward this hypothesis, which states that "perpetual peace can be achieved by developing a federation or league of free republican nations. Representative democracies, organized in an international organization, would bring peace.

Political scientists who have explored this hypothesis have focused on one of two versions: democracies don't make war against each other, or democracies don't initiate war at all. There is certainly evidence of the former, and some evidence of the latter."[14]

4. India's Soft Power

4.1 Diplomacy

Since its independence in 1947, India has not gone to war with any other nation with territorial ambitions. Rather when tensions arose between and among nations, India has always advocated diplomacy as a means to resolve conflicts. The country has always upheld the legitimacy of the United Nations as the organ to bring peace in troubled areas and situations. During the Cold War between the superpowers, the United States and the then USSR, India along with Egypt, and erstwhile Yugoslavia took the lead to form the Non-Aligned Movement (NAM) rather than join with either of the parties involved in the Cold War.

NAM, under India's leadership, played a great role in lessening tensions and resolving conflicts in international relations. Today even under great provocations from its neighbours – China and Pakistan – India has been advocating diplomacy to solve outstanding issues. China, being a one party dictatorship fail to understand democratic language and Pakistan's democracy is in shambles due to the constant interference of the armed forces and the ISI. Over decades India's soft power used through its diplomats and diplomacy, has been held in high esteem by the international community. Member countries in the UN support India's view-points because of attraction and not coercion. In some circumstances aggressive postures can destroy rather than create soft power. The latest example is China's aggressive posturing with regard to the South China Sea, which has been opposed by most countries in the region.

4.2 Democracy

India has always been a democracy since its independence as a modern nation-state. In the Rising India story, its democracy is an important component of its soft power. This aspect has come into the global limelight where a civilization-state with more than one billion diverse people is growing economically at a good pace under a democratically-elected government. Nye argues that India has a considerable soft power advantage over China in being a democratic country.[15] "One anonymous Chinese scholar believes that it is India's decentralized democracy that has managed to hold together a poor, populous, and linguistically and religiously diverse country... for the first time ever, the Chinese are finding that India's democracy is an advantage."[16]

4.3 Religious Diversity

India is a cradle of many world religions – Hinduism, Buddhism, Jainism and Sikhism. At the same time, the country has whole-heartedly welcomed other religions and facilitated their practice and spread along the length and breadth of its territory. Shortly India will have the largest number of people in the world who will practice Islam. This religious pluralism of India adds to its soft power for India's religious diversity is unique as no other.

4.4 Culture

Indian culture is an amalgamation of many, varied, regional and state cultures. It has been influenced by a history that is several millennia old. Today its culture is manifested mainly through a variety of dance forms and films, especially Bollywood. The Indian diaspora have played a major role in carrying and transmitting Indian culture across the world and this culture has been one of the most important components of its soft power.

4.5 Language

It might be difficult to find another country other than India where 22 major languages with 13 different scripts and nearly 720 dialects are spoken. This is the linguistic beauty of our country which forms yet another component of its soft power. An average Indian speaks three to four languages, which makes his ability to learn a new language that much easier. Internationally Indians are recognized to have an easier facility to learn new languages.

4.6 Economy

India is the third largest economy, after the US and China, in the world in terms of purchasing power. Some scholars talk about the "New Delhi Consensus", meaning economic development under a democratic rule. This is seen as a better model for Third World economies than the "Beijing Consensus" based on economic development under tight political control. Here, we might also recall what Nobel-laureate economist Amartya Sen said regarding the necessity of freedom for true economic development.[17] To put the issue of economic development in perspective one has to look at China. It is said democratic India's economic success over the last couple of decades has caused Chinese citizenry, at least among the intellectual class, to develop an extremely positive outlook towards Indian democracy.[18]

4.7 Media

As mentioned earlier one of the components of India's soft power is its democracy. But democracy can survive only with the existence of a free press. India is the largest democracy in the world. If it is considered a vibrant democracy by the international community, then it cannot be so without a free press. Since independence, with the exception of the Emergency period (1975-77)[19] the press in India has been fairly free. Jawaharlal Nehru, the first Prime Minister, had said he would rather have a completely free press with all dangers involved in the wrong use of that freedom than a suppressed or regulated press. Freedom of press does not enjoy any special mention in the Indian Constitution, but courts have ruled that it is synonymous with the right to freedom of speech and expression under Article 19(1) (a).[20]

4.8 Population

India is the second most populous country in the world - 1.252 billion (2013). Until a few years back this large population was seen as a great burden on the country. But today the whole world speaks of India's demographic advantage or dividend. In other words, the country's demographic weight will be such that she will not need to approach Western standards of living to achieve great-power standing. India has the largest number of young people in the world in the age group of 18-25. It is set to become the youngest country in the world by 2020 with 64 percent of its population in working age group. Current predictions suggest a steady increase in the youth population to 464 million by 2021 and finally a decline to 458 million by 2026.[21]

4.9 Other Soft-Power Skills (managerial, relational, IT, educational ...)

Indians are acknowledged to make good managers. This is due to the human resource management abilities, which comes to them almost naturally. This is credited partly due to the family ties that Indians maintain. As I write this paper many multinational corporations such as Google, Microsoft, Pepsi, to name a few, are headed by persons of Indian origin.[22] Besides aspiration, and the advantage of being fluent in English, what makes Indians stand apart is their understanding of the emerging markets, which is where the future is for many multinational corporations (especially tech ones), engineering ability (builders rather than sellers), and above all basic humility in the work place, which is helpful in "rolling back the dice so that they can make amends before a situation spirals out of control."[23] Even with the inherent limitations that the country is facing the education system is considered as one of the best in the world today – in Science and Maths Indian students excel much better than their counterparts in the Western world.

4.10 India's Deployment of Soft Power

India's largely free media – newspapers, television channels, online sites - have been the primary vehicle of its soft power. The digital revolution has enabled the nation to spread Indian ideas – Ayurveda, Yoga, Bollywood films, and other cultural products – to all corners of the globe, largely through the increasingly vocal and visible 25-million strong Indian diaspora. And the mostly English-fluent diaspora have made their presence felt internationally through global corporate, publishing, and marketing networks.

5. India's Hard Power

According to Shah "India, which has traditionally talked of the power of argument began to talk of the argument of power."[24] India's annual military budget is nearly $51.3 billion. In recent times the country has begun to realize the role of hard power to secure its national interests and also to make her voice heard in international politics. India's growing military profile is more significantly felt in the maritime domain. The prime military focus of India seems to have overshot Pakistan as it attempts to obtain a place in the international arena. By 2020, it seems as if Pakistan will lie on the periphery of India's military focus.

5.1 Military

With 1,325,450 active personnel and 1,155,000 personnel in reserves, India's armed forces are the third largest in the world. Since independence, the country has fought four wars: with China in 1962, and with Pakistan in 1965, 1971 and 1999. With the exception of the 1962 war with China, India has won the other three wars. Sections of the Indian armed forces have regularly been deputed by the United Nations as peace-keeping forces in various parts of the world. India's geographical location (a peninsular country), its neighbourhood (existence of unfriendly countries in the west and the north), and size (ranked seventh) make it imperative for it to have a very large force. And with a coastline of 7,516.6 kilometres, which is very vulnerable to external threats, the armed forces guarantee the safety, security, and integrity of the country.

5.2 Nation's Size

India is the seventh-largest country in the world, with a total area of 3,287,263 square kilometres (1,269,219 sq miles). It measures 3,214 km (1,997 miles) from north to south and 2,933 km (1,822 miles) from east to west. It is Asia's second largest country after China. Generally, and to an extent, the large size of a country reflects its might and helps the country to exert its influence and apply pressure on a whole lot of issues in the neighbourhood and beyond, mainly in a positive manner.

5.3 India's Deployment of Hard Power

India is known among the international community as a pacifist country, and it has an image of being a "soft country". And yet India has a very large military force, the third largest, after the US and China. In political parlance to possess such a large military power for a country with the size of India, in terms of territory and demography, is a given. But its hard power is meant primarily for self-defense and for preserving its territorial integrity. Increasingly India has been deploying its hard power along its borders, without in anyway threatening its neighbours, due to the prevailing security scenario in the South-Asian region. India cannot be expected to be a mere onlooker in the present geo-politico-economic situation of the world. India has deployed its hard power at UN's behest for peace-keeping in various parts of the world. Besides, the hard power is transformed into soft power when the armed forces engages in disaster relief in various parts of the country.

6. India's soft power and hard power in comparison with that of China

India and China are seen as the global movers of the twenty-first century giving legitimacy to the now familiar saying that this century would belong to Asia. One-third of the global population will be living in these two countries. Hence, it is relevant to compare the soft and hard power of these two Asian giants.

To all appearances, India is predominantly a soft power nation whereas China is perceived as a hard power nation, with the largest military in the world. "India, just like China, is not only a nation-state, it's also a civilization-state which is a very important element of soft power, as Nye says. India is the only country that can share the Chinese claim to great power status based on its 5000 year-old civilization."[25] When compared to China, India's soft power is seen through her vibrant democracy, which by now has been sited world-wide as a model for many countries especially in the Asian continent. "The fact that India could grow economically at more than seven percent over the last two decades under a democratic government is an ideological threat to the authoritarian China."[26] But realizing the increasing importance of soft power China is leaving no stone unturned to promote its soft-power side. It has started establishing 'Confucius Centres' in many countries of the world to promote its Chinese language, culture, cuisine, art, architecture, and tourism. Besides, China has embarked on giving financial and infrastructural help to many countries specially the ASEAN countries.

7. Challenges faced by India's soft power

Democracy, religious and ethnic diversity have been significant pointers over many decades to India's soft power. Lately however, with the Bharatiya Janata Party (BJP) in power and supported by Hindu fundamentalists, there have been much misgivings with regard to the survival of democratic institutions and the acceptance and respect for religious diversity by the majority community in India. For instance, tribals, Dalits, and other religious and ethnic minorities have been discriminated on various counts, especially on the basis of caste. A report also says that a demographic dividend is very unlikely to accrue to India anytime soon, as a large share of the country's youth lacks education (quality education) as well as jobs to deliver this productivity.[27]

8. Challenges faced by India's hard power

Resource crunch – both financial and human – are challenges to India's hard power. Considering the security scenario in India's neighbourhood, especially with China and Pakistan, it needs an enormous amount of financial resources to update its armed forces. Limitations placed by the national budget makes this task difficult. Though, India's military are ranked third in the world in terms of strength, the budget ranking is only sixth in the world with $51.3 billion amounting to only 2 percent of GDP.[28] Qualified personnel are another challenge. Thousands of officer-level posts are vacant in the armed forces due to a shortage of qualified personnel. The country's dependence on importing its required quantity and quality of defense equipment is yet another challenge. Its efforts to produce such equipment indigenously have not produced the desired result as its R&D has been lackluster and below international standards.

9. India's soft power and hard power: The future scenario

By 2050, India is expected to have the largest pool of skilled workers in the world. In this sense it will be in an advantageous position, compared even to China. Indian workers might have to span out to other countries to assist them. Indian culture would have made its presence felt in many parts of the world through its films, music, language, various dance forms, Yoga, cuisine, tourism, medical practices (especially Ayurveda), etc. As the emphasis is increasingly on the use of soft power in international relations and diplomacy there is bound to be less relevance to hard power which will of course take new forms in the shape of laser wars, robotic, and other high-tech space equipment.

10. Conclusion

The philosophy of soft power arose primarily from the recognition of the failure of using hard power to solve the myriad problems confronting humanity. In fact it will not be too far-fetched to state that the Philosophy of Non-violence had its genesis in soft power, which is in vogue today in international relations across the globe. As an emerging power of the twenty-first century, India would do well to take care that its policies at home and abroad are consistent with democracy, transparency, human rights, and respect for the opinion of others. In short the nation's stature in the global community will depend upon her developing a deeper understanding of the role of soft power and hard power in the present global scenario and balancing them in her foreign policy – that will be smart power.

Notes

1 <http://www.economist.com/news/leaders/21574511-indias-lack-strategic-culture-hobbles-its-ambition-be-force-world-can-india> (12 September, 2016).

2 <http://www.economist.com/news/leaders/21574511-indias-lack-strategic-culture-hobbles-its-ambition-be-force-world-can-india> (12 September, 2016).

3 Joseph S. Nye, Jr., *Soft Power: The Means to Success in World Politics* (New York: Public Affairs Books, 2004), xi.

4 Joseph S. Nye, Jr., *Soft Power: The Means to Success in World Politics* (New York: Public Affairs Books, 2004), x.

5 Joseph S. Nye, Jr., *Soft Power: The Means to Success in World Politics* (New York: Public Affairs Books, 2004), 6.

6 Nye, Jr., 6.

7 Joseph S. Nye, Jr., *Soft Power: The Means to Success in World Politics* (New York: Public Affairs Books, 2004), 5.

8 Nye, Jr., 5.

9 Nye, Jr., 32.

10 Roger Scruton, *Dictionary of Political Thought* (New York: Palgrave Macmillan, 2007), 462.

11 Max Weber "Politics as a Vocation," in H.H. Gerth and C. Wright Mills (Translated and Edited) (New York: Oxford University Press, 1946), 48.

12 Carolyn Stephenson "Nation Building." Beyond Intractability. Eds. Guy Burgess and Heidi Burgess. Conflict Information Consortium, University of Colorado, Boulder. Posted: January 2005 <http://www.beyondintractability.org/essay/nation-building> (12 September, 2016).

13 James Dobbins "Nation Building" http://www.rand.org/pubs/periodicals/rand-review/issues/summer2003/nation1.html (24 September, 2016).

14 Stephenson<http://www.beyondintractability.org/essay/nation-building> (12 September, 2016).

15 S. K. Shah, *India and China: The Battle between Soft and Hard Power* (New Delhi: Alpha Editions, 2005), 29.

16 S. K. Shah, 30.

17 See Amartya Sen, *Development as Freedom* (New York: Anchor, 2000).

18 S. K. Shah, 30.

19 Mrs. Indira Gandhi, Prime Minister of India, declared a national emergency during which the press freedom was curtailed almost completely.

20 See Francis Arackal, *The Indian Media: How Credible*? (Bombay: Better Yourself Books, 2010), 57-61.

21 Girija Shivakumar, *India set to become the Youngest Country by 2020*, April 17, 2013 http://www.thehindu.com/news/national/india-is-set-to-become-the-youngest-country-by-2020/article4624347.ece (22 September, 2016).

22 Indira Nooyi, the Chairperson & CEO of PepsiCo attributed her success to her Indian upbringing (One can read more about this in the following link<http://www.thehindu.com/news/national/indra-nooyi-attributes-her-success-to-indian-upbringing/article5615675.ece> (22 September, 2016).

23 Sahil Mohan Gupta 2015 "Five Reasons Why Indians Make Great Tech CEOs"<http://www.dailyo.in/technology/india-born-ceos-sundar-pichai-satya-nadella-rajiv-suri-shantanu-narayen-larry-page-sergey-brin-google-microsoft-nokia-adobe/story/1/5608.html> (22 September, 2016).

24 S. K. Shah, 18.

25 S. K. Shah, 29.

26 S. K. Shah, 29.

27 "Democratic Dividend Unlikely to Accrue to India Any Time Soon" (*Economic Times*, 6 April, 2016) <http://articles.economictimes.indiatimes.com/keyword/demographic-dividend (25 April, 2016).

28 2016 Figures.

13

Multiculturalism and Recognition in the Context of Nation Building

Western Questions and the Indian Experience

Dolreich Pereira
St. Pius X College, Mumbai

Abstract: In what seems to be a global phenomenon, many public institutions, including government agencies, educational institutions, and even international sports associations, have been criticized for failing to recognize or respect the particular cultural identities of citizens. In the context of nation building, what does it mean for citizens with different cultural identities, often based on ethnicity, race, language, gender or religion, to recognize themselves as equals in the way they are treated in a political and civil society? Are the reflections of Western thinkers open to the various achievements of different cultural eras or are their discourses poor and fixed in a monochrome perspective? Proponents of multiculturalism policies, argue that cultural exclusion is a by-product of economic and political exclusions and that once they are resolved, cultural exclusion will disappear by itself. They state that these policies are not only effective but even indispensable. Philosophically, the concept of cultural liberty goes beyond the liberal-communitarian debate. In fact, it no longer attempts to reconcile the individual cultures and universal values but seeks to complement and strengthen human rights. In this essay we take a look at multiculturalism, its challenges and the politics of recognition which plague democratic societies today, especially in the context of a liberal Indian democracy.

Introduction

In what seems to be a global phenomenon, many public institutions, including government agencies, educational institutions, and even international sports associations are criticized for their failure to recognize or respect the particular cultural identities of citizens. In India, the controversy involves issues such as reservations for Dalits and OBCs, various problems that involve minority groups of all types, taboos on what may be eaten and what is prohibited, etc. "It is hard to find a democratic or democratizing society these days that is not the site of some significant controversy over whether and how its public institutions should better recognize the identities of cultural and disadvantaged minorities."[1]

So in the context of nation building, this raises the question: what does it mean for citizens with different cultural identities, often based on ethnicity, race, language, gender or religion, to recognize themselves as equals in the way they are treated in a political and civil society? How does this affect the way their children are educated in government schools or the manner in which social and economic policies are formulated? This essay focuses on the challenges of multiculturalism and the politics of recognition which plague democratic societies today.

The term "recognition" does not belong to any traditional political vocabulary or to the classical vocabulary of humanities. Yet, it has become essential recently as the subject of collective concern as well as in philosophical, sociological and psychosocial theories. On the stage of labour and, in particular, social exclusion, the theory of recognition helps us to deal with social problems and political rights.

There are various debates today which involve the subject of recognition: acts of genocide committed in the past, "marriage" of homosexuals and gay parenting, and participation of the Church in the dark episodes of slavery and colonization among others. In addition, social struggles have emerged claiming recognition rather than rights or wage increases. The burning question of "contempt" and the increasing demands for "respect" which are associated in many parts of the world are clearly part of a recognition problem. Finally, the struggle for the defense or the preservation of collective identities, cultures, or minority or regional languages are presented sometimes as fighting for recognition.

This poses a question all democratic societies, whose basic principle is the equal treatment of all citizens: can they recognize different identities? Today, communities or groups with differing philosophical convictions, religious or moral principles, cultures, lifestyles and sexual practices, live in the same territory. What would be the political principles that govern their coexistence while, at the same time, recognize their different identities? John Rawls and

Jurgen Habermas respond to this fundamental issue by proposing a system based on a common minimum which unites differences, the principles of justice and human rights for the former and communication and constitutional patriotism for the latter. But in the eyes of communitarians, these models, based on universalism and the Kantian conception of autonomy of the subject are incapable of recognizing the various identities and produce ethical-political deadlocks which are difficult to overcome.[2] Developed in the United States and Canada since the late 1970s, the communitarian thinking has tended to become almost a new ideology in the USA. Against the excesses and trivial manifestations of liberal individualism, communitarianism proposes a return to family, religious and cultural values as well as the reconstruction of social ties based on the cross-community network.

In this essay, we will first study the thought of Charles Taylor and some other reflections on multiculturalism. Then, we will attempt a brief study of Indian democracy to evaluate how it addresses the problem of multiple affiliations and recognition. Finally, we will attempt a synthesis between the pragmatic construction of this territory and theorizing.

Let us now take a look at multiculturalism according to Taylor, one of the main theorists of communitarianism, and who is most written about on the subject. He remarks that the universal principle inherited from the Enlightenment had reached its limits and can no longer meet "the demand and the need for recognition of different cultural identities. It generates non-recognition or ignorance of those who do not share the same values as the majority and becomes the cause of many social conflicts."[3] In "Multiculturalism: difference and democracy", Taylor introduced the issue of recognition while referring to the development of the notions of honour and dignity.

Conducted in varied fields of philosophy (epistemology, hermeneutics, philosophy of language, ethics, etc.), Taylor's investigations combine to emphasize the primary role of community belongingness in the formation of identity - both individual as well as collective. They also converge towards an ardent defense of the plurality of conceptions of the good that reinforce the ethical and political life of democratic societies.

In addition, the central role that recognition plays, is due to two changes which, according to Taylor, have marked the history of democratic modernity. With the collapse of the society of the old regime,[4] the "egalitarian revolution" substituted dignity for honour. It showed a concept of identity that was deeply universal and egalitarian. But referring to Johann Gottfried Herder, Taylor isolates a second "turning point", described by him as an "expressivist revolution"[5]: the Romantic ideal of authenticity enjoins us to cultivate our cultural differences as many specific ways to realize our humanity. Linked to each other, these two changes lead to recognition becoming pivotal in the quest for identity, and also the direction toward which all human activity moves.

An individual's identity which occurs in an era of equality should be "internally generated" that is, it must be associated with a pre-existing structure. This is not an identity assigned to them according to their situation and their position in a hierarchical order.

Thus, Taylor proposes a model of recognition that can be summarized in two aspects. The first is the need of a point or a base unit where people can feel united in the same project (the community). The second is the negotiation of identity by recognizing each other - recognition signifying "acceptance of equal value". That's why Taylor puts forward this strong thesis: "Recognition is not just a courtesy that one does to people, it is a vital human need."[6]

Taylor also aims to make political liberalism more "hospitable to difference". He outlines a republican mode which is close to the doctrine of "civic humanism". In order that this statement may also apply to minority communities we must ensure through public measures the survival of the community, so that future generations can enjoy capacity, rights or values we consider essential for ourselves.

Collective rights as conceived by Taylor concerns the rights granted to endangered cultural groups, and to ensure the achievement of collective purposes of minorities.

However, there are several elements in Taylor's philosophy that make the conflict between individual rights and collective rights more acute. Most importantly, when there is a conflict, Taylor recommends the extremely perilous exercise of distinguishing within the system of human rights, on one hand, the "fundamental freedoms" that are really inviolable and, on the other hand, all the "immunities and privileges" that can be "revoked and restricted for public policy reasons."

Multiculturalism also poses some questions for a democracy. Faced with such uncertainty, there is some concern about the presence of shadows in Taylor's thinking. For example, how to define multiculturalism? It corresponds to a cultural, political or religious diversity. It can be a prescriptive model of integration, a willingness on the part of states to control cultural difference, or an established fact, unique to modern society that characterizes the coexistence of different cultural or ethnic groups.

In France, multiculturalism occurs due to immigration, but also on account of strong regional identities such as Basque or Corsican cultures. France, however, is an old nation state, whose national society is highly integrated.[7] It is attached to Republican values and secularism (*la laïcité*), which requires the complete separation of politics and religion, the latter being confined to the private area. It thus resists any recognition of cultural particularities in politics, and acknowledges only individual citizens. On this point, it is unlike India which recognizes that minorities are a component of the state. Let us now take a look at multiculturalism in the context of a liberal Indian democracy.

India sought to integrate multiculturalism in its political and social life since its creation as a modern State in 1947. The Indian Union recognizes the linguistic diversity of its population: Hindi is the official language of the federal state alongside English and 20 other languages which have official status in the States where they are mainly spoken. Furthermore, a trilingual education is practiced in schools. Children are educated in the official language of their state (Marathi in Maharashtra, for example) and also learn both official languages, Hindi and English. The Indian Union also recognizes the religious diversity of its population officially celebrating five Hindu holidays, four Muslim holidays, two Christian holidays, and one holiday each for Buddhists, Sikhs, Jains and Parsis. The Central government is even trying to exercise legal pluralism, recognizing the role of standards and judicial institutions of communities. Finally, it ensures the representation of tribes and scheduled castes by reserving seats in the assembly.

As demonstrated by the constitutional structure of India, it is possible to respect cultural diversity without challenging the nation state. In multicultural, multiethnic and multiracial societies like ours, social justice, economic progress and democracy can only be achieved by reconciling the requirements arising from identities and diverse interests. The legal and judicial systems derive their legitimacy from the fact that they cannot allow the needs of one group to move ahead of others or, even worse, make them fall into oblivion. Therefore, in India, at least in principle, pluralism combines different cultures with the spirit of liberal democracy.

In a multiethnic society, it is not enough to balance majority and minority; in a liberal democracy, one must also address the issue of social and distributive justice. If a multicultural democratic society does not demonstrate openness to diverse identities that constitute it, it will risk remaining a majoritarian democracy that harms its minorities.

The framers of the Constitution were fully aware of the fact that India formed a multi-ethnic society, but they have not neglected so far its aspiration for integration and unity. Such concerns seemed natural given the aftermath of the partition of the country that led to the creation of Pakistan in 1947, and it is in this context that a very particular kind of federal governance was considered. Over time, it became clear that a multipolar federalism was the best way to satisfy the wishes of cultural groups. The socio-economic diversity of the country has given its importance to the transactional dimension of Indian federalism: decentralized decision-making has led to a consensual democracy.

In India, the formation and reorganization of States took into account many elements: geographical proximity, common language, similarity of customs, equivalence of levels of socioeconomic and political development, community traditions and historical experiences, approximation of lifestyles, looking for administrative opportunities and, more importantly, the widespread feeling of social unity, i.e. a certain common identity. This effort of recognizing multiple cultures present in the country, however, leaves open the question of "Indian identity". For some, this identity is in Hinduism, which deeply structures Indian society and in particular the caste system, which in itself causes other problems of recognition. Let us now look at the politics of recognition of the Dalits and its consequences.

In terms of the Constitution that Dr. Ambedkar succeeded in crafting, untouchability was abolished by law and its practice recognized as criminal. Given the historical handicap of Dalits and tribals, two quotas were established by decree. In all places of higher education, as in all government jobs, a quota of 17 percent was allocated to Dalits. A fixed number of seats are also reserved for them in Parliament.

How have these measures served the Dalits? The practice of untouchability is certainly illegal, but it still persists widely, especially in the villages. Bereft of economic and political means, Dalits have few opportunities in seeking recourse to judicial justice. If they turn to the police to complain about this or that abuse, the police may refuse to register their complaint, or drag out the investigation over a very long period of time. In case of legal proceedings, they may not find witnesses willing to testify. The state and the police apparatus are controlled by the dominant castes. However, we can estimate that the situation is changing, albeit slowly, at least in some places. The more aware and better organized Dalits have begun to retaliate: violence for violence, life for life, so that in some areas a balance of terror maintains an uncomfortable peace.

Insofar as there is no real literacy and development programme, it is the poor Dalits among others who are paying the price: they do not have much access to the quotas under which they have a right to higher education and government services. In Kocheril Raman Narayan, India had a Dalit President, but he was the exception that proves the rule. In politics, Dalits elected to Parliament belong to different political parties and cannot do much to improve their lot without the support of their party. They often acquire support in words but not in deeds as their parties cannot really act because they are controlled by the dominant castes and are beholden to them.

From this point of view, the situation seems rather worse: new parties and political alliances are being formed increasingly on the basis of caste. This has led to Dalits forming their own political parties, which are mindful of the limitations of being caste based. And given the percentage of population they represent, they cannot hope to exist without political support from other parties. The positive side is that, around the country, Dalits have become aware of their situation and fight stubbornly for their empowerment.

The caste system, as a whole, must be transformed. However, it is extremely difficult to change socio-cultural attitudes. If Dalits, as a group, are to be liberated, assume their identity and enjoy social and political freedom, it would require that the other groups "recognize" their new status. It is within this context that the debate on multiculturalism and the politics of recognition can be useful and should be explored. The acuteness of the question of castes, however, should not overshadow other areas where the question of diverse identities remains an issue.

Like federal India, which is multiethnic and heterogeneous by nature, several states have developed a social cohesion based on heterogeneity rather than one identity. So they often form coherent political and administrative entities, even if they do not embody a single identity, but synthesize several. Some states pride themselves in defending a very specific culture. Others claim ethnic particularism, like Tamil Nadu, Karnataka and Kerala. In yet another grouping, regional identities are subsumed by the dominant language, such as in Maharashtra, Gujarat and Bengal. They all represent what might be called single-identity states. On the other hand, large composite states like Uttar Pradesh reflect a mosaic of settings: language/dialect, social composition of communities, ethnic regions, demographic characteristics, territorial contiguity, cultural pattern, economic, historical antecedents; all these constitute the political and psychological background to be taken into account to allow conscious identification with a group and as state citizens.

Thus, the importance given to territory has proved to be more useful to establish a system based on diversity within nation states and ensure that the cultural and ethnic differences do not lead to further disparities between groups. In addition, at least in principle, different groups do not perceive each other as superior or inferior. The Indian national spirit is generally based on the development of a societal ethos that facilitates the coexistence of a variety of groups within one country by the sharing of skills. To adopt pluralism as a fundamental value is a giant step in promoting equity and identity within a single political system.

For many observers (including those who are not hostile in principle to multiculturalism), multiculturalist policies would be a failure, not only because of their limited effectiveness, but also the danger they seem to convey.

First, their effectiveness would be limited insofar as they would not change the foundation of social inequalities but mainly benefit the "community leaders" who tend to manipulate or divert them to their profit. Second, it would be dangerous to the extent that they threaten to reify cultural phenomena, which are however by definition fluid. How does one define, in fact, the people to whom multiculturalist policies should apply without fragmenting society into arbitrary categories? In addition, multiculturalist policies that aim to fight against the injustices suffered by certain cultural groups would lead to the "freezing" of these groups. It also leads to a form of "racialization" of public policy and strengthens the hostility of groups that do not benefit from multiculturalism policies towards those who benefit.

In an era of "globalized violence", especially wanton terrorist attacks and their aftermath, the tendency would be to agree with the critics of multiculturalist policies. To cite a few examples, we see that violence is erupting in several parts of India, where Hindu nationalist hardliners are trying to impose by force a single Hindu identity in the country.

According to the World Report on Human Development 2004, affirmative action policies have been successful in reducing inequalities between ethnic groups. The Indian experience shows that affirmative action can reduce inequalities between groups.[8]

For instance, the allocation of jobs in the public service, admission to higher education and parliamentary seats allocated to scheduled castes and tribes have helped some members of these groups to get out of poverty and join the middle class. Moreover, not only would affirmative action be effective to fight against inequality, but it would also be favourable to economic development. India has managed its diverse cultures with pluralist policies and 22 official languages, and has made remarkable progress in economic growth and in the areas of health and education. These successful experiences in culturally diverse countries show the importance of pluralistic policies. Finally, the limits of multiculturalist policies, frequently referred to challenge these policies, are questionable: they would not be due to the policies themselves but the lack of effort made in their favour or sometimes clumsy implementation. None of these policies is devoid of complexity, but the experience of many countries shows that there are solutions.

In several countries where multiculturalism is practiced, it would seem that public opinion is not predominantly negative. Proponents of multiculturalism policies, however, go further: according to them, in fact, these policies are not only effective but even indispensable. Some claim that it is enough to guarantee civil and political rights such as freedom of religion, speech and association, to give individuals the opportunity to practice their religion and speak their language without being discriminated against in areas of employment and schooling, or many other types of exclusion. They argue that cultural exclusion is a by-product of economic and political exclusions and that once they are resolved, cultural exclusion will disappear by itself. This is not confirmed by facts. Many rich and democratic countries that claim to treat all citizens equally, are nonetheless places where minorities are inadequately represented in politics and for whom harassment and difficulty of access to public services is a frequent experience. Cultural freedoms can be expanded only by means of explicit policies which address the restrictions on such freedom, thus the necessity for multiculturalist policies.

Philosophically, the concept of cultural liberty goes beyond the liberal-communitarian debate. In fact, it no longer attempts to reconcile individual cultures and universal values but seeks to complement and strengthen human rights.

The ethical force of these rights depends ultimately on the importance of human freedoms and cannot be separated from that relationship. This basic recognition has far reaching consequences. Even without going into complex debates surrounding the idea of collective rights, we can easily recognize the basic need to link rights and freedoms. Will the defense of cultural diversity require us to support cultural conservatism, by asking people to stick to their own cultural history and not to experiment with other lifestyles? This would place us immediately in a position contrary to the freedom that would impede the ability to choose or change one's lifestyle, a choice that many people wish to enjoy. We would then find ourselves in the presence of a form of exclusion of a different nature: exclusion from participation, as opposed to exclusion based on lifestyle, since individual minority cultures would be excluded from participation in society in general. Nothing can be justified in the name of freedom without actually giving one the possibility of exercising that freedom, or at least without assessing how a possible choice would be exercised if it arose. In addition, cultural liberty is not opposed to equity but can be combined with it: "There is no fundamental tension - as is sometimes suggested - between freedom and equity. In reality, equity may be perceived in terms of equitable growth freedoms of all (rather than purely in terms of income distribution, or in the more limited perspective of "redistribution" from a starting point which ultimately is arbitrary)."

From a political perspective, cultural liberty is a true guide for action, separating unambiguously what falls into what category within cultural conservatism. For example, the continuation of many practices in a traditional society dominated by men may go against the interests and opportunities of women. Practices approved by the rules of some current cultures can affect the ability of a person to lead his own life and to exercise their own freedoms.

In seeking the answer to this question, it is important to place cultural liberty in a broad enough perspective. It is sometimes said, in defense of these practices, that the victims themselves typically accept these cultural rules without protest. But many injustices persist and thrive in the world by allying with the victims, and thereby depriving them of the opportunity to consider other alternatives. It is particularly important not to confuse and consider an insufficiently considered traditionalism as part of the exercise of cultural freedom. One must ask whether the poor in society had the opportunity to consider other alternatives and if they are free to know how other people live in the world. The need for serious reasoning and freedom is essential to grasp what is really at stake here.

In conclusion, it is clear that through these different topics of collective concern, the term recognition is not always taken in the same sense. In some cases, recognition means to admit that something took place, while in others, to recognize the legitimacy of a claim or, conversely, the granting of a claim is unfounded (or even to admit it to be wrong). In yet other situations, the term "recognition" can evoke a positive or negative image which others, or society itself may use to refer to individuals. Finally, it can signify not only the value of being or the actions of an individual but also collective entities that are cultural, linguistical, religious, customs, social uses, etc. The term "recognition" therefore can mean different things that in a certain way also ensures its strength. The fact that the same term is designated for so many burning issues seems to legitimize its use. The social movement of meaning through various topics of collective concern helps to prove that the issue of recognition is today a political problem worthy of attention.

Should the equal dignity of individuals be relative to all the universal rights that go with the exercise of individual freedom, as constitutional texts of both the English and French revolutions would seem to suggest, and are still supported even today by all those who are part of the tradition of political liberalism? Or should one also accept that individuals have a right to the recognition of the dignity which makes them different from each other, since the legal guarantee of freedoms may lose all meaning if the fundamental values enshrined in cultures, language and manners are not recognized?

If one chooses to retain the second of these two options, it is, according to Charles Taylor, because the contempt of cultural differences produce forms of oppression which are just as serious as a violation of universal human rights. According to him, one must accept in principle, the legitimate claims of differences in recognition. But that does not mean that in practice, any such difference is legitimate. It can only be so if it is compatible with the universal recognition of the requirements of dignity. It is in this sense that Taylor can write that "the politics of difference grows organically out of the politics of universal dignity."

Taylor's notion of "politics of recognition" gets its meaning by reflecting on the politics of difference, and this is framed in the debate between liberalism and communitarianism. There is now a broad discussion on these issues. However, if the reflections of Western thinkers are not open to the various achievements of different cultural eras, their discourses are likely to remain poor and fixed in a monochrome perspective.

Notes

1 Amy Gutman (ed), *Multiculturalism: Examining the Politics of Recognition*, (New Jersey: Princeton University Press, 1994), 3.

2 Cf. Alasdair Macintyre, *After Virtue. A Study in Moral Theory*, (London: Duckworth, 1987).

3 Charles Taylor, *Multiculturalisme: Différence et démocratie*, (Paris: Flammarion, 1997), p. 41-42.

4 L'Ancien Regime.

5 Charles Taylor, *Sources of the Self*, (Cambridge, Massachusetts: Harvard University Press, 1989), 374-375.

6 Ibid.

7 In the light of recent happenings in France, one can argue whether this is still the case.

8 Accessed from: http://hdr.undp.org/sites/default/files/hdr_2004_summary_en.pdf. Accessed on 10 September 2016. p. 21.

14

Politics Governing the Reservation Policy

S. Sekar Sebastin
St. Paul's Seminary, Trichy

Abstract: One of the demands people make in a politico-social sphere is of reservation based on caste and community. It becomes a genuine demand as it fosters the representation of the unrepresented and neglected people. To have fruitful and reasonable representation, the policy should be acceptable, which could govern the reservation. This paper makes an attempt to highlight the politics behind the policy of reservation. It is true that the subject of reservation, as the creation of statutory quotas for specific groups in the legislature, public services and institutions of higher education, has reportedly emerged as one of the critical issues in the political history of twenty-first century India. This paper elaborates the evolution of the policy of reservation with the principle of representation, the policy of reservation in the private sector, the debate with advocates and antagonists of reservation, the legal prospects of reservation and other salient features. The purpose of a reservation policy is to encourage a move to go beyond formal equality and to insure substantive equity or egalitarianism in society. The demand for reservation is to get rid of social injustice meted out in the name of caste system. It is a vital device that enables them to retrieve opportunities that are denied to them. Thus, a well-thought rational policy is imperative to provide opportunities for development for those who are economically and socially backward. It is hoped that this paper will set in motion a new thinking to save society as well as provide opportunities for the holistic development of those who will benefit most from such policies.

Introduction

The policy of reservation is an important socio-political issue in India today. India is the only democracy in the world that makes explicit constitutional and legal provisions, which are popularly known as reservations for the advancement of the historically depressed and socially backward sections of society. It is unique to this country with its objective to establish an egalitarian society and to ameliorate the traditional underprivileged position of the untouchables, tribals and other backward classes. In India, there are caste communities whose average welfare by many social and economic indicators is significantly below that of the population as a whole and a policy of positive discrimination[1] has been introduced to historically reduce persistent lags in the social and economic welfare of relatively poor communities. As there is the experience of different kinds of discrimination which give rise to certain basic theoretical, constitutional and legal issues relating to the contemporary reservation policy, the system of reservations provides a mechanism of peaceful transformation of the caste-centred system and a redefinition of merit in India. While it is true that the subject of reservation, as the creation of statutory quotas for specific groups in the legislature, public services and institutions of higher education has reportedly emerged as one of the critical issues in the political history of twenty-first century India, it involves fixing of quotas in legislative bodies, in educational institutions and in public employment.[2] As our research seminar focuses on the processes and prospects involved in making a nation, this paper exhibits the need to design an egalitarian policy and politics in order to govern and promote an acceptable reservation policy for those in need.

The Evolution of the Reservation Policy

Any system predominant in a society evolves in a historical context. Thus, the origin of reservation policy can be traced to the days of pre-independence. In 1925, the British who then governed India initiated the policy of reserving a certain percentage of posts in government service for minority communities on the basis of caste and community. This facility was extended to other minorities especially Schedule Castes in 1943. In 1946, the percentage of jobs reserved for SCs was raised to correspond to the percentage of their population.[3] In post-independence India this policy was continued for SCs and STs in educational institutions and public services, while at the same time the concessions for the minority community was removed. At a later stage, it was modified with a view that "except the backward classes who are economically and socially backward and SCs and STs who have special claims of their own, no other minority should be recognized in the Constitution."[4] Thus, the Constituent Assembly was not sympathetic to the demands of the minority communities. When a few members of the Constituent Assembly opposed reservations, Dr. B. R. Ambedkar defended them on the ground that "we have quite a massive opinion which insists that there shall be a provision made for the entry of certain communities which have so far been outside the administration."[5]

Hence, it is clear that the policy of reservations evolved and was based not merely on economic or political but on social as well as cultural factors. It is one aspect of public policy through which the interests of the underprivileged in our society are sought to be safeguarded. It is eventually believed that the policy of reservation is considered as a device through which the underprivileged can climb up the social ladder and stake their claim to positions of power and influence like other sections of society.[6]

Reservation and the Principle of Representation

The evolution of politics in the reservation policy entails the principle of representation as well. It is a great demand that all communities in a nation or society should be respected equally and also their differences are to be recognised. The principles of both the equality and difference must enhance communities, especially those from the backward communities, and resolve conflicts incumbent in society. The principle of representation is a hallmark to augment the lives and status of the underprivileged communities.[7] It is a fact that every community must be invested with a legitimate amount of power to function in the social order. But the subaltern communities do not enjoy and exercise much power compared to others in Indian society. Unless such groups are articulated as 'political community with proper representation,' they are likely to be ignored in the democratic processes and in the allocation of common resources.[8] Thus at the socio-political realm of representation, it was deemed necessary that all communities have a proportionate share of representation at the legislative, executive and judiciary levels of common and societal life. Without adequate representation, the demands and opinions of the weaker groups would be muted at the national and regional level, and this would result in dissatisfaction and eventual conflict. Hence, the socio-political representation and reservation is indispensable for all communities in India, especially the weaker ones, since the need for representation is unquestionable.

The Policy of Reservation in the Private Sector

The principle of representation has sparked a debate on reservations in the private sector. There is a radical change taking place in the current economic system. While jobs in the public sector are shrinking those in the private sector are swiftly expanding. Those who oppose reservations in the private sector say that it would affect merit and efficiency. This is an oft-repeated baseless proposition. So far the SCs have not been given any opportunity in the management of public sector units and only recently have the backward classes been given opportunities by reservation. For many centuries educational and other opportunities have been denied to the deprived sections. As people are handicapped due to the caste system, those who are suppressed should be given favourable treatment by means of a reservation policy. Hence, it is inevitable that companies have a social responsibility to uplift the under-privileged.[9] As we have reservations in government departments and undertakings, the demand of this favoured treatment to be extended to the private sector is on the rise. The underprivileged are unitedly trying to raise their voice in order to achieve aspirations.

The uncertainties surrounding reservations in the private sector will, to some extent, be extended with the implementation of OBC reservations in all the central educational institutions. With the present system of merit in IIT, IIM and medical and educational institutions in force, the private sector will have to fall in line. The notions of merit must be reset to relate to the levels of living conditions coupled with improved productivity in both the agrarian and industrial sectors. Development of innovative technologies and evolution of non-discriminatory management systems in all spheres of life do not depend on marks-centred merit. They depend on social connectivity, socially relevant knowledge and good institutional training.[10]

The Debate on the Policy of Reservation

The reservation policy has proved to be the most controversial public policy in recent times which has vertically divided society into two opposite camps - namely supporters and critics. The main debate about the policy of reservation is whether it violates the principle of merit and leads to the lowering of standards resulting in the incompetence and inefficiency which finally damages the larger interests of society. It is also debatable that despite continuation of the reservation policy for the last four decades, the overall condition of the weaker sections in society has not improved significantly. Thus these debates have created two groups namely the advocates and antagonists.

Arguments in favour of Reservations

Indian society has been rigidly compartmentalized since time immemorial. It is based on the hierarchy of caste and each caste occupies a specific position on the social ladder. The caste system has given rise to social inequality and discrimination which resulted in the condemnation of some sections to subhuman life. To overcome centuries of subjugation, to reshape society on democratic lines and to promote and safeguard the interests of the underprivileged, the policy of reservations was conceived. India's commitment to the cause of realising a democratic polity is well known. Democracy has its meaning only when all sections meaningfully participate in the political and social processes. Hence, the advocates of reservations claim that it is one of the surest means to enable the underprivileged to participate in the political process. It provides opportunities for vertical mobility in the society; promotes neglected talent and achieves social justice.

Further, the pro-reservationists argue that caste is a relevant criterion in the determination of backwardness. They want to compensate members of the backward castes for their age-old social handicap by giving them better representation, better opportunities and better facilities.[11] If the fruits of development have to be distributed equally, preferential treatment for the backward castes is a must. Such treatment is nothing but promoting the policy of reservation which would then eradicate parochial tendencies and strengthen national integration.

Preferential treatment for the SCs is generally proposed, demanded and justified not mainly on grounds of their educational and economic backwardness, but on account of extreme social discrimination they suffered for several centuries. Although, there has been perceptible change in inter-caste relations in the present century, caste discrimination persists, either overtly or covertly.[12] The crucial test is how it treats those at the bottom. Reservations in India are aimed to give the depressed and backward castes a helping hand without which competition with the upper castes would have become unfair and uneven. They are to reorder the social relationships of an iniquitous situation and close the social, educational and economic gap between the upper castes and the lower castes.[13]

Arguments against Reservations

The policy of reservations has been under attack from different quarters on the ground that the benefits are cornered by well-off sections among the underprivileged sections and not the needy. Thus, it creates further inequalities among the deprived sections rather than solving them.[14] The policy has also been criticised on operational grounds. The policy of reservation followed since independence has failed in yielding the desired results and indicates that something has been wrong with the policy both in its frame work and implementation though not in the spirit behind it. Critics of the reservation policy point out that it is against the principle of merit as well. On account of reservations, meritorious candidates are being denied admission/selection/opportunities to provide berths for undeserving candidates. Thus, reservations are promoted and propagated against the principle of merit and in favour of incompetence.[15]

Any policy of compensatory discrimination that is designed to restructure social relations is bound to be controversial and gives rise to resentment and conflict between the groups favoured and those adversely affected by such a policy. Thus in India the reservation policy encounters opposition and resistance mainly from the upper caste sections who feel threatened by the loss of opportunities and the erosion of their traditional position of dominance. The magnitude of resentment of non-preferred groups and the intensity of backlash against preferential policies is highest in India compared to that in any other country in the world. When the V. P. Singh government announced its decision to institute reservations for the backward castes there was a sudden adverse reaction to reservations, followed by violent protests and struggles. A group of Delhi University teachers protested that the reservations for BCs will disastrously divide Indian society, creating conditions of a virtual caste war. Some observed that it would only ignite dissension in society and reinforce casteism. A well-known constitutional expert, Nani Palkhivala, lamented that providing reservations for the BCs was a 'Himalayan blunder' and warned that the unity and security of the state was at stake.[16]

The standard arguments of critics of such reservation policies are that they destroy the democratic right of equality before the law, foster caste feudalism, polarise people on caste lines and endanger social unity, perpetuate dependence of the reserved communities on the state, subject the upper caste persons to destructive discrimination, and that the system cannot survive if merit, efficiency and achievement are disregarded. Most of the opponents of the reservation policy express sympathy for the disadvantaged groups but reject any quota system in their favour. They approve only compensatory action in the form of state support for free education, training or coaching and such other efforts to enhance the competitive potential of the low caste persons so that they can meet the meritocratic standards.[17] All these arguments appear to be all right unless one views the question of compensatory discrimination in a historical perspective and the need and ways to change deep-rooted social inequalities.

In India fierce opposition to reservations is built upon the plank that reservation benefits are mostly enjoyed not by the really backward, but by the better off sections among the depressed or backward castes. It is only natural that the more fortunate sections among the reserved communities would take advantage of the benefits. The reservation policy too, has led to the emergence of an elite among these communities. These advanced sections, in turn, are able to repeatedly make use of the reservations from generation to generation and keep moving up the socio-economic ladder. A question arises as to whether a member of SC, ST or BC remains backward even after he climbs up the ladder, being benefited by the reservation policy. It appears to be paradoxical. The condition of the bulk of the people in the caste remains unaltered. In fact, the beneficiary identifies himself/herself with his/her new class and not with his social group.[18]

The Legal Prospects in the Policy of Reservations

Reservations for the weaker sections of society is a guarantee of the Indian Constitution. It is to be ensured and implemented legally to support representation at the socio-political locus and to level economic imbalances with greater participation and equality of all.

The problem of reservations can be properly understood if one views it in the context of changing social relations in India, particularly in rural areas. Due to legal protection and guarantee, the upper castes are experiencing a loss of social respect which they hitherto commanded from the lower castes. Their economic control is also petering out. Land is generally passing from the hands of upper caste owners to the members of depressed and backward castes. Education and employment have also grown among these groups in most of the areas. The inability to develop respect for low castes and cope with the new realities is making upper caste people aggressive. The increase in violence is a measure of economic and social change and the rise of the erstwhile low castes through education, greater political consciousness and participation and increasing economic and political power.[19]

Most of the upper caste people feel that political leaders are trying to appease the depressed and backward castes for their selfish interests at the cost of the former's legitimate share in the valued societal goods. Using caste for political purposes is not something new to India. What is new is that it is blatantly used by every party as something perfectly normal, legitimate and even necessary. There is a pervasive feeling that the ruling parties are extending reservations to newer groups not with the intent to promote a just social order but to jack up their own electoral support. Apparently, there is a conflict between the short-term goals of political mobilisation and the implications of the current approaches to the health of the polity in the long run.[20]

The Constitution of India directs states to take special legal care to promote the interests of the weaker or disadvantaged sections of the society and, in particular, the Scheduled Castes and Scheduled Tribes and protect them from social injustice and all forms of exploitation.[21] In pursuance of these constitutional provisions, governments at the Union and state levels are allocating funds for preferential welfare programmes for the SCs, STs and Other Backward Classes; reserving seats in educational institutions and jobs in government and all other organisations aided or managed by the state. The legal prospects express an outstanding feature of the reservation policy in India that it is the reservations for the SCs and STs in the Lok Sabha, in the Legislative Assemblies of the states and in elected councils of local government. The number of jobs, seats and political positions for the SCs and STs is fixed in proportion to the population of the respective groups.[22]

Unlike reservations for electoral constituencies no time frame in the legal process is prescribed for reservations in employment and education. For the SCs and STs, reservation is legally provided in all educational institutions supported by the state. In employment at the federal or state levels reservation is provided at the time of selection, confirmation and promotion.[23]

The Salient Processes in the Politics of the Reservation Policy

Indians, rooted in cultural pluralism, are known for their capacity to accommodate conflicting interests, reconcile opposing views and cope with crises. In the context of the problem of caste reservations, what is required is a new national consensus in the light of the experience of the last four decades. Political parties and leaders can play an important role in this direction if they restrain from acting arbitrarily. All must be aware that the question of reservations is a highly sensitive, controversial and combustible one. It affects the individual psyche, social perceptions and material conditions. As such, the policy on reservations needs approval of more than one side in the contention. Any measure of compensatory discrimination should be based on the consent of those who are likely to get adversely affected. Rules are considered to be just if they are inclusive and capable of being accepted by all.

To arrive at such a consensus in India is extremely difficult and unfeasible in view of the formidable impediments. There will be competing interpretations of social justice. But conflicts can be resolved by taking only the claims that can be justified from all the relevant perspectives.[24] A consensus can be evolved if the issues involved in and the experiences borne out by the reservation policy are subjected to examination by competing groups as 'objectively' as possible. The discourse on reservation is affected more by bias and prejudice rather than level headed thinking. The need of the time is to develop a sense of respect for each other's feelings and legitimate interests instead of harbouring prejudice, nurturing animosity and developing contempt. There is no other way open for India except that the people of various castes have to coexist in such a way that inscriptive status is rendered insignificant.

Another pertinent issue is how long should reservations should remain in force. It appears to be more likely that reservations are irreversible so long as the inequalities among castes remains until the number of people from the reserved communities is in the same proportion in education and public employment as their proportion is to the total population. Once these proportions are satisfied, which is likely in the near future, at least for some castes, the moral basis for the reservation policy will gradually erode. For the reservation policy to retain its legitimacy, the state has to evolve institutional mechanisms for establishing rational criteria of "backwardness" and "forwardness" in a fair manner. In such an event, it becomes easier to build consensus on various issues involved in the reservation policy.[25]

The advocates of reservation policy criticise that the implementation of quotas is tardy, the orders relating to reservations are deliberately violated, and the overall impact of the reservations in the amelioration of the conditions of the reserved communities. It is also true that the representation of these communities in the military and judicial services and faculties of many universities is still low. Such criticisms tend to provide ammunition and put pressure in favour of specific reserved groups. But at the same time, it should be kept in mind that reservation policy cannot change the whole situation all of a sudden. The fact is that without these reservations it would not have been possible for a large number of SC and ST persons to enter high positions in the government, state services and education.[26]

Concluding Remarks

The purpose of the reservation policy encourages a move to go beyond formal equality and to ensure substantive equity or egalitarianism in the society. We cannot neglect the fact that reservations are also beset by weaknesses and have led to abuses. First, most of the politicians use reservations as a pre-poll ploy to increase 'quotas' that make them 'patrons' and the polity 'paupers' with the result that many weaker sections rally for reservation quotas and forget about their rights for social justice and equality. Second, instead of generating solidity and solidarity among the weaker groups to challenge the repression of castes/class hierarchies, reservations have, on the one hand, given birth to a 'creamy layer' of weaker groups who are assimilated into, and consolidate, caste hierarchy and hegemony, and, on the other, created "Dalits among the Dalits and backwards among the backwards" whose socio-eco-political status remains largely unaltered. Third, in the absence of real structural reform, reservations mask governmental inadequacies, and are thus deemed demeaning by some subaltern groups who question their efficacy.

While accepting that there are these lacunae in the implementation of reservations, given the glaring inequalities present between the privileged and the disadvantaged groups in India, we can endorse the need for reservations, albeit ensuring that inherent dangers are minimized. Reservation cannot be demanded as a compensation for historical wrongs. If so, it provokes animosity and resentment, and it does not help to develop a sense of self-respect among the beneficiaries of reservation. The demand for reservation is to get rid of social injustice meted out in the name of the caste system. The policy of reservation is the egalitarian principle that inspires historically disadvantaged sections of people to demand reservations as their legitimate right. It is not correct to say that reservation offers only minimal concessions to the deprived. On the other hand, it is a vital device that enables them to retrieve the opportunities denied.

The arguments placed by pro- and anti-reservationist groups have valid grounds. In a democratic socialist country, the advancement of the backward and weaker sections in the society is the responsibility of the state and the public. The reservation policy should be based on a rational basis which must eliminate any basis of caste. It's time for a new thinking to be infused to save society as well as to provide opportunities for the holistic development of the less privileged and remember that reservations and nation building are not antagonistic. The democratic and rational path charted by Ambedkar should be allowed to run its course; otherwise; an anarchist trend is bound to set in.

Notes

1 Positive discrimination means preferential selection of members of the under-represented ethnic, communities to desirable position in society. Ref. S. N. Ambedkar, *Reservation Policy: Issues and Implementation* (Jaipur: ABD Publishers, 2008), 171.
2 Anirudh Prasad, *Reservation Policy & Practice in India: A Means to an End* (New Delhi: Deep & Deep Publications, 1991), 7.
3 Sharma, B.A.V. and Reddy, K.M., (Ed.), *Reservation Policy of India* (New Delhi: Light and Life Publications, 1982), 2.
4 *Ibid.*
5 *Ibid.*, 6.
6 J. Laxminarasimha Rao, "Reservation Policy and the Principle of Merit: A Study of Indian Bureaucracy" *The Indian Journal of Political Science*, Vol. 53, No. 4 (Oct. - Dec. 1992), 479.
7 Francis Gonsalves, SJ, *God of Our Soil: Towards Subaltern Trinitarian Theology* (New Delhi: Tercentenary Publication, ISPCK, 2010), 118.
8 Shefali Jha, "Representation and Its Epiphanies: A Reading of Constituent Assembly Debates" *Economic and Political Weekly* 39 (September 25, 2004), 4358.
9 K. Veeramani, *Social Justice – Multi-Dimensions* (Chennai: Dravidar Kazhagam, 2008), 90.
10 Kancha Ilaiah, "Merit of Reservations" *Economic and Political Weekly* 23 (June 17, 2006), 2448.
11 Shyama Nand Singh, *Reservation Problems and Prospects* (New Delhi: Uppal Publishing House, 1991), 229.
12 Yogendra Singh, *Modernisation of Indian Tradition* (New Delhi: Thompson Press, 1973), 36.
13 K. C. Suri, "Caste Reservations in India: Policy and Politics" *The Indian Journal of Political Science*, Vol. 55 No. 1 (January – March 1994), 38.
14 J. Laxminarasimha Rao, "Reservation Policy and the Principle of Merit: A Study of Indian Bureaucracy" *The Indian Journal of Political Science*, Vol. 53, No. 4 (Oct. - Dec. 1992), 481.
15 *Ibid.*, 483.
16 K. C. Suri, "Caste Reservations in India: Policy and Politics" *The Indian Journal of Political Science,* 44.
17 Ramaswamy Iyer, "Towards Clarity on Reservation Question, *Economic and Political Weekly* 12 (March 2-9, 1991), 500.
18 *Ibid.*, 46.
19 Robert L. Hardgrave, *India Under Pressure: Prospects for Political Stability* (Boulder: Westview Press, 2006), 43.
20 K. C. Suri, "Caste Reservations in India: Policy and Politics" *The Indian Journal of Political Science*, 49.
21 Andre Beteille, "Distributive Justice and Institutional Weil-Being" *Economic and Political Weekly* 14 (March 19, 1991), 591.
22 K. C. Suri, "Caste Reservations in India: Policy and Politics" *The Indian Journal of Political Science*, 39.
23 Recently the Supreme Court ruled against the provision of reservation in promotions.
24 Michael Rosenfeld, *Affirmative Action and Prejudice: A Philosophical and Constitutional Inquiry* (New Haven: Yale University Press, 1991), 249.
25 *Ibid.*, 52.
26 *Ibid.*, 43.

15

Symbols of Indian Nationalism
Past Glory and Present Crisis

Vianney Maria Joseph
Salesian College of Higher Education, Dimapur, Nagaland

Abstract: From time immemorial, symbols have played a significant role in the life of humans and too a great extent, they have grown with these symbols. Symbols are an integral part of man, of his communication dynamism. Moreover, they are an important and integral element in understanding culture. They reinforce our norms and values, and provide an operative in which we can manifest our meanings. They can also evoke emotional responses from us. Simple things such as a national flag or anthem, the festivals and holidays linked with national heroes and patriots, enrich our insights and emotional associations with the 'motherland' and bind categories of peoples into a nation. Symbols and ideologies that glorified our motherland to the rest of the world have become instruments that are manipulated by sectarian groups to stir the emotions of individuals, thus leading to communal unrest and divisions. While we can think of several 'symbols' that promoted patriotic nationalism in the past, this paper attempts to look at some of them in the light of the present day crisis that we are witnessing.

Introduction

From time immemorial, symbols have played a significant role in the life of humans. To a great extent, humans have grown with the symbols and these days it has become well-nigh impossible to dissociate symbols from any field of work and profession. The media-savvy and high tech world use symbols in all their ramifications. Institutions have grown up because of their symbols.

For instance, the Life Insurance Corporation of India is synonymous with the two hands protecting a burning lamp. State Bank of India's symbol of a key hole in a circle will indicate even to an uneducated person in a rural area that it is a bank. There are religious symbols, like *swastika*, *AUM*, cross or the crescent moon to name a few. In terms of colour, red warns of danger and green is for prosperity. There are safety symbols in industries and for roads and other means of transport.

We are living in a period of human history in which Media and Communication are advancing far beyond our imagination. It would not be wrong to say that symbols form a vital component in the field of communication. Simple things such as a national flag or anthem, the festivals and holidays linked with national heroes and patriots enrich man's insights and emotional associations with the 'motherland' and bind categories of peoples into a nation. Symbols are an integral part of man, of his communication dynamism. Moreover, symbols are an important and integral element in understanding culture. They reinforce our norms and values and provide an operative in which we can manifest our meanings. They can also evoke emotional responses from us.

The aim of this paper is to present some of the symbols and ideals of our motherland that gave birth to the spirit of nationalism and played a significant role during the freedom struggle, as well as some of the symbols that have emerged in the recent past – propagated by certain sections of the society – symbols and ideologies that can be manipulated to stir the emotions of individuals, thus leading to communal unrest and divisions.

Evolution of Hindu nationalism

The various reform movements that led to the Hindu Renaissance in the first half of the nineteenth century laid the base of the idea of Hindu nationalism. The growth and development of such a movement can be seen in these successive phases.

The first phase: Era of Patriotism (1850 – 1875)

At a time when Keshab Chandra Sen had accepted the British subjection of India and himself had strong leanings toward Christianity, Raj Narain Bose placed before his countrymen a complex and comprehensive picture of nationalism, with the intention of reviving the old ideas, traditions and customs of every walk of life. In this period, we see the birth of 'Hindu Mela.' At this time, through his writings, Bankim Chandra Chattopadhyaya raised nationalism to the dignity of a religion. The "Anand Math" of Bankim Chandra, which contains the patriotic song "Vande Mataram", has rightly been called the Bible of Hindu nationalism. His 'mother' as conceived in Vande Mataram referred both to the land of Bengal and to the deity, which was a subject matter of religion, and formed the real basis of Hindu nationalism. This idea of the patriotic Mother or of the divine Motherland and this equation of the love of the country with the love of God, instinctively appealed to the nationalist Hindus. Bankim Chandra gave a religious significance to the idea of the motherland. We cannot ignore the First War of Indian Independence of 1857 that evoked a great spirit of nationalism and the seed of patriotism that it planted in the minds of Indians.

The second phase: Era of Aggression (1875 – 1905)

Hindu nationalism became aggressive, militant and more popular in this period. We also see the formation of organizations like the Arya Samaj, Ramakrishna Mission and the Theosophical Society. The role of Vivekananda was distinct and his contribution notable. With him, religion was the inspirer of nationalism. He infused in the new generation a sense of pride in India's past, faith in India's future and a spirit of self-respect and self-confidence.

The third phase: Era of Extremism (1905 – 1920)

With the partition of Bengal in 1905, the Nationalist movement became more violent. While the moderates were impregnated with Victorian liberalism, the extremists dominated the political scene. Vinayak Damodar Sarvakar and K.B. Hegdewar were inspired by the extremist movement led by Bal Gangadhar Tilak.

The fourth phase: Era of 'One Nation', 'One Language' and 'One Culture' (1920 – now)

The country saw the birth of the Hindu Maha Sabha, the RSS and Bharatiya Jana Sangh and the political wing, BJP. Today we are witnessing the fruits of their aggressive activities, carried out behind the mask of 'national integration' and 'cultural nationalism.'

Hindu rashtra

In the context of the contemporary religio-political scenario of India, wherein we are witnessing the emergence of Hindu cultural nationalism or Hindutva as a movement in the country, J. Kuruvachira, in his book *Hindu Nationalists of Modern India: A Critical Study of the Intellectual Genealogy of Hindutva*, opens our eyes to the truth that this movement has its roots in the past and its core concepts are provided by certain Hindu nationalists of modern India. He re-reads the writings of Swami Dayananda Saraswati (1824-1883), Swami Vivekananda (1863-1902), Bal Gangadhar Tilak (1856-1920), Vinayak Damodar Savarkar (1883-1966), Madhav Sadashiv Golwalkar (1906-1973) and Sita Ram Goel (1921-2003), thus tracing how the present day cultural nationalism and fundamentalism of the *Hindutva* has an intellectual history.

While none can deny the great good done by these 'patriots and freedom fighters' for the nation, one cannot be blind either to the fact that they have also sown the seeds of narrow-minded nationalism, anti-secularism, intolerance and religious-fundamentalism. Today we are witnessing the dictatorial style of governance by the BJP-led NDA government with the *Rashtriya Swayamsevak Sangh* (RSS) and the *Sangh Parivar* steering it as an invisible force.[1]

All the above mentioned six Hindu nationalists were anxious to preserve the Hindu religion and culture. In that process, both Christianity and Islam were seen as the greatest threats to their Hindu nation and culture. Projecting "India is a *Hindu Rashtra*" as their ideological framework, they challenged the very constitutional concept of India as Unity in Diversity – in its cultural, religious and ethnic plurality. Manipulating politics to promote the Hindu religion, they labelled non-Hindus as not being part of the Hindu nation, assigning to them the status of 'descents of migrants or converts from Hinduism'. It would not be an exaggeration if one assumes that Hindu nationalism is essentially an ethno-religious movement of the upper caste Hindus, for while Sita Ram Goel was an upper caste Agarwal, the remaining five nationalists were *Brahmins*. Guided by a negative ideology of Hindu nationalism and patriotism, their speeches, activities and writings promoted hatred of non-Hindus and persons with a secular frame of mind.[2] And the ordinary Indian masses, who can be easily indoctrinated and are fascinated by the narrow concept of Hindu *rashtra* built upon Hindu cultural nationalism, become the victims of the manipulative tactics of the Hindu nationalist groups.

As part of their concluding statement in their 23rd annual meeting, held in Bangalore in April 2000, the Indian Catholic Theologians made the following observation: "*Hindutva* is a dangerous ideology. It is a falsification and distortion of Hinduism that should be resisted and rejected by all true Hindus of our country. We call upon all the peoples of India to be united and face this challenge, and expose its dangers, distortions and fallacies."[3] It is true that several symbolic and metaphorical expressions were used by those who fought for the freedom of India in order to build the nation. These expressions, while they fuelled the flame of patriotism, brought about unity. However today, the very same expressions are being manipulated to sow the seeds of hatred and intolerance, while outwardly garbed by the expression '*Hindu Rashtra*', 'One Nation', 'One Language' and 'One Culture.'

"*Khun kharaba hona hai to ekbar ho jane do*" (If there has to be bloodshed, let it happen once and for all) - These were the words uttered by Sadhvi Rithambhara, a young female ascetic, during the *Ramjanmabhoomi* campaigns organized by the *Hindutva* forces between 1986 and 1992. And the country witnessed the horror of communal conflicts and riots, certain sections of humanity becoming savage beasts. Communalism is often shrugged off far too easily as plain politics masquerading as religion. While communalism is certainly part of a political agenda, religion, however instrumentally used by certain politicians, possesses separable categories and practices. In the last few decades, religions, religious beliefs and practices have gone through profound breaks and transformations. Communalism is part of a process in which modern political concepts draw many of their valences from the realm of sacred meanings. While it cannot articulate its authentic and specific agenda, it redraws the boundaries of religious identity and community in exclusively antagonistic and vindictive terms.

Vande mataram and Bharat mata

The idea that *Bharata* (India) personified the Mother Goddess (the supreme Mother) became popular during the freedom struggle. The slogan "*Bharat mata ki jai*" (Glory to Mother India) rent the air as patriots gathered for a meeting or went in a procession. *Vande Mataram* ("Obeisance to the Mother") was another battle-cry.

The expression of reverence to the motherland as found in *Vande Mataram*, was first used by Bankim Chandra Chatterjee (1838 – 1894) in his famous Bengali novel '*Ananda Math*' (The Abbey of Bliss). It became the national song sung at the Congress sessions from 1906 onwards. *Vande Mataram* became a form of greeting among the freedom fighters, especially the extremist groups.

Ananda Math is a story set in the context of the dreadful Bengal famine in the eighteenth century and the sufferings of the people under a tyrannical regime. The song *Vande Mataram* describes the greatness of the Mother in a number of ways:

> "Mother, I bow to thee! Rich with thy hurrying streams, Bright with the orchard gleams, Cool with the winds of delight, Dark fields warring, Mother of might, Mother free."

Its patriotic overtones can be felt in another stanza: "Who has said thou art weak in the land; When the swords flash out in twice seventy million hands; And seventy million voices soar; Thy dreadful name shore to shore? To thee, I call, Mother and Lord! Thou who saves, arise and save."

While Muslim nationalists accepted the song as an expression of patriotism, some sections of Muslims protested that it symbolized idol worship. The 'Mother' in the song is India perceived variously as *Durga*, *Laksmi* and *Saraswati*; the author sees the motherland in the *Durga* deity in temples. He says in *Ananda Math* that *Kali* is the symbol of the present degraded state of India. She is black in colour due to the intense misery of the country. She is naked as India has been denuded of all her wealth. She wears a garland of human skulls because the whole country has become a vast burial ground.

She has *Siva* under her feet to show that Indians are trampling upon their own welfare. The author calls upon Indians to sacrifice their lives at the feet of Mother India (seen in *Kali*). Thus, patriotic sentiments were roused through religious faith.

The song *Vande Mataram* was on the lips of those who participated in the agitation against the partition of Bengal Presidency in the first decade of the twentieth century and it became their battle-song. Due to this, the then British Government banned the song.

Among those who had faith in Mother India, Sri Aurobindo Ghosh (1872 – 1950) was the foremost. Starting as a revolutionary, he changed to a spiritual life and settled in Puducherry, a French colony at that time. He worshipped *Bharat mata*, as a living form of the Divine Mother. To him, India was not just a piece of land; it was power, *śakti* of millions of units that constituted the country just as *Bhavani Mahisa Mardini*, i.e. *Durga* sprang into being out of the *śakti* of all the gods assembled in one mass of force and welded into unity.

Sri Aurobindo famously exclaimed how in the map of *Bharat* one could find the portrait of *Bharat mata*. He described the cities, the mountains, rivers and forests as the materials which go to make up her body. The people inhabiting the country are the cells, which go to make up her living tissues. Indian literature is her memory and speech; the happiness and freedom of her children are her salvation. He called upon the people to behold *Bharat* as a living Mother, meditate upon her and worship her in the nine-fold way of *bhakti*. A picture of *Bharat mata* within the map of India was designed, printed and widely distributed.

Mahatma Gandhi was much impressed by the spirit of the song *Vande Mataram*. He declared that its aim was to arouse in Indians a sense of patriotism, and that the poet attributes to Mother India all the good qualities one finds in one's own mother. He said that just as we worship our mother, so in this song there is a passionate prayer to India.

Patriotic slogans in national integration[4]

While images and ideologies played their role in creating the spirit of national integration, we cannot sideline some of the popular slogans that aroused the sense of patriotic nationalism in the masses. I mention the following, as I found it in the internet, for our consideration:

1. "*Jai Hind*" = "Hail India", "Long Live India", "Victory to India": This was the first commemorative postmark of our independent country, popularised by Subash Chandra Bose, now used as a slogan and salutation almost everywhere in India.

2. "*Vande Mataram*" is a poem from Bankim Chandra Chattopadhyay's novel "Anandmath" in 1882, written in Bengali and Sanskrit. Being a praise to the motherland, it has played a vital role in our freedom movement, eulogizing India as a Goddess and glorifying the patriotic fervour.
3. "*Swaraj Mera Janamsiddh adhikar hai, aur main ise lekar rahunga*" (Swaraj is my birth right and I shall have it.) is a popular slogan adopted by Bal Gangadhar Tilak. It was coined by Kaka Baptista in our fight for independence. Not only did this slogan motivate people to fight for their rights, but it also provoked the love for country in the hearts of thousands of people.
4. "*Jai Jawaan, Jai Kisaan*" (Hail the Soldier! Hail the Farmer!) by Lal Bahadur Shastri is a slogan that awakens the inner-most sentiments of 'Jai Hindustan' in the hearts of Indians even today. Acknowledging the efforts of our soldiers and farmers, this slogan gave a new dimension to our freedom struggle.
5. "*Satyamev Jayate*" ("Truth alone triumphs"), popularized by Pandit Madan Mohan Malaviya, has not only been adopted as the national motto of India but is also inscribed in script at the base of our national emblem.
6. "*Inquilab Zindabad*" (Long live the Revolution!), synonymous with Bhagat Singh and coined by Muslim leader Hasrat Mohani, this slogan awakened the feeling of patriotism in the youth of India during those days with the urge to lay down their lives for their motherland and to get her free from the clutches of Britishers, this slogan marks an important event in the fight for freedom.
7. "*Sarfaroshi ki Tamanna, Ab hamare dil mein hai*", a patriotic poem by Bismil Azimabadi, later used as a slogan by Ramprasad Bismil in the struggle that challenged the authority of British rulers. Enlightening the need of the hour, this slogan urged people to fight for what was right.
8. "*Dushman ki goliyon ka hum samna karenge, Azad hee rahein hain, Azad hee rahenge*": The Jallianwala Bagh Massacre, that left hundreds of unarmed innocent people dead, led to a profound effect on Chandra Shekhar Azad that made him use this slogan and fight for his country.
9. "*Araam Haraam hai*" by Jawaharlal Nehru was an invitation to our freedom fighters not to seek even a sigh of relief until they freed their motherland from the claws of British Government.
10. "*Tum mujhe khoon do, mai tumhe azaadi doonga*": Urging the youth of India to join the Indian National Army in the struggle for independence of India, Netaji Subhash Chandra Bose used this slogan. This inspired thousands of young minds to sacrifice their lives for their motherland.

Spinning wheel[5] and patriotic nationalism

Deh charkhe nu geda, lor nahin topan di
(Ply the spinning wheel and you will not require cannons)
Tere bamban nu challan nahin dena Gandhi de charkhe ne
(The spinning wheel of Gandhi will not allow your bombs to explode)
Sada desh azad karaya Gandhi de charkhe ne
(The spinning wheel of Gandhi brought us freedom).

These folk ballads *(bolis)* of Punjab typified by *charkha* convey the spirit of nationalism before 1947. The *charkha* had been the source of livelihood of artisans as well as the companion and helpmate of women. It began to acquire a mystique during the freedom struggle when it became the symbol of the *Swadeshi* movement, so as to bring about an economic revolution by discarding the machine-made goods of Manchester and Lancashire and replacing them with Indian hand-made cloth. The emphasis on the *charkha* had as its goal the removal of the poverty of villagers who could supplement their income by working at home and to impede the flow of Indian money to the British industries.

Gandhi gave a novel interpretation to the *charkha*. He used the *charkha* to aim at building a new economic and social order based on self-sufficient non-exploitative village communities of the past. Growing industrialism and materialism were making man a slave of machine and Mammon. The use of the spinning-wheel was to counter that growth. To quote him: "The message of the spinning wheel is much wider than its circumference. Its message is one of simplicity, service of mankind, living so as not to hurt others, creating an indissoluble bond between the rich and the poor, capital and labour, the prince and the peasant. That larger message is naturally for all."[6]

For Gandhi the revival of hand-spinning and hand-weaving would make the largest contribution to the economic and moral regeneration of India. He wrote: "The spinning wheel represents to me the hope of the masses. The masses lost their freedom, such as it was with the loss of the *charkha*. The *charkha* supplemented the agriculture of the villagers and gave it dignity. It was the friend and solace of the widow."[7]

While for Gandhi the *charkha* had become an obsession - as evidenced by his speeches and writings on khadi economics, khadi science, khadi learning, khadi spirit, khadi epoch, khadi franchise for Congressmen, yarn currency and khadi romance – some of his contemporaries, like Rabindranath Tagore, felt that the spinning wheel had been turned into a cult, "thereby distracting attention from other more important factors in our task of all-round reconstruction."[8]

Has the cow become a national symbol?

In a modern day democracy what one should eat or should not eat should be decided by the person concerned. The government should not interfere in it unless the animal or bird is an endangered species. The religion of a person has no role in deciding what another person eats.

Sadly, it seems India is walking backwards. The BJP governments in many states are interfering more and more in what people should eat. The Maharashtra government has extended the anti-cow slaughter law to cover not only cows but also bulls and bullocks. Sale of these animals for slaughter is punishable with a jail term of up to five years and a fine of Rs. 10,000/-. Even possessing the meat of these animals is now a crime attracting a jail term of one year. The Haryana government has passed a more stringent law banning even the sale of packaged beef.

Why are the cow and its progeny singled out for special protection laws? If you ask any Indian, the answer will be that in our culture going back to the Vedic period, it is a sacred animal. The cow and its progeny should never be killed but have to be worshipped. This message of cow worship and sacredness being the basic values of Hinduism are proclaimed so loudly day in and day out by leaders of Hindutva movement all over the country that it became an indisputable truth. The Sangh propaganda made everyone in India believe that cow slaughter began here only after the the invasion of Muslim rulers.

Is this the truth? Was cow slaughter a cardinal sin throughout the history of Hinduism? Was the cow and its progeny never killed in ancient India? When we carefully study Vedic literature as well as the evidences provided by the Archaeology Society of India, we realise that though the cow and its progeny did have a higher position among animals in ancient India it did not mean it was not killed and eaten. Beef was considered to be a special dish. Sacrificing a cow when a special guest comes home was the rule. Also, in *yagnas* and *Sraddhas* killing a cow was considered as a higher sacrifice than killing other animals. Cow protection was not a gift of Vedic Hinduism to the world and its slaughter in India did not begin with invaders professing other religions.

The agenda of the Hindu nationalists of India to have a militaristic nation-state with a culturally homogeneous population of Hindus resembles the nation- and empire-building projects of nineteenth century Europe. They redefine many of their preferred aspects of Indian tradition and culture, and present them as eternal and immutable, interrupted only by alien Muslims and other 'unclean' foreigners. They fear the kind of scholarship that reveals that Indian tradition, like all other traditions, is a man-made thing, vulnerable to endless change, revision, and appropriation.

But the cow wasn't sacred to the nomads and pastoralists from Central Asia who settled in North India in the second millennium BC and created the high Brahminical culture of what we now know as Hinduism. These Indians slaughtered cattle for both food and the elaborate sacrificial rituals prescribed by the Vedas, the first and the holiest Indian scriptures. After they settled down and turned to agriculture, they put a slightly higher value upon the cow: it produced milk, ghee, yoghurt and manure and could be used for ploughing and transport as well.

Indian religion and philosophy after the Vedas rejected the ritual killing of animals. This may have also served to protect the cow. But beef eating was still not considered a sin. It is often casually referred to in the earliest Buddhist texts. The great Indian emperor, Ashoka, who instituted non-violence as state policy in the third century BC, did not ban the slaughter of cattle.

It is only in the early medieval period that the eating of beef became a taboo, if only for upper-caste Hindus. But the cow was far from holy. It is significant that no cow-goddesses, or temples to cows, feature in India's anarchically all-inclusive polytheisms.

Conclusion

Today, the biggest challenge to the Indian nation comes from forces claiming to represent the mainstream majority. There is an emergence of extremist voices that claim to speak for Hindus and they are laying down demands that threaten the very idea of a secular India.

Communal forces are actively propagating the myth that secularism is a new mask of fundamentalism. They denigrate secular policies, which are a hindrance to the Hindu Right's unobstructed march to subjugate the oppressed in general and minorities in particular. They are equating fundamentalism with Islam; and the policies of Indian rulers with secularism, and the appeasement of *mullahs* as being synonymous with secular policies. Further, *Hindutva* forces allege that secularism pampers the Muslims as a vote bank. The Muslims are accused of extra-territorial loyalty. The Christians, who are much lesser in number, are accused of being more loyal to the Vatican, another outside force, and of trying to convert poor Hindus with inducements of education and food. Who can forget the brutal burning of Graham Staines and his two minor sons by a member of the *Bajrang Dal* in the name of religion? Or even the rape of some sisters in Gujarat, their fault being the spreading of the word of their God.

There is a blatant attempt to subvert history, change school curricula and create a new set up in line with a *Hindu Rashtra*. It is not so much a question of defending or preserving the existing secular character of the Indian polity, but rather a need to create and build a secular polity in the nation. Only the ideal of building a secular democratic nation can stem the tide of communal fascism in the country. Religious clergy, bigotry, dogmas and rituals cannot be allowed to guide the state.

Mahatma Gandhi has rightly said: "I swear by my religion, I will die for it. But it is my personal affair. The State has nothing to do with it. The State would look after your secular welfare, health, communications, foreign relations, currency and so on, but not your or my religion. That is everybody's personal concern!"[9]

Hinduism is a faith that on the whole is favourable to the development of the secular state in India. It also has a strong tradition of freedom of conscience and tolerance of religious diversity that is not rightly projected by the *Hindutva* forces.

This strength of the Hindu religion is now viewed as a weakness. Secularism in the Indian context should imply respect for pluralism and a non-coercive, voluntary recourse to change. Respect for diversity not only embodies the democratic spirit, it is the real guarantee of unity. We should value democratic, not fascistic, unity. No democratic society can downgrade diversity and pluralism in the name of unity. Secular ethics can be strengthened only when acts of vandalism are sternly dealt with and the guilty are made to pay for it. With secularism that insists on the inalienable rights of the citizens and a due process of law, it will be easier to mount public pressure against sectarian killers and those who promote hatred. The battle of secularism and democracy has also to be fought at the grassroots levels where a set ideals generating strong idealism are required to mobilize and prepare the masses for struggle.

In the end, secularism begins in the heart of every individual. There should be no feeling of "otherness" as we all have a shared history. India, being a traditional society that contains not one but many traditions owing their origin in part to the different religions that exist here, has so far managed to retain the secular character of its polity. Ours is a society where *Sufis* and *Bhakti* saints have brought in a cultural acceptance for each other. Are we going to let it all go to waste and listen to people who have concern for their careers as politicians or leaders rather than our welfare at heart? Let us instead concentrate our efforts at making India a progressive secular nation, and turn the dreams of Mahatma Gandhi, Jawaharlal Nehru and Dr. B. R. Ambedkar into a reality, to be lived and cherished by us and by our posterity.

Notes

1 Kuruvachira 2006, ix-5.
2 *Ibid.*, 228-235.
3 *As quoted in* Kuruvachira 2006, 235.
4 Tulsiani 2015.
5 Kapoor 1999.
6 M. Gandhi, The Essential Writings 2008, 15.
7 Chakrabarty 2006, 140.
8 Kapoor 1999.
9 M. Gandhi, All Men Are Brothers: Autobiographical Reflections 2004, 72.

Part 3

Aspects of Nationalism

16

Ushering in a New Dawn
Making Poverty History in India

Ashley Miranda
Divyadaan Institute of Philosophy, Nashik

Abstract: The public debate on India's development between Amartya Sen and Jagdish Bhagwati has caught the attention of not only specialists but also the common man. While some have been greatly impressed by India's achievements, others feel that not enough has been done for India's poorest. In this article the author contends that the difference between Sen and Bhagwati is more a difference of emphasis than of substance. Both Sen and Bhagwati say very categorically that economic growth makes the resources available to promote the building of capabilities of the poorest; they also agree that if a nation does not invest in building human capabilities, the train of economic growth will derail. Therefore, rather than saying one of them is right and the other is wrong, India needs people like Sen and Bhagwati to disagree, to dialogue and to point out directions that others lack the experience to see. However, the author goes on to add that if one had to choose between the two, his vote would be in favour of Sen. Not because he is right and Bhagwati is wrong, but because Sen seems to focus on the poor first before looking at the welfare of the country as a whole, whereas Bhagwati's priority is on development and not the other way around. History – both world history and that of India – shows that it is amazingly easy to forget the poor, to see right through them as if they did not exist at all. When it comes to the poor, it would not be an exaggeration to say that we must work for their interests first before attending to anything else.

Introduction

Ruth Prawer Jhabvala, the well-known novelist and screenwriter, who died in 2013, had some very unsettling things to say about India. In her introduction to her collection of short stories *Out of India* she writes, "The most salient fact about India is that it is very poor and very backward. There are so many other things to be said about it but this must remain the basis of all of them. We may praise Indian democracy, go into raptures over Indian music, admire Indian intellectuals – but whatever we say, not for one moment should we lose sight of the fact that a very great number of Indians never get enough to eat. Literally that: from birth to death they never for one day cease to suffer from hunger."[1] Thankfully, Jhabvala wrote this and for that matter lived before the dawn of the age of the Indian troll. Today, it is dangerous to say anything even remotely negative about India. Those foolish enough to do so are usually advised to pack up and leave.

We live in the age of Indian jingoism. We are and have always been the greatest nation on earth. When the rest of the world was still living in the forests we built up a great civilization of grand cities with state-of-the-art sanitation facilities. In ancient times we had universities which were in the vanguard of research and creativity, especially in the areas of science and technology. The prototype of practically every major scientific invention was first created in India. Not too many years ago, India was the richest country in the world with more than 25% of the world's wealth. And the list goes on. This is the new narrative we must all mouth; otherwise we forfeit our right to live here. Patriotism today is something that must be on display, it must be worn on one's sleeve. In such a situation to question or to poke holes in the politically correct narrative is fraught with risks.

While all the wonderful things we say about India are true and worthy of celebration, it is also true that we have much to do to raise our nation from the grip of poverty that seeks to strangle it. The fact that every year more and more Indians find their names on the millionaires' list or the Forbes billionaires' list, means nothing to the vast majority of Indians who are desperately poor. The glorious things we say about our nation does little to ensure that they have food to eat, a roof over their head, schools to send their children to, and jobs to support their families. In fact, with each passing day the economic divide in India is getting more and more pronounced and stark. Statistics show that in 2015, the richest 1% of the Indian population had 53% of the nation's wealth, up from 2000 when the richest 1% owned 36.8% of the nation's wealth.[2]

How do we bridge this economic divide? How do we ensure that at the micro-level there is food on the table? Perhaps the question itself is incorrect in a nation where innumerable homes do not even have a table? Maybe we need to ask, how can we ensure that not a single child is forced to sleep on an empty stomach? On the macro-level we need to ask, how can we translate our immense resources both human and material into development that is equitable and sustainable and which becomes the foundation for further integral growth and holistic progress?

In 2005, Jeffrey Sachs wrote a compelling book with an eye catching title, "The End of Poverty: How we can make it happen in our lifetime."[3] In his 'Foreword' to this book the Irish singer-songwriter Bono highlights some of Sachs' key claims, namely, [1] "The destinies of the "haves" are intrinsically linked to the fates of the "have-nothing-at-all." [2] We must work to create a world that is more equitable, in which the senseless loss of human potential and human lives is no longer accepted as inevitable. A just world is possible and achievable in our own lifetime. Striving for equality is not just a question of heart, "it's smart". [3] There can never be any genuine peace and stability if the concerns of the poor are not addressed and redressed.[4]

Sachs, an internationally renowned economist who was special advisor to many governments all over the world, firmly believes that we – individuals, NGOs, governments, world organizations, and banks - can, if we are serious about it, work together to end extreme poverty by 2025. He thinks that the first set of problems we need to address is the lack of awareness and lack of will. Most people are simply unaware of the scale of poverty and injustice in the world. He says that the stories of the poor are not considered newsworthy. "Most people are unaware of the daily struggles for survival, and the vast numbers of impoverished people around the world who lose that struggle."[5] With regard to his claim that there is a lack of good will, he points out that the money needed to address the plight of the poorest of the poor is available; in fact, he holds that the money necessary to tackle the issue of extreme poverty that contributes so much to the unrest, violence and instability in the world is just a small percentage of the money spent on fortifying defenses and manufacturing arms.[6]

This article focuses on India, but the issues we have to deal with are very much those that Sachs has identified. The reasons why we urgently need to address the issues of equitable development and eradication of extreme poverty apply to India as well. Equity and justice are not a choice we can choose to make or on how charitable we feel. It is a question of common sense, of reading the writing on the wall. The India of today is bursting with hopes and expectations. The sheer number of those who feel left out is way too high to take lightly. We have got to address the question of development and equal access to opportunities and wealth urgently.

Two outstanding economists have written on how to deal with issues connected with the World economy in general and on questions related to India's development for years: Amartya Sen and Jagdish Bhagwati. In the build up towards the 2014 Indian National Elections the differences in their viewpoints came to be highlighted and presented by some in the media as representative of two different and opposing political and economic ideologies. While ascribing political hues to their economic theories may be bit of a simplification, it is true that leading up to the elections of 2014 the difference of view of these two economists and their supporters developed into a kind of personal spat where the two economists went beyond discussing ideas to making personal insinuations about each other. Sen apparently did not refer to Bhagwati by name every time he spoke to discredit one or another point made by Bhagwati, but Bhagwati on his part dispensed with the subtleties to explicitly name Sen in his criticism. Bhagwati opined that far from helping India's poor, Sen and his policy prescriptions 'have hurt the masses of India's poor twice.'[7]

But before we take sides, we need to ask what exactly do Sen and Bhagwati say about the path that India needs to take to make poverty a thing of the past? Are there any real significant differences in their views? Or are their differences only on emphasis, in real terms more cosmetic than substantial?

Amartya Sen and the Capability Approach to Development

Amartya Sen is often referred to as the "Mother Teresa of Economics."[8] While only the professional student of economics in India may have read his works, most educated laypersons have heard of him. This is largely because he was awarded the Nobel Prize for Economic Sciences in 1998. Sen has written extensively on development economics and has explored themes such as development, justice, plurality, poverty alleviation, democracy, freedom and human wellbeing, among others.

Sen is noted especially for his "capability approach to development". His main contentions, especially when speaking about India and other developing countries, are: (1) True development is not merely a matter of economic progress; an increase in GDP or per capita income. Development is best understood as "an expansion of people's basic freedoms or human capabilities."[9] (2) Economic prosperity is not an end in itself. The goal ultimately is the expansion of human freedom and capabilities. Economic "growth generates resources with which public and private efforts can be systematically mobilized to expand education, health care, nutrition, social facilities, and other essentials of freer and fuller human life for all." (3) Focusing on building human capacity in the present will lead to solid and sustainable economic growth in the long run. Prioritizing rapid economic growth in the hope that it will eventually lead to development of human capacities is likely to create an artificial and short lived bubble of progress that is likely to blow up quickly in the face leaving everyone concerned worse off.[10] Economic growth without a planned and systematic investment in human development is unsustainable and also unethical. (4) Despite the impressive economic [read GDP] growth that India has achieved since Independence, it has failed to achieve equally significant growth when it comes to a number of important social indicators [life expectancy, nutrition, sanitation and public hygiene, literacy, maternal mortality, etc.]. In an extremely complex nation like India where social inequality is so entrenched much more than increase of GDP is needed for a proportionate rise in these important social indicators.[11] (5) Liberalization of the economy must go hand in hand with "'ambitious social programmes' set in motion by the government with private sector participation to address problems in the fields of education, health, transport and other public services.'"[12] (6) At the risk of being termed spoil sports we need to have the courage to ask inconvenient moral questions. Questions such as, "Are the glaring disparities in wealth and access to opportunities justified?" "Do I have a right to be rich in a world of so much poverty and inequality?"[13] (7) The Market Economy and Globalization while inevitable are not absolute goods. Democracy and concrete initiatives to eradicate inequalities are equally, if not more, important. We need to recognize the value of different types of freedoms – economic, social, cultural and political – which are interrelated.[14] (8) In a country with deeply entrenched inequalities of caste, gender, education and income, economic growth which is not inclusive often only fuels more corruption and makes the poor only more vulnerable to exploitation.[15]

Jagdish Bhagwati and the Human Face of Globalization

Bhagwati is not as well-known as Amartya Sen is. However, in recent times he has caught the attention of the layman for his audacity to express his view that calling Amartya Sen the "Mother Teresa of Economics"[16] as many in India have rather over enthusiastically done, is an insult to Mother Teresa's memory.[17]

Bhagwati is often described as the most creative international trade theorist of present times. Way back in the 60s, when economists still spoke the language of protectionism, Bhagwati was a pioneering advocate of free trade.[18] His main contentions, especially with regard to development and poverty alleviation in India are: (1) Focusing on robust economic growth is the surest path to poverty alleviation. For this to happen policies need to be implemented that open up trade, free up foreign direct investment (FDI) and remove unnecessary red tape. (2) Creation of wealth in a liberal democratic set up, like that of India, has the potentiality to create a "revolution of perceived possibilities" which is basically a strategy that creates credible hope. When the poor see in their actual day to day lives that they can do better, their aspirations increase and they begin to work to fulfill them.[19] (3) The fundamental challenge of development is the creation of this credible hope in the hearts of the poorest. (4) Only if there is substantial growth can we meaningfully speak about redistribution. Significant redistribution in India could not have preceded growth because there were too few rich people and too many poor. Prioritizing growth will create the revenues necessary to undertake redistribution that is truly empowering.[20] (5) The economic reforms post-1991 have touched the lives of all, including the poorest in a very positive way. To say that reforms have increased inequality and have done more harm than good is clearly a position that is rooted in bias. While it is true that some have benefited way more than the others, we need to ensure that the pie grows larger before significant redistribution begins to make any sense. (6) The worst enemies of the poor are often those who profess to be their friends. Over-regulation, nationalization, reserving so-called core sectors only to the public sector, protectionism and other such policies that apparently aim at protecting the interests of the poor end up doing them more long term harm by creating stagnation in the economy that actually hurts the poorest the most. (7) Those who claim that the reforms of 1991 have only benefitted a few and have left the poor even more disadvantaged have got their facts wrong. Since the reforms the absolute number of poor people in India has fallen by more than 200 million. The percentage of people living below the poverty line has fallen from 40 percent in the pre-reform years to 20 percent in 2010. (8) The way ahead calls for more liberalization not less. India needs to re-jig its outdated systems of land acquisition, planning and its tightly regulated labour market. (9) Future reforms must proceed along two tracks, with track one focusing on accelerating and sustaining economic growth and track two seeking to making already existing redistributive programmes more effective. (10) Free trade encourages competition and innovation. Globalization, contrary to popular perception, does have a human face. It advances rather than inhibits the "achievement of social agendas as wide-ranging as the promotion of gender equality worldwide, reduction of poverty in the poor countries and the shifting of children from work to schools."[21]

'Who is right?' and 'who is wrong?'

Now that we have presented in brief the views of both Sen and Bhagwati, we could go on to ask, 'Who is right and who is wrong?' However, the question itself is a bit too simplistic, I think. Both are noted, passionate and committed economists; each with a huge following that include the who's who of the world of economics, development and government. Besides it is not that they are two economists who represent two diametrically opposite approaches to the question of development and justice. Sen and Bhagwati are temperamentally different; both say it as they see it. Both see water in the glass, one of them is inclined to say "the glass is half empty", while the other says "the glass is half full." One thinks that if we do not point out what is lacking there is a real danger that these important elements will be forgotten. The other thinks we have got to celebrate small and big victories; a winning formula should not be tampered with, and if we put real money in people's hands they themselves will make choices that will enable them to enhance and fine tune their capabilities in accordance with their own perceptions of what is truly needed. In his article, "Bhagwati versus Sen: What's going on?", Mihir Sharma points out that "both are liberal, neoclassical economists, who support deregulation and disapprove of existing subsidies."[22] He seems to think that the difference between the two has become a slugfest but the actual differences in their views is relatively minor, more a difference of emphasis than of substance.[23] Sen says building capabilities and fostering freedoms among the poorest is a sine-qua-non for equitable economic development. Bhagwati argues that if we focus on growth, incomes will rise sufficiently for those who are presently poor to invest in their own health, education and other social indicators that make for a good life. Sharma is of the view that both Bhagwati and Sen are right in a way, since neither of the paths suggested can be abandoned for the other. The question instead is which of the mechanisms suggested by the two great men will work faster and more effectively.[24]

The way ahead

Which path should India take? Which of the two roadmaps for development is likely to take India towards progress and integral development? The map given to us by Bhagwati or the one presented by Sen?

I think it would be better to use the imagery of a train running on tracks. In fact, Bhagwati does use the words 'track one' and 'track two.'[25] In the light of this debate we should perhaps look at them as parallel tracks. Both of them after all say very categorically that economic growth makes the resources available to promote the building of capabilities in a sustainable and equitable manner. Both also agree that if a nation does not invest in building human capabilities sooner rather than later the train of economic growth will derail. It is a question of 'the chicken or the egg' really!! India needs both Amartya Sen and Jagdish Bhagwati. The country needs them to disagree and to dialogue. It needs them to ask questions that others perhaps do not have the courage to ask, to point out directions that others lack the experience to see.

If one has no choice but to take sides in this debate, then I guess, the vote would have to be in Sen's favour. Not because Sen is right and Bhagwati is wrong, but because the former seems to say focus on the poor first before looking at the welfare of the country as a whole, whereas the latter seems to say we must look at development the other way around. History – both world history and that of India – shows that it is amazingly easy to forget the poor, to not notice them at all. They may be all around us but our eyes may see right through them as if they did not exist. When it comes to the poor – and India has more than a hundred million of them – it would not be an exaggeration to say that we must work for their interests first before attending to anything else. They often seem to be just pawns in the political struggle for power; not flesh and blood people with real aspirations and dreams, with certain definite human rights, but people who don't matter except for the one day every few years when they cast their ballot on Election Day.

By way of conclusion, I think it would be appropriate to highlight some considerations that all of us need to keep in mind as we work to create a new India and make poverty history. Whether we belong to the Sen camp or the Bhagwati camp, I am sure, we all agree on the following fundamentals: (1) India may not exactly be "shining" at the present moment, but the air is pregnant with hope. We cannot disappoint our people. Nobody wants an India in which all her citizens are equally poor; rather we all hope to build a nation that not only gallops along the road of economic growth and prosperity but also knows how to make all its citizens willing participants in this process. (2) Economic growth may not benefit all equally at the present moment but it surely needs to offer credible and tangible hope to those who may not be benefitting to the same degree. Disparities of income and opportunities can be tolerated to a certain extent, but once these swell beyond a particular threshold of acceptability the only consequence will be violence and revolution that will sink everybody and reduce us all to losers. (3) While all must contribute to the process of nation building, it is reasonable to hold that those who have benefitted more must also contribute more. To expect that one group of people pays the price for development while another group altogether reaps the harvest of development is unreasonable and unjust. (4) Any development plan, especially in India with more than 70 percent of the population living in rural areas must have as one of its principal constituents a detailed and integrated roadmap for the renewal, reinvigoration of the agricultural sector.[26] (5) Creation of wealth and growth in GDP are not ends in themselves. These are but means to enhance freedoms and to build capabilities that will contribute to integral well-being of all. However, there is unlikely to be any increase in wellbeing without a significant increase in wealth at the micro and macro level. (6) Economic growth must go hand in hand with generational, gender and ecological justice. Ruthless exploitation of the earth's resources, marginalization of indigenous peoples from their traditional holdings, and wanton destruction of other plant and animal species is an unacceptable price to pay for so called progress. (7) There can be no true development without good governance and systems of accountability. Democratic institutions – an unbiased and fair judiciary, a free and independent media, a balanced and integrated educational system, an incorruptible police force, free and fair elections, etc - which safeguard freedoms and provide the possibility for both the enhancement and the expression of capabilities must in turn be safeguarded. (8) In a country like India where the track record as far as equality and social justice is concerned is not so great, reservations and entitlements for the oppressed and marginalized classes are inevitable. However, these must have a time frame and must be empowering. Entitlements that only weaken the poor and create dependency and a shifting of responsibility for personal happiness onto other groups or the state for that matter do more harm than good. (9) Governments, Institutions, strategies and economic theories create possibilities for progress and development, but it is committed individuals who bring about change. Without large hearted and generous individuals committed to causes larger than themselves no nation can truly progress. (10) Of the many resources India is blessed with its greatest wealth is its human capital. Quality and universal education must be one of the most important priorities of any nation that has any pretensions to greatness. (11) A spirit of free enterprise, creativity and innovation promote economic development and progress. This calls for the relaxation of unnecessary regulation and protectionist measures that stifle and intimidate. (12) Differences of caste, creed, culture and language can either be a source of beauty or a cause for division and strife. No nation can hope to prosper without genuine unity, equity, cooperation and a respect for the uniqueness of individuals and groups. (13) No nation can hope to take significant strides ahead along the path of development in isolation from its neighbours and the larger world community. While it is imperative to protect one's borders and interests, the best way to ensure growth is that of engagement and interaction, the sharing of expertise and the welcoming of new ideas.

India is an enigmatic country for many people. It is a country that has much to boast about and also much to be ashamed of. It is often described as a rich country with desperately poor people. I agree with Jhabvala that one needs nothing less than a dead conscience to be able to turn a blind eye to the poverty and injustice that stares one in the face every day. Making poverty history in India may be a kind of "Mount Everest" as far as goals go. That day may not dawn in our own life time. Some among us may even think it to be a utopian dream. One thing that needs to be said of both Sen and Bhagwati is that while they may have their differences and may occasionally even be uncivil to each other, they are both believers who are convinced that a new dawn is indeed possible and it is something we all can make happen.

Notes

1 Ruth Prawer Jhabvala, *Out of India* (London: John Murray Publishers, 2003), 14.

2 Cfr. Manas Chakaravarty, *Richest 1% own 53% of India's Wealth*, http://www.livemint.com/Money/VL5yuBxydKzZHMetfC97HL/Richest-1-own-53-of-Indias-wealth.html, accessed on 16th September 2016.

3 Jeffrey Sachs, *The End of Poverty: How we Can Make it Happen in Our Lifetime* (London: Penguin Books, 2005).

4 Cfr. Bono, "Foreword", in Jeffrey Sachs, *The End of Poverty*, xvi –xvii.

5 Sachs, *The End of Poverty,* 1.

6 Sachs, *The End of Poverty,* 1.

7 Jagdish Bhagwati, "Why Amartya Sen is wrong" in Live Mint (July 23, 2013), http://www.livemint.com/Opinion/9Qzg05zypjEUbiogK9N1UM/Why-amartya-Sen-is-wrong.html, accessed on 10th September 2016.

8 https://www.questia.com/library/economics-and-business/economists/amartya-sen, accessed on 18th September 2016.

9 Cfr. Jean Dreze and Amartya Sen, *An Uncertain Glory: India and its Contradictions*, (Princeton: Princeton University Press, 2013), pdf, 39.
10 Cfr. Jean Dreze and Amartya Sen, *An Uncertain Glory,* 7-8.
11 Cfr. Jean Dreze and Amartya Sen, *An Uncertain Glory,* 15-17.
12 Cfr. Jean Dreze and Amartya Sen, *An Uncertain Glory,* 62.
13 Cfr. David Barsamian, *Amartya Sen* (Interview), http://www.progressive.org/amartya_sen_interview.html, accessed on 1st September 2016.
14 Cfr. David Barsamian, *Amartya Sen* (Interview).
15 Cfr. "why the world's biggest democracy still fails too many of its people", *The Economist,* http://www.economist.com/node/21580124/print, accessed on 8th September 2016.
16 Cfr. "The Mother Theresa of Economics", *Independent,* http://www.independent.co.uk/news/the-mother-teresa-of-economics-1076009.html, (January 24, 1999), accessed on 5th August 2016.
17 Cfr. Cfr. Jagdish Bhagwati, "Why Amartya Sen is wrong".
18 Cfr. Uttara Choudhury, "Jagdish Bhagwati: The World's Preeminent Free Trade Evangelist", *Braingainmag,com,* https://www.braingainmag.com/jagdish-bhagwati-the-worlds-preeminent-free-trade-evangelist.htm, accessed on 21st September 2016.
19 Cfr. "Five Questions for Professor Jagdish Bhagwati On the Indian Economy And Prime Minister Modi's Next Steps", Interview with Jagdish Bhagwati by Alyssa Ayres, Forbes Asia (May 27, 2014), http://www.forbes.com/sites/alyssaayres/2014/05/27/five-questions-for-professor-jagdish-bhagwati-on-the-indian-economy-and-prime-minister-modis-next-steps/#2d5d2880579c, accessed on 18th September 2016.
20 Cfr. Jagdish Bhagwati, "Why Amartya Sen is wrong".
21 Jagdish N. Bhagwati, "In Defense of Globalization: It *Has* a Human Face", in *Rivista di Politica Economica* (November-December 2004), pdf., 14,
22 Mihir S Sharma, " Bhagwati versus Sen: What's going on?", *Business Standard* (25th July 2013), http://www.business-standard.com/article/economy-policy/bhagwati-versus-sen-what-s-going-on-113072400516_1.html., accessed on 20th September 2016.
23 Cfr. Mihir S. Sharma, "Bhagwati versus Sen: What's going on?". Also Cfr. Axel Hameit Sievers, "The Big Indian Development Debate: Growth And/vs. Inclusion", *Heinrich Böll Stiftung, The Green Political Foundation* (March 24, 2014), https://www.boell.de/en/2014/03/03/die-grosse-entwicklungsdebatte-indien-wer-soll-vom-wachstum-profitieren, accessed on 20th September 2016.
24 Cfr. Mihir S. Sharma, "Bhagwati versus Sen: What's going on?"
25 Cfr. Cfr. Jagdish Bhagwati, "Why Amartya Sen is wrong".
26 Alex Hameit Sievers in his very insightful article on the Bhagwati-Sen tussle says that one of the most glaring limitations of both the camps of this debate is the surprisingly little that they have to say about 'the agricultural sector' where a significant majority of the poorest of India's people are employed. Cfr. Alex Hameit Sievers, "The Big Indian Development Debate: Growth and/vs. Inclusion".

17

Winners and Losers in the Development Game

Anthony Dias
Xavier Institute of Social Research, Nashik

Abstract: "Development" is a complex game and involves local, national and international players. It produces winners and losers. This article attempts to find out who the winners and losers are. It discovers that there are indeed winners but that there are many more losers whose losses are both tangible and intangible and which render them impoverished. They are the Project Affected Persons (PAPs) displaced and dispossessed by the draconian colonial law of land acquisition. Though replaced by a new law in 2013, it does not offer hope to the losers. The law is based on the doctrine of eminent domain which empowers the state to acquire any private land for a "public purpose" after paying a "just compensation". However, both these conditions have failed to control indiscriminate acquisition. Instead of expanding their freedoms the PAPs join the ranks of the "new poor", and are deprived of their basic rights and freedoms. In its concluding section, the article attempts to show that only the genuine praxis of sustainable development would guarantee protection of the rights of present and future generations and contribute to nation-building. It therefore explores ways of checking the acquisition power of the state by re-interpreting its core requirement - which is "public purpose".

Introduction

Describing the Bhakra Dam as "A New Temple of Resurgent India", India's first Prime Minister (PM), Jawarharlal Nehru dedicated it to the nation in 1963. In August 2016, the country's current PM Narendra Modi, referred to by his supporters as the *vikas purush*,[1] dedicated the *Kudankulam* nuclear plant jointly with Mr. Vladimir Putin, President of Russia and Ms. Jayalalitha, Chief Minister (CM) of Tamil Nadu to the nation.[2] He stated unequivocally that nuclear energy is clean and much needed for development of the country. His party, the Bharatiya Janata Party (BJP), won a landslide electoral victory in 2014 on the plank of development. Opponents of development projects say that these projects do more harm than good to the people and to the natural environment. Their clarion call is summed up in their slogan, "*vikas chahiye, vinash nahin*" (we need development, not destruction).[3]

"Development" is a high stakes game of and involves several players. In Kudankulam, where the plant is located, Mr. Putin, Russian companies, PM Modi and his government, and Ms. Jayalalitha, are all involved in the nuclear energy development project. The media is itself an influential player. Other players like intellectuals and grassroots workers joined the local people in protesting against the project. The locals risked arrests and threats to their lives and took their protest to the sea to draw the world's attention to their cause. The police attacked men, women and children. Sedition charges were filed against some people and their leader and anti-nuclear activist Udaykumar. The central government froze the bank accounts of local church NGOs and there were threats to stop their foreign funds. BJP leaders denounced priests and nuns for participating in the protests.

Winners and Losers

Politicians and big business promise a win-win situation. They tell the people that "development" would be seen and actualized through mega projects, which would contribute to the development of the whole country. There would be more production and exports, many jobs and more wealth. All these processes, the people are told, are part of nation-building. There would be no losers, only winners because wealth would "trickle down" and those who lose land and/ or jobs would be adequately compensated. Hence, at the end of the day, there would actually be only winners.

There are indeed several winners. When large dams and big industries were launched, several people benefitted, especially big farmers and industrialists. As the Gross Domestic Product (GDP) rose, particularly after liberalization with impressive growth rate of the economy, the Indian State benefitted although these benefits were cornered by big business and landed farmers, the elite and those in power. For instance, it is well known that politicians, who want to gain influence and want to win elections, wrest projects from the ruling government and bring them to their constituency. The public interests/benefits component of the project is subservient to the main goal of the politician, which is to become more powerful by projecting herself as the messiah of development.

Then there are other players, such as the companies which actually build the massive structures such as dams.[4]

The dam-builders have a nexus with an array of contractors who sub-contract and outsource their jobs. All these networks gain financially in the process of construction of mega projects. Large transnational corporations and big Indian corporate houses, which manage to get cheap land and other facilities such as water and electricity from the government, rake in a huge amount of profits which is shared with their shareholders. At the international level, there are other players, such as the World Bank, for instance, which wants to be known as a bank interested not in profits but in development. Although, on paper the bank insists on certain basic requirements such as fair policies of compensation and R&R, in practice it is known to honour its own commitments in breach. Who then are the losers; what do they lose?

There are several actual and potential losers. Their losses may not only be hard to quantify but they are also difficult to identify and understand. To begin with, there are the losers of the Law - the Land Acquisition Act, 1894 (LAA), which is at the heart of land acquisition - displacement - compensation/R&R regime. Projects launched under its "public purpose" clause are the cause of the direct and indirect displacement of millions of people since its enactment.[5] When the State wants to take land for "development", it uses the LAA's "public purpose" clause. A legislation of British vintage, it is based on the archaic doctrine of eminent domain, which empowers the State to acquire any private land compulsorily for a "public purpose", after paying "just compensation."[6] The Courts have also been categorical in ruling that there cannot be legal acquisition of land without a genuine public purpose.

However, "public purpose", which has an open-ended definition, makes it vulnerable to any interpretation by the government which has the final say in deciding what constitutes "public purpose". The Judiciary generally does not intervene in the eminent domain actions of the government which are ostensibly based on public policy. This has made land acquisition very easy for the governments. There was no law for rehabilitation, except for some states where laws were passed but by and large there were project-specific R&R policies, which were unsatisfactory. There were procedural lapses in the implementation of this stringent law. For instance, even its limited protective provisions such as giving adequate notice to the people before their eviction, were almost routinely ignored. Although, the sheer number of the displaced is staggering,[7] the record of rehabilitation has been dismal.[8]

When land is acquired forcibly, a lot of persons lose. Their loss is not only cultivable land but also the Commons which provide them with material and tangible livelihood resources, safety and security and a sense of well-being. Furthermore, the losers are also those who are dependent on other people's land and the Commons. All these losers, the displaced, are known as the "Project

Affected Persons/Families" (PAPs/PAFs). When not adequately compensated they continue to be losers till such time as they are "rehabilitated". In the case of tribals[9] who are not used to a cash economy, compensation money disappears and soon they have neither land nor livelihood. There is yet another class of losers and these are the excluded ones, those not recognized either by law or by R&R policies. Their names are not found in the list, although they qualify for compensation, due to their inability to provide proof of ownership of land. They are often termed "encroachers". In a non-literate economy documents such as title deeds are either not complete or are not available. Other losers are the landless dependent on landowners and these may include labourers and/or sharecroppers.[10] Women lose when families are displaced. Compensation and R&R policies focus more on men; women are routinely ignored. Another distinct category of losers is future generations who will inherit the present stressed and deteriorating environment. Apart from humans, another loser is the natural environment, the flora and fauna which continue to be damaged, often irreversibly, due to unrestrained developmental activities.

Understanding Losses and their Consequences

Development projects studied over decades reveal that the millions displaced suffer following recurrent losses whose consequence is impoverishment[11]: *Landlessness* is the primary and comprehensive loss because land is the foundation upon which the productive system, commercial activities and livelihoods are constructed. Land is not just an economic entity but an emotion for those who inherit it from their ancestors; a food security; a status symbol that provides guarantee for easy access to loan and helps in getting better marriage alliances in the family and represents self-sufficiency and independence. It causes a cultural marginalization, which has psychological implications like loss of self-confidence. Landlessness not only affects the owner of the land but also his family, children, as well as future generations because land provides hidden employment for every member of the family.

Joblessness, for those whose existence depends on jobs, the effects of displacement are destabilizing and debilitating. It results in helplessness. *Homelessness* is a loss that occurs when R&R policies and laws do not provide improvement in housing conditions, or if compensation for demolished shelters is paid at assessed market value rather than replacement values. A home provides a psychological, even spiritual attachment with ancestors; it provides a familiar environment for living and meeting the social and cultural demands. *Food Insecurity* happens because forced uprooting makes people fall into chronic food insecurity, caused by loss of land, livelihood and access to non-timber produce. These losses affect food production, availability of food and also the patterns of food consumption. *Loss of Common Property Resources* (CPRs) for the asset-less means loss of fruits, other edible forest products, firewood and deadwood for use and sale, common grazing areas, use of public quarries, and so on which account for a significant share of poor households' income and sustenance.

Morbidity happens due to stress and unhygienic conditions and when projects do not incorporate preventative epidemiological measures the situation can get worse. They become easy victims to diseases of poor hygiene, such as diarrhea and dysentery, to outbreaks of parasitic and vector-borne diseases such as malaria and schistosomiasis caused by unsafe, insufficient water supplies and inadequate sanitary waste systems. *Social Disarticulation* takes place when the disintegration of social support networks compounds individual losses with a loss of social capital. Dismantled patterns of social organization, which enable mobilization of people for actions of common interests and for meeting pressing immediate needs, are hard to rebuild. Such loss is higher when people are resettled in a dispersed manner. Such disarticulation processes undermine livelihoods and form part of the complex causes of impoverishment.

Distress migration: when the displaced have no means of survival, they migrate, either permanently or seasonally to cities where they are exposed to a number of risks. *Women's loss* happens when compensation money is usually paid to the head of the family, generally a male, who spends it on alcohol and/or gambling. If access to the commons is not available, women suffer because they lose additional sources of income and also their influence within the family. Schools in the new location are either non-existent or are far away and so children's education suffers. *Marginalization* finally occurs when families cannot fully restore their lost economic strength. Middle-income farm households do not become landless, but become small holders and families previously in precarious balance above the poverty line may fall below it and never recover, even without becoming landless. Marginalization is the cumulative effects of the preceding losses.

Nature's distress and losses of future generations: Development projects devour forests and damage bio-diversity which are then lost to the present and future generations. Land, air and water pollution have crossed critical thresholds and have reached "tipping points". Pressure on eco-systems is beyond their carrying capacity and hence compromises their power of self-regeneration. Harm done to nature is in most cases irreversible. This in turn harms humans who depend on nature not only as a livelihood base but also as sites of well-being and security, particularly tribal communities which live close to nature and who depend on it. Industries, dams, power plants and consumerism in India and all over the world have belched into the skies gases that have caused climate change which is harming the poorest of the poor since they do not have adaptive and coping mechanisms and resources. This is unsustainable development which harms the interests of not only the poor of the present generation but also of future generations. Hence both, *intra- and inter-generational justice* stand compromised.[12]

Observation and Analysis

The *process* of development and its *outcome* have not been entirely sanguine. There is indeed no gainsaying the fact that there has been impressive economic growth manifest in rising incomes and wealth production, external displays of which are visible in the form of goods and services, development of infrastructure such as expressways, airports, industrial estates and corridors and massive irrigation projects, all meant to fuel further economic growth. In its invisible form this wealth is hidden in tax havens. To entertain the business elite and the political class, swanky hotels and resorts, golf courses and boating clubs are mushrooming. To house the growing middle class with their strong purchasing power, there are plush bungalows and elite housing societies. Alongside these, one cannot miss seeing with one's naked eye not only poverty but also destitution all around in the form of sprawling slums, squatters on pavements and on the open grounds, children, the aged and the invalid begging. Along with the rising class of the *nouveau riche*, there is evidence of a burgeoning category of the 'new poor', the project-affected persons and families (PAPs/PAFs) for whom their very survival with human dignity is a daily struggle. Wealth has not trickled down. Inequality has increased and is posing a threat to human dignity and to society.

Across the country, acquisitions have triggered protests, some of them turning violent. In pre-independent India, there was fierce resistance to the building of the *Mulshi* dam.[13] Other protests continued during the post-independence period and despite Nehru's exhortations to the people to suffer willingly for the nation.[14] These protests became more violent as more land was acquired. In recent times, the wave of protests in *Singur* against Tata's Nano (small car) project and the reverberating sound of gunshots emanating from *Nandigram* in West Bengal that killed protesters and shook the nation as big business began to be implicated in dubious deal-making with the government of the day, is still fresh in the minds of the people. The tribal heartland is seeing extremist Naxal violence which has shaken the establishment. The State says that Naxal violence is the single biggest threat to internal peace and accuses the Naxals of unleashing terror; the latter say that they are countering State terror disguised as "development".

The response of the government to rising protests is to treat it as a law and order problem and to crack down on protesters instead of dealing with the people's genuine grievances concerning exploitation and development deficits. The response to extremist violence was to promote armies of tribals to fight tribals, effectively putting one oppressed group against another.[15] Finally, the State replaced the draconian LAA with a new one law. Enacted in 2013, the new law which as a Bill was known as "The Land Acquisition, Resettlement and Rehabilitation Act, 2013" (LARR) now has a long and interesting title, "The Right to Fair Compensation, Transparency in Land Acquisition and Rehabilitation and Resettlement Act, 2013." Although this law's focus is to acquire land quickly, it does provide for enhanced compensation and incorporates some other salutary provisions for land losers. Nonetheless, it also fails on many counts. The coercive eminent domain power continues to vest in the State and the definition of "public purpose" continues to be open-ended.

The whole purpose of the new law is an attempt to circumvent the hurdles before acquisition, such as rehabilitation of land losers and other affected persons, without substantially increasing the cost of land.[16] Several attempts have been made to amend the new law to dilute some of its provisions. The amendment Bill is still pending in Parliament with no resolution in sight. There are ongoing protests by villagers against land acquisition under the new law in the new State of Telangana. State repression in the form of censorship and restrictions on fundamental rights, have prompted villagers to say that they are being held "hostages in our own villages."[17] With the present government's push towards more foreign direct investment in industries and manufacturing, displacement and environmental degradation will continue unabated.

In the development-displacement discourse, it is often said that next to killing a person the worst you can do is to displace her. "Displacement" is a misnomer and hides the violence - physical, verbal and psychological - associated with coercive acquisition. It is actually deracination, which connotes violent uprooting. Coercive power of taking is used to uproot people from their habitat when those considered "encroachers", even when they have been residing for decades are evicted without just compensation it is a form of violence and raises fundamental questions about ownership and/or control of land and the commons. It leads to questioning the existence and role of the State and its power of eminent domain. Those who are somewhat lucky are forcibly relocated, but those who are not are forced to join the swelling ranks of the landless, the laboring and toiling classes, marginalized and impoverished.

Deprivation and the new poor

The PAPs are the impoverished "new poor", people who earlier generally led subsistence level dignified existence. From the perspective of the "Capability Approach", their poverty is a result of deprivation. There is not only income poverty, in the sense of lowness of income, but "capability deprivation."[18] The new poor suffer from multiple deprivations. They were either landowner, or were employed on the lands of others[19] or were share-croppers. Public purpose projects deprived them of their ancestral land, their homes and livelihoods. Joblessness robbed them of self-reliance and confidence and produced a sense of hopelessness and loss of dignity. These projects also deprived them of their food security. They were deprived of their homes. Displacement and/or relocation to a new and unaccustomed place, facing shortages of necessities and hostility from the host population, produced stresses of all kinds resulting in morbidity or deprivation of health. Distress migration brought in multiple risks especially when they settled in slums with inadequate or no access to civic amenities. Those who were forced to migrate seasonally and were employed at various sites faced exploitation of many kinds, ranging from non-payment of wages to sexual harassment in case of young girls and women. Children who accompanied migrant parents dropped out of school and were deprived of even basic education.

Instead of building capabilities, expanding freedoms and enhancing dignity, these situations produced the opposite. They reduced the capabilities of the displaced to lead the lives they valued. Instead of producing more and stronger freedoms, these situations made them less free, even helpless. Not only was there no expansion of freedoms, but whatever rights, freedom and dignity they possessed were taken away from them. "*Beghar se, hameh behaal kar diya*," said one Bhil tribal to this writer ("They have made us helpless, after making us homeless"). This is active deprivation *caused by the state* in the *process of development*. Furthermore, this process takes for granted that some people would have to *make sacrifices* for the good of the nation, for development. It is generally observed that it is the vulnerable sections of the public which are called upon to make the sacrifices; sometimes repeatedly by the same persons.[20] Often they are *sacrificed* at the altar of development. Those not lucky enough to receive compensation or resettlement face not only poverty but destitution, with starvation and death stalking them wherever they go or reside.

These “new poor” are those who have been “made poor” by the State. This is not merely *passive* poverty but *active* impoverishment, signifying that an external agency interfered with the lives of those who lived peaceful and dignified lives at the subsistence level. In this sense, impoverishment is state caused. On the other hand, some sections of society, especially companies and their officials, contractors and politicians, have gained *at the expense of* the losers. There has been “accumulation through dispossession”, which has increased inequality.[21] This is not only exploitation but an abuse of eminent domain[22] which is unjust and contrary to the vision and values of the Constitution which promised to herald freedom and a social revolution based on democratic ideals. The process of development has resulted in the transfer of resources to a few resulting in concentration of income and wealth in the hands of a miniscule minority. From the perspective of the Constitution and the expansion of rights and freedoms by some judges, these are not only grave deprivations *caused* by the state, through its acts of omission and commission, but also violations of rights. This is denial of justice guaranteed by the Constitution and eloquently articulated in its Preamble. It is not the Constitution that has failed us but it is we who have failed it.

The Promised Land is nowhere in sight; the promised win-win situation does not seem to exist. On the contrary, there is land and livelihood loss accompanying uneven growth. As a result, agrarian distress has deepened leading not only to an unprecedented wave of suicides by farmers but also mass distress migration, with its concomitant risks and woes. Inequality is stark and stares us in our face. Only a few have won and a large majority of people, especially the poor and powerless among those displaced from lands and livelihoods and ways of living, have lost. This is unsustainable development.

Conclusion

"Development" or "Public Purpose" should enhance the dignity of human persons and communities instead of depriving and impoverishing them. Poverty understood as deprivation, inequality, inequitable access to resources, unequal distribution of wealth and degradation of the environment leads to violence which threatens human dignity. People cannot be used as objects or as instruments to promote mere economic growth. Development should empower people by building capabilities and expanding their freedoms to lead the lives they value, both as individuals and as part of a community in which they can freely participate as equals and realize their full potential. Development should also not only not harm nature but it should be so undertaken that eco-systems are protected and promoted knowing full well that it is the livelihood base of the poor and that ecological balance is necessary for the well being of not only humans but also flora and fauna and the entire planet.

The boundaries of nature go beyond those made by humans; so is the case with pollution and environmental degradation. Not only are humans inter-related but this relationship extends to other creatures and to nature as a whole. It extends in space and time to future generations. We are one family living in one home, which is our "common home" and we share a "common future" that is at stake. The same is the case with justice. "Injustice anywhere is injustice everywhere." Intra-generational injustice will extend and adversely affect inter-generational justice. Authentic development happens only if there is *sustainable development* as conceptualized and articulated by the Brundtland Commission in its influential report.[23] For this to happen, there is a need to move away from the GDP-centric, top-down economic development model which privileges economics over other vital factors - such as environmental promotion, human rights and rights of distinct vulnerable groups - to a People-centric model in which people's free participation in their development is promoted through public hearings, devolution and decentralization of power, all of which recognize the wisdom of the local people to decide what is good for them, their environment and their nation.

Hence, it would be incumbent upon us to interrogate the State and question its power of acquisition. It would therefore be necessary to check the eminent domain and make it more accountable to the people and the Constitution. To rethink "public purpose" that forms the core or the basis for exercising the fearsome coercive power of acquisition in order to eliminate abuse of state power would be an imperative, an immediate task. Public purpose should be re-defined in such a way that it serves not private but genuine public interest by submitting to the foundational requirements of sustainable development - intra and inter-generational justice. Intra-generational demands that the rights and freedoms of the present generation guaranteed by the Constitution, and expanded by the Judiciary, are protected and promoted. It should be guided by the vision and values of the Directive Principles of State Policy (DPSPs) that "are fundamental in the governance of the country,"[24] which fundamentally includes development planning and implementation. This would include distributive justice that would be served when wealth is distributed in an equitable manner. Inter-generational justice requires that the rights and freedoms of future generations are not compromised by the projects undertaken by us in the name of development.

Secondly, "public purpose" should not be delinked from the requirements of "just compensation", as has been the case, but be intimately linked to it. If any project is either not capable of or deliberately excludes full compensation, it should not be considered as a project that meets the requirements of sustainable development. Compensation should enable people to not only restore their former standards of living and the freedoms enjoyed by them, but also help them to better their lives through bringing in more socio-economic and cultural opportunities to realize their full potential. Hence, it should take into account a more meaningful cost-benefit analysis that will factor in all the costs, including the full human costs involved in complete rehabilitation, and environmental costs as well. It should also tackle the conundrum of valuation as expressed in the concept of "constitutive incommensurability" through negotiations with unwilling sellers, such as indigenous people with strong ties to land and who find the whole idea of fixing a price on land and water and trees in order to sell them disturbing, if not revolting. This process should be made transparent and participative so that costs and benefits reflect present reality. Local bodies and village *gram sabhas* will have a big role to play. There are instances of best practices and success in this.[25] Civil society, academia and grassroots movement have also to play their respective roles in terms of raising awareness, mobilizing people and collecting data to check any abuse of State power and to protect the rights and freedoms of people and the environment.

Notes

1 Such a person epitomizes development. The PM is known as the architect of the "Gujarat Model" of development, which is one of the factors that catapulted him to the post of PM.

2 *The Indian Express*, August 10, 2016.

3 This is the slogan of the *Narmada Bachao Andolan* (NBA), a people's movement which critiques the existing model of development and proposes alternatives.

4 Patrick McCully, *The Silenced Rivers - The Ecology and Politics of Large Dams*, (New Delhi, Orient Longman), 2001, 243-254.

5 Smitu Kothari, "Whose Nation? The Displaced as Victim", Economic and Political Weekly, 31(24), (1996): 1476-85.

6 For a detailed discussion on this doctrine see Anthony Dias, *Development and Its Human Cost - Land Acquisition, Displacement and Rehabilitation of Tribals in India*, (Jaipur, Rawat Publications, 2012), 53-78.

7 Walter Fernandes and Vijay Paranjpye (eds), *Rehabilitation Policy and Law in India*: A *Right to Livelihood*, (New Delhi/Pune, Indian Social Institute/Econet, 1998), 149-168.

8 Only 25 percent of the displaced have been rehabilitated; Walter Fernandes and Vijay Paranjpye, *Ibid*. In Odisha those displaced by the Hirakud Dam built in the 1950 have still not received their compensation; see Rajat Kujur, "Underdevelopment and Naxal Movement", *Economic and Political Weekly*, 47/07, (2006): 557-559.

9 Tribals constitute 40 percent of all displaced and bear the brunt of displacement; see Patrick McCully, op. cit., 9.

10 Interestingly, in a recent protest, the main protesters were not the losers of land but those who worked on the land of others - the landless labourers. (Sreenivas Janyala, "Telangana Police clampdown on village opposing water project," *The Indian Express*, Sept. 14, 2016.

11 Michael Cernea, "Development's Painful Social Costs – Introductory Study by Michael Cernea" in S. Parasuraman, *The Development Dilemma: Displacement in India*, (London, Macmillan Press, 1999), 3-15.

12 The Brundtland Commission defines Sustainable Development as development that meets the needs of the present without compromising the ability of future generations to meet its own needs. The concept includes intra- and inter-generational justice.

13 The Mulshi dam protests in Maharashtra against land acquisition are considered the first anti-dam movement in pre-independent India and are a precursor to later anti-mega projects resistance all over the country.

14 Nehru spoke to the people affected by the *Hirakud* dam in 1948 thus, "If you are to suffer, you should suffer in the interest of the country."

15 The *Salwa Judum* militia that fought alleged Naxals was supported by the State, which also launched its own campaign Green Hunt to hunt them down.

16 For a detailed discussion on the Act, see T. K. Rajalakshmi, "A Law and its Losers", *Frontline*, January, 2013.

17 Swati Vadlamudi, "Landless, they fought land acquisition", *The Hindu*, August 6, 2016.

18 Economist-Philosopher Sen views poverty as "capability deprivation". For a detailed discussion on the subject, see Amartya Sen, *Development as Freedom*, (Mumbai, OUP), 2000, 33-43; also see Amartya Sen, *The Idea of Justice*, (London, Penguin, 2009), 225-290.

19 Swati Vadlamudi, op. cit., 17.

20 The phenomenon of "multiple displacement" happens, where those displaced and resettled are again displaced for another project.

21 C. P. Chandrasekhar, "The Myth of Growth", *Frontline*, August 5, 2016, 4-8; also see S. Subramanian, "Growth of Inequality" *Frontline*, August 5, 2016, 53-55.

22 In the Singur case verdict, the Judges admonished the previous Left Front government for abuse of this power. One of the judges even said that there was no "public purpose" in the acquisition, which makes acquisition void *ab initio*.

23 UN Document, *Our Common Future*, http://www.un-documents.net/our-common-future.pdf, 10th August, 2016.

24 Art. 37 of the Indian Constitution states that the Directive Principles are not enforceable but the principles therein laid down are nevertheless fundamental in the governance of the country; the article further adds that it shall be the duty of the State to apply these (principles) in the making of laws.

25 In Odisha, the *Gram Sabhas* were successful in rejecting the Korean company's POSCO project.

18

Clash of Nationalisms
Calling for a Gandhian Alternative

A. Pushparajan
Madurai Kamaraj University, Madurai

Abstract: The Indian Constitution is a momentous step towards the establishment of an egalitarian society, based upon modernisation and development. But it must be noted that any human progress also involves the spiritual dimension, which does not even find mention in the Constitution. The Constitution's vision is achievable not merely by political techniques, like legislation, but by simultaneously bringing about a change in the mind set, and attitudes to life. However, one cannot accept the blueprint of any one religion in a multi-religious society. In particular, one must clearly be aware of the domination of the so-called majority community's religion, precisely because it is not one single community, but is composed of myriad varieties each with its culture, beliefs, and practices. In such a situation then, what is required is a trans-religious approach of Gandhi and an interreligious dialogue and cooperation advocated by him. By being 'trans-religious' Gandhi meant that each one will be rooted in one's own religion and yet will go beyond it so as to co-operate with other religious believers. There can be no question of having mono-cultural model, trying to impose one's own world view upon others, but accepting that the worldviews of multi-religious and multi-cultural groups have co-existed for ages. This pluriformic, yet trans-religious, model is not meant for theoretical purposes but will be used to establish a just and new society, by pooling the resources of all so that all creatures will be able to live in dignity, equality and in harmony. This is what Gandhi succinctly termed *antyodaya* and *sarvodaya*. My submission is that if the Gandhian paradigm of trans-religious secularism was taken seriously, the whole set of problems regarding nationalism would not have arisen.

Introduction

A year after Shri Narendra Modi became the Prime Minister, Amartya Sen, a Nobel laureate who is an Indian citizen expressed a note of concern: "I think the threat to Indian secularism right now from the governing party is rather stronger than it has been in the past."[1] Such fears came true already within a couple of years since then: with Modi's exuberant promise of creating a "New India,"[2] immediately after the landslide victory of the BJP in the politically crucial state of Uttar Pradesh in March 2017 there is a clear indication that India is moving towards a Hindu state. No wonder, then, the India bureau chief at Reuters, while reporting at the swearing in ceremony of the UP chief minister on 12 March 2017, remarked: "The choice as Uttar Pradesh Chief Minister of Yogi Adityanath, a firebrand Hindu ascetic with a history of agitation against minority Muslims, stunned observers who said it marked a departure from the platform of 'development for all' on which Modi rose to national power in 2014."[3]

When Modi rose to national leadership, many forms of intolerance were unleashed across the country. Concerned journalists and authors like Saba Naqvi stated that, "The secular model currently offers no counter narrative to challenge Hindutva that claims to unite people above caste and religion in a national symphony."[4] Gautam Adhikari even spoke of a 'clash of nationalisms.'[5] In India, the one is inclusive and pluralist, as enshrined in the Constitution and, the other is Hindu nationalism which is envisioned by the Hindutva ideology and embedded in the slogan 'one culture, one nation and one religion.' This article tries to suggest that the Gandhian vision, if taken seriously, will prove a viable alternative to resolve the conflict between the two strands of nationalism.

1. Indian Nationalism

At the outset we need to make certain nuances clear regarding the use of concepts.

1.1 Nationalism is a modern concept

A cursory reading of world history will reveal that there was no idea of 'nationhood' anywhere in the world before the middle of the seventeenth century. The idea of 'nation-states' emerged only in the eighteenth century, perhaps as an aftermath of the industrial revolution. It was only in the nineteenth century that clearly defined states sprouted up, each with a central government. With technological evolution, the process of harnessing of people into imagined communities subject to a central state became simpler. It is only in the twentieth century that new ideas spread to the rest of the world.[6] As a corollary to nation, 'nationalism' became a driving force to define the state's identity, rivalling religion.

1.2 Nationalism is an ideology

Here there are two factors, distinct but interrelated: (1) People's 'attitude' towards their identity in terms of common origin, ethnicity or cultural ties with reference to the native land. (2) People's 'authority' to mould their domestic and international affairs with complete sovereignty. The former is designated by the term 'nation' and the latter by the term 'state.'

1.3 Secularism is also a modern concept

It became a political concept in the nineteenth century. In a word, secularism that arose in the modern west meant a clear separation of religion and state. This sort of political secularism was reinforced philosophically by the School of Rationalism which declared that the basis for morality could be found not necessarily in the principles derived from belief in God, but purely in the concern for the wellbeing of society. It even asserted that public morality ought to be seen solely as a social necessity, never appealing to the dictates of religion nor being influenced by religious authority.

1.4 Indian nationalism

Indian Nationalism, built around principles of Liberty, Equality and Fraternity, which were actually the values of rising classes, embodied mainly in the persona of Bhagat Singh, Ambedkar, Gandhi, Maulana Abul Kalam Azad and many others. Obviously thanks to the unquestionable leadership of Mahatma Gandhi in the freedom struggle against British colonialist rule the seed of Indian nationalism began to sprout and grow into a healthy plant. Muslim and Hindu communalists were not part of freedom movement because while freedom movement was all inclusive and aimed at secular democratic values, Muslim and Hindu communalists drawing from glories of respective kings of the past and kept aloof from anti-British struggle. From the decade of 1920 Hindu nationalists clearly opted to be on the side of British to oppose the Muslim Nationalists just as Muslim League had already curried favour with the British Raj as it regarded Congress as a Hindu party. Finally with tragic partition of subcontinent, India got the independence in 1947 and became a nation in the modern sense. It became a state as well, wen the Constitution of India was promulgated in 1950.

1.5 Indian secularism

Obviously the Indian nation-state is secular right from the beginning of its birth. The very fact the nation's founding fathers did not opt for a theocratic state while, Pakistan, the other partitioned part of British India, opted to be a theocratic state is itself a clear proof of Indian nationalism being secular. However, in contrast to the western idea, Indian secularism is not 'nonreligious' nor 'anti-religious'. As Sen put it, 'the roots of Indian secularism can be traced back to its long and diverse multi-faith history, including agnostic and atheistic trends.'[7]

It is important to note that Gandhi, while leading the freedom movement, followed certain principles unflinchingly. One of them was his interreligious approach, which he formulated in the formula *sarva dharma sama bhava* (equal respect to all religions).

Thus, Indian nationalism is secular and implies the following:

- Assurance of non-discrimination to minorities religious and linguistic, guaranteeing constitutional protection provisions such as Article 29 and 30.
- Right to establish their religious and cultural institutions.
- Some privileges to the minorities precisely because they are minorities they need some safeguards.
- Religious freedom to celebrate, to practise and profess their religion both in private and corporal sense.

1.6 Indian secularism in practice

Jawaharlal Nehru, the first prime minister, was an agnostic as he was the product of a rational secular tradition of a modern Western Europe. He felt that all religions would one day fade away, and was convinced that religion should not come in the way when state policy is being made.

The only aim of the nation builder was to create a modern and secular nation out of the diverse groups that constituted the people of India, liberating society from several kinds of bondage, and transforming it through application of science and technology without bringing in any religious consideration.

Moreover, he took a personal interest to codify Hindu personal laws even against the wishes of some sections of Hindus, although he allowed the personal laws of Christians and Muslims to be followed by their respective believers. Here again, his prime intent was not to meddle with Hindu religion, but to modernize society in the process of which the age-old practices of degeneration and immorality had to be removed at least by legal sanctions.

2. Hindu Nationalism

It is a historical fact that in the process of the liberation struggle of the Indian people, there were two groups which did not agree with this idea of nationalist movement as well as the leadership of Gandhi. Rather they clamoured for a religion-based nationalism: the Muslim and the Hindu. Vinayak Damodar Savarkar was the one who mooted the ideology of establishing a *Hindu Rashtra* and coined the term 'Hindutva' or Hindu-ness to mean the state of mind of a person who considers this land not only as his fatherland *(Pitrubhuh)* but also as his holy land (*Punyabhuh*)[8]. He maintained that Hindus were one nation (*Rashtra)*, one race (*Jati*), and one culture (*Samskriti*), mediated by one language (*Samskrta*). Savarkar's contention was that Hindus must have a privileged position and the various other religious minorities must accept the Hindus' way of life.

Taking a cue from the ideology of Hindutva, Keshav Baliram Hedgewar founded the Rashtriya Swayamsevak Sangh (RSS) in 1925 with the path of Hindu Nationalism and goal of Hindu Nation.[9] Its avowed purpose was "to train young Hindu men to stand up to the temptations of the secular society and revive the traditional values of Hindu India."[10]

As against Gandhi's attempt to draw the masses into anti-British struggle, Hindu Nationalists in the form of Hindu Mahasabha as well as the Constitutionalists like Jinnah and the traditionalists of Muslim League further drifted away and consolidated themselves after 1920s. Especially, after the formation of the RSS, Hindu nationalists gradually started asserting themselves, beginning with murder of Mahatma Gandhi.

Even within the Congress there was the division between the Hindu traditionalists and the liberal secularists which widened at the outbreaks of communal violence (1949-50). This in turn gave birth to the Bharatiya Jan Sangh (BJS).[11] Nehru wanted India to "lessen her religiosity and turn to science."[12] However, the tension between the secular and the religious remained strong. However, Nehru's government kept them under control. The RSS was even banned and silenced on the ground that the secular nation-state was created. But the Hindutva ideology did not die out. When the Congress-led government collapsed in July 1979, the BJS reorganized itself as the Bharatiya Janata Party in 1980 under the leadership of Atal Bihari Vajpayee, Lal Krishna Advani and Murli Manohar Joshi.

In 2014, the BJP formed the government with a simple majority and did everything possible to achieve its goal of converting Indian secularist nationalism into Hindu nationalism. The Hindu momentum spread far and wide and since then there has been a significant communalisation of the Indian society and politicisation of religion. Issues such as 'Cow as our mother', Ram Temple in the so called Ram Janma Bhoomi, Ram Setu, Abolition of article 370 and Uniform civil code have been made identity-related issues, and are coupled with 'Hate other' slogan, leading to communal violence with a view to polarization of communities along religious lines.

Modi, though himself a dedicated RSS *swayamsevak*, steeped in the ideology of Hindu nationalism, projected himself as the most powerful promoter of development, powerfully appealing to the economic aspirations of the masses. Asaduddin Owaisi, chief of Majlis-e-Ittehadul Muslimeen (MIM) puts it, with 'development' as username and 'hindutva' as password logging in to massive mandates becomes automatic.[13] No wonder then that under Modi's leadership, Hindutva-vad is working to revive Hindu nationalism with the sole view of converting India into Hindu nationalist state. To mention just a few of them:

1. **Using education for communicating saffron ideology**: The Vidya Bharati Trust (the RSS academic wing) runs thousands of schools and was given a statutory footing in the then BJP government in Madhya Pradesh. It allowed them to function in parallel to the state government's Educational Board and was permitted to incorporate any changes in the school curricula.
2. **Catching the young:** For many years the RSS has undertaken to poison the tender formative minds of children with hatred and distrust about the non-Hindu communities by undertaking its own schools, independent of the state boards like *Saraswati Shishu Mandirs*, *Vidya Bharati* primary and secondary schools and Rama Krishna Mission schools.[14]
3. **Distortion of historical facts**: The National Council for Education Research and Training (NCERT) the apex Central government body in charge of text books, observed that Vidya Bharati text books were "designed to promote bigotry and religious fanaticism in the name of inculcating knowledge of culture in young generation."[15] Further it has stated that the power, the resources and the authority of the state government were being used to foster among the young children a communal outlook to produce a generation of bigots."[16]
4. **Tampering with textbooks:** Under the auspices of the BJP-led government, the NCERT developed a new curriculum framework for school education.[17] In the name of correcting history, Hindutva ideology is being introduced in history books, despite heavy opposition from the intelligentsia.
5. **Manipulation of state institutions** like the legislature, bureaucracy, police department, and lawyers' associations has been done so systematically and so zealously that they don't bother about eruption of communal violence, even when characterised by riots and even genocide. Even the country's premier research sponsorship agencies like University Grants Commission (UGC) have not been left to function independently. The UGC under the Vajpayee's government was keen on introducing subjects like Vedic Astrology as a science. It called for proposals to set up Departments of *Karmakand* in selected universities. The stated objective is to "produce a trained group of young scholars with proficiency in rituals (Vedic, of course) and other cognate subjects" who in turn "will meet the requirement of a

larger segment of the society desirous of knowing and practising the path of action (*karma*) coupled with *Jnana* (knowledge) and *bhakti* (worship)."[18] Maybe it did not succeed. So, there is a talk about abolishing the UGC or modifying it.

6. **Attempts at tampering with the Constitution:** Even at the risk of facing severe criticism from all quarters, some bold attempts are being made to manipulate public opinion in favour of changing the secular fabric of the Constitution. Today, the BJP is clearly set to reorient the vision of the Constitution in favour of its communalist ideology under the name of review of the Constitution.[19]
7. **Intimidation of minorities:** There are instances of persecution of peace-loving Christians e.g. burning of missionaries alive, stripping priests naked and parading them in public and gang raping nuns, the consecrated persons. There has also been a series of incidences of churches being vandalized across the country. All this coincides with the rule of the BJP at the centre. These are all clear signals to tell the minority communities "in hard, harsh, stringent tones and action that their freedom to practice and propagate religion is under fire."[20]
8. **Curtailing the freedom of expression in universities:** We have seen the issue of Kanhaiya Kumar of Jawaharlal Nehru University, who was jailed for sedition, and that Rohith Vemula, the doctoral student from the University of Hyderabad committed suicide after he was thrown out of his hostel room. These are but a few examples of how the ABVP student wing creates problems even to the extent of pushing students to commit suicide. An M.Phil student in JNU, who belongs to a scheduled caste from Salem, and is a supporter of Vemula, stated in his blog: "These people claim dissenters as anti-nationals and seditious. They are going to kill many Rohiths like us, just for eating beef, for being rational, for being intellectually productive for the country."[21]
9. **Misrepresentation of truths** so as to create hatred among the masses against the minorities. For example, the subject 'Knowledge of Culture' prescribed as one of the core curriculum by Vidyarti Parishad seeks to pass off as historical truth that the site where Babri Masjid stood was the birth place of Rama, that it was invaded no fewer than seventy-seven times between 1528 and 1624 AD. It has described 2 November 1990, as a black day, because Hindutva forces tried to demolish Babri Masjid was repulsed by the police. Again it says that "India was partitioned on account of the conspiratorial politics of the followers of Christianity."[22]

10. **Indulging in sedition politics**: On her return from Pakistan, after participating in a SAARC Young Parliamentarians Conference, Ramya, actor and Congress member, had refuted Defence Minister Manohar Parrikar's remarks on that country, saying: "Pakistan is a good country, not hell. Parrikar's comments (that going to Pakistan or hell is the same thing) are not true." She made the remarks during a rally in her former constituency Mandya." She was accused of 'sedition' on 23 August 2016. A Karnataka-based advocate Vital Gowda lodged a complaint that "Ramya had insulted the Indian patriots by praising Pakistan."[23]
11. **Organizing *gharwapsi* or *suddhikaran* programmes** on Indian Muslims and Indian Christians on the assumption that they had to be given a ritual purification as sign of their repentance for abandoning their ancestral faith and thereby effecting their 'homecoming' into the fold of their former dharma. Though, it has met with opposition from many quarters and for many reasons,[24] yet the RSS leader Mohan Bhagwat declared in Kolkata that India is a Hindu country and there is nothing wrong in getting stolen 'maal' (goods) back.[25] How denigrating are these words to identify the converts as goods and objects.
12. **Appropriating and displacing the Father of the Nation**: In the early stages of its formation in the 1980s, the BJP described itself as "Gandhian socialists". They even took to the idea of Gandhi's *Rama Rajya* as their goal, and hijacked it, which some perceptive minds could grasp. Likewise, when Modi declared the '*Swatch Bharath*' project of his government, everybody thought he is appropriating the constructive programmes of Gandhi. But with the release of the 2017 calendar and diary by the Khadi Village Industries Commission, everybody now understood why his picture has replaced Gandhi's. Thus, it is clear that their technique is to first appropriate the Father of the nation and then replace him as a national icon.[26]
13. **Appropriating Dr. Ambedkar** in order to woo the Dalits. In October 2015, Modi performed the *bhumi poojan* in Mumbai to erect a 350 feet tall bronze statue of Ambedkar ('Statue of Equality'). It would be taller than the Statue of Liberty in the US which is 330 feet tall.[27] Then, on 15 November 2015, he inaugurated the Ambedkar Memorial in London, converting the house where Ambedkar lived between 1921-22. He also paid a high tribute to him in the British Parliament. He has exhorted the BJP MPs to work relentlessly for a fresh Dalit outreach to be crafted around 125th birth anniversary celebration of Ambedkar and a week-long celebration from 6-14 April 2017.[28]

14. **Engaging in double speak,** is much more evident in the case of the prime minister himself. As veteran journalist and commentator Shekhar Gupta told Reuters: "Modi is saying India is a Hindu country and shall remain so," ... "Hindus will rule, so you had better behave."[29]

All these measures, put together, clearly point to sealing "what appears to be a shift in course by Modi that could redefine the world's largest democracy as a Hindu nation."[30]

3. An appraisal: The Gandhian alternative, a way out

From the above accounts, it is clear that secularism in India practically seems to be no more than a political reconciliation of many religious communities and a political harmonisation of multiple communalisms.[31] Taking advantage of the fact that the basic features of secularism namely adherence to scientific temper and rationalistic spirit have not been defined in the Constitution each one began to interpret it according to their own background.

An agnostic like Nehru took religion to mean, in practice, as a private affair, and began to make a series of reforms in Hinduism. He went all out to push through the Hindu Code to reform Hindu marriages, inheritance and adoption laws. Questions may be raised as to why he did not reform the personal laws of the Muslims and Christians?

Meanwhile, the more powerful communal lobbies from the Indian Muslim community and the Sikhs began to voice that their religious minorities, culture, and identity were in danger. This in turn boomeranged on the crusading defenders of Hindu nationalism, who in turn began to voice that Hindu culture was in danger. They even came out with such slogans: "Secularism in India was essentially meant to weaken the Hindu solidarity". The so-called secularism enshrined in the Constitution is branded as "pseudo-secularism".

In this sort of argument there are certain flaws. (1) If the clarification of concepts explicated in the beginning of this paper is correct, and valid, then it is wrong to say that India was a 'nation' even centuries before the Freedom movement started. (2) Granted that the very term 'Hindu' originally signified a geographical stretch of land beyond the river 'Sindhu' seen by the Persians and Greeks, then it is clear Hinduism did not really mean a homogenous religion. It is further confirmed that what is today accepted as Hindu religion does refer to a variety of belief-systems, set of practices and code of conduct, practised by various communities. (3) The claim that Hindus alone are natives of the land and their assumption that religious minorities like Muslims and Christians are not natives, is totally untrue. They are very much children of this soil. In fact the traditions of South Indian Christians and Muslims is as old as their respective religions and thoroughly enculturated to the local environment. (4) Even otherwise, the culture of this land is so varied from community to community that it is essentially pluriformic, even contradictory to one another's. Right from ancient times the culture of the subcontinent has been one of heterogeneous framework. As Sen rightly remarks:

> The cultural inheritance of contemporary India combines Islamic influences with Hindu and other traditions, and the results of the interaction between members of different religious communities can be seen plentifully in literature, music, printing, architecture, and many other fields.[32] … The religious sects within the so called Hinduism is too varied. The numerous religious cultures of the tribals, even non-religious of Charvakas, Lokayatas, sceptics, atheists and agnostics.[33]

Needless to say that the Indian Constitution is a momentous step towards the establishment of an egalitarian society, based upon modernisation and development. But it must be noted that any human progress also involves the spiritual dimension, which does not even find mention in the Constitution. Here, the genuine concern of the traditionalists must be granted. The Constitution's vision is achievable not merely by political techniques, like legislation, but by simultaneously bringing about a change in the mind set, and attitudes to life. Hence, proper weightage must have been given to the Hindu sensibilities. True. However, one cannot accept the blueprint of any one religion in a multi-religious society. In particular, one must clearly be aware of the domination of the so-called majority community's religion, precisely because it is not one single community, but is composed of myriad varieties each with its culture, beliefs, and practices.

In such a situation then, what is required is a trans-religious approach of Gandhi and an interreligious dialogue and cooperation advocated by him. By being 'trans-religious' Gandhi meant that each one will be rooted in one's own religion and yet will go beyond it so as to co-operate with other religious believers, not merely at the socio-economic level but by truly drawing from the well-springs of each one's religious resource and sharing with others in a concerted way so as to solve the common problems of society collectively.

As against Nehruvian Secularism, Gandhi was never in favour of an a-religious approach, but he advocated for a deeply religious commitment. However, his view of religion was never sectarian. Personally, Gandhi was a Hindu, and he openly said "he prized it above all religions". But he immediately added that by religion he 'meant not a sectarian but that which transcends Hinduism, which engages one's very nature, which binds one inextricably to Truth within and which purifies.[34]

How significant is the comment made by a third person like Louis Fisher, the great American journalist and biographer: "Yet, the irreligious Jinnah wanted two religious states, while the religious Gandhi would countenance only a united secular state."[35] Should we say that this remark could possibly be attributed to the present day Hindutva-vad in an almost parallel term? Is not politicization of religion that seems to impel them to argue for a Hindu nation, and to adopt all sorts of means and strategies, which are crude, violent, barbaric, even immoral and uncivilized?

Even granted that some of them might be genuinely religious and are eagerly wanting to establish truly a Hindu Rajya and with a Hindu worldview, would they be able to say that they want to apply the same paradigm of the Gandhian *'Rama Rajya'* which he equated to the Christians' Kingdom of God and the Muslims' Kuda Raj?

The implication of such a paradigm, ultimately, is twofold: (a) There can be no question of having mono-cultural model, trying to impose one's own world view upon others. But it has to be essentially a pluriformic, but religious model, accepting the worldviews of the already multi-religious and multi-cultural groups co-exiting for ages. (b) This pluriformic, yet trans-religious, model is not meant for theoretical purposes but will be used to establish a just and new society, by pooling the resources of all in order that even the least of the human beings, nay, of all the creatures will be able to live in dignity, equality and in harmony. This is what Gandhi put in succinct formula working for *antyodaya* and *sarvodaya.*

My submission is that the Gandhian paradigm of trans-religious secularism, if taken seriously with both the implications (a) and (b) mentioned above, the whole set of problems regarding nationalism would not have arisen.

Unlike Gandhi, the western educated Nehru, despite all his respect and esteem for his *Bapu*, felt uncomfortable with the Gandhian paradigm. For him it was (b) and not (a). On the contrary Muslims, except for a few leaders, were frightened by the (a) component of his vision. They saw Gandhi's attempt to apply his trans-religious paradigm to the socio-political issues as a process of 'Hinduisation' of the nationalist movement and therefore demanded a separate nation. Still worse, the militant Hindus felt that Gandhi was too sympathetic to Muslims to be considered a genuine Hindu leader. They clearly saw that his reinterpretations of Hinduism was detrimental to their vested interests. They even went to the extent of terminating his life and career by assassinating him.

Now that we have witnessed the evil consequences of choosing one or the other aspects of Gandhian vision, and are face to face with the challenge Hindu nationalism, we can easily see the urgency to take Gandhi all the more seriously in the sense both the components (a) and (b) will have to be appropriated and applied to our present day context. To put it differently, the question now is: "Could we not think of being committed to secular ideas as well as to poverty removal, healthcare, elimination of undernourishment, lack of value education, etc.? Is one problem in India bigger than the other? It is worth remembering the words of Amartya Sen: "If there are two problems bothering you then address both the problems, and do not try to say which one is more important of the two, as if we cannot do both together."[36]

Conclusion

From the above, it is hopefully clear that there is a need and even an urgency to revisit Gandhi and accept and apply both the implications (a) and (b) of his trans-religious approach. The Gandhian approach is a clear and comprehensive understanding of nationalism integrating the values of both strands of thought that are at odds with each other.

In this connection, it is important to note that Gandhi had chalked out an 18-point constructive programme as the core component of any independent nation. The most basic of which are "Communal Unity," "Removal of Untouchability", and "Equality of religions."[37] It is in and through these programmes people can really establish their sovereignty. Whereas the nation-state relies very much on the use of legalization as its main weapon, Gandhi was relying very much on the sovereignty in terms of self-rule (*Swaraj*).[38] It is in pursuance of the constructive programmes that civil society can also play its role most effectively. It is in relation to such a role that the minority religions can contribute to the maximum by taking up the constructive programmes seriously.

On the part of Indian Christians, we could take up Gandhi's Constructive Programmes as indicators to new avenues of our Christian mission in India. If we really pursue them with a missionary zeal and as new missionary paths, it would be a significant contribution to nation building. This can never give room for Hindutva-vadies to level criticisms such as that we convert people with a view to denationalizing or making them anti-nationals and the like. Incidentally, it would remove the 'missionary crisis' that the clergy is feeling today in the Catholic Church.

Notes

1 Amartya Sen, in an interview with Siddharth Singh, "Amartya Sen: Threat to secularism stronger than in the past", http://www.livemint.com/Politics/bsW9sbkBQUeH1ntj9uxAAK/Threat-to-secularism-stronger-than-in-the-past-Amartya-Sen.html, First Published: Wed, Jul 08 2015, accessed on 19th Mach, 2017.

2 *The Times of India:* Bengaluru, 13 March 2017, p1. Also see on Twitter: "Together let us build an India of our dream so that when we mark 75 years of freedom in 2022, we have an India that will make Gandhiji, Sardar Patel and Dr. Babasaheb Ambedkar proud. Be a part of this India".

3 Douglas Busvine, "Hardline Priest Yogi Adityanath's Elevation a Sign Modi is Moving toward Hindu India" http://www.msn.com/en-in/news/newsindia/hardline-priest-yogi-adityanaths-elevation-a-sign-modi-is-moving-toward-hindu-india/ar-BBymkvg?ocid=spartanntp, 20th March, 2017, accessed on the same date.

4 Saba Naqvi, "Secular Manifesto for Change", in *The Times of India,* (Bengaluru: 21.3.2017), 12.

5 Gautam Adhikari is Senior Fellow at the Center for American Progress in Washington DC. He has been Executive Editor of The Times of India, and Editorial Page editor.

6 Gautam Adhikari, *art.cit.*

7 Amartya Sen (1998), 6-17.

8 V.D. Savarkar, *Hindutva: Who is a Hindu*, (Bombay: Veer Savarkar Prakashan), 102-111.

9 For years the main activities of RSS consisted of weekly meetings in urban houses and summer camps, teaching its members "nationalist, religious ideology and training them in self-defence, so that the undying vitality of Hindu manhood would assert itself so vigorously as to make the enemies of Hindudom tremble." V. D. Savarkar, "Foreword" to Savitri Devi, *A Warning to Hindus,* (Calcutta: Hindu Mission: 1939).

10 Walter Anderson and Shridhar Damle, *The Brotherhood in Saffron,* (Boulder, Westview Press, 1987).

11 Sardar Vallabhai Patel favoured an exchange of population and called for a hard line to be taken with Pakistan. But Nehru was against an exchange of population. Instead he suggested he and the Prime Minister of Pakistan (Liaquat Ali Khan) should make a joint statement assuring the minorities in both the countries of protection and fair treatment. When Nehru signed the agreement with Pakistan, known as the Delhi Pact on April 8, 1950, Shyama Prasad Mookerjee resigned from the Cabinet in protest, saying that the limited agreement would not protect the Hindus of East Pakistan and claiming that the riots formed part of deliberate and cold planning to exterminate minorities from East Bengal. He continued to advocate the need for a firm stand against Pakistan. Mookerjee proposed the idea of a new party with Golwalkar, agreeing on the Hindu Rashtra ideas. Golwalkar in turn agreed to send several "Pracharaks" as the first administrators of the proposed party. Impatient with the delay, Mookerjee started a 'West Bengal People's Party' on 28 April 1950, and in 1951 in Greater Punjab, in UP and Madhya Bharat. Finally, in a convention of all these units at Delhi on 21 October 1951 S. P. Mookerjee founded the Bharatiya Jana Sangh, a political wing of the Rashtriya Swayamsevak Sangh (RSS) "National Volunteers Corps" with the sole goal of rebuilding India in accordance with Hindu culture.

12 Jawaharlal Nehru, *Discovery of India,* (New Delhi: OUP, 12th Impression, 1992), 529-534.

13 Quoted by Sagarika Ghose "Can Hindutva deliver Vikas?", in *Times of India*, March 29, 2017, p. 22.

14 Aditya Mukherjee, Mridula Mukherjee and Sucheta Mahajan, *RSS, School Texts and the Murder of Mahatma Gandhi*, (New Delhi:, Sage Publication 2008), 18.

15 *Frontline* (Nov. 20, 1998).

16 *The Hindu* 'Editorial' (23.10.1998).

17 Shaukhat Ullah Khan, "On the verge of Saffronisation?" in *The Hindu* 5.6.2001, p. OB-2,

18 Cf. the UGC Circular from Dr. (Mrs.) Pankaj Mittal, the Deputy Secretary, and F. No 1-28/2001(CPP-11) dt.23 Feb. 2001.

19 A lot of materials may be found in the discussions that have come up in the dailies. Particularly one will be benefitted by the numerous feature articles that are published in *The Hindu*, especially during February 2000.

20 Nadirshaw K. Dhondy, "Minorities in India: Constitutional Rights and Actual Governance," in *Journal of Dharma*, XXV/3&4 (July-Dec. 2000), 326.

21 *The Times of India* (Bengaluru: 14.3.2017), 5.

22 *Frontline*, 20.11.1998.

23 'Sedition' charge against actor Ramya for 'Pakistan is not hell' remark" http://indianexpress.com/article/india/india-news-india/ramya-sedition-case-filed-against-actor-divya-spandana-for-pakistan-is-not-hell-remark-manohar-parrikar-2991772/

24 Francis Gonsalves, "Gandhian Perspectives on Religious Conversion: Garwapsi and its Effects on community in India" in Ed. Johnson J. Puthenpurackal, *Enhancing our Home: Re-Reading and Re-Living Gandhian Thought, A Festschrift in Honour of Prof. Dr. A. Pushparajan,* (Bengaluru: ATC and ACPI Special series 4, 2016), 294-311.

25 Vivian Fernandes,"National law needed on conversions: Jaitley" in thehoot.org, accessed January 5, 2015.

26 *The Times of India,* (Bengaluru 20, January, 2017), 8.

27 http://www.dnaindia.com/india/report-dr-ambedkar-s-statue-of-equality-in-mumbai-to-be-taller-than-statue-of-liberty-in-us-2244094, accessed on 18.3.2017.

28 *The Times of India*, (Bengaluru: 17.3.2017), 13.

29 Douglas Busvine, "Hardline priest Yogi Adityanath's elevation a sign Modi is moving toward Hindu India" http://www.msn.com/en-in/news/newsindia/hardline-priest-yogi-adityanaths-elevation-a-sign-modi-is-moving-toward-hindu-india/ar-BBymkvg?ocid=spartanntp, 20th March, 2017.

30 Douglas Busvine, "Hardline priest Yogi Adityanath's elevation a sign Modi is moving toward Hindu India" http://www.msn.com/en-in/news/newsindia/hardline-priest-yogi-adityanaths-elevation-a-sign-modi-is-moving-toward-hindu-india/ar-BBymkvg?ocid=spartanntp 20th March, 2017.

31 Rasheeduddin Khan (op.cit.), 137-139.

32 Amartya Sen (1998), 315.

33 It is significant that Amartya Sen, after an elaborate analysis of what constitutes the Indian identity, arrives at this conclusion: There cannot be any "proposal here to seek a single-factor explanation of India's past and present through an exclusive and separate focus on one particular feature out of multitude that be found in India's constantly evolving traditions", Amartya Sen, op.cit. (1998), 30.

34 M. K. Gandhi, *The Voice of Truth*, (Ahmedabad: Navajivan Publishing House, 1969), 263.

35 Louis Fisher, *Gandhi: His Life and Message for the World* (signet:1950), 150.

36 Amarty Sen's Interview referred to in footnote no.1 above.

37 M. K. Gandhi, *Constructive Programmes*, (Ahmedabad: Navajivan Publishing House), 1941.

38 Anuradha Veeravalli, "Swaraj and Sovereignty" in *Economics and Political Weekly*, Vol. XLVI, No.5, (Jan. 29, 2011).

19

The Nation as an Antinomy
A Note on the Conceptual Logic of Tagore's Dissenting Voice on Nationalism

Devasia M. Antony
Hindu College, University of Delhi

Abstract: In this paper, my aim is to analyze conceptually the logic inherent in Tagore's dissenting voice on nationalism. I argue for the case that this conceptual logic is found in the dialectic of *advaya-advaita* present in the works of Tagore. After offering clarifications on the use of certain terminologies and a rather explanatory justification for the use of the expression *advaya-advaita,* I will analyze the narrative of nationalism and the inbuilt problematic of exclusive predication and hermeneutic violence in the antinomy of the nation. After a brief description of the various nuances and significance of the twin concept "nation-nationalism", I will attempt to analyze the use of this concept in some of Tagore' chosen works. Various interpretations of Tagore's dissent are presented and analyzed. The problem of relationality or relativity between the "Self" and its "Other" becomes very important in the context of 'domesticated' nationalism. The *advaya-advaita* model employed here calls for universal humanity and not a parochial humanity as nationalism is often taken to mean.

Ami prithibir kobi [I am a poet of the world].

Tagore[1]

I love India ... but my India is an Idea and not a geographical expression. Therefore, I am not a patriot

– I shall ever seek my compatriots all over the world.

Tagore[2]

India has never had a real sense of nationalism. Even though from childhood I had been taught that the idolatry of Nation is almost better than reverence for God and humanity, I believe I have

outgrown that teaching, and it is my conviction that my countrymen will gain truly their India by

fighting against that education which teaches them that a country is greater than the ideals of

humanity.

Tagore[3]

When anyone asked ... [Diogenes] where he came from, he said, "I am a citizen of the world."

Diogenes[4]

Introduction

In one of his writings, Tagore unequivocally states that he is "neither a scholar nor a philosopher."[5] Then what is he one might justifiably ask? Elsewhere he says that he is a poet of the world: *Ami prithibir kobi*.[6] Parenthetically I believe that here lies in an embryonic manner a hidden and embedded conceptual logic in the thought-world of Tagore, in that he thought through human life, in all its myriad forms, *philosophically* and yet lived his life *poetically*. Further I want to suggest that the very condition for such synchronicity and mutual fecundation of the philosophic rationality and the poetic rationality in Tagore is to be located in his immaculately crafted and simultaneously sophisticated metaphysical-cum-poetic vision of *advaita* or non-duality.[7] It is in this context that I wish to hear, decipher and understand dialogically Tagore's dissenting voice on the very idea of the nation and its logical-cum-conceptual corollary, that is, nationalism.

Terminological Clarifications

Before we proceed, certain heuristic terminological clarifications might be in order. I have chosen to characterise the twinned ideas of nation and nationalism as an "antinomy". In modern logic, "antinomy" is seen as referring to a logically impossible conclusion though it might be seen as resting apparently on a correct proof. Frank Ramsey made a distinction between semantic antinomies which employ concepts like meaning and truth and logical antinomies. The much celebrated critical philosopher Immanuel Kant in his works uses the expression "antinomies" in the sense that a given antinomy is said to have a pair of thesis and antithesis based on sound proofs.

Kant attempts to solve this conflicting nature of antinomies by asserting that in an antinomy, a given thesis can rationally be said to belong to the domain of the *phenomena*, meaning things as they appear to us. And its counter or contradictory thesis can be seen from the domain of the *noumena*, meaning things as they are in themselves or things *per se*. And in this way the antinomous character can be resolved.[8]

In the Indic tradition both Ādi Śaṁkara in his *advaita* philosophy (*Kevalādvaita Vedānta* tradition) and Nāgārjuna in his *advaya (Mādhyamaka* Bauddha tradition) philosophy look at this problematic in a different way. The *advaita* tradition basing itself in the axiomatic principle of *ananyatva* – the categorial principle of relationality as fundamentally non-otherness or non-alterity -- argues for the case that a rigorous conceptual analysis of the dialectic of the Self and its Other shows that the categories of "Self" and "Other" are not ontologically oppositional but in a radical sense appositional. That means for the "Self", the proclaimed "Other" is not a radical "Other" but "non-Other."[9]

Ācārya Nāgārjuna, who historically predates Ādi Śaṁkara, counter-intuitively emphasises the epistemic character of the relationality of constructing concepts from the matrix of *partītyasmutpāda-vāda* or the theory of dependent origination which functions as the fundamental law of causality in Buddhism. He makes this cardinal thesis on the idea that a concept cannot but be relative to a certain cluster of conditions that allows the very possibility of the creation of that concept. Further this would mean that necessarily a given concept has no own-nature, that is, *svabhāva*. Hence, *niḥ-svabhāvatā* (the character of having no-own-essence) and its logical corollary *sūnyatā* (the character of non-substantiveness or 'no-thingness') being the very conditions of concept making, the significant conclusion that emerges is the leitmotif of *advaya* – meaning [epistemologically] not-two -- which is primarily a heuristic construct. That means *ācārya* Nāgārjuna is making a revolutionary thesis here: every concept built on the relationality or the relativity principle of *partītya-smutpāda-vāda* is ultimately a logico-linguistic-cum-conceptual fictional narrative having only pragmatic and empirical purchase value as it operates as the *samvritti satya* (empirical truth) in the horizon of human linguistic intercourse.[10] It is here that I want to argue for the possibility of the dialectic of *advaya-advaita* canon[11] which can be christened as the very locus of the conceptual logic embedded in the Tagorean dissenting voice on nationalism.

The Narrative of 'Nationalism' and the Problematic of Exclusive Predication and Hermeneutic Violence

The above discussion on the conceptual logic of *advaya-advaita* canon can justifiably be objected to especially from the disciplinary matrix of political science and history. Moreover after Gilbert Ryle, one can even raise here the issue of committing the fallacy of "category mistake". My contention is that the fundamental intellectual activity of theory building and concept formation has a primitive philosophical character and for that one can fruitfully recollect the philosopher Aristotle's idea that philosophical practice is fundamentally "thinking about thinking." This reflects to my mind the umbilical cord between philosophy and political science on the one hand and that of history on the other. Extending the reasoning further I wish to argue that the same symbiosis holds true for philosophic rationality as well as poetic rationality; thinking philosophically and thinking poetically. It becomes very significant in the context of Tagore's self-assessment that he is a world-poet which I have referred to earlier.

In the domain of theory building praxis in politics and other related disciplines, the twinned concept of "nation – nationalism" gets a sharp theoretical articulation enmeshed in various narratives. The universal principles that constitute nationalism are said to be mainly the following:

1) "... [A]n assertion of the primacy of national identity over the claims of class, religion, or humanity in general" with the assumption that "people can be better understood in terms of the linguistic, cultural, and historical factors which bind them to a territory than by reference to their general human capacities."[12]
2) "The economic dimension of such nationalism is the belief that the ownership and control of important resources should be maintained firmly within the nation itself."[13]
3) "The political application is the principle of self-determination which seeks to base political life on the nation-state, a sovereign entity dominated by a single nation."[14]

Elsewhere delineating the many meanings associated with 'nationalism', Anthony Smith has picked out the most important ones in this way: "(1) a process of formation, or growth, of nations; (2) a sentiment or consciousness of belonging to the nation; (3) a language and symbolism of the nation; (4) a social and political movement on behalf of the nation; (5) a doctrine and/or ideology of the nation, both general and particular."[15]

One can definitely list the advantages of such a given theory of nation and nationalism. Primarily and in an important sense it does generate a singular affirmative sense of identity, belonging and security that becomes a hallmark of a given particularized human collectivity. But my contention is that in the Tagorean *weltanschauung* the disadvantages of such an imagined, fossilized and socio-culturally fabricated reality[16] as singularity of the twinned concepts of nation–nationalism are much more perilous and tend to de-humanise the very soul of the human person as it is built solely on the fallacious foundation of exclusive predication which generates radical othering! That is to say, to my mind, the very notion and narrative of "nationalism" commits hermeneutic violence.

Tagorean scholars writing on the singular idea of nationalism, despite their hermeneutic multiplism/singularism debate,[17] are unequivocal in emphasizing the unique theoretical trajectory of Tagore's dissenting voice on nationalism. Ashis Nandy in his provocatively titled work *The Illegitimacy of Nationalism* offers a psychological biography of modern nation-state in India with particular emphasis on Tagorean *weltanschaaung.* Nandy points out the distinction Tagore makes between governmentality by kings and human races which symbolize civilizations and governmentality by nations which for Tagore meant rule of the nation-state. The latter for Tagore is universal and impersonal and predictably effective unlike the former where there is fluidity in its texture and gaps that call for individual life-affirming participation. Further the latter for Tagore imprisons the human soul whereas the former, however imperfect its extant model might be, liberates human consciousness. Nandy goes on to buttress his interpretation of Tagore's undiluted critique of nationalism by making a study of three classic novels of Tagore: *Gora*, *Ghare-Baire* ('The Home and the World' in English) and *Char Adhyay* ('Four Chapters' in English).[18] Elsewhere making a distinction between nationalism and patriotism *per se* where the former category is seen primarily as "an ideology configured in human personality" and the latter being taken to mean "a non-specific sentiment centering on a form of territoriality that humans share with a number of other species", Nandy contends that in Mahatma Gandhi we have a spirited critique of conventional nationalism whereas in Tagore we encounter the outright rejection of nationalism *per se.*[19]

Amartya Sen in a thought-provoking article makes an attempt to strike a middle path between nationalism as an unmitigated evil and as a universal virtue and says that it is the contextual felicity that makes the very idea of nationalism a boon or a curse. Further he interprets Tagore's dissent as a critique of aggressive nationalism which is nothing but another form of imperialism.[20] Another celebrated Tagore scholar Sabyasachi Bhattacharya warns one against taking a singular, monolithic view of Tagorean nationalism and the desire to locate it in the stereotypes of internationalism or pigeonhole it into what has been bracketed as antinationalism. Bhattacharya finds many accounts of Tagorean nationalism committing reductionist fallacy. For example, he sees Nandy's account of Tagore's idea of nationalism as reductionist as the effort is to fit Tagore into the worldview of what is called 'anti-modernism.'[21] In the same way, Bhattacharya critiques Michael Collins[22] for presenting Tagore's thoughts through the prism of what has come to be known as 'post coloniality'. According to Bhattacharya, a much sophisticated and nuanced view of Tagorean nationalism must include Tagore's attack of naked obscurantism which tends to be forgetful of the inclusive character of Indian civilization.[23] Martha Nussbaum, in her piece on cosmopolitanism and the practice of patriotism discusses the trajectories of transnationalism available in Tagore and in particular focuses on the novel *The Home and the World* to portray the "tragic story of the defeat of a reasonable and principled cosmopolitanism by the forces of nationalism and ethnocentrism." Further for Nussbaum, "... Tagore sees deeply when he sees that at bottom nationalism and ethnocentric particularism are not alien to one another, but akin – that to give support to nationalist sentiments subverts ultimately, even the values that hold a nation together, because it substitutes a colourful idol for the substantive universal values of justice and right."[24] This idea becomes incarnate in the dialogue between Bimala and her husband Nikhil over the issue of *Swadeshi*, the chanting of *Bande Mataram* and the ideology of patriotism in *The Home and the World.* To the complaint that his wife makes that he has not whole-heartedly accepted the spirit of *Bande Mataram*, [which to my mind, in a narrow sense is axiomatic of crystallised nationalism and hyphenated patriotism in a fundamental sense], Nikhil, the non-nation or trans-nation theorist and protagonist, makes this insightful remark: "I am willing to serve my country; but my worship I reserve for Right which is far greater than my country. To worship my country as a god is to bring a curse upon it." In philosophical terminology, one finds here the dialectic of the particular and the universal, as well as the need to respond to the call of universal humanity while being rooted in one's country without succumbing to the perils of exclusivist nationalism which is built on the perceived and constructed irreconcilable binary of the "Self" and its hostile "Other".

Concluding Remarks

In the discussion that we have had thus far what emerges is the hermeneutic polyvalence of the conceptual logic of *advaya-advaita* inbuilt into the very dissenting voice Tagore poetically cultivates on the various nuances of the ideological construct called nationalism. Nationalism can degenerate into a brute, oppressively violent and banal force when it is conflated with exclusive predication of the human consciousness in absolutist canons of territoriality and political power accruing from the nation-state. The therapeutic philosophic insight is to listen incessantly and uninterruptedly to the call of universal humanity. And in the Tagorean *weltanschauung* only that can liberate the human spirit, where the apparent other becomes the radical non-other of the Self that is. Perhaps this is what Tagore had in mind when he thought philosophically and imagined poetically the following:

> The hungry self of the Nation
> shall burst in a violence of fury
> from its own shameless feeding.
> For it has made the world its food.

And licking it, crunching it, and swallowing it in big morsels,
It swells and swells
Till in the midst of its unholy feast descends the sudden heaven piercing its
heart of grossness.[25]

Notes

1 Rabindranath Tagore, *Janmadine* [On my birthday], 1941, poem #6, Quoted in Uma Das Gupta (ed.), *The Oxford India Tagore: Selected Writings on Education and Nationalism* (New Delhi: Oxford University Press, 2009), i.

2 Rabindranath Tagore, *Letters to a Friend.* Edited with Two introductory essays by C.F. Andrews, reprint (Delhi: Rupa, 2002), 119.

3 Rabindranath Tagore, *Nationalism* in Sisir Kumar Das, ed., *The English Writings of Rabindranath Tagore, Vol. 2: Plays, Stories and Essays* (New Delhi: Sahitya Akademi, 1996), 456.

4 Diogenes Laretius, *Life of Diogenes the Cynic*, quoted in Martha C. Nussaum, "Patriotism and Cosmopolitanism" in *The Boston Review* (November-December 1994), 1.

5 Rabindranath Tagore, *The Religion of Man* (London: George Allen and Unwin, 1931), 120.

6 See note no. 1 above.

7 For a succinct view of the classical Indic *advaita* philosophical tradition see Devasia M. Antony, "Advaita" in *ACPI Encyclopedia of Philosophy*, Vol.1, ed. Johnson Puthenpurackal (Bangalore: Asian Trading Corporation, 2010), 24-29. For a more nuanced and contemporary re-description of *advaita* see Devasia M. Antony, "Towards a New Hermeneutic of Self-Inquiry" in Shail Mayaram (ed.), *Philosophy as Saṁvād and Svarāj: Dialogical Meditations on Daya Krishna and Ramchandra Gandhi* (New Delhi: Sage Publications India Pvt. Ltd, 2014), 85-94 and Devasia M. Antony, "Play Theatre and Non-Dualism" *Philosophy East and West*, Vol. 66, No.1 (2016), 5-12.

8 See "Antinomy" in Thomas Mautner, *A Dictionary of Philosophy* (Oxford: Blackwell Publishers, 1996), 21-22.

9 See Ādi Śaṁkara, *Brahmasūtra-Śāṁkara-Bhāṣya*, [*Adhyāsa-Bhāṣya*] Ādi Śaṁkara's Introduction in *Vedānta Sūtras with the Commentary of Sankaracarya*, trans. George Thibaut (Delhi: Low Price Publications, 1996 [first published 1896], 3ff

10 See the chapter titled *pratyaya-parīkṣā* [An Analysis of Conditions]' in Nāgārjuna, *Nāgārjuna,'s Middle Way: Mūlamadhyamakakārikā*, Mark Siderits and Shoryu Katsura (Boston: Wisdom Publications, 2013), 17ff.

11 For a discussion on the philosophical import of the canon of *advaya-advaita* see Devasia M. Antony, *Interrogating the Humanus: Raimon Panikkar and the Interlude between Advaya and Advaita* [forthcoming publication]. Paper presented in the International Conference on 'Relearning to Be Human for Global Times: The Cross-Cultural Way' held at Manipal University, Jaipur, December 26-27, 2016.

12 "Nationalism" in Iain McLean and Alistair McMillan, *The Oxford Concise Dictionary of Politics*, Indian edition (New Delhi: Oxford University Press, 2006 [First published 1996]), 361.

13 Ibid.

14 Ibid.

15 Antony D. Smith, *Nationalism: Theory, Ideology and History*. Indian edition reprint (Cambridge: Polity Press, 2005 [First published 2001], 5-6.

16 Here, it does augur well to refer to the classic work of Benedict Anderson, *Imagined Communities*, which has brought into the centre of intellectual discourse across disciplines the very idea of nationalism. In interpreting the 'anomaly' of nationalism, Anderson contends that "… nationality … nation-ness, as well as nationalism are cultural artifacts of a particular kind … and they command … profound emotional legitimacy." Later he would contrast the political power of nationalism with its inbuilt philosophical poverty and incoherence. Benedict Anderson, *Imagined Communities: Reflections on the Origin and Spread of Nationalism*. Revised edition (London / New York: Verso, 2006 [First published 1983]), 4-5.

17 By the expression 'hermeneutic singularism and multiplism' I mean the very determination of the nature of the object that is amenable to interpretation and thus articulated in the categories of singularism or multiplism.

18 Ashis Nandy, *The Illegitimacy of Nationalism: Rabindranath Tagore and the Politics of Self* (Delhi: Oxford University Press, 1994), 4ff.

19 Ashis Nandy, "Nationalism, Genuine and Spurious: Mourning Two Early Post-Nationalist Strains", *Economic and Political Weekly* (August 12, 2006), 3500.

20 Amartya Sen, "Is Nationalism a Boon or a Curse?" *Economic and Political Weekly* (February 16, 2008), 40.

21 See Ashis Nandy, *The Illegitimacy of Nationalism* (footnote n. 18 above).

22 See Michael Collins, *Empire, Nationalism and the Post-Colonial World: Rabindranath Tagore's Writings on History, Politics and Society* (Oxford: Routledge, 2013).

23 See Sabyasachi Bhattacharya, "Antinomies of Nationalism and Rabindranath Tagore", *Economic and Political Weekly* (February 6, 2016) 39-41.

24 Martha Nussbaum, "Patriotism and Cosmopolitanism" *Boston Review* (October/November 1994), 2. http://www.bostonreview.net/BR19.5/Nussbaum.php#1. Accessed on 01/01/2017.

25 Rabindranath Tagore, *The Sunset of the Century* in Sisir Kumar Das, ed., *The English Writings of Rabindranath Tagore, Vol. 2: Plays, Stories and Essays* (New Delhi: Sahitya Akademi, 1996), 466.

20

Revisiting Narayana Guru, Periyar and Ambedkar for Secular Modernity in India

James Ponniah
University of Madras

Abstract: India claims to be one of the largest democratic, secular, modern states of the world. It has undergone mutations, conflicts and turbulent transformations to come to this level. In this context, this essay focuses on the initiatives and struggles of three leaders - Narayana Guru, Periyar and Dr. B. R. Ambedkar – who, basing themselves on the principles of equality, individual freedom and rationality, sought to make India a secular modern state, either through direct political activism (as in the case of Periyar and Ambedkar) or through spiritual activism (as in the case of Narayana Guru).

Introduction

Secularity and modernity are two important characteristics of Indian democracy. Fraught with struggles, the project of establishing secular modernity in India had to confront the iron cage of age-old Indian systems like the *varnashrama dharma* in an attempt to align them with the values of secular modernity such as rationality, equality, fraternity, justice and individual rights. Secular modernity is understood as the realization of certain principles and values of modernity that not only altered the then existing traditional values and practices in culture and religion but also affected the identity formation of the self (both individual and collective) and the state, and the relations such a process entailed between the state, the self and religion on the one hand, and among the citizens as equals on the other. The translation of modern principles such as equality, socio-economic justice, rationality, fraternity and individuality on Indian cultural soil met with multiple roadblocks as some of them were diametrically opposed to the already existing Indian idioms and ethos. Many attempts were made in this regard by a range of leaders to liberate Indian people from the tyranny of the dehumanizing aspects of India's past in as much as some leaders were inspired by Indian ideas to evolve a universal outlook. This essay focuses on the life and mission of three great leaders, namely, Narayana Guru, Periyar and Ambedkar, who contributed to the project of secular modernity in India. While Narayana Guru's attempts of translation embodied religious means such as building of *avarna* temples and ashrams, both Ambedkar and Periyar's project of translation involved direct political engagement. While Periyar's efforts of translation remained all through anti-religious, Ambedkar just before his death opted for Buddhism to invent his own version of it in neo-Buddhism to serve as a source of emancipatory identity for the Dalits. Thus while Periyar sought solutions to the problem of translation outside religion, both Narayana Guru and Ambedkar drew upon religious resources to achieve the same goal. What brings all of them into one camp is their passionate engagement with the project of low caste emancipation which steered them towards modernity as an agency of transformation. As described below, it is the emancipatory vision and actions of these three leaders that propelled them to embrace and promote the secular modern values of equality, fraternity and rationality.

Narayana Guru's Project of Emancipation

Central to the praxis of emancipation of Narayana Guru (1854 – 1928) was his famous slogan, 'one caste, one religion and one God.' He developed his emancipatory anthropology around the key organizing principle of 'humanity as one caste' that, he hoped, would put an end to all social and religious evils of his time. The princely Hindu state of Travancore into which he was born as an Ezhava was notorious for its infamous corpus of dehumanizing castes and untouchable evil practices. His idea of humanity as one caste was aimed at not only eliminating all these evils but also building up a casteless society. Through logical reasoning, he arrived at the idea of a world that had only one caste. Having defined caste as 'a special characteristic seen in several individuals of a species - which 'separates them from all others,'[1] he went on to assert "within a species, is it not, that offspring truly breed? The community of man thus viewed, to a single caste belongs."[2] He said that no two different species can, by their union, reproduce. Since any two caste people can reproduce another human being, they both belong to the same species, same caste. 'As bovinity is to the cow, humanness to humanity is a symbol of human caste or creed.'[3] As cows are distinguished from other animals and species by its bovine nature, so human caste is identified by its humanness.

To disseminate the idea of equality to his contemporaries, he employed philosophical ideas and idioms which already existed. For instance, his idea of the equality of all is founded upon the advaita philosophy of oneness of reality, according to which, there is no difference between soul and God, one soul and another, and therefore between one man from another. He once said, "One of kind, one of faith, and one in God is man; Of one womb, of one form, difference herein none.'[4] At another place he observes:

'All limbs suppressing and standing as a bolt
The limb-owner mere vapour enshrouds within
'This' man he takes different from 'that' therefore,
Owing to the weakness of unwisdom alone.'[5]

What underlies all the above said ideas is the belief that no one is superior or inferior. Hence divisions and distinctions such as Brahmins, Kshatriyas, etc., are all not innate and true, but man-made and false. At the time of birth, there is no caste. All are equal. Inequality and differences occur only later in the externalities due to variations in opportunities and social possibilities. Divisions occur not among animals but among the humans. In one of his press meetings he made clear this point: "A dog recognizes another dog of its own kind. All beasts possess this recognizing power. They live according to it. But man alone has doubts in this matter. He does not have the power to distinguish his kind or caste. Men are worse than beasts."[6] Narayana Guru was also a firm believer in the value of fraternity. His firm faith in advaitic equality also serves as a base for universal brotherhood and fraternity: "The other man's interest that is even mine, what to oneself is beneficial is so far the other man also; such is the course of discreet conduct; all acts aiming each man's self-happiness must spell at once the happiness of the other fellowman."[7]

Emancipation demanded that there was freedom in society to develop one's self according to one's choice. In this regard, Narayana Guru indicted the caste system once again as one's caste hampers the growth of a human being and takes away one's freedom to develop one's intelligence. He said "It hinders the freedom of man. It destroys intelligence. There is no advantage in reducing freedom and intelligence. Everyone should have the freedom to study and work one chooses to. Do not restrict one's study to one subject or one sphere alone. There should be no restriction on people regarding their study and practices."[8] He also critiqued the systemic discrimination that deprived the low castes of their intelligence. Emancipatory social justice demanded that new opportunities be created for the low castes to study and develop their talents. With his praxis-oriented approach he started schools in various poor neighborhoods to educate children – both boys and girls. In 1905, he spoke to the inmates of the ashram before they were sent out on mission: 'Explain to the people the need for education, highlight its advantages and the loss and dangers caused by the absence of education. Encourage them to feel proud that there will not be a man or a woman without at least primary education among them. Encourage the people to start schools, libraries and reading rooms wherever possible.'[9]

For Narayana Guru, emancipation involved not only social justice but also economic justice. Here also he denounced the caste system for its ill effects on the economic growth of a human person. "How can we improve our occupations without freedom and intelligence? Caste degrades occupations."[10] To defend people's freedom to choose their intelligence and careers, he cited the examples of Parasara and Vyusa, who in spite of their low caste background, rose to great heights to give us great scriptures: "In by-gone days of a Pariah woman, the great sage Parasara was born As even he of Vedic-aphorism fame of a virgin of a fisher-folk."[11]

In this regard, we can recall his instruction to his disciples on agriculture and industry. Before sending them out to serve the poor, he exhorted them as follows: "Speak about methods and means to improve agricultural facilities, trade, industries and handicrafts. Wherever necessary start factories. Encourage the people to learn technology and spread it."[12]

Another modern principle that Narayana Guru pursued was 'rationality'. Like renaissance thinkers such as Mohan Roy and others, he developed his religious system on firm rational grounds. About Narayana Guru one author observes, 'He discarded everything that was based on superstition or which offended the dignity of man. He therefore opposed the practice of determining the status of man by his caste, religion, race or class.'[13] In similar vein, Narayana Guru called upon his disciples to expose superstitions and dissuade people from worshipping evil spirits with weird rites like animal sacrifices. His advice to his disciples in this regard was: "Exhort the people to practice truth, cleanliness, fear of evil and faith in God; urge them to give up meaningless and harmful customs, and adopt better modes of conduct in tune with the changing times."[14] However, he held, 'Whenever there is a genuine demand for a temple encourage people in an intelligent manner.'[15]Anticipating the spirit of Indian secularism, i.e., equal respect for all religions, he advised his disciples: "Never criticize other religions in an objectionable way or hurt the feelings of those who follow other religions."[16]

Narayana Guru's philosophy of emancipation involved both thought and action. To advance his emancipatory project, he implemented a number of action-plans. First among them was the installation of Sivalinga at Aruvippuram in Kerala. In contravention of the accepted norms of his times, Narayana Guru, a non-Brahmin Ezhava installed a Sivalinga. By performing a ceremony which was regarded as the exclusive prerogative of Brahmins, he launched a decisive onslaught on the caste system. Later, when a Brahmin priest questioned the legitimacy of his act, Narayana Guru famously replied: "I have installed only the Ezhava Shiva."[17] However, Narayana Guru later on inscribed on the temple wall of the very same Sivalinga the following words which eloquently declared his vision of the oneness of man:

> "This is the model abode
> Where all men live in brotherhood
> Without any caste distinction
> Or religious animosities."[18]

To further realize his emancipatory vision for the depressed classes, he founded ashrams for the oppressed people and with the help of his prominent disciples Dr. Palpu and Ayyapan he started an organization called SNDP which started schools and many other programs for the upliftment of Ezhavas in Kerala. Narayana Guru, like the other two leaders translated his philosophy into a transformative programme of action that would bring hope to tens of thousands of the common folk. He had a grand vision which combined spirituality with social praxis. He never organized any protest against oppression but travelled extensively to illumine the minds of the ordinary people.

According to Jerald Pereira, the views of Narayana Guru come close to the concepts of equality, liberty and fraternity of modern socialism.[19] Another scholar writes: "His life was mostly devoted to up-lifting, to modernity and higher levels of humanism in this small part of the Indian sub-continent, Kerala, then hopelessly steeped in the quagmire of social taboos and superstitions to an extent that provoked Swami Vivekananda to condemn it as a 'lunatic asylum'."[20] 'Today we talk of the rights of man. We have the Declaration of Human Rights by the United Nations Organization. The Indian Constitution also envisages the creation of a secular, casteless and classless society. The fundamental ideas inspiring these documents were given to the people three quarters of a century ago by Sree Narayana Guru,'[21] extols Vishwanathan.

Periyar's Mission for an Egalitarian Society

Periyar (1879-1973) from Tamil Nadu is another important legend of the twentieth century who relentlessly worked for social transformation throughout his life. His contribution towards making India a modern secular egalitarian nation lies in his long-drawn battle to bring about social justice, gender justice, human rights and rationalism in a country that was deep-rooted in its own traditions of male-dominance, caste-discrimination, injustice and irrationality. This section below describes some of his efforts in this direction.

Seen against the background of the then prevalent caste discriminations in India where Brahminocracy (a term coined by Periyar) ruled the roost, Periyar's decisive battle for social justice that began with the founding of the Self-Respect Movement in 1925 was very commendable. The term 'self-respect' stands for respect towards the identity and dignity of individuals, which Periyar felt were reserved only for the high castes but denied to the *Sudras* and the scheduled castes. The mission of the self-respect movement was to remove social inequalities in Hindu society and to usher in an egalitarian and just society wherein there would be equality of status and opportunity to all castes. Indicting the hierarchical caste system on two counts, namely, for the loss of respect and human dignity which the Sudras and the SCs suffered, and for the lack of spirit of unity and brotherhood it produced in the nation, Periyar took manifold steps to overcome this sinister system.

For instance, Periyar fired the first salvo for social justice in Tamil Nadu in 1924 when he started a campaign against the Cheranmahadevi Gurukulam which enforced separate dining for the high-caste Brahmins and low-caste non-Brahmins with difference in quality of food.[22] He also fought for the removal of *agraharams* for the Brahmins and cherries for the 'untouchables', which in his view, was an apartheid worse than what was practiced against the blacks in South Africa. Secondly, in the first self-respect conference held in 1929, he passed two resolutions: one to condemn Varnashrama Dharma and the arbitrary division of society into Brahmins, Kshtriyas, Vaisyas, Sudras and Panchamas and to repudiate the belief in the superiority of Brahmins based on their birth; and, second, to give up the use of all suffixes and terms that bore caste-titles. Thirdly, taking cognizance of the fact that the Brahmins held disproportionately large number of posts in government services, he pressed for a communal government order (G.O.) that sought to ensure the representation of all communities in government jobs proportionate to their size in the population. Realizing that many posts reserved for the non-Brahmins remained vacant for the lack of qualified people from these communities, Periyar also fought for the introduction of Communal G.O. in all government-owned professional colleges and educational institutions. Later on when these G.Os were challenged in Madras High Court and knocked down as a violation of Article 14 of the constitution, Periyar campaigned for the amendment of the Constitution itself. It led to the first amendment of the Indian Constitution on 18 June 1951 that led to a new Article 15 (4) which 'empowered the state for making special provisions for the advancement of any socially and educationally backward classes of citizens and the scheduled castes and the scheduled tribes.[23]

To bring about an egalitarian India, Periyar also promoted gender-justice. He proposed many measures to remove discrimination against women. In the first self-respect conference held in Chengelpet in 1929, he invited women representatives to discuss their issues and passed many resolutions in support of their right of inheritance of the property of her parents and deceased husband, the right to divorce her husband and seek remarriage, widow's right to remarriage and the right of woman to exercise birth control. He also advocated the restrain and prevention of child marriage. He proposed that woman should be enrolled in the police department and should be recruited for military services. He advocated that the virtue of chastity should not be a one way traffic and should be enforced equally on men and women. Undue emphasis on women's chastity is a patriarchal conspiracy to enslave and subjugate women. He proposed that the initials before a person's name should be the mother's name and not the father's name. The best tribute for Periyar's work for women's emancipation was evidenced by the fact that the title of 'Periyar' (great man) was conferred upon him by the women themselves in a women's conference held at Madras in November 1938.[24]

Periyar's mission also included the promotion of human rights especially of the untouchables to restore their human dignity and to make them as equals with other citizens. In the 1922 Congress conclave, he sponsored a resolution that Hindu temples should be made accessible to the untouchables and the Nadars, a caste treated almost as bad as the SCs. Further, on special request by the Kerala Congressmen in 1924, he went to Kerala to lead the agitation of temple entry at Vaikom. When he was imprisoned for six months, his sister and wife carried out the struggles on his request. When a question was raised, why he, a militant atheist, who called temples the 'refuge of scoundrels', took part in the Temple entry agitation, his answer was that as long they existed, they should not be used as another agency of caste-based discrimination. Further, on 27 November 1957 he went to burn a copy of the Constitution of India for it had failed to abolish casteism in India.[25]

Another important contribution of Periyar to modern India is his campaign for *pakuthrarivu* (rationalism). The primary goal of this campaign was to liberate human beings from the bondages of customs and traditions, and to see humanity and life through the window of reason. He saw lack of rationality as a cause for conflict, enmity and folly. He observed: "In the society, the existing differences, enmity, hatred, disgrace, squalor, stupidity, and such other human qualities are caused by man's deficiency in knowledge, absence of rationalism or non-use of rationalism in a proper manner."[26] For him 'rationalism is the triumph of reason, in human affairs, in the life of individuals, at home, in society, and in the whole country. Rationalism consists in the spirit of inquiry and questioning everything, including what he said and wrote. Rationalism means bringing all things under the scrutiny of critical reason that would widen people's horizon of knowledge and outlook. It would help them 'not to be narrow-minded and dogmatic but to be liberal and tolerant in their views.'[27] He subjected everything to reason and evaluated it on that basis of usefulness and functional efficiency. Periyar stood for change guided by rationality. He said: "We welcome and accept changes taking place in the society. They are caused by the growth of knowledge and scientific research."[28] In another place, he said "Today things considered rational may tomorrow be brushed aside superstitious … why, our offspring may refer to me and comment, 'there was one Ramaswamy who was superstitious.' This is in the nature of things only, a symbol of change and a mark of changing times."[29]

Periyar's famous dictum '*Kadavilai mara manithanai ninai*' ('Forget God, think of the human') is a bold statement that not only enthroned 'rationality' as the reigning epistemological paradigm for modern Tamil Nadu, but also became the very motif of thousands of his meetings held in public squares and street corners during which he vociferously criticized the misuse of religion and ridiculed its Brahminic renderings. In this context he said "the religious minded man has neither self respect nor original mind. Religion is against man's progress and his unity."[30] He also went on to say: "Do not accept anything on the pretext that our forefathers have said so. Do not believe whatever is found in ancient scriptures simply because they are ancient and sacred."[31]

He was a bare foot rationalist 'who carried the message of rationalism to the people and delivered it in a language that was understood and well received by the illiterate masses. Periyar a born rationalist was the only leader who preached rationalism as a creed to be followed in day to day life.'[32] Rationalism became a mass movement – a movement that Periyar spearhead in the abolition of Brahminism and casteism as it took deep roots in the Tamil soil.[33]

Ambedkar's Project of Emancipatory Modernity

B. R. Ambedkar's (1891-1956) views on secular modern India involved a two-fold emancipation: political emancipation, i.e., freedom from foreign rule and social emancipation, i.e., liberation from tradition and socio-economic bondages. After independence, the first emancipation was realized just as Ambedkar carried out his relentless struggle to bring about socio-economic freedom in India. The first step in this regard was his framing of the Indian Constitution which at least on paper and in principle had provisions to safeguard the socio-economic-political rights for all, especially for the depressed classes. He feared that the lack of such a situation would effectively exclude large sections of the population from the democratic process as seen in his speech to the Constituent Assembly in 1949:

> On the 26th of January, we are going to enter a life of contradictions. In politics we will have equality and in social and economic life we will have inequality. In politics we will be recognizing the principle of one man one vote value. In our social and economic life, we shall, by reason of our social and economic structure, continue to deny the principle of one man one value. How long shall we continue to live this life of contradictions? How long shall we continue to deny equality in our social and economic life? If we continue to

> deny it for long, we do so only by putting our political democracy in peril.[34]

Thus, Ambedkar's idea of modernity is immediately related to the ideas of securing equality in socio-economic spheres and the emancipation of the untouchables from the then existing socio-economic systems that denied them equality. The liberation of untouchables from the oppressive caste system cannot come true without questioning the tradition that sanctioned and perpetuated caste-based discriminations and dehumanizing practices of Indian societies for many centuries. That is exactly what Ambedkar did, before he set out to delineate his project of modernity.

His critique of Hinduism is multipronged. First, its system of social organization, built on *jati* and its parent *varna*, is founded upon the 'principles of gradation and rank, in other words, of inequality.'[35] Ambedkar points out that caste system is not merely a division of labour but also division of labourers as unequals. Further he observes, "Inequality in status is not merely the inequality that one sees in the warrant of precedence prescribed for a ceremonial gathering at a king's court. It is a permanent social relationship among the classes to be observed to be enforced – at all times in all places and for all purposes."[36] It is the grammar of inequality which underscores the Hindu customs regarding education, occupation, marriage, and religious rights and duties. Second, the absence of equality and justice was also quite evident in the Hindu law. 'Rule of law did not mean equality before law.'[37] Instead, there were different sets of law for different castes. 'Punishment did not have so significant a correlation with the gravity of the offence as with the *varna* of the offender.'[38] Hindu law books like Manu *dharmasastra* prescribed laws on the premise that 'the higher the caste, the less rigorous the punishment.'[39] Thus, inequality was writ large in Hindu jurisprudence as evidenced in the Hindu law books that provided caste-based immunities to high caste people even if they committed heinous crimes. Third, Hinduism not only denied economic independence to the Sudras and *avarnas* by taking away their liberty to choose occupations of their choice but also enjoined that they must always serve others. To ensure that there was enough labour force to serve the high castes, Hinduism recognized slavery: "Manu recognized seven kinds of slaves, whereas Narada has put the number at fifteen.'[40] Manu's law of wages was an iron law that fixed wages so low that 'there was no fear of Shudra accumulating wealth and obtaining economic security.'[41] Fourth, Ambedkar indicted Hinduism for its discriminatory and inefficient literacy policies which (1) Denied to most of its people their right to study its sacred scriptures; (2) Worse still, it made any attempt of the common folk to acquire knowledge a punishable offence; (3) But, it reserved the privilege of acquisition of knowledge to a few castes. In particular, in made it possible for only the Brahmins to be 'inalienably vested with the authority of learning, teaching and interpreting the shastras' and they 'became the repository of knowledge;'[42] (4) Its system of education was restricted merely to the acquisition of routine practical skills and lacked new thinking and perceptions. "It did not widen the horizon… so that in a changing environment the skill turned out to be gross ineptitude. Illiteracy became an integral part of Hinduism by a process which is indirect but integral of Hinduism."[43] (5) Hindu rules of precedence not only put the Brahmins on the pinnacle of socio-religious privileges but denied most of them to other castes and all of them to the Dalits, especially in matters of commensality, i.e., inter-mixing, inter-dining and inter-marriage. "These conditions of commensality did create inferiority and superiority complexes in the Hindu society, but what added the most obnoxious and oppressive dimension to it was the purity-pollution syndrome. It was this very syndrome which categorized the Dalits into untouchables, unapproachables, unshadowables, or even unseeables."[44]

For Ambedkar, the dream of modern India will become a reality only when, equality – one of the central ideas of modernity – prevailed in all spheres of life, be it political, social, religious and economic. Baxi notes that 'Ambedkar's wide-ranging programme of equality and equity measures aimed at the fulfillment of a wide variety of material and non-material needs.'[45] Thus, Ambedkar stood for an egalitarian and more 'inclusive' society that ensured everyone equality of opportunities, rights, services, resources and freedoms. To achieve this on an economic front, Ambedkar's conception of modernity concurred with the Nehruvian approach that supported centralized planning and the strengthening of public sector in which the state was seen as an interventionist and a positive instrument. He endorsed modernity as a thesis of emancipation for India because 'modernity creates the idea of individual as a rational moral agent. Along with it come ideas about equal worth of individuals, individual dignity and fraternity of all citizens.'[46] Thus, modernity is capable of 'replacing stratified societies with horizontal direct access societies.'[47] Though, Western modern education had the potential to bring about social, economic and political and cultural modernization, colonial modernity had failed to effect fundamental changes in the India's hierarchical social structure as it benefited mostly the high-caste elites. Realizing that the caste-system served as a stumbling block that prevented the low-caste from reaping the benefits of modernity, he sincerely pleaded for provisions to ensure that the untouchables and depressed classes have access to education. For him, this is the first step towards achieving modernity in post-colonial India in which Nehru's efforts of industrialization and urbanization would deliver its desired result of equity in development.

Ambedkar's views on secular modern India is embedded in his vision of nation-building through constitutional democracy. Realizing that it was Hindu scriptural texts that produced and sanctioned the non-egalitarian and inhuman practices of caste-gender hierarchy, he provided an alternative text for modern India, namely the Constitution of India, to secure equal rights and representations for the erstwhile discriminated people, namely, the Dalits, women and the religious minorities. He understood the Constitution as a fundamental document whose purpose 'is not merely to create the organs of the state but to limit their authority, because if no limitation was imposed upon the authority of the organs there will be complete tyranny and complete oppression.'[48] According to him, the Constitution has to do with '(a) The organization of the State, (b) The rights of the State against the subjects and (c) The rights of the subjects against the State.'[49] It is in favor of this tripod vision that he considered parliamentary democracy as crucial to keep alive the Constitution so that justice is delivered to the oppressed groups through the provisions of secular modernity.

Conclusion

The focus of this essay is the religious and social changes that occurred in India due to the influence of western modernity and 'its gradually evolved more open forms of social justice.'[50] It has drawn one's attention to the transformations the three great leaders initiated on the social, economic and political landscapes which have to do with the impact of modernity upon the ancient, social and ideological structures. The strategies these leaders adopted helped the oppressed groups overcome their disadvantaged positions and restore their human dignity, which led to the formation of new identities. Having rightly understood that religious and social identities are very closely intertwined in India, both Ambedkar and Narayana Guru's efforts for the restoration of human dignity did not reject the roles of religion and tradition in providing deep-seated meaning to the dignity of their subaltern people. While Naryana Guru's philosophy of 'one caste, one religion and one god' reimagined and recast Hinduism in a new light, Ambedkar believed that the total divorce of Dalits from the religious system of Hinduism (which excluded them from society) was the only sane alternative. In addition, Ambedkar set out to reconceptualise and reinvent one of the Indic protest movements, namely, Buddhism in its new avatar called Neo-Buddhism as an emancipatory religion for the Dalits. While for Ambedkar and Narayana Guru the new identity was profoundly religious in character, the path taken by Periyar was a near total rejection of religion, which he called 'rationalism'. But all three approaches can be seen as a response to the demands and opportunities that sprang forth off secular modernity and its values.

Notes

1 Jerald J. Pereira, *Narayana Guru: A Social Educator* (Cheruniyoor, Varkala: R. R. Publishers) , 39.
2 *Ibid.,* 40.
3 *Ibid.,* 39.
4 *Ibid.,* 43.
5 *Ibid.,* 75.
6 *Ibid.*, 41.
7 *Ibid.*, 79.
8 *Ibid.*, 42.
9 "The Guru's Compassion for The World (Chapter–7)," Last modified October 10, 2016. http://www.sreenarayanaguru.in/book/export/html/183.
10 *Ibid.,* 42.
11 *Ibid.*, 43.
12 'Guru's Compassion.'
13 M. K. Sanoo, *Narayana Guru (A Biography)* Translated by Madhavan Ayyappath. Last modified October 11, 2016. http://www.sreenarayanaguru.in/book/export/html/560.
14 *Ibid.*
15 *Ibid.*
16 'Guru's Compassion.'
17 *Ibid.*
18 *Ibid.*
19 Jerald J. Pereira, *Narayana Guru,* 76.
20 M. K. Sanoo, *Narayana Guru.*
21 *Ibid.*
22 Dr. Justice P. Venugopal, *The Five-Pronged Battle of Periyar for an Egalitarian Society* (Chennai: The Periyar Self-Respect Propaganda Institution, 2005), *185.*
23 *Ibid.,* 191-192.
24 *Ibid.,* 193-198.
25 *Ibid.,* 199-203.
26 M. K. Subramanian, *Periyar E. V. Ramaswamy: His Life and Mission* (Chennai: Periyar E. V. Ramaswamy-Nagammai Education and Research Trust, 2004), 83.
27 Venugopal, *The Five-Pronged Battle,* 211-212.
28 Subramanian, *Periyar E. V. Ramaswamy.*, 83.
29 *Ibid.*
30 *Ibid.*, 82.
31 *Ibid.,* 80.
32 Venugopal, *The Five-Pronged Battle.,* 214.
33 Subramanian, *Periyar E. V. Ramaswamy.*, 83.
34 V. Bijukumar, "Politics of Contested Modernity: Gandhi, Nehru and Ambedkar," *Journal of Polity and Society* 5, No 1&2 and 6, No 1 (2013 & 2014): 29-46, 41.
35 S. K. Gupta, "Indian Society and Dr. Ambedkar's Idea of Equality" in Ranga (ed.), B. R. *Ambedkar: Life, Work and Relevance* (New Delhi: Manhor, 2000), 46.
36 *Ibid.*, 46-47.
37 *Ibid.*, 47.
38 *Ibid.*
39 *Ibid.*
40 *Ibid.*
41 *Ibid.*

42 *Ibid.*, 48.
43 *Ibid.*
44 *Ibid.*
45 As quoted in V. Bijukumar, 'Politics of Contested Modernity.,' 41.
46 *Ibid.*, 42.
47 *Ibid.*
48 Sanjeev Kumar, "Ambedkar on Constitution and Nation Building in India" *Asian Journal of Multidisciplinary Studies,* Volume 2, Issue 2, February 2014, 97-103, 97.
49 *Ibid.,* 98.
50 Bardwell L.Smith (ed.) *Religion and Social Conflict in South Asia.* Last modified October 13, 2016. https://books.google.co.in/books?id=xNAI9F8IBOgC&pg=PA1&source=gbs_toc_r&cad=4#v=onepage&q&f=false), 3.

21

Subaltern "Space" within the Fabric of Contemporary Indian Society

James D. Chellappa
Christian Academy for Advanced Theological Studies, Nagercoil

Abstract: This article deals with the struggle of subaltern communities within the fabric of the Indian society. The onslaught of Hindutva and other fundamentalist forces has raised a question in the minds of each and every Indian: that is there a "space" available for every individual in Indian society. Space determines the existence of any living being. Thus striving for space is an ontological necessity. The present Indian scenario has become difficult for subaltern communities to coexist with the hegemonic forces which are in power. A subaltern is a person who is excluded from representation in the structures of mainstream political power, in other words, a person who experiences powerlessness. Dalits, minority religious communities, tribals, nomads, immigrant workers, etc., come under the subaltern section of society. A case study was done on the subaltern religiosity based on the Ayyavali cult of the southern Kanyakumari region of Tamil Nadu. Interestingly, the Ayyavali cult emerged as a reform movement or as a protest movement from within Hinduism. Later it became independent with its own forms and rituals. The outcome of the study shows that the recent onslaught of Hindutva has made Ayyavalli into yet another form or strand of Hinduism. Originally strong reformers, they are now happy to assert their Hindu roots and traditions.

Introduction

India is a complex, multi-cultural, multi-ethnic/racial, multi-lingual and multi-religious society. Plurality and pluralism are norms which have brought people of diverse groups into one to establish this democratic nation known as India. Unity in diversity is a slogan that was once heard in almost every corner of the country. However, contemporary India is in crisis. Oppression of the weak, the downtrodden, the poor, and the powerless has become the norm of the contemporary era. Hegemonic forces are trying to remove this multifaceted image of Indian nation/society by imposing a single political/social/religious ideology. Hindutva has "claimed a nation-space where the major axis of exclusion is cultural – the 'others' who arouse anxiety are indelibly marked by an essential cultural difference."[1] An attempt is being made to systematically bring about a homogenous society in which the voice of the "others" can be or will be silenced and thus unheard. Unity is stressed subtly at the expense of the diverse. Felix Wilfred identifies that the negation of diversity and plurality is one of the most crucial issues facing today's humanity.[2]

Who is an "Indian"? This question can be continuously raised in the given contemporary situations of insecurity and political instability which are regularly witnessed in relation to identities of different people groups within the fabric of Indian society. Do all the so-called Indians have a "space" in all aspects of being a citizen in this nation? Or do we need to contest in order to get a "space." Why are people being marginalized? Why do people get oppressed? Why is Indian society not humane? Why are we forced to witness atrocities meted out on people regularly in the name of caste, creed and colour? Why is the Indian government impotent to ensure the fundamental rights of its citizens? Sometimes, it has been noted that cows have more protected spaces than some humans within the fabric of Indian society! One can easily observe in the Indian society a "socio-cultural crisis"[3] expressed explicitly through the discontent of the marginalized people. Many live in conflict zones across the country where violence is the norm of daily living.

In the Indian context social institutions like caste, religion, patriarchy, panchayats, even political parties, etc., are all behind the ongoing systematic oppression of the powerless and the economically poor marginalized subaltern sections of society. Across the world powerful communities strategically deny or seize the space of existence meant for powerless communities. According to Robert Rothman, "broad patterns of inequality are deeply set in the structure of the society and are constantly enacted and reinforced daily in social relations. At the most obvious level, class, racial, and gender incidents show up in countless small but maddening instances of distain, humiliation, hostility, and discrimination."[4]

An idea of space

Space is an abstraction, an idea, a concept. G. Aloysius suggests that, "space itself is viewed as a human product."[5] Doreen Massey comes up with five themes about space: (1) Space is a social construct. (2) The social is located in space. (3) Social space is always dynamic, constituted by social relations. (4) Space is also about power – real or symbolic. (5) Social space might consist of contradictory, even conflictual spaces: it is never one space, but many spaces.[6] According to Pramod Nayar the social construction of space defines spaces of work, spaces of leisure, spaces of consumption, and spaces of intimate relations.[7]

Animate and inanimate matter needs space in order to subsist. If mobile, the animate seeks better space for enhanced existence. Paul Tillich says, "to be means to have space. Every being strives to provide and preserve a space unto oneself. This means above all a physical location – the body, a piece of soil, a home, a city, a country, the world. This also means a social "space"– a vocation, a sphere of influence, a group, a historical period, a place in remembrance and anticipation, a place within a structure of values and meanings. Not to have space is not to be. Thus, in all realms of life striving for space is an ontological necessity."[8] Tillich further adds that, "the space of an animal is not only the space taken by the physical existence of its body but also the space of its self-directed movement, which can be very small, as in some lower animals, or very large, as, for example, in migrating birds. The space covered by their movement is their space."[9]

An ecological issue like deforestation has brought both humans and animals into conflict. Such conflicts are primarily based on the issue of space, whether humans and animals can coexist in a shared space. Aloysius feels, "that man is essentially a spatial creature just as he is a temporal one, and has begun to impinge upon critical consciousness."[10] Within the human community conflicts due to control of space is common because of the division and segregation of humanity based on race, caste, creed, culture and language. Within the greater human community the tribes, clans and kinsmen create geographical boundaries of the familiar space and claims it as their own areas of continued existence. Wars took place in human history when people tried to defend their space or when others came to occupy spaces meant to be one's own. Edward W. Said is of the opinion that, "this universal practice of designating in one's mind a familiar space which is "ours" and an unfamiliar space beyond "ours" as "theirs" is a way of making geographical distinctions that can be entirely arbitrary."[11] In the present political scenario the "other" is painted as a scary social symbol, a complex metaphor. Instead of gaining some knowledge about the "other" we have a hermeneutics of the "other". A fundamentalistic interpretation of the "other" is thus conceived. Consequently, the "other" has turned into a problem. Such symbolization is used to conquer the space of the "other."

In the Christian context the Hebrew Bible testifies that the major crisis addressed in it is the crisis of land or a quest for free space to survive. The theology of the Old Testament is basically a territory-based theologizing. The

"Call of Abraham"[12] in itself is significant that it comes with a promise of land, a social space, an empire. Said says, "underlying social space are territories, lands, geographical domains, the actual geographical underpinnings of the imperial, and also the cultural contest. To think about distant places, to colonize them, to populate or depopulate them: all of this occurs on, about, or because of land. The actual geographical possession of land is what empire in the final analysis is all about."[13] Here, we see God has called out a person and his family to be His own with a promise of a safer space for prosperous survival. If the people of Israel "the chosen ones" are faithful to Yahweh they then possess the land of Canaan and its prosperity and exist as a nation. If they rebel against Yahweh, we see that the enemies of Israel prevail over the land and its produce and thus the chosen people of God go through slavery and lose their land. Thus, the relationship with God is determined on a continuous struggle for spatial possession.

In the New Testament there is a paradigm shift. The space promised to the Church moves from an earthly or this worldly space to another worldly, celestial or heavenly abode/space. The followers of Christ are advised to live like pilgrims in this earthly life of finitude and temporality by not focusing on building earthly empires but in anticipation of a celestial body and a heavenly space which is the eternal kingdom of God. Tillich is of the opinion that, "God creates extension in the ground of his life, in which everything spatial is rooted. But God is not subject to it; he transcends it and participates in it."[14] It is the Christian hope that we will share God's space in eternity.

An important question can therefore be asked: What is the space of the subaltern in Indian society? For centuries, upper caste Hindus have oppressed the so-called lower castes and have denied them education, social life, religious life and human status. After independence, the Indian government has taken up the cause of the oppressed to some measure by abolishing untouchability. The government has introduced reservation policies in areas of education and employment, and also introduced reservation in housing and other basic necessities. But still in our country the subaltern people are in need of a decent space to bring forth their authentic self-respect and existence.

Subaltern discourses

The subaltern[15] is a rather popular term in contemporary postmodern and postcolonial philosophical and theological discourses. The term subaltern refers to "those groups in society who are subject to the hegemony of the ruling class."[16] Being subaltern refers to "the state of people who are excluded from representation in the structures of mainstream political power, and those who are dominated culturally and economically, and thus find themselves in a state of overall powerlessness. They are deprived of a position from which to address their situation of exclusion and powerlessness."[17] Swami Raju says that, the term subaltern refers to "the perspective of persons from regions and groups outside of the hegemonic power structure."[18] The term can also be "used to signify the many different people who did not comprise the colonial elite."[19] People groups termed as the depressed class, scheduled castes/tribes, primitives, minorities, uncivilized, Dalits, periphery and secondary citizens, etc., by the mainstream comprise the subalterns.[20]

The subaltern as a person is "one who is on a journey from eclipse to identity, dependence to autonomy and from contrary consciousness to critical consciousness. The primordial subaltern posture towards reality is the struggle for survival."[21]Hardiman observes that, "the subaltern are compelled through a wide variety of coercive and cultural mechanisms to accept their subordinate position; only occasionally and in exceptional circumstances do they resist in an outright manner."[22] In such circumstances Anthoniraj Thumma believes that, "it is essential that subaltern people themselves feel discriminated and deprived of basic necessities and legitimate rights and, more importantly, rise above the engulfing disappointment, discontent, despair and frustration of crippling crisis, to protest, struggle and mobilize themselves as a group to resist the oppression and exploitation."[23]

Subaltern religiosity and the *Ayyavali* cult: A case study

The subalterns, the marginalized and downtrodden face discrimination in all walks of life; especially, and it is well noted, in the religious sphere in Indian society. Felix Wilfred says that, "subaltern religiosity refers to a particular kind of religious experience that derives from the condition of being marginalized."[24] Subaltern religiosity transmits identity. It empowers the subaltern to voice their concern.

The ideal of *varna/caste* itself is a (Hindu) religious doctrine which divides humanity in hierarchal categories. It is understood that, "the caste system in India is an exploitative symbol of domination."[25] People in the lowest strata of society are denied space in the religiosity of the so-called upper or higher castes even today. The struggles to enter temples by the downtrodden are very well recorded in Indian history. It is noted that, "the Nadars in Tamil Nadu initiated the temple entry agitation at first in the second half of the nineteenth century."[26] They were considered a polluting caste and were denied entry into temples of the Pan-Indian or Brahminical deities. Nadars were prohibited from installing and worshiping Brahminic deities like Siva, Vishnu and Brahma as they were considered high caste gods.[27] Nadars had their own local deities like Chodalai Madan, Muttaramman, Murugan and Badra Kali, etc. Their priests were shamans from within their community.

This case study is based on a subaltern religious cult known as Ayyavali, which is named after Muthukutty Swamy -- popularly known as Vaikunta Swamy or just as Ayya[28] which emerged from the downtrodden Nadar[29] community. His parents named him Mudisoodum Perumal. At that time the high castes forbade the Nadars from using the name Perumal (king) so he was forced to change this name.[30] The rationale for choosing this case for a study is because "the Nadars could be singled out as a subaltern group that was definitely on a course of self-assertion for social empowerment in the emergent context of modernity. The experiences of economic exploitation, socio-political oppression, restricted civil space and fear psychosis had contributed to the emergence of various forms of social protest and assertion."[31] Ayya was a socio-political guru and a miraculous healer. He is seen mythically by his devotees as a deliverer or liberator born (circa 1808-1851) for the deliverance of the Nadar community.[32] He organized the '*Samattva Samajam*'[33] and fought against all disabilities of Nadars and other downtrodden communities of Southern Travancore region.[34] He was a forerunner among the social reformers of India and he was a religious reformer too.

Ayya called himself as the incarnation of Narayana or Vishnu. He said that he was the avatar in the Kali-yuga and has come to destroy evil. He accepted that Narayana was incarnated in many forms and he was one of them incarnated in the Nadar community.[35] According to Immanuel, Ayya was, "the first revolutionary in the eighteenth century to raise the voice of protest against the Brahminical exploitation, misrepresentation and misinterpretation of Hinduism by the Brahmins. He preached equality for everyone before God. He was the first one to give the call to all citizens to come under one umbrella to worship God in his temple without any difference of caste or creed."[36] He saw his mission as one to establish dharma under one banner which is love.[37] Ayya opposed idol and demon worship. Even now the Ayyavali temples do not have idols in the sanctum sanctorum; in it is installed a mirror through which the image of the worshipper is reflected as the worshipped. This contempt for idols may have originated because Brahminical Hinduism once prohibited the worship of their deities by the lower or indigenous castes.

The religious structure and doctrines of Ayyavali can be found in their sacred texts *Akilattirattu Ammanai* and *Arul Nool*. These books were written in Tamil, the local language. Ayya can be seen as a language reformer too. He wanted the people to know the truth and meaning of their worship. He insisted on worshipping God through the mother tongue when the norm of those days was to worship the deities using Sanskrit.[38] Ayya rejected the authority of the Sanskrit/Brahminical deities by claiming to have symbolically married them and thus incorporated them within himself.[39] He claimed to be the God of *dharmayugam* – the futuristic age.

Ayya taught many important social principles in religious disguise. He compelled men to wear a turban and women to be fully dressed in a context where the so-called oppressive upper castes have prohibited the Nadars, even their women from wearing cloths which cover the upper parts of the body. He taught them self-respect. He infused in them self-confidence and he kindled in them the fire that they are the children of God and thus not inferior to anyone. The turban emerged as a socio-religious symbol. The Nadars and other men of oppressed castes were not allowed to wear their turban in front of the upper castes. To change this social oppression Ayya instituted the wearing of turban as a religious symbol and made men to wear it while worshipping God. His teaching gave courage to his devotees to wear it with social dignity. In his most recent novel Ponneelan, a Sahitya Academy Award winner, has graphically recorded the importance of the turban in the then social struggles of the Ayyavali followers.[40] To learn how much people struggled to protect their self-respect is such an eye-opener.

Swamythoppu, a village near Kanyakumari, is the centre of this cult as it has the central pati or temple. The worship is led by gurus who are the direct descendants of Ayya. The peculiarity of this temple is that they never invite Brahmins to any of their special occasions.[41] Ayya instituted a common meal for his followers. All the offerings brought to the temple were utilised for this sacred meal which was made available thrice a day. The offerings were not stored for another day. Rajamani compares this practice with early Christian fellowship. He says, "the common meal of this cult is a powerful contemporary evidence for the fellowship of God's people, which is an evidence to confirm the possibility of God's people eating and sharing together even outside the church."[42] In order to abolish caste, Ayya encouraged inter-dining of devotees from all castes.

Ayyavali existed as a distinct subaltern cult for some time. They had a definite space in the religious sphere of the Travancore/present Kanyakumari district region. They were a cult persecuted by caste Hindus because of their ideologies like equality, fellowship and iconoclasm. They were even seen as a threat to the colonial Christian missionary enterprise in which the Nadar conversion to Christianity was a mass movement. Today Ayya Vali has lost its protestant character. The onslaught of Hindutva has not spared this revolutionary cult too as their religious space is already occupied by Hindutva ideologies. A recent tower built in the traditional Hindu/Aryan style at Swamitoppu central pati/temple of Ayyavali is witness to this. When questioned about the influence of Vedic Hinduism on the Ayyavali cult, especially in regard to the new tower, their chief guru Balaprajapati Adihal got irritated and annoyed. He said "once we were prohibited from building such towers by the Brahminical Hindus. Now we are politically as well as socially able to construct such a monument. We are not worried about critics. If Ayya was alive he too would have permitted us to have towers. The high tower is a symbol of social emancipation."[43] As Ayya himself claimed to be the avatar of Narayana/Vishnu it was easy for his later followers to be identified as Hindus. The present gurus of this cult have internal power struggles due to the high revenues the devotees bestow on the temples. Now Ayyavali exists as a mere Hindu sect and is slowly losing its unique space in the vast ocean of Hinduism. It is now viewed as just a Hindu renaissance movement.

Conclusion

In the words of Bergesen, "hegemonies do not last, and neither do their cultural forms."[44] In a just society there should be no space for hegemonic ideologies. Every one of the inhabitants should be accepted and included as equals. Everyone should have a shared space in the areas of education, employment, and in everything needed to lead a happy life in its fullness as human beings with dignity and respect. No one must be treated as high or low caste which is based on birth, colour, and creed. The idea of one God and oneness of humanity must be stressed. Only then can a country qualify to be a just and peaceful nation.

On the contrary India is a peril for the subalterns who are denied space for survival. Take, for example, a minority group like the Christians. To be a Christian is to be in solidarity with the oppressed and to stand for justice. It is what Jesus did or would have done. But do we have a space? It is hard to gather for worship. It is difficult to construct a church. It is becoming hard to run a school. It is even difficult to do social work through Christian NGOs. Everywhere Hindutva forces are gazing at us. Their gaze brings lots of disharmony and anxiety in the public space as we are forced to share the available space with them. Then situations become tense and violent. Unity among all the subaltern, marginalized and minority communities is a must in order to strive for a better space in the social fabric of Indian society. The sad part of the discourse is that there are subaltern people within the Church too. It is the duty of Christians to first eradicate imbalance based on caste bias and prejudice from within the Christian community. If the Church/Christians become a model of shared space, a model of the Kingdom of God on earth, then we can urge the nation at large to follow this model of success in which all the inhabitants/subalterns will have space in the nation.

Notes

1 Satish Deshpande, 'Hegemonic Spatial Strategies: The Nation-Space and Hindu Communalism in Twentieth-Century India' in *Community, Gender and Violence*, Partha Chatterjee, et.al, eds., (Delhi: Permanent Black, 2000), 186.

2 Felix Wilfred, *Asian Public Theology: Critical Concerns in Challenging Times*, (Delhi: ISPCK, 2010), 228.

3 Joseph Chittooparampil, *Cultural Hermeneusis on Caste Culture, its Discontents and Politics of Culture: A Model of Contextual Theologizing*, (Delhi: ISPCK, 2005), xvii.

4 Robert A. Rothman, *Inequality and Stratification: Race, Class and Gender*, (New Delhi: PHI Learning, 2005), 23.

5 G. Aloysius, *Conceptualising the Region*, (New Delhi: Critical Quest, 2013), 13.

6 Doreen Massey, *Space, Place and Gender*, (London: Polity Books, 1994), 3.

7 Pramod K. Nayar, *An Introduction to Cultural Studies*, (New Delhi, Viva Books, 2011), 180.
8 Paul Tillich, *Systematic Theology*, (Chicago: UCP, 1951), 1:194.
9 Paul Tillich, *Systematic Theology*, (Chicago: UCP, 1963), 3:317.
10 Aloysius, *Conceptualising the Region*, 13.
11 Edward W. Said, *Orientalism: Western Conceptions on the Orient*, (New Delhi: Penguin Books, 2001), 54.
12 *Bible, Genesis, Chapters 12, 13.*
13 Edward W. Said, *Culture and Imperialism*, (London: Vintage Books, 1993), 93.
14 Paul Tillich, *Systematic Theology*, (Chicago: UCP, 1951), 2:277.
15 The term 'subaltern' is popularized by a group of historians known as the Subaltern Study Group. Scholars like Ranajit Guha, Gayathri Spivak, and Partha Chatterjee, et. al., have brought out a 10 volumes series titled Subaltern Studies published by Oxford University Press, India.
16 Bill Ashcroft, et. al., *Key Concepts in Post-Colonial Studies*, (London: Routledge, 2004), 215.
17 Felix Wilfred, Margins: Site of Ancient Theologies, (Delhi: ISPCK, 2008), 103.
18 T. Swami Raju, 'Subaltern Movements: Insights for Interreligious Dialogue' in *The Yobel Spring: Festchrift to Rev. Dr. Chilkuri Vasantha Rao on His 50th Birthday*, Praveen PS. Perumalla, et. al., eds., (Delhi: ISPCK/ACTC, 2013), 1:250.
19 John McLeod, *Beginning Postcolonialism*, (New Delhi: Viva Books, 2011), 109.
20 John Peter Vallabadoss, 'Subaltern Historizing: A Study on Iyothee Thass' Indirar Desa Charithiram' in *History and Historizing*, John Peter Vallabadoss, ed., (Bangalore: ATC/ACPI, 2012), 305.
21 Jose Maliekal, 'Subaltern' in *ACPI Encyclopedia of Philosophy*, 2 vols. Johnson J. Puthenpurackal, ed., (Bangalore: ATC, 2010), 2:1334.
22 David Hardiman, *Histories for the Subordinated*, (Ranikhet: Permanent Black, 2006), 9.
23 Anthoniraj Thumma, *Voices of the Victims: Movements and Models of People's Theology*, (Delhi: ISPCK, 1999), 14.
24 Felix Wilfred, *The Sling of Utopia: Struggles for a Different Society*, (Delhi: ISPCK, 2005), 138.
25 George Panthanmackel, 'Castes and Metaphysics of Violence' in *Subaltern Perspectives: Philosophizing in Context*, George Thadathil, ed., (Bangalore: ACPI/ATC, 2005), 163.
26 G. Rengaraju, *Temple Entry Politics in Colonial Tamil Nadu*, (Chennai: Pavai Publications, 2006), 16.
27 D. Peter and Ivy Peter, *Liberation of the Oppressed, A Case Study, Since 1822 AD* (Nagercoil: KIDS, 2009), 9.
28 Ayya can be translated as master or as father. Thus Ayyavali means the Way of the Master/Father.
29 Nadars were previously known as Shanars. For detailed studies refer Robert Caldwell, *The Tinnevelly Shanars,* (Madras: Christian Knowledge Society Press: 1849); Robert L. Hardgrave, *The Nadars of Tamilnad: The Political Culture of a Community in Change,* (Delhi: Manohar Publishers, 2006).
30 V. David, *The Broken Shackles: Emancipation of Women in South Travancore 1819-1894*, (Kanyakumari: H A Publications, 2012), 71.
31 G. Patrick, *Religion and Subaltern Agency: A Case Study of Ayyavali – A Subaltern Religious Phenomenon in South Tiruvitankur*, (Chennai: University of Madras, 2003), 65.
32 M. Immanuel, *The Dravidian Lineages – A Socio-Historical Study: The Nadars through the Ages,* (Nagercoil: Historical Research and Publications Trust, 2002), 324.
33 Association for the Establishment of Equality.
34 Hugald Grafe, *History of Christianity in India: Tamil Nadu in the Nineteenth and Twentieth Centuries*, (Bangalore: CHAI, 1990), 4:2:209.

35 C. Rajamani, *The Cult of Muthukutty Swamy*, (M.Th. Thesis, Bangalore: United Theological College, 1981), 49.
36 Immanuel, *The Dravidian Lineages – A Socio-Historical Study: The Nadars through the Ages*, 324.
37 David, *The Broken Shackles: Emancipation of Women in South Travancore 1819-1894*, 72.
38 Rajamani, *The Cult of Muthukutty Swamy*, 65.
39 Patrick, *Religion and Subaltern Agency: A Case Study of Ayyavali – A Subaltern Religious Phenomenon in South Tiruvitankur*, 94.
40 Ponneelan, *The Dance of Flames*, (Chennai: New Century Book House, 2016), 241-260.
41 Rajamani, *The Cult of Muthukutty Swamy*, 78.
42 Rajamani, *The Cult of Muthukutty Swamy*, 100.
43 Informal interview at Swamithoppu on 10-08-16.
44 Albert Bergesen, 'The Art of Hegemony' in *The Underdevelopment of Development: Essays in Honour of Andre Gunder Frank*, Sing C. Chew and Robert A. Denmark, eds. (New Delhi: Sage, 1996), 277.

22

Sri Aurobindo
From Politics to Poetics in Post-Modern India

Kamladevi R. Kunkolienker
PESRSN College, Ponda, Goa

Abstract: Researchers and laymen alike find Sri Aurobindo's involvement and withdrawal from the Indian political scenario during the freedom movement, mysterious. This issue deserves to be looked into from various perspectives - such as his ideas about nationalism, the then existing struggle for freedom of India, the political circumstances, the leadership issues, and more significant, the nature of the Indian social set up. In his replies to letters appealing to him to return to the freedom movement, he made clear the reasons for his leaving active politics. This paper attempts to deal with the foundation and his ideas of nationalism, his contribution in awakening the people of India towards the freedom movement, and his retirement as a yogi in Pondicherry.

Introduction - Sri Aurobindo (1872-1950)

Sri Aurobindo was born in India on 15 August 1872. He was educated in England as his father wanted him to be a perfect English gentleman - in style and culture. More importantly, his father never wanted Aurobindo to know about the Indian freedom struggle and had instructed his guardians, Mr. and Mrs. Drewett to that effect. Despite this fact, the spark of fighting against harassments by the rulers or the colonial powers could be seen when he took part in agitations in England. However, even before going to Cambridge to study, he turned his mind towards his motherland, and started to take an interest in the political and social conditions in India. It is ironical to note that, his father who had instructed that his sons were not to be exposed to any Indian influence, himself helped Aurobindo to think and act towards his motherland. Aurobindo's interest in Indian politics also moved him to join the Lotus and Dagger, a secret society whose members had to take a solemn vow to work for the liberation of India and not to serve the alien government. Upon his return to India, he worked for the Maharaja of Baroda, Sayajirao Gaekwad, and lectured on English literature. On a request of his friend, K. G. Deshpande, Aurobindo wrote a series of political articles entitled, 'New Lamps for Old' in the journal, Indu Prakash that was circulated in Bombay during this period (August 1893 – March 1894). The articles severely criticized the policy of the Indian National Congress and created a furore in political circles. This shows a disagreement between his political philosophy and the ideas about the freedom movement in the Indian National Congress. He was imbued with the nationalist spirit, and he considered India as the Mother and a powerful force.

Sri Aurobindo was one of the most creative and influential figures in the Indian Renaissance movement. As a gifted intellectual, a great philosopher and a Yogi – he was unmatched when compared to present day Indian intellectuals. Rabindranath Tagore thought of him as the most pronounced exponent of the spiritual message of India to the world. Former president Sarvapalli Radhakrishnan accepted him as perhaps the most accomplished of modern Indian thinkers and after Aurobindo's death, declared him to be the greatest intellectual of our age. During the early period of the national struggle, he brought about a national consciousness within a short period of two years (1906-1908), through his electric writings in Bande Mataram. This was only a miracle that has remained unparalleled in the history of nationalism of the entire world."[1]

Foundation of Sri Aurobindo's political ideas and nationalism

The great aim of Aurobindo's life was to 'nationalise' India and it was the favourite shibboleth (custom, belief) of his life. We may notice that, his childhood studies and his getting influenced by the literature - both from the east and the west, contributed towards his concept of revolution and nationalism.

At the age of seven he was sent to England for studies. Aurobindo's guardians, the Drewetts, were very learned people and they tutored Aurobindo at home. During his childhood period he spent much of his time reading. At the age of 10, he was reading the King James Bible and was enchanted with the English Romantics. P.B. Shelley's poetry on 'The Revolt of Islam'[2] influenced him the most and had a decisive impact on Aurobindo. Inspired by the message of the poem, his 'vague' (at that point of time) commitment to "world change" soon developed into an aspiration to free India, his motherland, from British rule. At St. Paul's School in London in 1884, he studied the history of European revolutions and was much inspired by the Italian revolutionary, Mazzini. All his revolutionary interests later got channelized into his idea of liberation of his own country.

After his return to India, he worked for the Maharaja of Baroda, Sayajirao Gaekwad in 1893. He continued writing in English, as he did not understand either Bengali or Sanskrit or any other Indian language. The education that he received in England did not stimulate his interest in the spiritual life, as he termed it as mainly classical and which had a purely intellectual and aesthetic influence. However, Aurobindo admits that, his "first turn towards spiritual seeking came in England ... He was specially struck by the concept of Atman in Advaita ..."[3] Some thinkers are of the opinion that Romantic English literature might have played a role in his turning spiritual later, as the Romantics often wrote of the transcendent reality which can be distinguished from the beauty of the natural world.

His studies in Indian literature may be looked upon as an extension of his pursuits in England. Due to the life-changing influence that he had during his study of Indian literature, he observed that it penetrated far more deeply into the transcendent realm than Romantic literature. Thus, he started moving away from an agnostic's position that he temporarily had adopted for a short time, to that of a spiritualist, as he became more accepting of a transcendent reality. He writes, "The Hindu ... is passionate for the infinite, the unseen, the spiritual, but he will not rest satisfied with conceiving them, he insists on mapping the infinite, on seeing the unseen, on visualizing the spiritual"[4]

His spiritual and nationalistic interests were completely separate arenas in his life during this period. The teachings of some of the Advaitic schools, that the unity of Atman and Brahman is irrelevant to worldly action and that it annihilates the duality, did not impress him. He thought that this kind of yoga would not facilitate his nationalistic ideas, which required renunciation of worldly activities. To put it in his own words: "But I had thought that a yoga which required me to give up the world was not for me. I have to liberate my country. I took to it seriously when I learnt that the same Tapasya which one does to get away from the world can be turned to action. I learnt that yoga gives power, and I thought why the devil should I not get the power and use it to liberate my country? It was the time of 'country first, humanity afterwards and the rest nowhere.'"[5]

This evidences the fact that for Aurobindo there was no conflict between the practice of yoga and politics that one became the part of the other. He did experience the fact that, after practicing yoga for five or six hours, his brain became full of light – 'Prakashmay'. Aurobindo had started doing pranayam and yoga seriously even before meeting Vishnu Bhaskar Lele, who instructed

Aurobindo in his meditations, reaching up to the state of Nirvana. It is against this background that, when he was jailed at Alipore, his spiritual fervour deepened and he experienced still higher states of consciousness, and had visions of Sri Krishna as his protector and guide. During his Kashmir visit accompanying the Maharaja, he had felt the power and presence of Kali. Taking note of the growing agitation in Bengal and with all his spiritual experiences in 1905 he published a pamphlet, Bhavani Mandir, which is his first known synthesis of religion and nationalism. He gave instructions to set up a monastery, so that monks would be dedicated to the worship of the Goddess Bhavani, and to the service of the nation. Founded on Vivekananda's idea that the doctrine of the Atman can inspire heroic actions, Sri Aurobindo attempted to synthesize spirituality and nationalism in this pamphlet. He also reinforced Vivekananda's message of strength by synthesizing it, under the influence of Bankim Chandra Chatterji's 'Bande Mataram' slogan, with Shaktism.

His 'nationalism' demonstrates his passionate love for India as a living entity and not just as a piece of geographical land. It was his conviction that through spirituality, one can bring about desired changes in this world and can direct actions, which also played a role in nationalism.

Aurobindo was also much influenced by the ethics of the Mahabharata epic and its value system. He observed that Indian spirituality is not divorced from worldly life, but is firmly integrated with it. According to him the message of the Bhagwad Gita is also key to integrating spirituality and worldly life. Not only did he admire the message of action in the Bhagwad Gita, but he lamented that in the centuries following the composition of the epic Mahabharata, the people of India had fallen into passivity and unproductive 'otherworldliness'. He saw this message as a great source to integrate his ideas of nationalism and spiritualism.

In a similar manner, his account of historical ancient India and her ardent people and kings who restored her glory also shows a nationalism. According to him, this nationalism is of a different kind than what was shown during the freedom struggle by the Congress leadership during that time. So he tries to draw his idea of nationalism from ancient Indian heroes, exemplifying their valour fighting for their motherland. Aurobindo also notes that the consciousness of a cultural unity has been there in India and this is visible in literature, art, mysticism, religion and ethics of different parts from India. But, according to him, political nationalism in the sense that a people linked by a feeling of common belongingness should have the power of autonomous political self-determination, is a western phenomenon.

Sattvic religion was an important ingredient in Aurobindo's concept of nationalism and hence he stressed the necessity of spiritual and moral discipline both for the leaders and their followers. He insisted on harnessing of moral forces and this emphasis on moral idealism behind political nationalism shows the depths of Aurobindo's teachings.

We should also note that he conceived of nationalism as a necessary stage in the social and political evolution of humans. Undoubtedly, he was one of the early believers of having a completely independent India and, he correspondingly accepted the realization of the gospel of human unity as an imperative political necessity of mankind. Thus, literature and poetic influences played a very great role in the development of spiritual and nationalistic convictions of Sri Aurobindo.

Active participation in politics as a nationalist leader

Sri Aurobindo joined the revolutionary society of Bombay and in 1902 shouldered the responsibility of propagating these ideals in Bengal. He attended the Ahmedabad session of the Congress in 1902 and met freedom fighter B. G. Tilak, who took him out of the pandal "and talked to him for an hour in the grounds, expressing his contempt for the Reformist movement and explaining his own line of action in Maharashtra."[6] Aurobindo also authored a pamphlet, titled 'No Compromise' – his anti-partition position on the partitioning of Bengal.

He advocated non-co-operation and the policy of passive resistance as the means to achieve his goal of 'Swaraj'. "Secret revolutionary propaganda and preparation; a more overt collaboration with nationalist leaders like Tilak and a behind-the-scene jostling with a view to converting the Congress to a new programme of Swaraj-Swadeshi-Boycott; and finally, the nationwide mobilization of the people's idealism and energies through a movement of non-co-operation and passive resistance on the issue of immediate national independence, these were the three levels of Sri Aurobindo's political thinking and activity, at first distinct enough from one another, but really meant to coalesce sooner or later, into a single "triveni", facilitating our baptism of rebirth as a new nation and a new people."[7]

'Nationalism' for Aurobindo, is a religion that comes from God. The National College was established in Calcutta in 1906, and Aurobindo was appointed as the Principal of this college. He took this as an opportunity to move from Baroda to Bengal in order to become more active in his political activities. At the same time, he became the editor of Bande Mataram, which was started by Bipin Chandra Pal. He had a two-fold work - to vigorously carry out propaganda for nationalism and to teach on national lines.

Along with Tilak, Pal and other Bengali crusaders in the freedom struggle, he preached 'New Nationalism' - new because it distinguished itself from the prevailing politics of the Moderates. This 'new nationalist' programme emphasized "Chatuhsutri", that is, 1) Swaraj, 2) Swadeshi, 3) Boycott and 4) National Education. Aurobindo called the famous Surat Congress, the battle of

'Kuruhsketra'. At the Calcutta Congress session earlier in 1906, the nationalists had succeeded, mainly due to Aurobindo's influence and his efforts behind the scenes, in prevailing on the Congress to pass the resolutions adopting Swaraj as its goal and Swadeshi, Boycott and National Education as the effective means of realizing it. This was a serious setback for the Moderates, since they had opposed it, in particular to the idea of complete Swaraj. The growing cleavage between the two groups, turned into a battle during the Congress session at Surat. Aurobindo vehemently opposed the Moderates' policy of "politics of petition". He advocated the radical policy of boycott, and rejected the mendicant policy of 'prayer, petition and protest', which was based on "opposition-cum-co-operation" theory.

During his active career as a nationalist leader, he suffered imprisonments and persecutions. In 1907, he was prosecuted for sedition but was acquitted. He presided at some of the important meetings of the extremists group in Surat, where Tilak addressed the gatherings. In 1908, Aurobindo lectured extensively in Maharashtra on nationalism. From 4 May 1908 to 5 May 1909 was an under trial prisoner in Alipore jail. It was during this period that he had great spiritual experiences that brought about a profound spiritual transformation. In his 'Uttarapara Speech' he declared that, he had a vision of Lord Vasudeva in Alipore jail, who gave him a message to preach to India and the World of the glories of the eternal Sanatana Dharma.

After his acquittal, he found the political scenario in Bengal gloomy, as many of his associates were imprisoned. In order to dispel the gloom and despondency he launched the publication of two weekly journals - The Karmayogin in English and The Dharma in Bengali. The Karmayogin was a weekly review of National Religion, Literature, Science, Philosophy, among other subjects.

Sri Aurobindo's journey from politics in Bengal to poetics and yoga in Pondicherry

The erstwhile British government was confused when dealing with Sri Aurobindo. The bureaucrats wanted to deport him, but Viceroy opposed it fearing it would trigger violence in India and thought that it will provoke criticism in England. Suspecting his deportation, Sri Aurobindo wrote an article in Karmayogin in July 1909, calling it 'An Open Letter To My Countrymen', in which he exposed the government's intention and informed the countrymen about what he called, the 'last political will and testament' to guide them in his enforced absence.

On 15 February 1910, on learning that a warrant of arrest had been issued against him and interpreted by Sri Aurobindo as an 'imperative' or ' Adesha' from God, he left for Chandernagore, where he stayed for six weeks and from there went to Pondicherry, where he lived in retirement till his Mahasamadhi on 5 December 1950.

His sudden departure from active politics in Bengal created a vacuum, which was all the greater because of the powerful impact that he had made on the minds of people not only from Bengal but all over the country. The British government could not believe that he had withdrawn from politics, and they thought that he was secretly planning some revolutionary activities against them. On the other hand his nationalist followers deplored his retirement and thought that he was lost to India and the World, being interested only in his own spiritual salvation. Many called him an 'escapist'.

Reasons for leaving active politics

Aurobindo wanted to clarify his leaving of active politics and pursuing yoga at Pondicherry. In his book "On Himself" he writes, "I may also say that I did not leave politics because I felt I could do nothing more there; such an idea was very far from me. I came away because I did not want anything to interfere with my Yoga and because I got a very distinct adesha in the matter. I have cut connection entirely with politics, but before I did so I knew from within that the work I had begun there was destined to be carried forward, on lines I had foreseen, by others, and that the ultimate triumph of the movement I had initiated was sure without any personal action or presence. There was not the least motive of despair or sense of futility behind my withdrawal …"[8]

He retired from active politics in order to obtain increased spiritual strength and vitality for eventual use in the cause of India's independence. But it is also true that his intense yoga leading him to ever growing depths and splendours of spiritual life demanded his total absorption into it, making it impossible for him to return to politics. In his letter to Romain Rolland he explains the causes of his withdrawal from politics: "India possesses in its past, a little rusty and out of use, the key to the progress of humanity. It is to this side that I am now turning my energies, rather than towards mediocre politics. Hence the reason for my withdrawal. I believe in the necessity for Tapasya."[9]

A decade after Sri Aurobindo withdrew from active politics and settled in Pondicherry, two prominent nationalist leaders appealed to him to return to British India and to resume leadership of Indian politics. One of them was Joseph Baptista and the other was Dr. Munje, a congressman who visited Aurobindo at Pondicherry in 1920, after Tilak's death. It is worth noting that even after leaving active politics, Aurobindo retained his interest in politics. He expressed his views through the interviews and through occasional messages, where he continued to give his opinions on political problems. Most importantly he was committed to yoga and spirituality, which culminated into the future poetry, 'Savitri'. He also developed the system of 'Integral Yoga'.

Observations

What would have happened if Sri Aurobindo had not retired from active politics? He might have become a political leader, and that too was possible only after overcoming the agenda set by other leaders, which according to him would not have served his brand of nationalism. He was opposed to Congress' creed of 'petition, prayer and protest'.

There was a tension between the two preoccupations of Sri Aurobindo - to achieve complete freedom and to achieve the heights of spiritual evolution. As a revolutionary, he devoted himself to the freedom struggle, and aroused the feelings of nationalism in the minds of his countrymen. He soon realized that his concept of 'nationalism' required him to develop his spiritual powers to strengthen his political activity. He believed in 'transformation' of the social and overall set up of India leading to the awakening of Indians as true nationalists. His yoga became a source of powerful energy, through which actions could be directed. He could not have achieved such heights in his Tapasya if he did not pursue Yoga assiduously, without any interference. His achievements of sadhana are meant for the benefits of all, as he aimed "not only to realize the Divine and attain complete spiritual consciousness, but also to take all life and all world activity into the scope of this spiritual consciousness and action and to base life on the spirit and give it a spiritual meaning."[10]

Notes

1 Indrani Sanyal and Krishna Roy (Ed.) 2007: Sri Aurobindo and His Contemporary Thinkers, D.K.Printworld, New Delhi, pp.16-17.

2 Peter Hees (ED.) 2013: Situating Sri Aurobindo, A Reader, Oxford University Press, p. 68.

3 Ibid., p. 69.

4 CWSA 1: 212.

5 A. B. Purani, 1964: The Life of Sri Aurobindo, Pondicherry, Sri Aurobindo Ashram Trust, p.108.

6 Indrani Sanyal and Krishna Roy (Ed.) 2007: Sri Aurobindo and His Contemporary Thinkers, D. K. Printworld, New Delhi, p. 318.

7 Ibid., p. 319-320.

8 Sri Aurobindo, 1972: On Himself, Sri Aurobindo Ashram Trust, Pondicherry, p. 55.

9 Vishwanath Prasad Varma, 1960: Political Philosophy of Sri Aurobindo, Motilal Banarasidas, Delhi, p. 169.

10 Nirodbaran 1990: Sri Aurobindo for All Ages: A Biography, Sri Aurobindo Ashram, Pondicherry, p. 123.

Statement of ACPI Research Seminar on "Becoming a Nation: Processes & Prospects"

We, the Association of Christian Philosophers of India (ACPI), met at St. Albert's College, Ranchi, for our 41st Annual Research Seminar from 20th to 23rd October, 2016. There were 92 participants in attendance.

1. Our Context

- India is a sovereign, socialist, secular, democratic republic, having a Constitution which safeguards the fundamental rights of its citizens.
- India's tradition of plurality and diplomacy, its scientific advancement and tremendous natural and human resources are signs of its immense potentiality.
- India's variegated religious and spiritual traditions and its multi-cultural richness enhance the uniqueness of the process of becoming a nation. We are invited to affirm human dignity and equality in spite of cultural and religious differences.
- However, at present, there are unenlightened and dysfunctional attempts made to challenge and subvert many of the above-mentioned strengths and assets of Indian socio-political reality.

2. Seminar Insights and Deliberations

- There persists a colonial hangover resulting in religious polarization and politicization, the assertion of cultural supremacy, the homogenizing approach of certain people with vested interests, and the emergence of developmental projects which lack ecological sensitivity, traditional wisdom and popular acceptance.
- Current developments seem to lead to a narrow understanding of nationalism, with fundamentalist and anti-secular overtones

foregrounded by the politicized use of the media, resulting in unreflective mob violence and terrorist activities.

- While dissent is an integral part of democracy, what we are witnessing is the suppression of dissenting voices of intellectuals and the masses.
- Numerous challenges to the integrity of the Constitution via anti-democratic and anti-minority policies have emerged, resulting in cultural and economic exclusion which will have severe repercussions on various subaltern communities.

3. Proposals Stemming from the Seminar

- The process of "becoming a nation" invites us to celebrate differences, to recognize and accept one another, to affirm cultural liberty and plurality, and to appreciate a mutually fecund co-emergence grounded by an ethics of compassionate care.
- We affirm socio-political thinking that is in line with the Constitution, which employs democratic and rational approaches, and results in constructive activism.
- We support an egalitarian momentum which ushers in the welfare of all, especially that of the voiceless, trusting in their capabilities for empowerment and freedom.
- We will attempt to adopt methods of sustainable development which recognizes the mutuality of science and religion, and is aimed at integral and holistic growth.
- We will combine religious and moral education and enlightenment with relevant social activism.
- We will cultivate a spirit of pluralistic patriotism rather than chauvinistic nationalism.
- As Indian Christians, we will celebrate and share overlapping socio-cultural spaces with our fellow country men and women at the macro and micro levels.
- Our interrelationships and collaboration with diverse communities will be aimed at fostering a spirit of inter-becoming.

Contributors

A. Pushparajan (angelpura@gmail.com) is Professor and Head (Retired), Dept. of Interreligious Relations, Madurai Kamaraj University and Coordinator of the School of Philosophy and Religions in the same University. He has authored 30 books, contributed over 300 articles in research journals, and presented over 400 papers in national and international seminars, symposia and conferences. Been a Consulter to Pontifical Council for Faith and Culture, Awardee of Charles Wallace Fellow in Dept. of Religions and Theology, University of Bristol UK, Invitee to the UN Peace Summit of the Religious and Spiritual Leaders, Member of the Founding Meet of World Council of Religious Leaders, and Member of the Governing Body of the Indian Council of Religious Leaders, Member of the Governing Body of the NBCLC. Presently, resides in Bengaluru, giving guest lectures in his fields of specializations: Interreligious Dialogue, Gandhian Theology / Spirituality and Ecosophy and Eco-Spirituality and Family Spirituality.

Anthony Dias (anthonyda@gmail.com) is presently the Director of Xavier Institute of Social Research (XISR) and is based in Nashik. He holds a doctorate from the National Law School of India University. His Ph.D work was on development-induced displacement. His book, 'Development and Its Human Cost', published in 2012, deals with this subject and that of eminent domain. He has participated in national and international conferences on the subject and is consulted by NGOs, colleges and specialized institutions. His other areas of research are Distress Migration, Climate Change, Ecology and Human Rights, India's nomadic and de-notified tribes and corporate social responsibility.

Ashley Miranda (ashsdb@gmail.com) is a Salesian of Don Bosco who has been teaching philosophy at Divyadaan: Salesian Institute of Philosophy, Nashik, for more than 20 years. He has also taught at Don Bosco Philosophate, Pyin Oo Lwin, Myanmar. He is specialized in Ethics but is also deeply interested in Contemporary Western Philosophy, Epistemology, Philosophy of History,

Postmodernism, Political Philosophy and Ecosophy. At present, Fr. Ashley, while continuing to teach Philosophy, is also Rector and Administrator of Don Bosco School and Parish, Nashik.

Devasia M. Antony (devasia.m.antony@gmail.com) teaches Philosophy at Hindu College, University of Delhi. He has published over 25 articles and research papers in refereed journals as well as in edited volumes. He has presented about 28 research papers in conferences, seminars and workshops. His research interests include hermeneutics of religious language, Indian intellectual traditions, classical Indian metaphysics, continental philosophy, Advaita Vedanta and Buddhism.

Dolreich Pereira (dolreichpereira@gmail.com) is a Catholic priest of the Archdiocese of Bombay. He teaches philosophy at St. Pius X College, Bombay. He did his philosophical studies at Institute Catholique de Paris in France and is currently writing his doctoral thesis at Jnana-Deepa Vidyapeeth, Pune.

Francis Arackal Thummy (farackal@gmail.com) did his PG Diploma in Media studies from Griffith College, Dublin, Ireland, and Licence and Doctorate in Social Sciences, specializing in media, from the Gregorian and St. Thomas Universities in Rome. He has a Master's Degree in Philosophy from Nagpur University and a Licence in Philosophy from St. Thomas University, Rome. He was Director of *Gyandhara*, Institute of Philosophy, in Orlim, Goa. From 2012-15, he taught in the Mass Communication Department at St. Joseph's College (Autonomous) Bangalore. He was also the Head of the Department. He has published four books and presented papers in national and international conferences and seminars. At present, he is a Professor of Journalism and Mass Communication at Amity University, Gurgaon, Haryana.

Gayatri Mendanha (gayatri@ssla.edu.in) holds Masters' degrees in both English and Philosophy. She is currently an Assistant Professor at the Symbiosis School for Liberal Arts, Pune, where she teaches courses in Literature and Philosophy. She is a visiting faculty at Jnana-Deepa Vidyapeeth. She has presented papers at various conferences and has guest lectured at DePaul University, Chicago.

Gregory Mathew Malayil (gm6272@gmail.com) is a lecturer in the Faculty of Philosophy, Dharmaram Vidya Kshetram, Bengaluru. He has two Masters' Degrees (Physics and Philosophy) to his credit. He has a Doctorate in Physics from Cochin University of Science and Technology. His areas of academic interest include Cosmology, Consciousness and Science-Religion Interface.

James D. Chellappa (jameschellappa@gmail.com) is an ordained Pastor/ Priest in the Kerala-Kanyakumari Diocese of the Evangelical Church of India

(ECI). He is the Founder and Principal of Christian Academy for Advanced Theological Studies (CAATS), an interdenominational and ecumenical/evangelical seminary, in Kanyakumari, Tamil Nadu. His areas of interest are Contemporary Theology, Philosophy of Religions, Postmodernism and Post Colonialism.

James Ponniah (jamesponniah@gmail.com) is Assistant Professor in the Department of Christian Studies at the University of Madras. He previously was the Dean of the Faculty of Philosophy and an Associate Professor in the Department of Indian Studies at Jnana-Deepa Vidyapeeth University in India. Ponniah specializes in popular religious movements in India. Ponniah published *The Dynamics of Folk Religion in Society* in 2011 and has co-edited three other books; in addition, he has written numerous articles about popular religious movements in India. Ponniah was also a part of the Christianity and Freedom Project headed by the Berkley Center's Religious Freedom Project. He holds an M.A. and Ph.D from the University of Madras.

John Peter Vallabadoss (petercapu@gmail.com) is a Franciscan Capuchin and has taught Philosophy for 15 years. He is presently Dean of studies at St. Joseph's Capuchin Philosophical College, Kotagiri, Tamil Nadu, and a visiting faculty at Jnana-Deepa Vidyapeeth (JDV), Pune. He is also Secretary of Association of Christian Philosophers of India. He has convened three national seminars. He has published two books (*Methodology for Scientific Papers, Ecological Crisis Re-addressed*) and edited three books (*Openness to the Other, History and Historizing, Journey of Represencing St. Francis of Assisi*) and published 22 research articles till date.

Jose D. Maliekal (jose.maleikal@gmail.com) teaches systematic philosophy and social praxis, at St. John's Regional Seminary (Institute of Philosophy, Religious Studies and Social Sciences), Kondadaba, Vizianagaram District, Andhra Pradesh, and at Don Bosco Vishwa Jyothi College, Warangal, Telangana. His doctoral thesis, in Subaltern Fundamental Theology, based on a five-year long field research, among the Dalit Madigas of Godavari Delta, East Godavari district, A.P., defended in the Department of Christian Studies, University of Madras, is soon to be published by ISPCK, Delhi, under the title, *Standstill Utopias?: Dalits Encountering Christianity*. His areas of research are subaltern perspectives on the production of knowledge, Dalit identities, and the impact of religion on socio-economic transformation.

Jose Pennaparambil (frpenjoe@gmail.com) belongs to the diocese of Thamarassery. He has a Master's degree in English Literature and served the diocese as Forane director of K.C.Y.M and Mission League. He secured a Licentiate in Philosophy from Santa Croce University, Rome on the subject of artificial intelligence and a Ph.D in Islamic Philosophy at Dharmaram Vidhya Kshetram Bangalore with a thesis on "Terrorism Versus Justice: Islamic Terrorism and Fundamentalism, A Philosophical Analysis on the basis of Rawlsian Theory of Justice". He now serves the diocese in varies capacities as, Director of Family Apostolate and Pro-Life Movement, Asst. Director of Pastoral Center and Priest Home, and Coordinator of Social Department of the diocese. He is visiting professor of Islamology in St. Joseph's Seminary, Aluva, Little Flower Seminary (CST) Aluva. OCD Seminary Trivandrum, Pilar Niketan, Nagpur, De Paul Institute Kengeri, Bangalore.

Kamaladevi R. Kunkolienker (kaamakhya_k@rediffmail.com) is Associate Professor, Department of Philosophy and Head of the Department of Philosophy and Vice Principal of P.E.S'. R.S.N. College of Arts and Science, Farmagudi, Ponda, Goa. She has been teaching Philosophy for the last 29 years. She has a Master of Arts (Philosophy) and Ph.D (Philosophy of Mind) on "The Perspectives on Mind and Consciousness: A Critical Evaluation." She is Secretary of Science – Religion "SANGAM", Goa. Her book on "World Philosophies", in the Konkani language, was awarded "SAHITYA ANDBHASHA SEVA PURASKAR 2014" by Goa Konkani Academy. She has presented several papers on Sri Aurobindo's Philosophy at international conferences in Pune and at state-level seminars at Sri Aurobindo Society, Panaji, Goa.

Keith D'Souza (keith@jesuits.net) teaches Philosophy and Religious Studies at St. Pius X College, Mumbai. He has degrees in Science (B.Sc. in Physics), Theology (M.Th. in Systematic Theology) and Philosophy. He did his doctoral studies at Marquette University in Wisconsin, USA, with a specialization in philosophical hermeneutics (Hans Georg Gadamer and Paul Ricoeur). He has edited two books and published around forty journal articles in the areas of hermeneutical theory, socio-political philosophy and religious studies. He is a member of the Bombay Philosophical Society, and is currently the President of the Association of Christian Philosophers of India (ACPI).

Nishant A. Irudayadason (nishant@jdv.edu.in) is a professor of Philosophy and Ethics at Jnana-Deepa Vidyapeeth: Pontifical Institute of Philosophy and Religions (JDV), Pune, India. After having completed his doctoral studies on Philosophy and Ethics at Université Paris-Est and in Institut Catholique de Paris, France, he has been actively pursuing academic life. He is currently the Chairperson of the doctoral programme in the Faculty of Philosophy at JDV. His regular courses include History of Contemporary Philosophy, Ethics, Politics and Poststructuralism. He has presented research papers in many National and International Conferences. He has authored two books, edited two books and published nearly 30 research essays in National and International Journals as well as in edited books. He is a regular contributor to contemporary political analysis in "Light of Truth," a bimonthly published from Kochi, Kerala.

Noel D'Costa (noelcost75@yahoo.co.in) is a diocesan priest of the Archdiocese of Goa. He is the Dean of Philosophy of the Patriarchal Seminary of Rachol, Goa. He teaches Philosophy of Science, Cosmology, World Religion and Science and Technology. He holds a Master's degree in Interfacing Science, Philosophy and Religion from the Jnana-Deepa Vidyapeeth, Pune. He has presented paper on science-religion dialogue at various places in India. He is also the Convenor of the Inter-Religious Dialogue in the Archdiocese of Goa. His area of interest are Philosophy of Science, Cosmology, Historiography and Science and Technology.

Peter Ladis F. (peterladis@rediffmail.com) is Assistant Professor, Chanakya National Law University (CNLU), Patna. He is a Catholic priest of the Archdiocese of Patna presently holding various administrative responsibilities in the Archdiocese of Patna as well as CNLU, Patna. He has undertaken various legal researches and presented papers in National and International Conferences many of which have been published in reputed journals. He is a visiting faculty at Jnana-Deepa Vidyapeeth. He is also an Academic Counsellor of IGNOU.

S. Sekar Sebastin (sekarsebastin@gmail.com) is a priest from the diocese of Trichy, Tamil Nadu. He holds a doctorate in philosophy from the Pontifical University of St. Thomas Aquinas, Rome. After teaching philosophy for fifteen years with various capacities as Dean, Registrar at Sacred Heart Seminary, Poonamallee, Chennai, he is at present Dean of philosophy at St. Paul's Seminary, Trichy. The area of his interest is Moral Philosophy, Philosophical Anthropology, Postmodernism and History of Western Philosophy. Besides many scholarly articles to his credit in different philosophical journals, he is the author of two books and editor of a book in the ACPI series.

S. Stephen Jayard (sjayard@gmail.com) belongs to the Diocese of Tiruchirapalli, and is a Professor in the Faculty of Philosophy, Jnana-Deepa Vidyapeeth, Pune, since 2008. His Ph.D in Philosophy of Science is from the Central University of Hyderabad, had the Post-doctoral research on Science and Values, at the Lonergan Institutes, Washington DC and Boston College, Boston, USA and Regis College, Toronto, Canada, He is a visiting faculty at various Institutes of Philosophy and Religion in India and abroad. He has conducted workshops on 'Integrating Science and Spirituality' and sessions on motivation for the faculties and the students in Schools and Colleges, published several articles in the National and International journals, and five books; including Towards a Theory of Rationality in Science: A Plea to Reasonableness (2012) and A Book That Cannot Be Titled (2015).

Vianney Maria Joseph (joevianney@gmail.com) belongs to the Salesian Province of Dimapur in North-East India. He graduated in English (Honours) from NEHU (North Eastern Hill University – Shillong, Meghalaya) and has done his M.A. in Indian Philosophy from Madras University. He teaches Metaphysics, Theodicy, Introduction to Indian Philosophy & Culture, Introduction to World Religions, Social & Political Philosophy and Indian Philosophy (Vedas & Upanishads, Astika & Nastika Darshanas, Contemporary Indian Thinkers) to the Salesian and Diocesan Clerics doing their B.Ph. Course as well as to the Students of B.A. in Philosophy in Salesian College of Higher Education – Dimapur, Nagaland. Currently, he is pursuing his Ph.D in NEHU – Shillong, looking at the aspect of Religious Experience as contained in the two Religious Texts: Gita and St. John's Gospel.

Victor Ferrao (victorferrao@yahoo.co.uk) is a priest of the Archdiocese of Goa, and teaches at Rachol Seminary, Goa. He has doctorate in Philosophy from Jnana-Deepa Vidyapeeth, Pune, with a specialisation in Philosophy of Science. His primary interest is in the area of Science and Religion Dialogue. He has attended as well as organised several international as well as national conferences in this area. He is the Co-founder of Science-Religion Sangam, a science and religion dialogue movement in Goa. He is a co-coordinator of the special study centre of IGNOU at Rachol Seminary. He has published five books and several research papers in reputed and peer reviewed journals and has been an active member of the ACPI.

ACPI Books

Annual Series

1. The Postmodern: A Siege of the Citadel of Reason (2000)
2. Faith, Reason, Science: Philosophical Reflections with Special Reference to Fides et Ratio (2001)
3. The Constitution of India: A Philosophical Review (2002)
4. Truth, Power, Money: A Postmodern Reading (2003)
5. Philosophical Methods: Through the Prevalent to a Relevant (2004)
6. Subaltern Perspectives: Philosophizing in Context (2005)
7. Pluralism of Pluralism: A Pluralistic Probe into Philosophizing (2006)
8. Romancing the Sacred?: Towards an Indian Christian Philosophy of Religion (2007)
9. Culture as Gift and Task: Philosophical Reflections in the Indian Context (2008)
10. Enigma of Indian Tribal Life and Culture: Philosophical Investigations (2009)
11. Violence and Its Victims: A Challenge to Philosophizing in the Indian Context (2010)
12. Tradition and Innovation: Philosophy of Rootedness and Openness (2011)
13. History and Historizing: Philosophical Reflections (2012)
14. Identity, Difference and Conflict: Postcolonial Critique (2013)
15. The Dynamics of Development: Negations and Negotiations (2014)
16. The Symbolic World: Constructions and Re-Constructions (2015)
17. Philosophizing the Body: Physical, Social, Psychosomatic & Spiritual Dimensions (2016)
18. Becoming a Nation: Processes and Prospects (2017)

Special Series

1. ACPI Encyclopaedia of Philosophy, 2 Vols (2010)
2. Authentic Existence: A Philosophical Probe (2012)
3. Raimon Panikkar: Being Beyond Borders – A Commemorative Volume (2012)
4. Enhancing Our Home: Re-Claiming and Re-Reading Gandhian Thought (2016)